Jewish Bialystok and Its Diaspora

Jewish Bialystok and Its Diaspora

REBECCA KOBRIN

Indiana University Press
Bloomington and Indianapolis

Publication of this book is made possible in part by generous support from the Koret Foundation.

This book is a publication of

Indiana University Press
601 North Morton Street
Bloomington, Indiana 47404-3797 USA

www.iupress.indiana.edu

Telephone orders   800-842-6796
Fax orders   812-855-7931
Orders by e-mail   iuporder@indiana.edu

♾ The paper used in this publication meets the minimum requirements of the American National Standard for Information Sciences—Permanence of Paper for Printed Library Materials, ANSI Z39.48-1992.

Manufactured in the United States of America

Library of Congress Cataloging-in-Publication Data

Kobrin, Rebecca.
Jewish Bialystok and its diaspora / Rebecca Kobrin.
p. cm. — (The modern Jewish experience)
Includes bibliographical references and index.
ISBN 978-0-253-35442-6 (cloth : alk. paper) —
ISBN 978-0-253-22176-6 (pbk. : alk. paper)
1. Jews—Poland—Bialystok—History. 2. Jews—Poland—Bialystok—Migrations—History. 3. Jews, Polish—Cultural assimilation—Foreign countries. 4. Jews—Migrations—History—20th century. 5. Jewish diaspora—History—20th century. 6. Bialystok (Poland)—Ethnic relations. I. Title.
DS134.66.B53K63 2010
305.892'4043836—dc22
2009039149

1 2 3 4 5 15 14 13 12 11 10

To my parents,
Lawrence and Ruth Kobrin

CONTENTS

Contents

ACKNOWLEDGMENTS

It seems almost impossible after so many years of working on this project, which has gone through numerous transformations and alterations, to remember and give full credit to all the people who helped me. This book represents the culmination of a long journey, along which I have been most fortunate to have had the support of a number of individuals, institutions, and fellowships. I must begin by thanking my parents, to whom this book is dedicated. Ruth and Lawrence Kobrin have always supported and nurtured my quest for knowledge. Their boundless love, along with the countless hours of babysitting when I ventured on research trips, made the completion of this project possible.

The seeds for this book were planted when I heard Professor Nancy Green at Yale College give a talk concerning comparative Jewish migration and her growing frustration over her inability to find good bagels, let alone bialys, in Paris. But this writing would never have come to fruition had it not been for the wonderful teachers I encountered along the way. From the moment I stepped into David Ruderman's and Paula Hyman's classrooms as a Yale undergraduate, I was inspired by their passion for teaching and commitment to rigorous scholarship. At the University of Pennsylvania, I thank Michael Katz, Deborah Dash Moore, Ewa Morawska, and Israel Bartal for introducing me to new ways of thinking about the process of migration and East European Jewish history. I am especially grateful to Benjamin Nathans, Deborah Dash Moore, David Ruderman, and Beth Wenger, whose thoughtful comments and exacting academic standards helped me see this project to its completion. Benjamin Nathans's incisive questions, sage advice, and steady encouragement pushed me to rethink how one effectively narrates a transnational history of East European Jewry.

But my early drafts would not have crystallized into this book without the constant support, and sage advice of Paula Hyman and Deborah Dash Moore. I thank them for including me in their series and their gentle prodding. Together they demonstrated to me how one negotiates with grace between the conflicting demands of scholarship, family life, and a commitment to Jewish communal life. My postdoctoral fellowships at Yale and New York University not only provided me the opportunity to work closely with Paula Hyman and David Engel, but also afforded me the time to expand my research, improve my Polish, and learn from many distinguished faculty members, most notably Laura Engelstein, Matthew Frye Jacobson, and Timothy Snyder. My colleagues in Yale's Religious Studies' Department and in New York University's Hebrew and Judaic Studies Department—Ivan Marcus, Shannon Craigo-Snell, Hasia Diner, Gennady Estraikh, Steve Fraade, Christine Hayes, Tony Michels, Jonathan Ray, and Ludger Viefhues—welcomed me and engaged me in stimulating discussions that helped me to refine my overall project.

Procuring documents for this transnational study was a daunting challenge but was made much easier by the tireless and generous efforts of many archivists and librarians around the world. I am very grateful to Gennady Pasternak at Tel Aviv University, who found space for me to look through the rich collection of the Goren-Goldstein Center for the Study of Diaspora Jewry at Tel Aviv University. I did not have the opportunity to meet the late Chen Merhavia of the National Library's Rare Book and Manuscript Division, but had it not been for his efforts, I could not have completed this project. Professor Merhavia tirelessly devoted himself to amassing materials related to Bialystok, his birthplace, for a work he planned to write that would bring to life the vitality and diversity of Bialystok's Jews as it assessed this city's significance to the broader modern Jewish experience. Soliciting documents over the course of a lifetime from friends, colleagues, and acquaintances, Merhavia left no stone unturned in his search for information about Bialystok. As I gathered from his close friend Menachem Lewin, Merhavia was a most exacting scholar who envisioned his planned book on Bialystok as the crowning achievement of his life's work. I only hope that the following pages do justice to his dream. In Buenos Aires, Silvia Hansman graciously helped me navigate through Fundacion IWO's rich collections. At the YIVO

Institute for Jewish Research, Zachary Baker, Herbert Lazarus, Yeshayu Mettle, and Dina Abramowicz z"l all patiently addressed my queries. In Warsaw, Natalia Aleksiun, Yale Reisner, and Helise Lieberman helped me navigate Poland's rich archival collections and immediately made me feel as though I were a beloved member of their families. In Bialystok, Kataryzna Sztop-Rumkovska provided me not only guidance through the various collections of Archiwum Państowe Białymstoku but also a place to stay. Not only did Deborah Yalen offer warm hospitality in Moscow, but her persistence is the reason this book contains documents and information acquired from archives in Russia.

Aside from historical documents, this book owes much to the hundreds of former residents of Bialystok I had the chance to interview over the last decade. I can never thank them sufficiently, as they met me on my short research trips throughout the United States, Argentina, Israel, and Australia, sharing pieces of their lives with me. As I explored new areas, I benefited from the counsel of many. Eric Goldstein, Nancy Green, Eli Lederhendler, Michal Lemberger, Adam McKeown, Mae Ngai, Annie Polland, Jonathan Sarna, and Daniel Soyer all generously gave of their time and read portions of this book. Their useful suggestions enriched this project. I am particularly indebted to Betsy Blackmar, Jonathan Frankel z"l, Olga Litvak, Ron Meyer, Derek Penslar, and Jeffrey Shandler, whose insight, candor, and close reading of my entire manuscript helped me make my final revisions. Janet Rabinowitch and Katie Baber at Indiana University Press were both precise and patient as I completed this work. All mistakes, needless to say, are mine.

The research and writing of this book were generously supported by a number of institutions and foundations, to whom I am sincerely indebted: the Wexner Graduate Fellowship, the U.S. Department of Education (IEE Fulbright program), the Memorial Foundation for Jewish Culture, the Pew Program for the Study of Religion, the National Foundation for Jewish Culture, the Center for Jewish History, the YIVO Institute for Jewish Research, the Institute for Latin American Studies at Columbia University, the Harriman Institute, the Cahnman Family Foundation, the Koret Foundation, the American

Council of Learned Societies, and the American Philosophical Society. Neither they nor the readers whose comments helped refine my work are responsible for the views expressed in this book.

Finally, I wholeheartedly thank my siblings, Jeffrey Kobrin, Michelle Greenberg-Kobrin, Debra Levy, and Dan Levy, who always make me laugh, particularly at myself, and who refrained from asking when I would finish working on "that book on Bialystok." I am profoundly indebted to my husband, Kevin Feinblum, whose migration, love, and strength has informed this project in more ways than he will ever know. For over a decade, he endured the endless copies of obscure documents from Polish archives scattered throughout our apartment, trips overseas, the printing out of documents, and the scanning of images of long-deceased Polish Jews. His unflagging support helped me through the ups and downs of this project in countless ways. Last, but most important, I must thank my daughters, Ariela and Simone. There was nothing better than returning home after a long day of research or writing to be asked when they could design and color with their markers the cover of my book. I thank my girls for their snuggles, giggles, and smiles that continue to be a constant source of joy and that sustain me every day.

Note on Orthography and Transliteration

In transliterating Russian and Hebrew words, I have generally followed the systems used by the Library of Congress, with the exception of certain well-known names familiar to American readers for which other transliterations (e.g., Dubnow rather than Dubnov; Trotsky rather than Trotskii) are commonly used. Many of the people mentioned in this book use different names in different languages. For consistency, I have used the name by which I believe they are most widely known. In general, Yiddish words, phrases, titles and names of organizations, places and persons have been rendered according to the transliteration scheme of the YIVO Institute for Jewish Research, except for names familiar to English speakers in a different form, such as *kehilla*. Moreover, I have made no attempt to standardize nonstandard orthography. Many Yiddish periodicals used in this study, notably the *Bialystoker Stimme,* possess Yiddish titles that were transliterated at the time of publication by the editors and they did not follow the YIVO guidelines. So, for example, the *Bialystoker Stimme,* one of my main sources, would be rendered *Byalistoker shtime* according to the YIVO standard but I have chosen to render it as it appears in its Library of Congress listing. Hebrew words that appear as integral parts of Yiddish titles or phrases are spelled as they are pronounced in Yiddish (*goles* for the biblical term *galut* [exile]). Foreign words are italicized only the first time they appear, at which point they are explained. All translations are mine unless otherwise indicated.

European place names in the text follow the main entry in Mokotoff and Sack, *Where Once We Walked: A Guide to Jewish Communities Destroyed in the Holocaust.* Where Yiddish spelling of a location differs significantly from the main term used in another language (Bialystok [Yiddish], Białystok [Polish], Belostok [Russian]), I use the Yiddish name and do not use the diacritical marks deployed in East European languages. When referring to Jewish natives of a particular place, I use the Yiddish form (Bialystoker for a person from Bialystok). I have used the spelling of organizational names as they appear in English in *Di yidishe landsmanshaften fun Nyu York, the Jewish Communal Register,* or *From Alexandrovsk to Zyrardow: A Guide to YIVO's Landsmanshaftn Archive.*

Jewish Bialystok and Its Diaspora

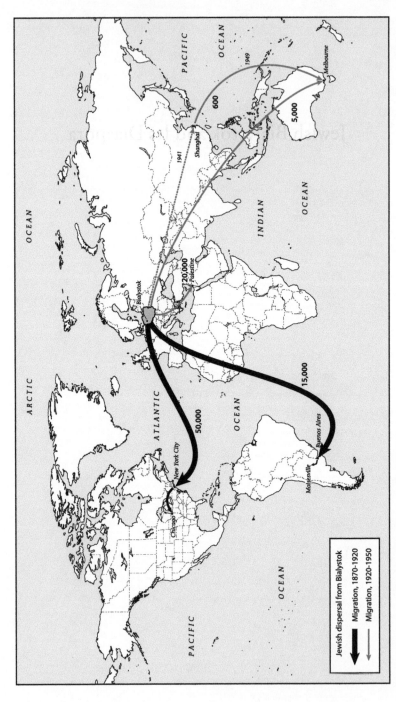

The Dispersal of Jews from Bialystok, 1870–1950.

Between Exile and Empire: Visions of Jewish Dispersal in the Age of Mass Migration

In 1921, Chaim Horowitz (1885–1962), a Yiddish journalist fresh off the boat in New York, was approached to write the feature piece for a debut journal, *Der Bialystoker Stimme* (The Voice of Bialystok). Overwhelmed by his new home, Horowitz appreciated the opportunity to make his name known in New York's Yiddish literary world through a *landsmanshaft* (Jewish immigrant hometown association), one of a network of organizations claiming close to a million members.[1] Groping for the correct metaphor to convey his mood, Horowitz opened with a lament: "We Jewish immigrants from Bialystok suffer from an acute homesickness . . . as we wander [*navena'd*] throughout America . . . discovering it is impossible to feel at home, like we had in Bialystok."[2] Summoning the biblical phrase *navena'd,* used to describe Cain's wandering after being expelled from the Garden of Eden, Horowitz cast migration as akin to divine punishment in the powerful eulogy he devised for his lost Eden in Eastern Europe. In contrast to portraits of migration prevalent in American and Jewish history that echo American nationalist mythology—America was a "promised land" for the Jews, filled with "golden opportunities," and "exceptional" in its warm welcome—Horowitz saw Lady Liberty as standing at the mouth of New York harbor not bearing a lantern to lead him to a new utopia, but a sword inaugurating a new type of Jewish exile.[3] His image resonated with the new journal's readership: dozens wrote in to the *Bialystoker Stimme* from cities and towns scattered throughout the United States, South America, and Europe to echo Horowitz's deep ambivalence over leaving Bialystok;[4] one respondent even summoned the term *goles,* the Yiddish rendering of the biblical word *galut* (exile), to advance the idea that migration from Bialystok resembled the Jewish people's divinely ordained existential and physical dispersal from the biblical land of Israel two thousand years earlier.

David Sohn (1890–1967), executive director of the Bialystoker Center and editor of the *Bialystoker Stimme,* shared Horowitz's passion for Bialystok but not his despondent view of migration. Rather, he marveled at the vitality of the "various Bialystoker colonies scattered throughout the world," whose members all felt compelled to respond to Horowitz's lament.[5] With creative wit, Sohn went as far as to deploy the word *koylonia* (colony) to depict the satellites of the ever-expanding world of Jewish Bialystok. Voraciously contributing to and reading each issue of the *Bialystoker Stimme,* these Jews dedicated themselves to making audible "the 'voice of Bialystok.'"[6] Summoning imperial imagery in place of an exilic metaphor Sohn reiterated Horowitz's galvanizing vision of Eastern Europe as an inspirational homeland. But he rejected a vision of East European immigrants as helpless exiles, suggesting instead that Jewish Bialystok's "expansive array of colonies" demonstrated the power of migrant dispersal. Having just returned from Eastern Europe, where he had distributed millions of dollars in remittances collected in New York, Sohn appreciated the ways in which Bialystok's Jews living abroad were viewed as akin to powerful colonial emissaries, mining the riches of their new homes so that they could maintain, rebuild, and expand their former homes. Their presence in Bialystok altered how Poles viewed Jewish migrant "colonies," "the empire" of America and Jews' place in it.[7]

To be sure, both Horowitz and Sohn appreciated the ironies in using the metaphors of exile and empire as they sought to engage a wide readership. Indeed, they succeeded in their goal, as they excited an estimated forty thousand readers to continue to read and contribute to the publication for the next seventy years. While many today would either laugh at or ignore these images as descriptive of the bonds tying millions of East European Jews scattered throughout Europe, the United States, Australia, Africa, and Asia by 1920, Benedict Anderson rightfully points out that "communities are not to be distinguished" or analyzed "only by their genuineness, but by the style in which they are imagined."[8] So why would these immigrant Jewish writers—who, though not revered intellectuals, cared passionately about ideas and the issues of their time—employ such ideologically and politically loaded terms to describe the new community they had become a part of as a result of the silent revolution of East European Jewish migration?[9]

Indeed, as the following pages argue, the choice of these terms by two writers living in New York City and their readers scattered throughout the world opens up a larger set of questions concerning the conceptualization and narration of East European Jewish migration in modern Jewish history, American history, and the field of migration studies. Many scholars discuss Jews' migration from Eastern Europe, but few locate this profound population shift in its larger global context. The triumphant experience of Jewish immigrants in the United States continues to garner the lion's share of scholars' attention, obscuring how East European Jewish settlement in the United States represented part of an ongoing process of migration that reshaped Jewish life, first in nineteenth-century Russia and later in early twentieth-century Europe, Africa, Australia, Asia, and South America. The United States, the *goldene medina* (golden land), was not a self-contained Jewish immigrant enclave, as so often depicted, since it was only one satellite or "colony" in a dense web of East European Jewish migrant settlement.[10]

As they highlighted the wider lens needed to evaluate the havoc wrought by migration, Horowitz and Sohn's diametrically opposed images also engaged a deeper question: should one view the mass departure of Jews from Eastern Europe—an exodus that constituted the largest voluntary population shift in modern Jewish history—as illustrative of Jews' power or their powerlessness?[11] Are the millions of East European Jews who immigrated abroad best understood as exiles chased from their homes, as Horowitz implies and as scholars and popular writers have traditionally rendered them?[12] Or were they rather economic opportunists who sought better lives for themselves and channeled the riches of the New World to rebuild their former East European homes? Indeed, as East European Jews acted like many other migrant groups, one must consider how to cast their dispersal in this era of worldwide mass migration and expanding empires.[13] In the coming pages, as I narrate and analyze the fate of

Jewish Bialystok and its dispersed émigré community in its larger global context, I highlight the ways in which East European Jewish immigrants remained bound together by their self-perceived, new, exilic state as well as their newfound empowerment. As they struggled as ethnic minorities carving out niches in foreign lands, they also enjoyed relative economic power, which they used to form new organizations, philanthropies, and newspapers that forever changed Jewish life in Eastern Europe, as well as the practice of Jewish diasporic identity in the new emerging centers of Jewish life.

In Horowitz's bemoaning of his exilic state, we hear echoes of the discontent voiced by many migrant groups who have arrived in the United States. In the previous century, Irish immigrants similarly had mourned their collective and individual fates.[14] Italian and Polish immigrants, Horowitz's contemporaries, also penned paeans to their former homes. But their articulations of longing for home differ from those captured on the pages of the *Bialystoker Stimme* in that they belie a well-developed biblical tradition of Jewish alienation. For centuries, both traditional and popular writers constructed Jewish identity[15] as primarily shaped by the Jewish people's immutable links to the biblical land of Israel and their dispersal from it two millennia earlier.[16] These traditional writings helped Jews emerge as the model diasporic group for the contemporary field of "diaspora studies." But few, as Horowitz's eloquent anguish highlights, correctly understand how diaspora, or dispersal, actually informed twentieth-century Jews' affiliations and self-conceptions.[17] Far from being united by their traumatic dispersal from the ancient land of Israel, many Jews saw Eastern Europe as their archetypal Jewish homeland. Their migration forced them to rethink the fundamental data of their Jewish identities, namely, diaspora, exile, and homeland, and to forge a multi-diasporic Jewish identity, tied to both their temporal and mythic homelands.[18]

While Horowitz drew on a rich biblical tradition available to few other groups, Sohn's use of colonial language to describe those East European Jews who spread not only to the United States, but also to Western Europe, Argentina, and Australia, could have only been crafted in the early twentieth century, when *empire,* a useful, but frustratingly vague term, gained currency to describe various bonds and political formations.[19] To be sure, while today the terms *empire* and *imperialism* often are used in reference to political entities who dominate through military force, trade enterprises, or political bullying, these terms in the early twentieth century, as historian Andrew Thompson points out, "were like empty boxes continuously being filled up and emptied of their meanings."[20] Sohn, a sarcastic man, certainly appreciated the comic value in comparing immigrant Jews scattered throughout the world to an expansive and powerful colonial entity, but he nonetheless specifically chose this term because it conveyed to him not only the power that migrants' possessed but also the international sphere in which they operated. As scholars increasingly discuss America, its culture, and overseas ventures within an imperial framework, the following pages open engagement with Sohn and his contemporaries' invocation of colonial terminology underscores the ways in which even immigrants' foreign attachments shaped American culture. Indeed, as the case of Bialystok suggests, East European Jews in America envisioned their overseas entanglements with their former homes as part of a larger imperial mission to spread the New World's riches and ideals to less fortunate parts of the world.[21]

While East European Jewish immigrant writers at the turn of the century only had the terms exile and empire to discuss their ties to those in other countries, contemporary scholars eschew such terms and embrace the concept of transnationalism—generally defined as the continued alliance of peoples across national borders—in their discussions of such ties among migrant groups.[22] Casting transnationalism generally as a late twentieth-century phenomenon, aided by the ideology of globalization and advances in travel and communication technology, few consider the experiences of migrant Jews, who for decades defined the field of immigration studies.[23] Thus, while we know much about the intricate web of foreign and domestic entanglements among contemporary Asian, Mexican, and South Asian immigrant communities,[24] early twentieth-century East European Jewish immigrants' transnational financial, literary, political, and cultural entanglements are virtually unexplored.[25] As *Jewish Bialystok and Its Diaspora* demonstrates, transnationalism is nothing new: East European Jews behaved like the quintessential

David Sohn, editor of the *Bialystoker Stimme,* sitting at his desk in the Bialystoker Center, circa 1955. *Courtesy of William Kavee, Steven Kavee, and Rona K. Moyer.*

transnational migrants, to use the words of Nina Glick Schiller, as they "forged and sustained multi-stranded social relations link[ing] together their societies of origin and settlement."[26] But East European Jews distinguished themselves by having emigrated at a rate unparalleled by any other East European ethnic group.[27] As a result, they forged new types of solidarities through print culture, organizations, and philanthropies simultaneously animated by very local concerns—namely their members' undying loyalty to a specific East European city or town—but also cognizant of the global network in which they now found themselves.

The city of Bialystok, which inspired both Horowitz and Sohn, provides an ideal window through which to view the ways in which Jewish migration brought global, national, and local concerns into collision with one another. Over the course of the nineteenth and early twentieth centuries, approximately one hundred thousand Jews migrated to and from this city situated in a heavily forested region dividing Poland from Belorussia and Lithuania. Its growth from a commercial town to a major industrial center was typical of many regional capitals in late imperial Russia,[28] when Russia's uneven industrial development forced millions to move from small towns to large cities.[29] As one can see vividly in the example of nineteenth-century Bialystok, the dramatic movement of Jews within the western areas of the Russian Empire provoked development of new types of political, religious, and communal institutions that sought to facilitate the Jewish migrants' adaptation to urban life. While these organizations struggled to protect Jews from the economic vicissitudes of the era, political instability and episodic violence compelled thousands of Jews to abandon Bialystok for faraway lands such as the United States (50,000), Argentina (20,000), Australia (5,000), and Palestine (20,000). Whether they settled on the crowded streets of New York's Lower East side or on small farms on Argentina's Pampas, Jews from Bialystok dedicated themselves to transplanting their understanding of the political, welfare, and communal institutions they had developed in Eastern Europe to their new homes.[30]

Like any large city, Bialystok possessed distinctive geographic and political features; accordingly, its diaspora exhibited particular social formations. But Bialystok and its émigré outposts were not exceptional: what was true for Bialystok could also be said of Pinsk, Vilna, or a host of other East European cities or towns transformed by tsarist Russia's uneven industrial development. Each city engendered among its former inhabitants a deep sense of loyalty. While the following pages do not seek to argue that Bialystok presents a paradigm for the study of Russian Jewish urban life, its transformation from a small provincial town into a major industrial city and then a center for Jewish emigration offers relevant insights into the global tale of East European Jewish migration.[31]

The Global and the Local
in the Writing of Jewish History

Jewish Bialystok and Its Diaspora shifts the lens of analysis away from a specific nation in its narration of East European Jewish migration. To be sure, the saga of the mass dispersal of Jews from Eastern

Europe is far from uncharted scholarly terrain. In general, as Nancy Green and François Weil note, literature on migration, and in particular East European Jewish migration, has been "resolutely a literature of *im*migration."[32] Framed almost entirely from the perspectives of the countries of arrival, we know much about East European Jewish immigrants in New York, London, or Buenos Aires but little about the transnational character of their movements or the links forged between them.[33] Even those scholars who compare Jews' experiences with those of other ethnic groups almost exclusively focus on their convergence in one country, most often the United States.[34] While innovative work has shed light on the worldwide network of Italian immigrants, few, as Nancy Green points out, have yet to conduct sustained transnational analysis of the divergent paths taken by East European Jews,[35] obscuring how state-formation, timing of migration, and economic development (in both region of origin and final settlement) shaped the experience of migration as well as the process of adaptation across space and time.[36]

Spanning five continents, this book illuminates what scholars of modern Jewish life can contribute to current debates about all things "transnational." But in writing such a "transnational" history of East European Jewish migration I do not intend to dismiss the heuristic value of the nation-state in historical analysis. Indeed, the fundamental differences between the experiences of Bialystok's Jews in the United States, Argentina, Australia, and Palestine highlight the continued centrality of the state to modern Jewish life, particularly for those interested in the dynamics of immigrant adaptation.[37] But in its concurrent attention to the power of the nation-state as well as the transnational sphere in which Jewish immigrants operated, *Jewish Bialystok and Its Diaspora* highlights the ways in which one cannot fully understand the havoc wrought by migration on Jewish life during the twentieth century if one solely depicts Jews in dichotomous frameworks dictated by nation-states. East European Jews often saw the complexion of their daily lives shaped in spheres located both above and below the purview of the state as they engaged, contested, and debated the pressing question of their lives: what did it mean to be an East European Jew when one lived beyond the confines of Eastern Europe?

While states implicitly shaped immigrant Jews' lives, loyalty to these political entities did not figure so large for East European Jews in the early twentieth century. East European Jews, like their European counterparts, saw their identities as intricately tied to their cities, towns or regions of origin.[38] As Israel Beker, director of Israel's renowned Habima theater troupe, summed up: "I am not just from Bialystok, I am a Bialystoker, and that means much more."[39] Yiddish folklore registers such local loyalties, associating different character traits with different regions: Jews from Vilna, for example, the Jerusalem of Lithuania (*Yerushalyim de lita*), were renowned for their piety and learnedness; Jews from Odessa, Russia's port city on the Black Sea, were seen by Yiddish folklorists as hedonistic and assimilated, causing their hometown to be encircled by seven miles of figurative hellfire (*zibn mayl arum Ades brent der gihenum*).[40]

The physical abandonment of Eastern Europe did not erase but rather reinforced regional identities. Through newly formed organizations, commonly called *landsmanshaftn*, East European Jews sought to remap their regional identities onto a transnational terrain by continually drawing and redrawing the boundaries of their distinctive communal identities.[41] Scholars of Jewish immigrant life have long commented upon the ways in which Jews delineated their collective identities along religious or political lines.[42] Few scholars, however, have addressed the continued centrality of regional identity, even as Isaac Rontch, head of the Works Progress Administration's Yiddish Writers' group, posited in 1937 that one out of five Jews in the United States still affiliated with associations organized around the principle of regional loyalty.[43] As the following pages demonstrate, regionalism may not have supplanted Jews' political or religious identifications, but it dovetailed with these convictions and framed their articulation, pushing migrants to craft myths about creating a new Jewish diaspora or a powerful empire anchored in Eastern Europe with extensions throughout the world.

The East European Jewish Diaspora
and the Field of Diaspora Studies

My discussion of one slice of the larger East European Jewish immigrant world intervenes in the vigorous academic discussion that has sprung up around the concept of diaspora, a growing field of inquiry that often summons the "Jewish diaspora" as its archetype but is uncannily devoid of Jewish actors. The term *diaspora* first became popular for a wide variety of groups in the 1980s, when scholars interested in both voluntary and involuntary migrant groups from regions as diverse as South Asia, the Caribbean, and Africa saw the category of diaspora as the best heuristic to analyze the intricate matrix of identifications exhibited by immigrants as they moved across national boundaries, settled in new lands, and developed subnational and/or ethnic identities.[44] Soon many scholars summoned *diaspora* as the category of analysis for their examinations of the dilemmas of identity in an age of mass migration and modern nationalism: as Khaching Tölölyan quipped, "where once were dispersions, there now is diaspora."[45]

In their expansive discussions of contemporary migrant groups, most scholars now devote great attention to migrants' diasporic mentalities. Jews, whose diasporic condition is often held up as a paradigm, however, are fundamentally misunderstood. While initially, to be sure, the term *diaspora*—derived from the Greek root for the verb "to scatter"—was coined to describe the Jewish people's expulsion from their ancient homeland, over the course of the next two thousand years, Jews constantly reconfigured and revised their understanding of their diasporic situation.[46] Indeed, as scholars Daniel and Jonathan Boyarin provocatively suggest, there has long been a disconnect between the existence of a Jewish diaspora and Jews' practice and performance of their diasporic identities.[47] The Jewish past highlights that Jews' understanding of such key terms as home, exile, and power were not shaped by their imagined exile from the biblical land of Israel but in the crucible of their connections to other homelands.[48] In fact, "Jews never imagined their home exclusively in

Israel or Zion," as Yosef Yerushalmi observes, "but in a whole myriad of places, such as Toledo, Amsterdam, and Granada." As it turns out, Yerushalmi continues, "Jews felt at home within exile itself," with the "Jewish mentality betray[ing] an intrinsic oscillating duality" between maintaining "ongoing links to the ancient land of origin and endow[ing] the place of exile with familiarity, perceiving it as Jewish."[49] While the biblical land of Israel remained Jews' mythic diasporic homeland, Eastern Europe was the "lived diasporic" homeland for millions of Jews at the dawn of the twentieth century.[50]

In its focus on strategies used by immigrant Jews to remain tied to both a real and imagined Eastern Europe, *Jewish Bialystok and Its Diaspora* highlights the problem in viewing diaspora as a trans-historical concept or condition. Diasporic centers and peripheries shift over time, provoking Jews to revise their understanding of what it means to be a "dispersed people" and to rethink the roles diaspora and exile play in the Jewish *Weltanschauung*. The traditional rendering of Jewish diasporic identity contends, from the moment of their first dispersion in 586 BCE, that Jews articulated a yearning for the ingathering of the Jewish people to its mythic homeland in the historic land of Israel.[51] But a Jewish diasporic mentality was first created by the rabbis in the third century, as they reshaped exilic themes introduced in the Bible to emphasize the sacredness of time rather than place (Jerusalem) in their writings.[52] By sacralizing acts of learning and prayer, the rabbis articulated a new vision of Jewish exile and redemption that revolved around an activity (learning) that could be accomplished anywhere in addition to a fixed place (Jerusalem). Even as biblical literature compelled the rabbis to maintain the mythic notion of *shivat tsiyon* (return to Zion), rabbinic writings actually made diaspora sites of learning almost as sacred as the land of Israel itself.[53] By elevating learning above all else, the rabbis converted a place in the Diaspora that was "peripheral" to the Israelite religion into a "center," with rabbinic texts evincing loyalties to two homelands—one temporal (Babylonia, the center of Jewish learning) and the other ultimate (Zion).

In medieval and early modern philosophical and kabbalistic works, particularly following the expulsion of Jews from Spain in 1492, Jews often drew upon traditional rhetoric concerning exile to describe their longings to return to their former homes in the Iberian Peninsula. For example, Moshe Ibn Ezra, who was forced to leave Granada in the eleventh century, wrote a collection of poems incorporating biblical passages of longing to return to Zion in which he described his painful exile from Granada and Andalusia.[54] Jews living in early modern Europe often employed biblical rhetoric to convey their continued longing to return to the places of their birth, which they imagined as their true "homes."[55] Portuguese Jews in seventeenth-century Amsterdam constantly referred to themselves as *os da nação* (those of the nation) to demarcate their perceived fundamental difference from other Jews as a result of their dispersion and imagined connection to their temporal homeland in Spain, while also acknowledging they were part of *Mikve Yisrael,* those who longed to return to mythic Zion.[56]

During the modern period, few political or intellectual movements transformed the ways in which Jews talked about the condition of diaspora more radically than Zionism.[57] Modern articulations of Jewish diasporic identity, in short, are inseparable from Jewish nationalism and nation formation. In response to many intersecting trends, including Jewish assimilation, antisemitism in Western Europe, and continued political and economic oppression in Eastern Europe, a cluster of Jewish political and national movements sprouted up that would eventually become known as Zionism, with the goal of Jewish self-redemption through the creation of an autonomous Jewish nation-state. As early Zionist thinkers, such as Theodore Herzl, politicized the idea of a return to Zion, they also portrayed the Jewish diaspora in starkly negative terms, emphasizing the hopelessness and powerlessness of Jews subject to oppressive governments—epitomized by tsarist Russia. Indeed, amid all the divisions among European Zionist ideologues, one of the few beliefs that united Zionist thinkers across the spectrum—from labor Zionist A. D. Gordon to cultural Zionist Ahad Ha'am (Asher Zevi Ginzberg)—was their firm commitment to a "negation of the diaspora."[58] While few American Zionists adopted this aspect of Zionist ideology, vehemently denying that it was impossible for the diaspora to nurture Jewish life, their voices were overwhelmed by leaders in Europe who maintained that

Jews' historical suffering and persecution would only cease when Jews had a land of their own. No Jew, Zionists thinkers in Europe insisted, regardless of their religious or national beliefs or where they lived, could ever be truly "at home" in the diaspora.

Many Jews, most notably the world-famous Russian Jewish historian Simon Dubnov, refused to accept the notion that Jews could not harbor allegiances to their temporal homelands. Indeed, thousands of East European Jews held fast to the ideology of *doykeyt* (lit., "hereness," an ideology dedicated to maintaining Jewish life in Eastern Europe). Dubnov argued for Jewish "autonomism," a sociopolitical system allowing Jews to contribute to political and civil life in their host societies while retaining freedom of self-determination. All, in their own way, vociferously challenged the view that Palestine offered the only and ideal circumstance for Jewish national renewal.[59]

In the clashes over whether Eastern Europe or Palestine provided a better home for Jewish renewal, few have accounted for the voices and actions of thousands of East European Jewish émigrés. Advancing the notion that their temporal "promised land" was none other than Eastern Europe, Jewish immigrants offered up a vision of migration as placing them in a new kind of Jewish exile. To remain connected to Eastern Europe, they developed imaginative communal institutions, philanthropic organizations, and literary journals. While the actual institutions focused on Eastern Europe may have lasted only several decades, as the following pages illustrate, the strategies and behaviors they encouraged among their members and their children did not disappear with the immigrant generation. Rather, they were incorporated into how East European immigrant Jews and their children—who by the 1950s comprised the majority of world Jewry—related to the "ultimate" Jewish homeland embodied by the newly formed state of Israel.[60]

To fully appreciate the ways in which migrations and dispersals reshaped Jewish diasporic identity in the last two centuries, one must begin with a consideration of the Jewish dispersal within Eastern Europe. Indeed, as chapter 1 highlights, Jewish immigration to America can only be fully understood if one appreciates that, on the individual level, it was often experienced as part of a longer series of migrations, first to larger cities within the Russian Empire and only later overseas.[61] Jews flooded into Bialystok from the north-western Pale during the nineteenth century, demographically over-whelming the city's indigenous population as they did in Warsaw, Lodz, and other large urban areas in Poland. Despite the striking parallels between Bialystok and other cities, Bialystok was distinct in its disproportionately large Jewish migrant population: according to the 1897 Russian census, 47,783 Jews lived in Bialystok, constituting over 75 percent of the population. While the same census counted more than 210,526 Jews living in Warsaw, Jews only comprised 34 percent of the city's population.[62] Thus the massive influx of Jews into Bialystok left a more substantial imprint on the city's economic, political, and social development. As they financed industrial expan-sion and developed new political and welfare organizations, these Jewish migrants destabilized traditional authorities and helped transform Bialystok into a Jewish space. Whether or not they also chose to identify themselves with national or international move-ments, such as Zionism, socialism, or Esperantoism, Jews in Bialystok saw their identities as deeply intertwined with their city. Thus, even after they left Bialystok in response to economic recession and politi-cal instability, their experiences in Bialystok, the city in which they first encountered industry, nationalist politics, and "modern" Jewish organizations, shaped the way they approached challenges in their new homes. That intense identification with Bialystok was due to its transformation from a small provincial town into a large industrial center, a process that mirrored their own personal transformations into modern urban Jews.

Chapter 2 explores how Jews from Bialystok laid the foundation for a new type of dispersed Jewish community by forming new orga-nizations as they spread around the world. The Bialystoker Center in New York—which became the economic epicenter of the Bialystok diaspora—played a central role in galvanizing this transnational community through its publications and philanthropic endeavors. Yet the tale of Jewish Bialystok and its diaspora is not an exclusively American tale; America was only one of many destinations pursued by Bialystok's Jews. Indeed, aside from New York, one finds in Buenos Aires, Tel Aviv, and Melbourne new "centers" devoted to transplanting the essence of Bialystok to new "colonial outposts" throughout the world. While all Bialystoker organizations offered financial support to their constituents, they each reframed its constituents' regional identities in a manner that spoke to their practical and existential needs. Through its cross-cultural juxtaposition of these four self-proclaimed "new Bialystoks," chapter 2 highlights not only the shared but also distinct domestic, political, economic, and cultural structures shaping East European Jews' encounters with the New World. By exposing the intricate links between Bialystok's Jews support of welfare in New York, working-class politics in Buenos Aires, and Jewish philanthropic development in Melbourne, this chapter provides a deeper understanding of the wider trends shaping patterns of Jewish adaptation and acculturation over the last century.

Chapter 3 explores how, after the First World War, philanthropy became the defining focus of the dispersed Bialystoker Jewish community, offering émigrés a way to affirm their new identities as American, Argentine, or Australian Jews as well as to articulate how they wished to reshape the world by rebuilding Bialystok in their images.[63] Between 1919 and 1939, Bialystok's Jewish émigrés raised more than $9,000,000 (equivalent to approximately $107,000,000 2008 dollars), which they donated to rebuild the now-devastated communal institutions of their former home. Jews in America, for whom philanthropy played a major role in defining their sense of self, spearheaded these efforts in the 1920s.[64] By demanding active participation of women and encouraging distinct patterns of leadership, philanthropy created a particular culture among Jewish émigrés from Bialystok. The linking of philanthropy with the language of the marketplace reminded émigrés of their connection to Eastern Europe, as it pushed them to see philanthropy as a vehicle through which they could convey to those in Europe and scattered throughout Bialystok's diaspora how successful they had become in their new homes.

How did Bialystok's Jewish émigrés' growing economic power affect life in Eastern Europe? The philanthropic drive not only changed émigrés' understanding of themselves, but also fundamentally reconfigured how Jews in Bialystok imagined the parameters of their community. The long, controversial, and complex story of interwar Polish–Jewish relations rarely considers how the vast sums that migrant Jews funneled into Poland influenced interethnic relations on the local level. Bialystok's Jewish émigrés created innovative philanthropic organizations that confounded partisans of the new Polish state by transcending national categories. As a result, Jewish residents of Bialystok were compelled to question the authority of the state during this era of dramatic social and political upheaval. While Poles who left Bialystok also sent money back to their relatives, as migrants often do, their generosity was more meager and did not attract the same attention given to the dozens of Jewish émigré philanthropists who visited during the 1920s and distributed millions of dollars to build schools, hospitals, and cultural organizations. Indeed, the massive influx of Jewish émigré money into Bialystok (as in other cities throughout Poland) had several unintended consequences, transforming how Poles viewed Jewish power, interacted with local Jewish leaders, and viewed Jews' place in the new Polish state.

Chapter 4 interrogates the ways in which the press reinforced the financial ties laid by the philanthropy of this transnational Jewish community. Beginning in 1921, the Bialystoker Center in New York began publishing a quarterly magazine, *Der Bialystoker Stimme,* to rouse support for its namesake in Europe. Yet this publication went beyond galvanizing the immigrant community, as it deployed a wide array of innovative idioms that pushed Jews on both sides of the Atlantic to rethink the parameters of their identities. In their depictions of Bialystok as a motherland, a colonial empire, or a second Jerusalem, émigré writers repeatedly searched for a "usable past" upon which to build their new identities as Jews in New York as they claimed Eastern Europe as their inspirational homeland and conceptualized migration as a new form of exile.[65] Chapter 4's examination of the literary reinvention of Eastern Europe in the transnational Bialystok press aims to recover émigrés' "inner world," recounting not only what they experienced but also the worldview through which they experienced it.[66] In many ways, the creative process of adaptation to their new homes became entwined with, and in some cases even aided by, a pious devotion to Eastern Europe in the Bialystoker émigré mind. Through an almost liturgical telling and retelling of the story of their shared past and dispersal, Bialystoker émigrés solidified the ties of their scattered community and negotiated their evolving relationship with their new homelands.[67]

As the final chapter explores, these fortified ties with their temporal homeland were put to a difficult test in the years following the Second World War. The growing literature on migrant diasporas discusses the role that trauma plays in the formation of diasporic communities, but few have been forced to contemplate the dynamics unleashed when a migrant group confronts the complete destruction of its inspirational homeland. While still envisioning themselves as powerful leaders as a result of the dollars at their disposal, Bialystok's Jews, like thousands of East European Jews, found themselves unable to make sense of what had taken place during the Holocaust. What type of response should they devise in the aftermath of such complete destruction? Initially, Bialystok's Jews who survived around the world could not abandon their former home despite its complete eradication. Between 1945 and 1949, thousands of dollars was sent to rebuild Bialystok for those several hundred Jews who had survived and returned to the city. But the persistence of violent antisemitism in Poland and the power of Zionist leaders in postwar Bialystok's Jewish community compelled émigrés to reevaluate their commitment. As a consequence, Bialystoker philanthropic organizations in New York shifted their fundraising efforts away from their "temporal" homeland in Bialystok and toward their "ultimate" homeland in Israel. Exercising their economic power through the erection of a "new" Bialystok in the state of Israel, Bialystok's Jews donated ambulances, buildings, factories, and synagogues. But even as Israel's institutions supplanted East European institutions as the main recipients of Bialystoker philanthropy, one aspect remained the same: just as the Bialystoker Center encouraged its members to nurture and support their homeland in Eastern Europe in the interwar period— with no expectation of a permanent return—it now encouraged East European Jews in America to support the Jewish homeland in Israel, knowing quite well that few would settle there. Thus, the behaviors developed during the interwar period with regard to philanthropy and devotion to a "homeland" in Poland shaped the ways in which the dispersed East European Jews and their children viewed their relationship to the new state of Israel and their philanthropic endeavors on its behalf.

The tale of *Jewish Bialystok and Its Diaspora* conveys up close how the simple decision of millions of East European Jews to abandon their homes not only reshaped the demographic centers of nineteenth century Jewish identity; it also radically revised and reconfigured the ideological cornerstones of modern Jewish life. This tale of Jewish migration seeks to encourage others to move beyond the territorial boundaries of nation-states when assessing not only Jewish migration but also the Jewish past writ large. Moreover, in its relinquishing of a narrow definition of diaspora, the following pages demonstrate the ways in which immigrant Jews harbored different, at times competing, longings and loyalties. To be sure, contemporary immigrants rightfully see themselves as politically disenfranchised and culturally alienated in the new homes, as did Chaim Horowitz in 1921. But they too, at times, must acknowledge the power they wield, as they deploy the funds at their fingertips to alter local elections in Mexico, or to provide funds to finance reform efforts in the Dominican Republic. Indeed these contemporary migrant groups are also caught, like Bialystok's Jews were in the first half of the twentieth century, between the dilemmas of exile and empire.

CHAPTER 1

The Dispersal Within: Bialystok, Jewish Migration, and Urban Life in the Borderlands of Eastern Europe

In 1862, when the young Russian writer Nikolai Leskov first saw the town of Bialystok, it boasted little more than a few paved roads and seventeen thousand residents. First settled in 1320, the town was bequeathed to Count Jan Klemens Branicki in 1703, who immediately welcomed Jews to his new home. By the late nineteenth century, Bialystok boasted few buildings taller than two stories, its landscape punctuated only by a large palace erected by the Branicki family at the eastern end of the town that was said to resemble Versailles and a clock tower standing at the center of the main marketplace. Although devoid of the clear markers of a large metropolis such as the wide boulevards of St. Petersburg or the towering turrets of Moscow, this "new" city's bustle along its main thoroughfare that sloped gently west from the Palace overwhelmed Leskov. As he noted in his diary, "the main street [Lipowa Street] is packed with people . . . [and] swarming with Jews."[1] "The entire city felt like a market place," Leskov observed, because Jews, who at the time constituted 70 percent of the town's population, "filled the streets" with "conversation," "quarrels," and "noise." More than simply populating the landscape, Jews also brought with them a resolute entrepreneurial spirit that Leskov concluded fueled the city's economic growth, transforming it from a small provincial town into an industrial center many called the "Manchester of Lithuania."

The lure of the potential riches one could reap from industrial production indeed drew thousands of Jews to Bialystok, where by 1897, when tsarist officials conducted an official census, they comprised

Street scene, Bialystok, 1930s. *From the Alter Kacyzne Photography Collection, Archives of the YIVO Institute for Jewish Research, New York.*

75 percent of the city's 62,993 residents.[2] The first Jewish migrants who streamed into the city over the course of the late nineteenth century set up their homes in an area due west of the palace and at the southern end of the town's main square. As one mid-nineteenth-century memoirist recalled, "every year" when "I walked down Surazer Street [the main street of the Jewish area off the city's main square], I always found new side streets opened up" where families who had just arrived in the city had set up their homes.[3] Such overcrowding prodded Zvi Masliansky, an itinerant preacher who visited the city in 1892, to note that thousands of Jews jammed into this "new city." Awed by the merchants, workers, industrialists and "men of action" whom he encountered, Masliansky proclaimed that Bialystok's Jews, with their firm commitment to Zionism and philanthropy, had made "Bialystok into the Jaffa of Lithuania."[4] Indeed, this comparison was most apt, he concluded, since like Jaffa, Palestine's burgeoning port city, Bialystok owed its development to the efforts of Jewish migrant

pioneers.[5] In short, Masliansky understood Bialystok's growth from a small town into a large industrial center as part of the revolutionary migration reshaping Jewish life throughout the world.[6]

As a growing industrial center and a center of Jewish migrant settlement, Bialystok did resemble both Manchester and Jaffa, suggesting the complex ways in which urban industrial development and Jewish migration became fundamentally entwined in nineteenth-century Russia–Poland. Józef Ignacy Kraszewski, the noted nineteenth-century Polish nationalist writer, once observed that actually what made "every Polish city feel Polish . . . [was] . . . the presence of Jews."[7] Yet few Jews resided in Bialystok until 1658, and by 1807, only two thousand Jews called Bialystok home. By end of the nineteenth century, however, approximately fifty thousand Jews lived in Bialystok, drawn to the town by its central position along the Russian railway system and tsarist authorities' support of Jewish settlement in Congress Poland as a means to quell Polish nationalist agitation. Many Jews saw Bialystok as the answer to their harsh economic predicament.[8] Owing largely to social pressures stemming from Jewish demographic expansion as well as to discriminatory state policies, Jewish artisans and petty merchants living in smaller towns, as Eli Lederhendler points out, were "reduced to a single caste-like status" over the course of the nineteenth century, with few social or economic distinctions existing between Jewish laborers, artisans, and petty trades people.[9] By 1912, almost all of the 73,950 Jewish residents of Bialystok were migrants or children of migrants who had arrived over the course of the late nineteenth century as part of a desire to improve their economic prospects. Indeed, such growth was not particular to Bialystok: the Jewish population of Łódź, another Polish industrial center, swelled even more dramatically—from 259 in 1820 to 98,676 in 1897.[10] Demographically overwhelming the indigenous populations, migrant Jews fundamentally transformed the economic, political, and civic life in these and other emergent East European industrial centers.[11]

Population shifts of this nature had a profound effect on daily life. The massive influx of Jewish migrants into Bialystok affected existing systems of control and authority, posing challenges to both

Postcard of Bialystok's central marketplace, circa 1920. The clock tower, which had stood in the center of the city's main square since 1742, was recognized by all as symbolic of the city. *Courtesy of the Merhavia Collection, Jewish National Library, Jerusalem.*

local Jewish communal authorities as well as to the state. While it was painfully apparent to most turn-of-the-century Poles, few contemporary scholars of late Imperial Russia address the unsettling effects that Jewish migration and urbanization had on life in Russia's Polish provinces, where prior to the First World War Jews played a dominant role in founding theaters, literary clubs, schools, newspapers, and charity institutions that defined many dimensions of the Polish urban life.[12] When we consider Bialystok's growth and development from a provincial town into a bustling city over the course of the nineteenth century, we immediately become aware that Jewish migrant newcomers revolutionized Poland's economy by financing industrial expansion, generating new ethnic antagonisms, creating addition grounds for political opposition against the Russian government, and developing innovative political and welfare organizations to address their needs. All of these features contributed to the destabilization of traditional authority, challenging—as Peter Gatrell notes in a later period—the "prevalent political, social and cultural practices" of tsarist Russia's estate system.[13]

The political turmoil in the region aided the efforts of migrant Jews to remake the city: over the course of two and a half centuries, Bialystok found itself under the aegis of the Polish–Lithuanian Commonwealth (*Rzeczpospolita*), Prussia, France, the Russian Empire and finally, in 1919, the Second Polish Republic. Each of these regimes left an imprint on the city and its inhabitants, forcing Germans, Russians, Poles, Lithuanians, and Jews to coexist in a patchwork of social and economic relations. Even when Bialystok remained part of tsarist Russia, as it did for most of the nineteenth century, the absolutist state's pursuit of modernizing reforms in an uneven and haphazard manner created tremendous ferment in this city, as exemplified by the strikes and anti-Jewish violence at the dawn of the twentieth century. Bialystok is representative of many cities in tsarist Russia, such as Kiev, Minsk, or Warsaw, in the ways it combined radically modern modes of production with significant features of pre-industrial life, such as rabbinical control of Jewish welfare distribution.[14] It is within this context of accelerating change, social dislocation, and economic transformation that one must situate Bialystok's development as a center for industry and Jewish migrant life within the rapidly evolving Russian Empire.[15]

While the hope of improving their economic lot motivated many Russian Jewish migrants to settle in Bialystok, economic success often became interlaced with their desire to integrate into their new home's cultural milieu. The development of a wide array of new Jewish welfare organizations and Jewish political parties, such as the socialist Bund Party, the Zionist Hibbat Zion (Lovers of Zion) Party, or the Esperanto language movement provide vivid illustrations of ways in which Jews established new organizations and employed new strategies to confront their needs as uprooted migrant workers. These organizations—whether traditional philanthropic associations or more radical political enterprises—transformed life in Bialystok by encouraging Jews to challenge the authority of the *kehilla* (local

Jewish communal authority) and the tsar while simultaneously making them see their Jewish identities as having a pronounced regional character: as Eliyahu Oran and Yisroel Prenski summed it up, "We are not just from Bialystok; we are Bialystoker Bundist Jews."[16] To be sure, the fact that Jews in Bialystok resided in a region characterized by intense nationalist agitation—with the nascent Polish, Belarussian, Ukrainian, and Lithuanian national movements all fighting for recognition—reinforced Bialystok Jews' localized base of their self-identity. However, what is most intriguing about these new organizations is that as they linked their constituents to larger ideological movements—such as Zionism or socialism—they also encouraged Jews to see their regional affiliation as intertwined with their religious, social, and political identities.[17] Needless to say, Bialystok was by no means exceptional in this regard: despite their shallow roots, having only recently arrived in burgeoning cities such as Odessa, Warsaw, and St. Petersburg, many Jewish migrants believed that their adopted hometowns defined their identities. Jews throughout Eastern Europe identified with their new homes since the transformations of these locales from small market towns into centers of industrial capitalism, revolutionary nationalist politics, and progressive welfare organizations mirrored their own personal transformation into modern people with urban sensibilities. They were united with the developing cities of the Russian Empire not only by place but by experience as well.[18]

Bialystok and Eastern Europe's Shifting Political Sovereignty

Located in the Pale of Settlement—the mandated area of Jewish residence in tsarist Russia's western borderlands—Bialystok sat at the crossroads of this empire (see table 1 and map 1). Administered successively by four different regimes, its geographic location attracted Poles, Russians, Germans, Lithuanians and, of course, Jews drawn from many different regions.[19] Although demographically dominant, Jews represented a non-native population and so struggled with issues of identity and assimilation. Like other immigrant or minority peoples in other times and places, Jews in Bialystok desired both to integrate into their cultural surroundings and to maintain independent religious, social, and political identities. In place of national affiliation, then, these Jews—like those in Odessa, Warsaw, and St. Petersburg—viewed themselves through an urban regional lens. They were loyal Bialystokers, first and foremost, ambivalent and uncertain whether to identify themselves as devoted Russian subjects or as Jews of the Polish nation.[20]

The absence of a demographic pressure to assimilate into one nation-state or imperial mold, however, should not obscure the subtle shifts in Jewish life as the city became incorporated into each new regime.[21] When Bialystok fell under Prussian control in 1796, for example, officials actively sought to "Germanize" the city by limiting Jewish migration, restricting the number of professions open to Jews, and encouraging German entrepreneurs and Prussian administrators to settle in the area.[22] They also reformed Bialystok's secondary school system in order to "Germanize" the local population.[23] While the native Polish population remained steadfastly loyal to their "Polish province," as Prussian officials dejectedly admitted, Jews embraced German culture. They quickly became proficient in German, entered new professions and championed the ideals of the German-Jewish *haskalah,* or Jewish enlightenment.[24]

Exposure to these new ideas led many in Bialystok's Jewish community to behave like acculturated German Jews, and some leaders identified with the German *maskilim* (proponents of the haskalah), devoting themselves to disseminating the "enlightened" works and ideological tracts produced by German Jewish maskilim throughout Poland.[25] Rabbi Eliezer Halberstam epitomized Bialystok Jewry's embrace of the ideals of the haskalah: he opened a new school to train Bialystok's Jewish youth in maskilic ideals and contributed extensively to the Hebrew maskilic newspaper *Ha-magid* (The Declarer).[26] Rabbi Aaron Halevi Horowitz set up Bialystok's first Hebrew printing press in 1804 to spread ideas of Jewish modernization. The ambivalence experienced by Jews regarding their relationship to the dominant culture is best illustrated by the reception of these efforts. Although embraced by Halberstam and others, these "modern" ideas opened a rift in the Polish Jewish community. More traditionally minded rabbis, who clung to older ways, proclaimed that Bialystok

Table 1.1. Political Shifts and Demographic Growth in Bialystok, 1795–1939

YEAR	POLITICAL	POPULATION	
		TOTAL	JEWISH (% OF WHOLE)
1795–1807	Region is part of Prussia.	4,145	2,116 (51%)
1807–1831	In 1807 Bialystok is incorporated into Russia. Bialystok is administered as its own autonomous *oblast*.	9,248 (from 1830)	4,716 (51%) (from 1830)
1832	Bialystok's autonomy vanishes as it becomes part of the Grodno *gubernia* (province)	n/a	n/a
1897	Part of Grodno *gubernia*	62,993	47,783 (76%)
1916	Annexed by Germany in 1915. Many flee Bialystok.	54,260	40,000 (73.7%)
1921	Bialystok is incorporated into the Second Polish Republic.	76,792	37,186 (48.4%)

was a "heretical city, filled with *haskalah* and *bildung* [enlightenment and secular education]" and should be avoided at all costs.[27]

After 1807, however, when Bialystok was annexed by the Russian Empire, "Germanization" lost some of its appeal, prodding Jews in Bialystok to mitigate their identification with German Jewry.[28] At the moment the Russians seized power in Bialystok in 1807, the town council was led by a Christian mayor, but its deputy mayor was Jewish and two of the town's four councilors were also Jewish. Jews maintained a prominent role in civic affairs under Napoleon, who ruled Bialystok between 1812 and 1815. After Bialystok was returned to Russia in 1815, Jews shifted away from municipal service and focused on expanding their commercial ties, both within the Russian Empire and beyond its borders.[29] Until the 1830–1831 Polish uprising, the tsarist government respected the local residents' loyalty to their Polish heritage and culture and made few efforts to "Russify" the province. The city retained its role as an administrative center

Russian Poland and the Jewish Pale of Settlement circa 1900.

and even served as the capital of its own independent *oblast* (administrative district).[30] Once Polish nationalist agitation intensified in the 1830s, though, the tsarist government reversed course, instituting an intensive program to refashion the local population into loyal Russian subjects.[31] As part of this plan, the government encouraged Jews, who despite their ambivalent relationship to the Russian state were viewed as more loyal than Poles, to settle in Bialystok in order to diminish Polish revolutionary fervor.[32]

Drawn to Bialystok by the economic and cultural opportunities it offered, Jews streamed into the city, causing the city's Jewish population to grow from 2,116 in 1807 to more than 79,350 by 1914. As revealed by a cursory glance at the birth, death, and marriage records of the Jewish community in 1862, some Jews hailed from surrounding hamlets less than fifty kilometers away, such as Tykochin, Most, and Knysan. Tykochin, the former provincial capital renowned for its wooden synagogue, vividly illustrates the rhythms of life in these small hamlets: Jews comprised 60 percent of the town's population that totaled a little more than 2,000 people in 1897. One memoirist recalled how his pious grandmother kept a cow in her yard to insure that even if there was no money for food, her family would always have milk and butter, because this "town was only known for its poverty, annual fair, and its deep rooted [observance] of Jewish traditions." Indeed, the main items produced in Tykochin were Jewish prayer shawls. Others came to Bialystok, however, from burgeoning cities hundreds of kilometers away, such as Minsk, a city in fact larger than Bialystok with over 91,494 inhabitants in 1897. It appears as though the great potential for quick economic success even attracted Jews to Bialystok from locales outside the Pale of Settlement, such as Konigsberg in Prussia, where Jews not only freely enrolled in university but also enjoyed membership in non-Jewish social clubs.[33] To be sure, natural population growth played a limited role in fueling this population explosion; nonetheless, it was generally recognized that, as Michael Flicker recalled, "everyday when the train arrived, another Jewish family would disembark to start their life anew."[34]

The flood of migration intensified even more during the last quarter of the nineteenth century. Bialystok's booming economy and easy accessibility attracted thousands of Jews from both near and far.[35]

Late-nineteenth-century Jewish settlers were forced to live in formerly desolate areas of the town near the Zverinetz forest: "with no paved streets or roads," complained one young Jewish resident, his daily walk to work over "hills and dales filled with snow" took over an hour.[36] In addition, when the tsarist authorities invested heavily in expanding the Russian railway system in the 1860s as a way to modernize the empire, Bialystok became a central transit point on the St. Petersburg–Warsaw railway line. Now Jews from most areas in the Pale of Settlement could reach Bialystok in less than a day's journey. Moreover, the Polish rebellion of 1863 cemented Russian authorities' support for Jewish settlement and industrial expansion in Polish lands; it also prodded Russian authorities to establish a military base in Bialystok, all steps taken with the hope that the increased military presence along with an influx of Jews and new economic opportunities would help eliminate Polish nationalist fervor.[37]

While these policies did not achieve their ultimate goal—eradicating Polish nationalism—they did indeed diversify the city's population and economy. As the 1897 Imperial census reported, tens of thousands came to Bialystok from nearby small market towns and neighboring small cities. The increased presence of the Russian military in the region diversified Bialystok's population, drawing thousands of men from distant regions in the Russian Empire such as Tver and Kazan (1,634).[38] The promise of work and investment opportunities in the city's growing network of factories enticed hundreds of settlers from cities scattered throughout the empire, such as St. Petersburg (198), Minsk (701), Vilna (752) and Warsaw (523). Many were also attracted to the city from outside the geographic borders of the Russian Empire: close to 600 residents of Bialystok came from the Prussian and Austro-Hungarian empires.[39]

Weaving the Fabric of Everyday Life: Jewish Migrants and the Development of Industry in Bialystok

Jewish migration to Bialystok did more than simply alter the city's demographics; it radically reshaped its economic life as well. Bialystok's rapid development into a center of industry was part and parcel of Russia's industrial transformation in the nineteenth century, but, as in other cities in Poland, this growth was to a large extent driven by Jewish productivity and ingenuity.[40] In Bialystok's industrial sector, Jewish workers constituted 83.9 percent of the work force, while Jewish merchants owned 88 percent of the city's shops.[41] These trends were particularly evident in the textile sector, an area in which Jews owned 80 percent of the city's 309 textile factories by 1898.[42] Thus, in the new world of industrial capitalism that developed in Bialystok around textile manufacturing, Jews constituted the majority of the elite entrepreneurial class, dominated the merchant class, and formed the core of the new working class.[43]

Textile manufacturing was introduced to the city's economy by settlers from Prussia in the early nineteenth century. Around 1800, several German industrialists established factories that catered primarily to an upscale market, producing only high-quality expensive woolen fabrics for wealthy customers. After the solidification of Russian control over Congress Poland in 1831, however, the Russian government made Bialystok the tariff barrier between the Congress Kingdom and the Russian Empire. Bialystok thus became a new border city. With this act, the stage was set for it to grow into a major industrial center that attracted many Jewish entrepreneurs in the 1840s and 1850s, among them Sender Bloch.[44] Bloch, a Jew from a wealthy entrepreneurial family in Vilna, set up a cloth factory in Bialystok in 1842. Interested primarily in making a quick profit, he turned away from the production of fine goods, focusing instead on lower-quality synthetic wool that he then marketed to Eastern Europe's lower and middle classes.[45]

Bloch's decision revolutionized Bialystok's textile industry. As Russia's middle class grew, the continued demand for these lower-priced fabrics forced a surge in the number of textile factories in Bialystok. Soon enough, the factories that turned out high-quality fabrics could not compete with those producing lower-quality items.[46] Eventually, these Jewish lower-quality fabric factories produced the vast majority of woolen uniforms for the Russian army.[47]

The impact that Jewish entrepreneurs had upon the textile industry of Bialystok went beyond the factory system. Because it cost relatively little to set up a business, many recent arrivals to the city took advantage of the opportunities available to them to set up their own shops. These men, known as *loynketniks* (lit. men of expediency), knew how easy it was to master the craft of weaving, and so ended up employing most Jewish migrants in small unmechanized shops.[48] Loynketniks, acting as contractors, provided finished goods for the larger, mechanized factories. In return, the factories supplied the loynketniks with looms and raw materials. In his memoir, Max Havelin, a Jewish migrant from a small village in the Mohilever region, described how his frustration with his low pay from toiling in a small factory prodded him to set up his own workshop. After months of painstaking labor on two borrowed looms, Havelin prospered, and he was able to hire several weavers and buy two more looms.[49]

Undoubtedly, Havelin was the exception to the rule. Most Jewish workers had few options, a factor that Jewish loynketniks gladly exploited, forcing many poor Jewish migrant workers to toil long hours for little pay. As one worker recalled in his memoir:

> In the summer, I would work from seven in the morning until eight in the evening while in the winter the hours were from eight in the morning until nine in the evening. Before holidays, I often worked the entire night. Only after six months of such hard labor did I start earning two rubles a week.[50]

Both the exploitation of the workers and the fact that textile production differed dramatically between the mechanized factories and the loynketnik shops led to a two-tier hierarchy of weavers in Bialystok. In 1885, for example, factory workers earned almost three times as much as weavers working in the loynketnik system.[51] By 1900, factory workers received about eight rubles a week for their work, while those working in the loynketnik system earned only four rubles a week.[52] In 1887 Jewish factory workers went on strike, not, as in other cities, to protest the working conditions in the mechanized factories, but rather to eradicate the loynketnik system, since they believed it undermined their status as skilled laborers and kept them from demanding higher wages during busy periods.[53] Throughout the next decade, factory workers repeatedly went on strike to protest the surplus of weavers created by the loynketnik system.[54]

Although Bialystok did present its Jewish migrant population with job opportunities, it also dealt them much hardship and suffering. Like other developing industrial centers, Bialystok experienced periods of stagnation as well as growth. Recession, as reports of the regional governor highlight, hit the local economy again and again between 1872 and 1909.[55] Long periods of unemployment were common for most Jewish migrant workers, especially for those working in smaller factories that closed during slack times to save money. Those who remained employed often avoided losing their jobs only by agreeing to work fewer hours or to split their wages with other workers.[56] In response to these periods of economic crisis, many Jewish textile workers left Bialystok and were immediately replaced by Polish Catholic workers, prompting one late-nineteenth-century Russian observer to remark "Bialystok [is] a Jewish city, [with] Jewish factory owners, but not a single Jewish worker."[57]

These periods of recession highlighted the precarious position of Jewish weavers, particularly those in the loynketnik system, in which employers were able to keep wages low because of the steady supply of available Jewish migrant labor. Jewish workers made up the vast majority of the workforce in unmechanized factories; however, as Jewish industrialists developed large, mechanized factories, they rarely employed Jewish workers in these enterprises because they did not wish to close their factories on both Saturdays, in honor of the Sabbath, and Sundays, the expected "day of rest" in Poland.[58] An 1886 survey of the 150 advanced mechanized textile factories in Bialystok found that less than one-fifth of the workforce was Jewish.[59] This trend changed little by the end of the century, when the 1897 Russian census reported that Jews in Bialystok comprised 83.9 percent of the workforce in nonmechanized, Jewish-owned factories and only 36.6 percent of those employed at mechanized, Jewish-run factories.[60]

The loynketnik's exploitative methods provoked Bialystok's Jewish migrant proletariat into political action. Labor unrest became more common among Jewish weavers than among their non-Jewish counterparts.[61] At first, Jewish workers turned to Jewish communal institutions to arbitrate their labor conflicts. For example, in 1882, the seventy weavers who abandoned their looms to demand increased wages at Aaron Suzarsky's textile factory—considered the first major strike in the city—turned to religious authorities for help.[62] Since most of the weavers were members of the same hasidic congregation as their employer, the congregation's rabbi adjudicated the conflict.[63] Religious considerations also played a role in the conflicts of the 1880s, when many Jewish factory owners replaced Jewish workers with Christian ones, as the latter demanded only Sundays off.[64] This enraged many Jewish workers, and rather than turn to religious authorities, they took matters into their own hands and coordinated several strikes.[65] Jewish workers used strikes to protest against factory regulations introduced by government inspectors that made their tasks more physically burdensome; they also walked out to demand higher wages and shorter workdays.[66] When Bialystok plummeted into recession in the 1880s, many Jews working in the loynketnik system decided to give up on Bialystok altogether and attempted to move to places with greater economic opportunity.[67]

The Politics of Charity: *Lines Hatsedek* and the Challenge of Jewish Migrants to Traditional Communal Governance

Despite their wishes, most Jews could not just leave Bialystok, and turned instead to the dense array of new Jewish welfare organizations that cropped up to address the needs of poor migrants living far away from their familiar support systems. Since the tsarist empire did not maintain an official welfare policy or system of public relief, Bialystok's poor, as in almost every city in the empire, were cared for by a web of institutions supported primarily by wealthy individuals as well as through some funding from the state and municipal authorities.[68] Newly arrived Jewish migrants turned first to the dozens of houses of worship—spanning from small intimate prayer quorums (*minyanim*) to large formal synagogues (*shuln*)—scattered throughout the city for help. With close to one hundred groups meeting daily for Jewish ritual prayer services, even new arrivals in the city had little trouble finding a place to pray.[69] But unlike in smaller towns, where charity and food were distributed to the needy after services, the overwhelming number of newcomers made it impossible for all to receive help. As one memoirist recalled after moving to Bialystok with his father from the small town of Most, his family showed up for services and spoke to the sexton "because we had no arrangement to eat." The sexton tirelessly sought "to have some synagogue member invite us," but his "effort was in vain" since there were "too many soldiers" and other newcomers for "whom homes had to be found."[70]

After the synagogue, the larger governing body of the kehilla bore the rest of the responsibility for dispensing charity and addressing poor Jewish migrants' needs. Even after the tsar's official abolition of the kehilla in 1844, it still exerted great power in the community as both a legal authority and a regulator of religious and charitable affairs.[71] Yet by the late nineteenth century, the kehilla's inability to address the pressing economic needs of the growing masses of Jewish migrants, who were not only indigent and working class but acculturating rapidly as well, compromised its position, prompting those more secularly minded Jews looking to challenge the traditional power structure in the Jewish community to establish competing organizations. These new charitable groups often operated outside of the kehilla's purview and broke its monopoly on power, unleashing, as historian Benjamin Nathans describes it, "a contest for power within Russian-Jewish society."[72]

Many of the new Jewish charitable organizations linked themselves to the late nineteenth-century Russian welfare reform movement.[73] Beginning in the 1880s, the tsarist state grew increasingly concerned about the governance of Jewish communal welfare and attempted to regulate Jewish voluntary welfare associations as part of a larger effort to modernize and reform elements of the entire empire. Tsarist authorities began to regard the unsupervised activities of traditional Jewish charitable organizations as suspect and demanded their reorganization to combat "Jewish isolation" and its oligarchic governance.[74] With these goals in mind, tsarist authorities encouraged Jewish communities to centralize their communal and welfare services by abolishing traditional Jewish associations, hevrot (hevrah, singular), and replacing them with modern voluntary associations (obshchestva).[75] As a result, Jewish charitable organizations proliferated rapidly: the editor of Khronika voshkoda observed in 1899 that there were numerous "Societies to Aid the Poor" springing up "all over the place, in every community," directly challenging the authority of old Jewish societies and the wealthy communal leaders who ran them and who, many claimed, were notorious for their corruption.[76]

In Bialystok and other cities, these *obshchestva* became the bastions of a younger, secular-educated generation that had studied in Russian schools and wanted to participate in Jewish organizations that openly identified with the larger Russian society. As they strove to insert themselves into Russian society, acculturating Jews saw philanthropy not only serving the needs of the Jewish poor but also their own needs, as new Jewish elites who deserved greater recognition in the community. These Jews—lawyers, physicians, and industrialists—sought to challenge the traditional leaders who often had exclusive access to *korobka* (the kosher meat tax) funds, a major source of power in most Jewish communities. The challengers hoped their new voluntary associations would spread their agenda: to integrate into the surrounding society.[77] Philanthropic organizations represented the best avenue to achieve their goals, since such institutions could easily underpin the idea that the true face of Judaism and Jews was to care for all, regardless of faith, and clearly to demonstrate Jews' commitment to the advancement of a multinational Russian Empire.[78]

One such social welfare organization was the self-help and medical aid organization *Lines Hatsedek* (lit., To Lodge the Righteous), established in 1885. Organized in a "democratic" manner, Lines Hatsedek allowed men of all social classes, and even women, to participate in its elections. Even more unusual, its mandate dictated that that anyone in need, Jew or non-Jew, would receive aid. In their new vision of the place of Jewish organizations in Russia's multinational society, the founders of Lines Hatsedek, comprised of recent arrivals from other developing nineteenth-century cities, openly challenged the more traditional kehilla leaders who maintained a strictly exclusivist approach to Jewish philanthropy.

The founding myths concerning the establishment of Lines Hatsedek demonstrate how a new cadre of leaders reacted to the kehilla's inability to address the pressing needs of the growing Jewish urban poor. According to one story, a migrant Jew living alone in

1885 was bitten by rats in his small, disheveled home. Unable to walk himself to the overwhelmed Jewish hospital, originally founded in 1830 to serve the Jewish community, this poor man died alone in his room.[79] His tragic death prodded members of the community to found a new organization to care for the ill members of the working class because *Bikur Holim* (lit., To Visit the Sick), the kehilla-sponsored organization charged with this task, was run by a "despotic dictator" who would not tend to those poor ailing workers in need.[80] A less gruesome tradition links the founding of Lines Hatsedek to the death of Meyer Szochet, a hospital attendant living far away from his family, who fell ill and died because of neglect. At Szochet's funeral, a group of Jews whose families remained behind in other towns established Lines Hatsedek to make sure that no other Jew in poor health in Bialystok would ever find himself in a similar situation.[81] Both versions are apocryphal, yet they sum up, as such tales often do, the main concerns and central facts of the case: in Bialystok, a city filled with swelling ranks of Jewish migrants living apart from their families, the fear of falling ill and dying because of lack of care was a lethal reality. The synagogues of the community, as one memoir writer recalled, "could never keep track of or care for all those who sought help at their steps."[82]

While indigent migrant Jewish workers feared dying alone, it was acculturated Jewish newcomers to the city who gave critical support to this organization in its formative years. Russian Jews were often portrayed in popular literature and the press as possessing poor health and hygiene, and the growing poverty among Jews often made that reputation seem apt. The crowded and unsanitary conditions of cities like Bialystok only made things worse. For acculturated Jews seeking to place a positive face on the Jewish community for the larger Russian society, sickly Jewish masses that put other populations in danger were to be avoided at all costs.[83]

The interests of these two groups thus came to together to found Lines Hatsedek, which was cast from the outset as a populist organization established "by the people."[84] Its founders stood in direct opposition to the kehilla-sponsored organization Bikur Holim, whose members were appointed by Bialystok's chief rabbi and represented

Lines Hatsedek Medical Society Volunteers, circa 1900. *Courtesy of the Goren-Goldstein Center for the Study of Diaspora Jewry, Tel Aviv University.*

a more exclusive and wealthy segment of Bialystok's Jewish community.[85] Over time, and in response to the demands of its members, Lines Hatsedek grew from simply providing care to the ill to establishing ambulance services, storage facilities to distribute food and clothing to the poor, and its own infirmary.[86] With an imposing building on Bialystok's main thoroughfare, Lines Hatsedek was recognized as the most reputable Jewish philanthropic organization in the city. By 1913, the association had grown into one of the most widely used charitable organizations in Bialystok, serving more than 29,000 people.[87]

Lines Hatsedek's success was due to its revolutionary structure as much as to communal need. First and foremost, it was the first Jewish welfare organization in the region not linked, directly or indirectly, with the kehilla. This independence allowed it to abandon the rigid hierarchical structure characteristic of other kehilla institutions in favor of unprecedented forms of organization.[88] It prided itself on requiring all of its members to serve overnight shifts regardless of their wealth or status in the community; hence, wealthy industrialists and uneducated factory workers served together. In most other Jewish charitable organizations, including Bikur Holim, wealthy members paid those with fewer resources to fulfill organizational duties, such as visiting the sick. In contrast, Lines Hatsedek demanded that all its members—whether they were wealthy industrialists or uneducated factory workers—work together to care for the ill. While at times wealthy members paid poorer ones to serve in their place, at Lines Hatsedek's annual banquet, rich and poor alike competed for prizes rewarding the member who had participated in the most night duties during the course of the year.[89]

Even more radical than its cross-class membership was Lines Hatsedek's inclusion of women in its membership. As in most of Russian society, where the wives of Russian nobles, high officials, and wealthy merchants often participated in local philanthropic causes, many Jewish women in Bialystok established and ran private relief institutions. But official state-affiliated institutions remained the domain of men.[90] Lines Hatsedek, recognizing the immense resources women offered, allowed them not only to participate in the institution's nightly watches, but even to vote in annual elections and sit on its governing board.[91]

The ideal of inclusiveness that drove its attitude toward membership also extended to the constituencies that Lines Hatsedek sought to serve. As part of their effort to distance themselves from the kehilla and advance a new vision of the role Jewish philanthropy could play in the Russian Empire, the founders claimed that they would "serve any ill resident of Bialystok, regardless of their faith, nationality or class."[92] In practice, Lines Hatsedek primarily helped Jews, since they made up the vast majority of the city's population. Nevertheless, the organization's leadership made great efforts to realize its multinational ideology, as exemplified by the tireless efforts of Dr. Joseph Chazanowicz, Lines Hatsedek's leader during its first two decades, who articulated a new vision of Jewish philanthropy, transforming how Jews and even non-Jews viewed their place in Bialystok and the larger Russian Empire.[93]

A New Jewish Leadership for Bialystok's Innovative Jewish Welfare Organizations

Considered by many to be "the most remarkable Jewish personality of Bialystok," Chazanowicz, a doctor and Zionist activist, epitomized the new type of educated and acculturated migrant flocking to Bialystok in the nineteenth century.[94] Born in 1844 in Grodno, Chazanowicz was raised by his paternal grandparents after his mother's death.[95] Committed to the ideals of the haskalah, his grandparents supplemented Josef's *kheyder* (traditional religious school) education with extensive training in Hebrew and Russian and sent him to the local Russian gymnasium.[96] In 1866, he enrolled in the University of Königsberg, in Prussia, to study medicine.[97] After completing his degree, he worked in St. Petersburg, serving as a military doctor, but returned to Grodno in 1878 to wed and then moved to Bialystok in order to open a medical practice. After his wife's sudden death, Chazanowicz decided that instead of remarrying, he would devote himself to the affairs of the community.

Chazanowicz was typical of the hundreds of Jewish men who embraced medicine in the late nineteenth century, who transformed the practice of medicine in the Russian Empire and thus created a new elite class in Russian Jewish society.[98] By 1889, for example, Jewish men represented 13.4 percent of the empire's practicing physicians, even though Jews accounted for less than 4 percent of Russia's total population.[99] This proportionally large number of Jewish doctors gave the medical profession in Russia a stigma of social inferiority among the Slavic majority. While Russian Jewish doctors—like all ordinary *vrachi* (doctors) who completed the five-year program at university— garnered little pay, they did earn the coveted right to live outside the Pale of Settlement. According to a law passed in 1879, any Jew of either sex studying to become or practice as a doctor (*vrach*), doctors' assistant (*fel'dsher*), or even midwife (*povival'naia babka*), enjoyed the right to live anywhere in the empire.[100] While many used their medical training as a ticket out of the Pale, others, like Chazanowicz, chose to return to it, as their degree translated into respect and higher social status within the Jewish community.

Chazanowicz used that status not only to assume the mantle of leadership in Lines Hatsedek but also to put forth a new vision of Jewish philanthropy as a means to facilitate Jews' integration into Russian society. Even though Jews were an overall minority in the tsarist empire, they constituted a majority of the population in Bialystok and several other expanding cities in the Pale of Settlement and Congress Poland. Thus, in these cities Jewish communal leaders were offered a rare opportunity to demonstrate through their institutions not only the ways in which Jews could integrate into the empire, but more importantly, the ways in which their institutions could play an integral role in the empire's modernization and expansion. Appreciating this great opportunity, Chazanowicz was the force behind the decision to provide Lines Hatsedek's services free of charge to every resident of Bialystok, including local Poles and Russians.[101]

Chazanowicz's commitment to universal care was soon put to the test. As his tireless efforts during Bialystok's 1896 cholera epidemic demonstrated, Jews, Poles, Russians, and Ukrainians all received medical attention. Working for days without sleep, Chazanowicz put himself in grave danger, earning himself the nickname "the crazy doctor."[102] Moreover, his steadfast dedication to serving all members of the community led the district governor to appoint him Bialystok's official city doctor, imprinting the tsarist's state stamp of approval on both Lines Hatsedek and the new group of Jewish leaders running this organization.

Beyond transforming how tsarist authorities viewed Jewish charity, Chazanowicz's efforts also succeeded in altering the ways in which other ethnic groups in Bialystok saw Jewish philanthropy: despite its Hebrew name, Lines Hatsedek was not considered to be an exclusively Jewish organization. A turn-of-the-century Bialystok Polish proverb describing the assets of a young suitor bespeaks this organization's success in entrenching itself in the city's greater popular imagination:[103]

Zgrabny—jak ułan z Dziesiątki

Zgrał sie—jak rzeka Biała

. . . Punktualnie—jak w Pogotowie Lines Hatsedek

He is as handsome as an uhlan from the tenth regiment

He is as melodious as the Biała river

. . . As punctual as the members of Lines Hatsedek's

Emergency service.[104]

As much a part of the Bialystok landscape as the Biała river, Lines Hatsedek's volunteers were admired throughout the region, helping the organization eclipse the kehilla in stature and entrench itself in popular consciousness as a model charitable institution.

Lines Hatsedek's pluralistic approach to charity became the pride of the city's Jewish community. As journalist Nahum Prylucki summed up in 1935, "in describing the work and achievements of the Lines Hatsedek society, I have never used the word Jews or Jewish. . . . This was deliberate, since, although it was founded and directed by Jews, supported by Jewish funds, and bears a Jewish name, no one is ever asked about his faith or nationality."[105]

As it grew in prominence under Chazanowicz's guidance, Lines Hatsedek had to concoct several inventive fundraising techniques to support its programs. During the recession of 1900, when few Jews in Bialystok had spare money, Chazanowicz sent appeals to several Yiddish newspapers in the United States, calling "on our brothers who are residents of Bialystok but are dwelling across the sea to help us here in Bialystok with our bitter situation."[106] Chazanowicz emphasized that the Bialystok Jewish community was a truly transnational community, and that Bialystoker Jews were "still members of Bialystok" regardless of where they lived.[107]

Chazanowicz's letter suggests not only that Lines Hatsedek's fundraising needs prompted Jews in Bialystok to dream up a new vision of the parameters of their community, but also how transAtlantic migration was reshaping life in Bialystok, creating new constituencies from which struggling welfare agencies trying to challenge the status quo in Russia could elicit support. By tacitly bypassing both the kehilla and the tsarist state in search of support and turning to Jews abroad for help, Lines Hatsedek's leadership created additional grounds for political instability.

While the implicit challenges of new Jewish philanthropies to traditional authority clearly changed the ways in which Jewish elites exercised power, the concern over these new philanthropies paled in comparison with the growing strength of other new Jewish organizations, in particular, the illegal socialist, and Zionist parties in Bialystok.[108] These organizations were openly revolutionary, demanding democratized systems of Jewish communal governance and altering how Jews in Bialystok envisioned the contours of their communal identities and engaged with political authorities.[109]

Jews' Political and Cultural Responses to the Migrant Dilemma: The Bundist, Zionist, and Esperanto Movements in Bialystok

At the same time that an innovative network of Jewish welfare organizations arose in Bialystok and other cities such as Minsk, Kiev, and St. Petersburg—a host of innovative (and illegal) Jewish political organizations were also being formed to address the dilemmas caused by Russia's rapidly changing economic, social, and political climate. Throughout Eastern Europe, Jewish leaders debated the larger existential question of Jewish assimilation. In Bialystok and elsewhere, Jews viewed this debate through the prism of their personal travails as migrants striving to incorporate themselves into new environs.[110] How should Jews balance their new economic and social realities with the powerful drive to preserve their former values? In other words, what shape should the Jewish path to modernity take in the Russian Empire? Three new Jewish political and cultural movements in Bialystok—the socialist Bund, the proto-Zionist Hibbat Zion (and from 1899 the Zionist movement), and the Esperanto language movement offered different answers to these questions. Their respective efforts to enact their radically divergent beliefs fundamentally transformed the structure and form of Jewish communal life in Bialystok.[111]

While the ideologies that shaped these movements originated in Jewish intellectual circles, their support was drawn from the thousands of Jews who streamed into large cities during the late nine-

Antique postcard printed in Russia circa 1895 depicting Chazanowicz and the intended Jewish National Library in Jerusalem. *Author's private collection.*

teenth century.[112] The success of these new political and cultural organizations thus hinged on their ability to link their larger ideological platforms with the economic and psychological hardships facing internal Jewish migrants in the Russian Empire. Economic vicissitudes in Bialystok led the Bund (the abbreviated name for the *Algemeyner Yidisher Arbeter Bund in Lita, Poyln un Rusland* [General Jewish Worker's Union in Lithuania, Poland, and Russia]), the illegal Jewish socialist political movement founded in Vilna in 1897, to attract many followers. Linking the pressing economic problems of the common Jewish worker to the larger political structure, Bund leaders in Bialystok strove to convince Jewish workers of the political nature of their economic struggles, arguing that only the elimination of the tsarist government would permit them to defend their interests effectively and legally. On a practical level, the Bund helped Jewish migrant workers raise their wages by organizing strikes, but they emphasized that such methods would provide only short-term solutions. Ultimately the tsar had to be removed and replaced.[113] Goaded by Bundist activism and rhetoric, Bialystok's peaceful labor protests of the 1880s and early 1890s came to be replaced by violent agitation as workers became infused with revolutionary fervor.[114]

The Bund was wildly successful in Bialystok, where hundreds of Jewish workers joined the party and redirected their anger from their bosses to the larger political structure. This success was partially rooted in the fact that Bund leaders in Bialystok never forgot that the Jewish migrants, despite having physically uprooted themselves from their familiar social networks, would not relinquish the deeply ingrained religious and cultural patterns of their former small-town lives.[115] Jews from these smaller towns still revolved their daily lives around the synagogue and the rhythms of the Jewish calendar. Few migrants would quickly abandon their traditional adherence to Jewish law, which forbade revolution against non-Jewish authorities, such as the tsar. A 1903 poster produced by Bialystok's *beys din* (Jewish religious court) captures this religious mindset:

> With great sorrow we note how recently some people with little understanding or knowledge have listened to the advice of some agitators who are leading them from the ways of the Torah and righteousness so that they will destroy the just order of the state police. . . . We the children of Abraham, Isaac and Jacob have been commanded to do the right thing and accept the sovereignty of the yoke of the lands in which we live with the hearts and souls of righteous men. . . . We the people of Israel, therefore, must love the tsar and fulfill every law he orders. . . . Any man with understanding can recognize the goodness of the king, who acts in kindness and in a just way with the people of his country. . . . Our brothers, the children of Israel, pay attention to our words which are the truth and do not go in the way of these agitators . . . and may we all loyally serve our tsar, the righteous one whom God preserves and may he succeed during all his days and may Judah and Israel only live in peace.[116]

In response to such deeply held beliefs, the editors of the Bundist newspaper *Der bialistoker arbeter* (The Bialystoker Worker) and the party's proclamations often employed religious terminology when trying to inspire revolution. Such rhetoric allowed Jews to feel that they still operated within the parameters of Jewish law, even as they directly challenged the authority of the tsar. An 1898 Bund proclamation summoned the words of "the great wise Jewish scholar, Rabbi Hillel," urging every Jewish worker to ponder "If I do not act for myself, who will act for me? And if I care only for myself, what am I?"[117] Beyond hoping these rabbinic words would convince Jewish workers to see their protest as rooted in Jewish law, the Bundist leaders in Bialystok hoped it would provoke immediate action, concluding their proclamation with Hillel's famous call to action: "If I do not act now, then when?" Rabbinic phrases and dictums were also deployed to emphasize the failures of the Russian state and the need for Jews to revolt: in 1899, after several weavers were arrested and sentenced to exile in Siberia for planning strikes, *Der bialistoker arbeter*'s editors mocked tsarist officials' investigative practices using the religious terminology of *drisha* (inquiry) and *khakira* (investigation)—terms employed exclusively in Jewish courts of law—to awaken a sense of moral outrage in religious readers, and to mobilize them to embrace the platform of socialism.[118]

In addition to galvanizing Jewish workers through the use of rabbinic rhetoric, the Bundist leaders also created fictitious religious characters in their publication (who, naturally, convert to socialism) to convey the compatibility of these different viewpoints. The story of "Khaim der veber" (Chaim the Weaver), which debuted in an 1899 edition of *Der bialistoker arbeter,* describes the conversion of a pious Talmudist and weaver, Khaim, into a union organizer. Through Khaim's voice, the writer persuasively argued that allegiance to the Bund did not present any theological problems. Constructing a direct parallel between his study of *heylik* (holy) texts and his *heylik* (holy) and *erlekh* (virtuous) commitment to helping poor working Jews, the writer drew a direct conclusion: joining the Bund did not require an abandonment of piety and devotion to Jewish text study; rather, it asked that religious devotion be rechanneled from texts into action.[119]

Contributors to *Der bialistoker arbeter* also helped Jewish migrant workers negotiate a wide array of social issues, from shifting gender roles to the dilemmas of integration. *Der bialistoker arbeter*'s coverage of the attempted strike of the female loom assistants (*shpuliarkes*) in 1902, illustrated that even though Jewish women were involved in almost every aspect of textile production in nonmechanized factories, their presence on the shop floor deeply disturbed Jewish men. When the women banded together to protest the expectation of the factory owners that they clean underneath the looms for no additional pay, the male workers refused to support their cause.[120] Rather, they encouraged the factory owners to hire non-Jewish women as strikebreakers. The male workers were outraged by their female coreligionists' assertiveness, as one weaver declared in *Der bialistoker arbeter:*

> What do they mean that they will no longer clean under the looms? Do they think that this work is not fitting for them? Who do they think they are? Polish countesses?[121]

The weavers' equation of Jewish female laborers with the pampered and lazy Polish countesses not only sought to degrade women's request for more money for more work, but also sought to advance the idea that Jewish laborers were as much a part of Bialystok's landscape as the Polish nobility who had founded the city centuries ago. Indeed, contributors to the newspaper would continue to debate the dilemma of these female workers as well as the weaver's derisive view of their efforts, but all implicitly accepted in their articles a similar vision of Jewish laborers as integral to Bialystok's landscape.[122] Throughout every issue of *Der bialistoker arbeter,* published between 1899 and 1903, the Bund's leaders in Bialystok addressed its readers as not merely workers but as both Bialystokers and workers.[123] In the same issue in which the weaver criticized the shpuliarkes, for example, the editors published articles urging workers to fight the "the war, the turmoil . . . in this city,"[124] urging members of the Bund to "reinforce the guard" against Bialystok's impending attack.[125] Proclamations published by the Bund similarly emphasized Jewish workers' deep links to Bialystok and to the larger movement by alternating addressing their calls to "the workers of Bialystok [*białostockich robotniów i robotnic*], the weavers of Bialystok [*belostokskim tkacham*] and to the general "working brothers [*bracia robotnicy*] of Bialystok."[126]

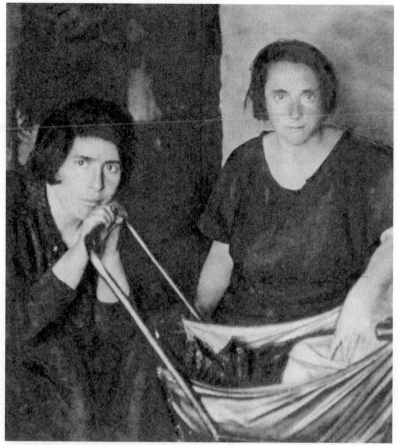

Portrait of two female weavers, circa 1930. Women were integrally involved in all aspects of Bialystok's textile industry throughout the late nineteenth and early twentieth centuries. *Courtesy of Forward Association/Alter Kacyzne.*

Such rhetoric, with its emphasis on Bialystok's residents' distinctive traits, encouraged Jewish workers to see their labor activism as simultaneously rooting them in their local environs and linking them to a larger ideological revolution. Even when Bialystok served as home to the Bund's central committee between 1900 and 1902, the editors of *Der bialistoker arbeter* still emphasized that readers' regional and class identities were intertwined. Jewish socialism, the editors argued, entailed a commitment to improving conditions in

Bialystok as well as to overthrowing the tsar.[127] By embedding their calls for revolution in both religious terminology and the language of regional loyalty, the editors of Der bialistoker arbeter attracted hundreds of Jewish workers to their ranks. Bundist leaders' talent for speaking in a language that resonated with Jewish migrant workers made the Bialystok branch of the Bund one of the strongest and most active in the Russian Empire.[128]

The Bund's initial success, however, planted the seeds for its slow demise. As the Bund grew in prominence, local Russian policemen began to threaten Jewish factory owners who did not expose those Jews who were members of the Bund.[129] Ironically, while such police action unified Jewish workers and factory owners, it also created tension within the ranks of the Bund itself. Some members of the Bund felt that the police's efforts must be countered with terror tactics, commonly used by the anarchists; the Bund's leadership in Bialystok vehemently opposed such a response. Addressing this new challenge the Bund argued: "the anarchists, with their small and short-sighted goals, [are] terrorists [who] create false hope in the masses; they blind their eyes with a false tactic that destroys the independence of the working class."[130]

The local committee's refusal to embrace terror as a tactic prompted many of its members to flock to more radical revolutionary parties. The abandonment of the Bund should not be viewed as evidence of this party's lack of influence; quite the contrary, the Bund had succeeded in its goal of convincing traditionally minded workers that they should challenge the tsar. Its success is vividly portrayed by the fact that virtually every revolutionary party in Russia and Poland in the late nineteenth century had active branches in Bialystok.[131] The Socialist Revolutionary Party, for example, which was dedicated to using violent terrorist tactics, had a particularly vibrant branch in Bialystok and successfully orchestrated the assassination in 1903 of Bialystok's chief of police.[132]

The revolutionary solutions offered by the Bund to the dilemmas confronting Jewish migrant workers, however, did not appeal to all; many turned to Rabbi Samuel Mohilever, chief rabbi of Bialystok, and his Zionist vision to negotiate life in their new home.[133] Arriving in

Bialystok from Radom in 1883, Mohilever was appointed chief rabbi of Bialystok, replacing Yom Tov Lipman Halperin, who had died in 1882.[134] Mohilever was considered by many (particularly Western Jewish leaders) to be "an outstanding national leader" whose talent became apparent in 1881, when he advocated that East European Jews resettle the land of Israel to solve the "Jewish problem" after the pogroms of 1881.[135] To achieve his overarching goal of resettling Jews in their ancient homeland, Mohilever actively raised funds[136] and inspired hundreds of Bialystoker Jews to rally behind his cause.[137] In 1882, Mohilever was among the prominent figures involved in the founding of Hibbat Zion, an organization that argued that the Jews in Bialystok must look upon themselves as possessing national ambitions similar to those of other East European groups.

The popularity of Hibbat Zion's ideology among Jews in Bialystok was linked to the fact that its fervent nationalist cry fit snugly within Bialystok's cultural landscape, where debates over nationalism kept segments of Bialystok's multiethnic populace in constant tension.[138] The idea of building a Jewish homeland in Palestine provided Jews in Bialystok with a national ideology like those of the Polish and Lithuanian minorities surrounding Bialystok's Jewish population. As a result, hundreds of Bialystok Jews were drawn to the Hibbat Zion chapter in Bialystok, even though it was only semi-legal and was frowned upon by some traditionalist rabbis.[139] A letter from the members of the Bialystok chapter of Hibbat Zion to prospective philanthropists in Paris illustrates the popularity and influence of this organization:

> We, the children of Bialystok, have awakened to the call of the desert and we aim to awaken in you this love of our land. . . . Many great men and leaders in our city have joined together and founded a society called Hibbat Zion in order to expand and spread this idea of resettling our holy land by buying land to farm and supporting colonists to live there. . . . We thank God that there are wonderful members of the Jewish people like you [in Paris] who support such an endeavor and who understand the terrible situation of many families in Eastern Europe among whom are many fine people in our city. . . . [140]

Identifying themselves as both the "children of Bialystok" and as loyal to Zion, the members of Hibbat Zion illustrated how entwined their vision of themselves as Zionists was with their understanding of themselves as residents of Bialystok. Through its efforts and activities, the Hibbat Zion chapter not only linked Jews to a larger national movement but also reinforced their regional ties. The Bialystok Association for Land Purchases, a Zionist organization based in the city, further illustrated this point: it raised money to resettle only Jews from Bialystok (not just any interested East European Jew) in Palestine. In 1913, the Bialystok Association for Land Purchases spent 140,000 francs for Kefar Uriyya, the largest private group purchase of land in Palestine prior to the First World War.[141]

Mohilever drew on this dual commitment of his constituents to promote Zionism in Bialystok and to help himself gain more power within Hibbat Zion, an organization, as historian Ehud Luz notes, whose leadership was divided between the beliefs of its traditionalist rabbinic founders and its predominately secularized and acculturated leadership in Odessa.[142] The commitment of these "children of Bialystok" to their chief rabbi and the Zionist cause helped Mohilever topple Odessa's Leon Pinsker and become head of Hibbat Zion in 1889.[143]

Similar to Lines Hatsedek, Hibbat Zion popularized Zionism through radically new organizational tactics, such as sponsoring frequent social and political events that included women and members of all classes in its activities. From Hibbat Zion sprouted dozens of organizations, such as *Bnos Tsiyion* (Daughters of Zion), for young women and *Po'alei Tsiyion* (Workers of Zion) for working-class Jews who sought to reshape the Jewish economy through Zionism.[144] Each of these offshoots of Hibbat Zion hosted numerous evening lectures, classes, and social events. Lev Koppleson, born in Bialystok in 1900, recalled how his father was rarely home, as he attended meetings almost nightly. Sonia Mazny recalled that her parents often complained that they never saw her since she spent so many long nights planning and attending activities as part of her involvement in Bnos Tsiyion.[145] Participants in these groups, which increasingly embraced a more revolutionary stance, took great risks: Hasya Feinsod, for example, born in Bialystok in 1889 and mother of prominent Israeli leader Yigal Yadin, was arrested three times for attending *Bnos Tsiyion* meetings (for which she was detained four days); she was incarcerated for three weeks when police discovered she was a member of *Po'alei Zion* and that she possessed stamps produced by the Jewish National Fund (Keren Kayemet). Puah Rakovsky describes in great depth her siblings' arrests for their involvement in Zionist "revolutionary" organizations as well as their campaigning for Jewish national autonomy, activities tsarist authorities came to fear only somewhat less than socialist revolution.[146]

Zionism's inventive organizational practices were matched by its revolutionary ideology of Jewish unity. Not only did Mohilever advocate the resettlement of Jews in Palestine, but he also maintained that the common link of Jews to Zion provided the key to preserving Jewish unity against the challenges of modern life. Arguing against the religious schisms and class divisions that he saw tearing apart Russian Jewish society, Mohilever stressed that Zionism taught all Jews that they must tolerate and support one another. He claimed that one of the greatest "evil[s] [he had seen] among the pious in [Russia] is how they . . . despise and persecute [those] who do not follow the Torah," ignoring the principle that "all Israel is responsible one for another [*kol yisrael arevim zeh lazeh*]."[147] While most Jews in Bialystok did not become members of Hibbat Zion, Mohilever's message of Jewish unity percolated down to inspire many in Bialystok, a city where poor migrant workers opposed Jewish factory owners and all lived alongside different nationalizing ethnic groups. Mohilever's message of tolerance and Jewish unity, in fact, became his lasting legacy once Jews emigrated abroad: when the members of the Bialystoker Unterstitzungs Verein Somach Noflim (Bialystoker Mutual Aid Society Somach Noflim) in New York established their organization in 1886, they noted that they had been inspired by Mohilever's teachings which did not involve building a new Jewish state but rather maintaining their "strong Bialystoker local patriotism [that] inculcated in [them] that everyone may live in their private lives as they please, as a radical or religious Jews . . . [as long as each remained] one hundred percent Bialystoker compatriot [*landsman*]."[148]

Mohilever's vision of Jewish unity and integration on a national scale inspired many but was rejected by acculturated and educated

Bialystok Jews, who saw linguistic assimilation as the correct blue-print for success in their new home. As scholars of contemporary migration note, language is the principal initial barrier to adaptation confronting many migrant communities after they settle in new homes.[149] For Jewish migrants in the multilingual Russian Empire, the question of language and its relationship to their integration was complex. For more than a century, Russian Jewish thinkers deliberated this question of linguistic assimilation as they pondered the best strategy to achieve Jewish emancipation. Should Jews relinquish their use of Yiddish? Should Jews switch to using the local vernacular, which in the case of Bialystok was Polish? Or should Jews learn to speak Russian as subjects of the Russian Empire?

One native son of Jewish Bialystok, Ludwig Zamenhof, attempted to address this linguistic issue and the larger question of Jewish assimilation by creating a new language, Esperanto. Esperanto offered to its followers not only an innovative language, but also a novel path to assimilation in a multiethnic world. Zamenhof hoped that Esperanto, a language which contained nine hundred root words and only sixteen grammatical rules, would create unity in his hometown of Bialystok by eliminating interethnic misunderstanding.[150] In essence, Zamenhof's Esperanto movement proposed a plan that facilitated Jewish assimilation by metaphorically forcing all residents of Eastern Europe to face the same struggle of learning a new language.

Born in 1859 in Bialystok, Zamenhof was the eldest child of a secondary schoolteacher of geography and foreign languages. Although educated in a Russian school, Zamenhof predominately used Polish in daily conversation. In his writings, he recalled his childhood experiences on the streets of Bialystok when he watched Jews, Russians, Poles, Ukrainians, and Lithuanians taunting each other.[151] This deeply troubled him, for he saw himself and other children of different ethnic groups as all tied to Bialystok; all were, in his words, "the natural sons of the same land and the same town."[152] These childhood experiences convinced Zamenhof that ethnic hatred resulted from misunderstanding rooted in the absence of one common language for all.[153] He therefore set out to create an international language that combined pieces of sixteen different languages and allowed people to communicate not as "Frenchmen with Englishmen, or Russians with Poles . . . but as men with men."[154]

Before dedicating himself to the dissemination of Esperanto, Zamenhof had been an active member of the proto-Zionist movement, clearly illustrating that competing affiliations often overlapped in individuals' lived experience. In 1883, two years after moving to Warsaw to study medicine, Zamenhof's experiences in Bialystok inspired him to form a local Hibbat Zion chapter. While he saw Hibbat Zion as a practical response to the plight of the masses of Jewish refugees, he also worked many hours on creating Esperanto, whose name literally meant *hope*, which he believed was the true solution to the Jewish problem. Upon completing his medical degree in 1885, Zamenhof moved to the Veiseyai region of Lithuania, about one hundred miles from Bialystok, to practice medicine. His experiences in this region populated by Jews, Lithuanians, Ukrainians, and Russians appeared to him to confirm the lessons he had learned as a child. Consequently, he abandoned Hibbat Zion in 1887, devoting himself to his medical career and to the development and dissemination of his international language.[155]

The first major step Zamenhof took to further Esperanto was the publication of his *Linguo Internacia* [The International Language] in 1887. In this primer for his new language, he outlined not only his rules of conjugation but also his dream of creating a world filled with mutual understanding and respect through the propagation of Esperanto. Appreciating the difficulty migrants faced in learning a new tongue, Zamenhof made the defining feature of his language the simplification of grammar and word declension.[156] The optimism of Zamenhof and his followers in their belief that a common language could "break down the walls which he saw separating different nations" gave hope to many Jews in Bialystok who questioned their long-term prospects in the city.[157] This became even more obvious to him after the outbreak of pogroms in 1905 and 1906, when he began to stress that Esperanto offered the answer to antisemitism, as he emphasized in his 1906 address to the International Esperanto Conference:

> We know that the Russian people are not responsible for the
> bestial butchery in Bialystok and many other towns; for the

Russian people have never been cruel or bloodthirsty. . . . It is quite well known that the guilt lies with a group of vile criminals, who . . . by broadcasting lies and slanders, have created a dreadful hatred between one race and another. But would the worst lies and slanders have such dreadful results if the races knew one another well, if between them there were not high thick walls which forbid them to communicate freely between one another and see that the members of one race are just the same human creatures as the members of another race?[158]

Zamenhof's speech at the international conference emphasized to his followers in Bialystok his continued belief in the inherent goodness of humanity and his hope that a common language could eradicate ethnic and racial hatred. Yet, as this speech illustrates, despite its internationalist claims, Zamenhof's Esperanto movement was shaped by local needs. In contrast to the growing nascent East European nationalist movements fueling intensified strife in the region, he argued for a Jewish identity that eschewed one national affiliation and instead emphasized a cosmopolitan multiethnic affiliation. Zamenhof's program for Jewish integration, however, was doomed to failure because it assumed that all Jews lived in a multiethnic cultural borderland like Bialystok and that language was the only issue dividing people.[159]

Few people learned Esperanto, let alone conversed in it on a daily basis; nonetheless, this movement made at least a minimal imprint on Jewish migrants in Bialystok, some of whom internalized Zamenhof's message that despite the senseless "atrocities and crimes of 1906," Bialystok was still their home in which "not ill will, but rather lack of knowledge" provoked violence.[160] His vision for the possibility of Jewish integration inspired many Jews in Bialystok. They would point to his birthplace with pride and named a street in his honor.[161] By the turn of the century, Zamenhof's childhood home was a tourist attraction, a shrine where visitors reflected upon Esperanto, a language and ideology that did not advocate political revolution but offered Jewish migrants in Bialystok a vision of a different world where they would not be linguistic outsiders.[162]

While leaders of the socialist, Zionist, and Esperantoist movements each advocated divergent approaches to the challenge of

Jewish life in Bialystok, their refraction of larger political debates through a local prism further entrenched in the minds of Jewish migrants the centrality of Bialystok to their identities. Bialystok was far from the only city in which larger movements were reconfigured to fit local needs. The same trend operated among Jews in a host of cities and towns, or with Polish peasants in Austria and Galicia.[163] The need for Jewish migrants to address their feelings of dislocation prompted these organizations to embed their larger ideological platforms within a discourse of regional loyalty, a useful strategy of adaptation that became even more pronounced once Jews moved beyond the Russian Empire.

The Revolution of 1905

By the turn of the century, nearly every illegal political organization active in late Imperial Russia had a vibrant branch in Bialystok.[164] As a result of the precarious economic situation, socialist parties, such as the Bund or the Polish Socialist Party, commonly known as the PPS, dominated the city's political landscape.[165] Their success in aligning workers' struggles with a larger socialist ideology is evidenced by the fact that between 1901 and 1903, 78 percent of all strikes were linked to political causes and directed by one of these illegal political organizations.[166]

Bialystok was far from the only city that nurtured revolutionary fervor; the besieged tsarist government faced increased agitation throughout the country.[167] Even as diverse groups were agitating for change, tsarist officials' response to the threat of insurrection remained connected with "the Jewish question" and often focused on cities such as Bialystok, where Jews constituted the majority of the population and where political opposition to tsarist authority was strong. Prince Pyotr Dmitrievich Sviatopolk-Mirsky, Governor-General of Russia's North-Western province including the *gubernias* of Vilna, Kovno, and Grodno, reported in 1903:

> The density, insecurity, and poverty of the Jewish population and the extreme restrictions of its rights have created among the Jews suitable ground for antigovernment propaganda. . . . Over the past years, the important industrial and trading center of

Bialystok in the North-Western territory has become a prominent arena for revolutionary activity, as revolutionary organizations find many supporters among the inhabitants of the Jewish
nationality and among the numerous members of the working
class, which is frequently made up of Jews. The abundance of
all kinds of proclamations and pamphlets of an antigovernment
nature . . . is one of the best proofs of the fact that this town is
selected by the supporters of the revolutionary movement as
one of the favorable areas. The two demonstrations which took
place in February and July 1903 . . . the two attempts upon the
life of the local chief of police, the repeated attempts by the
Zionists to organize their secret meetings, finally the proposal
of the Zionists to call a Zionist congress in Bialystok—all this
shows that the movement which has built its nest here . . . is
aspiring to bring about grave antigovernment actions. . . . Above
all, it seemed necessary to provide Bialystok with an appropriate
number of police staff, as the present numbers do not at all cor-
respond to vital needs . . . I personally want to report the lack
of supervision in Bialystok to Your Imperial Majesty, requesting
that new staff be brought into operation in view of the urgency
of the case.[168]

In response to Sviatopolk-Mirsky's plea, additional police and army
battalions were dispatched to Bialystok to control the revolutionaries;
little, however, could be done to abate the rising radical tide, especially after Russia's humiliating defeat in the 1905 Russo-Japanese
War. Throughout the Russian Empire, thousands participated in
strikes; many were led by Jewish laborers. In the Pale, Jewish workers tried to mobilize other ethnic groups such as Lithuanians, Poles,
and Belorussians, linking the fight for improved working conditions
with a program of national liberation.[169]

As revolutionary fervor mounted in Bialystok, tsarist police
clashed with Jewish workers, who often took to the streets to protest the government's mismanagement of the economy, the war, and
the country. Many of these clashes turned fatal. Dozens of Jewish
workers lost their lives between 1903 and 1905.[170] Jewish communal
leaders tended to view these events as examples of class conflict
rather than anti-Jewish violence, and so accepted the tsarist regime's
efforts to maintain order among the urban working class. The conser-

vative attitude toward law and order informed the weak communal response to a July 1905 massacre of twenty-five Jews, whom tsarist officials claimed were anarchists plotting a revolt, a claim local Jewish leaders made little effort to refute.[171]

By October 1905, the growing strength of the revolutionary movement and the spreading of political unrest throughout the empire forced Tsar Nicholas II to expand on his earlier reforms, such as broadening the power of the *Zemstvo* (local self-governments), and signing the liberal- and reform-minded October Manifesto. Jews in Bialystok greeted the issuing of the October Manifesto on October 17, 1905, with much enthusiasm.[172] The new law established a limited semi-parliamentary government, eased censorship, granted concessions to non-Russian subjects, and provoked a massive celebration, as one participant, Boris Tsipin, recalled:

> It was such a warm, beautiful day that no one could believe it was the middle of October. The whole city, children along with adults, was in the street . . . everyone, even the non-Jews who did not play a big part in political activities in the city, were congratulating one another and trying to see with their own eyes a copy of the manifesto [that the Police had posted in the central marketplace].[173]

The festivities, however, came to an abrupt end as local police opened fire on October 18, 1905, killing twenty-two Jews. This final provocation finally forced the Jewish community to ponder whether efforts to control political insurrection were truly manifestations of antisemitism.[174] While anti-Jewish violence had mounted throughout the empire in the years leading up to the revolution, few Jews were prepared for the six hundred vicious riots that took place in all corners of the empire in the fall of 1905. Shocked not only by the brutality of the violence, Jews were deeply disturbed that the outbursts often took place under the close watch of regional *gubernia* governors.[175] In contrast to the 1881 pogroms, as Shlomo Lambroza, I. Michael Aronson, and Hans Rogger note, local tsarist government officials in 1905–1906 were often complicit in the orchestration of antisemitic violence, reflecting the misguided notion that violence against Jews would eradicate the core of the revolutionary movement and channel the anger of the masses away from the autocracy.[176] Bialystok Jewry, while suspicious of the government, believed they were relatively safe since Jews constituted a majority of the population in the city. The pogrom of 1906, however, brought to the surface the disconcerting undercurrents of Russian life and forced the city's Jews to call into question tsarist authorities' commitment to the safety and security of its Jewish subjects.

Anti-Jewish Violence in a Jewish City: The Bialystok Pogrom of 1906

On June 1, 1906, a ferocious pogrom erupted in Bialystok. While dozens of pogroms had broken out throughout the empire between 1905 and 1906, few riots made as deep an impact on both Russian society and Russian Jewish culture as Bialystok's pogrom in 1906. No Jews would ever view tsarist policies or the place of Jews in the Russian Empire in the same way again. It all began during a religious procession of Catholic and Russian Orthodox clergy celebrating the feast of Corpus Christi. Following the religious procession was a battalion of soldiers. Suddenly revolver shots were fired, and someone yelled, "Beat the Jews." Immediately thereafter, a melee ensued, with "thugs," as one observer noted, "beating everyone with axes, crowbars, and slabs of iron." Not a single policeman could be seen; all the soldiers, who moments earlier had filled the streets, had vanished.[177] Over the next two days, "there was a continuous fusillade in the town, as if on a battlefield," reported an observer from the Duma. A total of 88 Jews were murdered, close to 700 wounded, 8 streets decimated, and 169 stores destroyed. Damages amounted to hundreds of thousands of rubles.[178] But what was most shocking, as the Duma's report concluded, was that the participants in the rampage included "not only hooligans but policemen and soldiers."[179]

The brutality with which all those involved attacked local Jews stunned witnesses: as Jews disembarked from trains in Bialystok's central railway station, for example, they were attacked by mobs and beaten to death with such ferocity that onlookers reported that the *pogromshchiki* (pogrom perpetrators) looked like "wild beasts, chewing on [their] clothes and biting [them]" even after they were clearly dead.[180] More disturbing than the scale of the violence was the fact that local events took place while the regional governor was present in the city, suggesting his direct complicity.[181] S. Ansky, a special correspondent for the Yiddish-language newspaper *Der fraynd*, whose reports are described in more depth below, depicted in graphic detail the flowing "rivers of blood" from "murdered and desecrated bodies" and "torn-apart children" that the governor failed to stop.[182] Consequently, the pogrom prompted both Jews in Bialystok and throughout the empire to reconsider their assumptions of security and safety: if Jews, the largest ethnic group in Bialystok, could become so vulnerable in a city where they enjoyed demographic and economic dominance, would any region, city, or town in Russia ever be safe for Jews?

Indeed, Bialystok Jewry's sense of security evaporated as local leaders, regardless of their political sympathies, could provide little protection against a backdrop of a seemingly official promotion of antisemitism.[183] While economic recession and general unrest had characterized the months leading up to the pogrom, no one could have predicted that such a brutal attack specifically against Jews would take place in Bialystok. Many factories closed and numerous strikes paralyzed the city. Police clashed with protesting workers; in some instances, these clashes turned violent and workers, who happened to be Jewish, were killed.[184] But few Jews took seriously the rumors that began to circulate about preparation for a pogrom following the appointment of S. D. Sheremetev, a well-known antisemite, as the head of the city's police force, in May 1906.

Lulled by a sense of comfort due to their demographic majority and their dominating role in the city's economic life, Jews petitioned the government to remove Sheremetev, convinced that his removal would prevent a pogrom. Their petitions were left unanswered. As more rumors continued to circulate about an impending pogrom, Jewish leaders took another step, composing the following open letter in Polish to local clergy and the residents of Bialystok:

> There are rumors that there is preparation for a large pogrom against the Jews [in Bialystok] . . . much has been done to incite the blind masses by members of the intelligentsia and other circles in society. . . . We the residents of the City of Bialystok

only want Jews and Christians to live together happily and freely. So we are asking all [local] leaders to help us keep life orderly and filled with joy.[185]

The tone reflected Jewish leaders' fundamental commitment to their city. Aware of Polish and tsarist officials' promotion of antisemitic violence in the press, Jewish leaders sought to convince the local Polish intelligentsia to stop the growing unrest by publicly condemning violence against Jews.[186] But this letter failed, as a Duma observer reported, as extreme nationalist political parties and the tsarist government officials inculcated local policemen and soldiers with the notion that "Jews were enemies of Russia . . . [and] it was [their] duty to fight revolutionaries and annihilate them."[187]

Unlike the government officials, many Polish, Russian, and international leaders outside of Bialystok were appalled by the events of June 1906. Particularly troubling was the news that while Jews were being beaten and their homes destroyed, neither local non-Jews nor tsarist officials tried to stop the violence. "In the non-Jewish areas of the city," a revolted journalist reported, "the mood is festive. People are in clubs, play[ing] cards, sing[ing] songs and eat[ing] snacks."[188] The wives of local gentile businessmen, along with a priest, unabashedly sorted through stolen Jewish property as it was thrown onto the streets.[189] Sheremetev, the police chief, not only stood idly by, but even urged locals to "exterminate" the local Jews who, he claimed, were "bloodsuckers and robbers."[190] All were aghast that the central tsarist government did not reprimand Sheremetev but rather promoted him for his role in the pogrom and his faithful service.[191]

Such actions provoked the Polish socialist movement to declare the pogrom a prime example of the tsarist government's brutality and despotism.[192] The largest Polish socialist party declared that Jewish workers no less than Polish workers "must be protected in order to protect our own freedom."[193] Other segments of the Polish press called for further reform in the government and demanded that the central government take action against those who participated.[194] The Duma openly opposed the central government for its handling of the pogrom. As has been indicated, the official Duma report chronicled the collusion of local officials, troops, and police during the pogrom.[195] Despite the Duma's petitions to "take vigorous" action to stop the pogrom, no measures were taken against the local governor or police.[196] News of this atrocity stirred protests abroad, prompting King Edward VII, for example, to hold the tsar directly responsible; the king argued that the British government should not deal with "such a government of murderers."[197]

Closer to home, the events in Bialystok stunned Russian Jewish society and forced its members to ponder their futures in the Russian Empire. *Der fraynd*, the most widely read Yiddish language newspaper in the empire, dispatched S. Ansky, the well-known public figure to cover the story. For more than two weeks following the outbreak of violence, he sent back reports that the newspaper featured on its front page, along with photographs of the devastation and the dead. While Ansky, like many others, was confused about how the pogrom actually unfolded, he was certain that even if some questions remained open, "from our vast, sad experience and knowledge of past pogroms, we already know the details with precision . . . rivers of blood, murdered and desecrated bodies, ravaged children, shredded books: the depths of hell, with all its suffering and anguish.[198]

Ansky was far from the only member of the burgeoning Jewish intelligentsia to have his faith in the Russian Empire shattered by the events in Bialystok. Across the spectrum, socialist, Zionist, and liberal Russian Jews absorbed the views presented by Jewish newspapers and grew particularly horrified, since Bialystok, with its Jewish majority, seemed to constitute a Jewish city. As the poet Moses Eisenstein exclaimed, "What was that terrible scream I heard from the terrible pogrom which stormed through the city of Bialystok . . . [a city] which up until now had only known trust and not the roar [of violence]."[199] While by the summer of 1906 the larger revolutionary movement had been virtually quashed by the government, in the Jewish community, the revolutionary fires still burned as organizations such as the Bund pointed to Bialystok's pogrom to inspire its members to overthrow the tsar.[200]

The pogrom left an indelible mark on Bialystok's Jewish population, forcing many Jewish migrants to question the price of resettlement or to evaluate whether they had chosen the best place to build a new life. Even in a city in which Jewish-owned factories dominated economic life and Jewish organizations defined civic culture, Jews could not be assured of their security. Many Jews became fearful; as Moses Eisenstein wrote in 1907, "I hear the great fear . . . [of] my brothers who fell by the hands of murders."[201] As the memoirs of Bialystoker émigré Jews narrate, this uncertainty and fear provoked tens of thousands to move to Western Europe, the United States, and Argentina, places they felt offered greater security together with economic opportunity.[202] Others, however, remained in Bialystok, where industrial expansion still offered economic opportunity. Their recent experiences kept them tied to revolutionary parties, like the Bund and the Anarchists.[203]

Jewish Bialystok's "Golden Age": Bialystok in the Waning Years of the Tsarist Empire, 1906–1914

Interestingly, the 1906 pogrom, as terrifying as it was, did not dull Bialystok's luster: thousands of Jews who felt marginalized in their economic pursuits in small towns of the Pale of Settlement flocked to cities such as Bialystok to take part in the flourishing industry.[204] They appear to have firmly believed, to use the words of historian Shaul Stampfer, that the city's "economic opportunities outweighed any risk of violence."[205] In fact, the period between 1906 and the First World War saw Bialystok's Jewish population grow from 41,905 to 61,500. Moreover, it witnessed the creation of so many new Jewish organizations that one contemporary observer declared the period before the First World War the "golden age of Jewish Bialystok."[206]

During this golden era, in addition to devoting energy to developing revolutionary political organizations as in earlier decades, Jewish migrants saw education and the press as the means by which to address their primary concerns: to prepare families to participate in the empire's economic and social life while simultaneously forestalling rapid assimilation.[207] Participation in the empire's growing commercial arena demanded linguistic competence in more than just Yiddish, and Jewish migrants founded new schools to serve this need.[208] To be sure, in the early twentieth century, many Jewish children were enrolled in state schools. But the desire for commercial success along with knowledge of Judaism led a dynamic group of young Bundists in Bialystok to found the Handworker School (Handverker shule) in 1905, a school that offered both a regular academic program in Hebrew and Yiddish as well as a rigorous vocational programming with training in such fields as tailoring and carpentry. Anna Gepner recalled the rigor of her Russian instructor at the Girls' Jewish school she attended, founded by L. H. Bogdonovsky, where daily drills incited fear in most of the students.[209]

With a similar linguistic agenda, Joseph Zeligman turned to the press to educate the masses and started publishing the Russian-language *Golos Belostoka* (The Voice of Bialystok) in 1909, a newspaper dedicated to discussing the political concerns of the Jewish community as it promoted the ideals of integration into Russian society. Zeligman's success prompted Avraham Hershberg to found *Bialistoker tageblat* (Bialystok Daily News), the city's first Yiddish daily newspaper, to cater to Jewish readers who may have not been fully comfortable in Russian, but were deeply distressed over the politics of integration and their children's economic prospects. Following in Hershberg's footsteps, several educators soon turned to founding Yiddish and religious schools for Jewish boys and girls to combat the gradual erosion of traditional Jewish practice, which they saw as rooted in Jews' relocation to the city. Of particular note is the proliferation of schools for Jewish girls, which as Paula Hyman states, reflects East European Jewry's belief at the turn of the century that women's education provided the key in their fight against assimilation.[210] Jews in Bialystok also experimented with other novel modes of Jewish cultural transmission—for example, founding a Hebrew theater troupe, Habimah, and several Yiddish literary groups—to contend with the growing alienation of young Jews from traditional Jewish culture.[211]

This golden age, however, came to an abrupt end in August 1915. In the aftermath of the assassination of Archduke Ferdinand and his wife, the city of Bialystok, like dozens of towns and cities in the Pale of Settlement, was invaded by the German army. Far from resisting occupation, Jews welcomed the Germans as their liberators and emancipators. Freed from tsarist restrictions, Jews embraced the

Portrait of one class in a new school opened for Jewish girls in Bialystok in the aftermath of the 1905 Revolution. *From the Archives of the YIVO Institute for Jewish Research, New York.*

German occupying force that allowed them to hold free elections for the first time and to bring clandestine Zionist, socialist, and cultural organizations into the open. As Hebrew writer and philosopher Simon Rawidowicz recalled, a Jewish cultural renaissance took place in Bialystok.[212] With the help of his sisters, he personally founded three Hebrew language elementary schools; with the aid of prominent journalist Avraham Hershberg, Rawidowicz also formed the city's first Hebrew teacher-training academy.[213] Through these new schools, literary societies, newspapers, and social and welfare organizations, Jews constructed a remarkably complex, cohesive, and variegated civil society. With their elected officials, they constructed an entity resembling a virtual Jewish polity.

The initial euphoria over these cultural opportunities faded quickly, though, as the war dragged on and thousands were forced from their homes. Jews in Bialystok became consumed with their immediate needs of food, clothing, and shelter. As German and

Russian forces both fought to recapture the area, civilians in Bialystok suffered acutely. By 1918, thousands had been killed and the entire region's economic infrastructure lay in ruins.[214] The Jewish hospital, along with many institutions, synagogues, and schools that had been built by Jewish settlers over the previous half century, were totally destroyed by bombardment and invasion; yet the contributions of migrant Jews to Bialystok did not fade into oblivion. When Jews sat down to rebuild their community in 1918, they looked at the efforts of their predecessors, reshaping not only the contours of Jewish life in this city, but the very essence of how the new multiethnic Polish state operated in this contested borderland region.

Conclusion

Pesach Kaplan, editor of *Dos naye lebn* (The New Life), the most widely circulated Yiddish newspaper in interwar Bialystok, once exclaimed the following in an editorial:

> Bialystok! My feelings toward you are not motivated by local patriotism alone [for] Bialystok is unique as a result of the boundless untiring energies of its populace. . . . [As a result,] wherever there are a few Bialystoker Jews, regardless of their number, they immediately organize themselves into a colony, [in order to keep] in touch with other Bialystoker communities and with their beloved birthplace.[215]

Kaplan's words represented the attitude prevalent among many Bialystoker Jews in the interwar period: while their home city was remarkable, they were also part of a larger transnational community linked together by common devotion to Bialystok. Jewish migration, which transformed Bialystok from a small town to a large industrial center in the nineteenth century, had once again reshaped the boundaries of the city's Jewish community. Jews from Bialystok who left the city in response to economic downturns or violence and moved to other parts of the world sought to remain connected to the city whose textile industry, social organizations, cultural movements, and political parties had shaped the way they viewed the world. Bialystok's Jews living overseas showed a lasting devotion to their former home, Kaplan argued, transforming the city once again into an entity akin to a colonial empire with outposts throughout the world.

Just as earlier generations of writers whimsically imagined Bialystok as Jaffa or Manchester, migration made Bialystok akin to a new type of imperial center in Kaplan's mind. All images reflected some element of reality: Bialystok's transformation from a small town founded in the Polish tradition (by a noble) into the third-largest textile-producing center in the Russian Empire was a direct result of the tireless efforts of Jewish industrial entrepreneurs and workers who migrated to the city over the course of the nineteenth century. The labors of Jewish migrants not only drove the city's rapid economic development, but also established Bialystok, a city already perched in the tense Polish–Russian–Lithuanian borderland region, as an arena of class and ethnic conflict. Tsarist policies did little to ameliorate the situation, turning the city into a multiethnic hodgepodge, where Jews, Ukrainians, Poles, Belorussians, Germans, and Lithuanians all struggled side by side to earn a living. As the Russian Empire in the nineteenth century solidified its borders and tried to define a national identity for itself, the internal conflicts created many quandaries for Jews in Bialystok, who faced violence and discrimination and were forced to conceptualize their religious identities as intimately connected to their regional environs and not linked to the larger empire.

It was within such a context that Jews became acquainted with an urban industrial environment and rearticulated their understanding of what it meant to be an East European Jew. Whether they chose to identify themselves as Zionist or socialist, Jews in Bialystok saw their identities as deeply intertwined with the city in which they first encountered industry, nationalist politics, and "modern" Jewish organizations. Bialystok never lost its prominence or sense of immediacy for how Jews there conceived of their identities. Such a regional affiliation was not peculiar to Bialystok Jewry, as Isaac Bashevis Singer once noted: "Jews from the Lublin area spoke in a different way and even, it seemed, looked different from Jews from Kalisz or Siedlce. . . . [Jews from] towns by the Vistula [saw themselves as] very different from those [Jews] in Volhynia."[216]

Portrait of Peysakh Kaplan, Yiddish writer and editor of Bialystok's *Dos naye lebn*.
This photograph was taken at a YIVO conference in Vilna by photographer Alter
Kacyzne on November 24, 1929. *Courtesy of Forward Association/Alter Kacyzne.*

Even when economic and political factors prompted many Jews to leave Bialystok, they harbored ambivalent feelings about their departure. On the one hand, they had freed themselves from Bialystok's ethnic, class, and political tensions; on the other hand, they appreciated how bereft they would feel without Bialystok, stripped of the only bearings they knew. Despite their shallow roots in Bialystok of less than two generations, most Jews in and from Bialystok saw the city as central to their vision of themselves. Thus, as Jews ventured forth to seek fortunes elsewhere, the guide provided for them by their experiences in Bialystok was the most salient force shaping the way they approached the world and addressed their new circumstances. When they arrived in their new homes, they founded hundreds of organizations dedicated to furthering the legacy of their former home, as discussed in full in the next chapter. While there was no consensus among these organizations as to what exactly constituted Bialystok's essence or legacy, all agreed that it was essential to offer both financial and spiritual aid to their former home particularly after the Great War. As these organizations developed and responded to the changing needs of their constituents, they not only molded the ways Bialystok's Jews throughout the world envisioned their identities, but also altered how Jews in Bialystok saw their own community: Jewish Bialystok, while geographically located in northeastern Poland, was actually part of a larger entity that spanned the world.

CHAPTER 2

Rebuilding Homeland in Promised Lands

With little fear or hesitation, David Sohn, a young man of twenty, approached the podium of the small dark auditorium at 246 East Broadway on New York City's Lower East Side. Clearing his throat, he began speaking to the sweaty crowd of hundreds who had assembled on July 17, 1919, to hear about Bialystok's fate during the Great War. Sohn, with his ink-dark hair and aquiline features, cut an impressive figure. His "fiery" eloquence, as Joseph Lipnick, head of the Bialystoker Bikur Holim society recalled, "deeply moved" everyone in the audience in a manner that no other speaker ever had.[1] Few were prepared for Sohn's vivid description of the horrors befalling their former home: the renowned Jewish hospital lay in ruins; the great synagogue along the main boulevard was now a heap of rubble; wealthy Jewish philanthropists found themselves begging on street corners; Jewish orphans lay starving in the streets; and the lines for the kosher soup kitchen stretched for blocks. All present at the meeting, Sohn thundered, "must do everything in our power to help our compatriots (*landslayt*) in their time of need."[2] Despite their initial shock and despondency, the crowd went wild. Within a few short weeks, the squabbles that had cropped up in America between Jewish émigrés from Bialystok since the late nineteenth century were forgotten; ideological differences that had earlier divided the dozens of Bialystoker organizations were ignored. Leaders, who had previously refused to sit in the same room, not only met with one another but even decided to merge their organizations. In less than a month, they formed the Bialystok Center with David Sohn at its helm and with a mission to coordinate relief efforts to rebuild Bialystok.

David Sohn maintained the mantle of leadership in this new organization for almost fifty years, during which time he nurtured

David Sohn in 1922, after his first trip to Poland on behalf of the Bialystoker Center. *Courtesy of Steve Kavee, William Kavee, and Rona K. Moyer.*

and sustained a new type of dispersed Jewish community and earned himself the title "Mr. Bialystok."[3] Sohn reached out to those who cultivated similar organizations in Buenos Aires, Palestine, and Melbourne, exerting tireless effort to raise millions of dollars to support Jewish life in Bialystok and its legacy abroad. To be sure, Jews from Bialystok were far from exceptional: dozens of other immigrants formed a wide range of civic, labor, religious, and cultural organizations to preserve their deeply ingrained cultural patterns in the early twentieth century. East European Jews exhibited a particular penchant for forming organizations that tied them to an idea of the Old World as they helped them adapt to the dramatically new political, economic, and social environments they encountered in their new homes.[4] By 1939, there were more than three thousand East European Jewish immigrant associations in New York City, and in Buenos Aires an estimated 40 percent of the adult Jewish community belonged to such a society.[5]

Scholars of Jewish migration have long commented upon the dense network of landsmanshaftn, Jewish immigrant mutual aid societies that helped struggling migrant Jews; far fewer have discussed the ways in which these organizations thrust East European Jews living in the United States, South America, Africa, Australia, and Europe into a transnational sphere in which they debated, conferred, and reimagined what it meant to be a Jew from Eastern Europe. Often casting these organizations as "an American phenomenon" or viewing them primarily within the framework of associational life, scholars have yet to analyze these organizations in a comparative framework or assess the ways in which they tied their members to Jews in other parts of the world.[6]

As Jewish immigrants from Bialystok strategically employed the term *Bialystoker* both in reference to a concrete place and as an abstract discursive term, they clearly demonstrated that Jews from different parts of Eastern Europe did not see themselves as belonging to one monolithic ethnic or religious group, as scholars often paint them, but rather saw Old World regional distinctions as still defining who they were.[7] Through a cross-cultural comparison of the functions and rhetoric of the organizations founded by Bialystok's Jews in New York, Buenos Aires, Tel Aviv, and Melbourne—the only four cities where these immigrant Jews founded Bialystoker "centers" dedicated to recreating and maintaining Bialystok—this chapter illuminates the divergent ways in which Jews from the same place of origin recast their identities as they searched for ways to translate their Old World predilections into fresh idioms appropriate for their new surroundings. Because of the diverse social, political, and economic demands of their new homes, the simple act of organizing a "Bialystoker" institution raised larger ideological questions: what did it mean to be a Bialystoker Jew outside of Bialystok? Why was it necessary to have a distinct Bialystoker organization? While these organizations all articulated a vision of successful adaptation as dependent on its members' ability to rebuild an imagined Bialystok in their new homes, the types of institutions Bialystok's

Jews actually erected and the diverse meanings they assigned to the term *Bialystoker* highlights the complex variables brought into play as East European Jews tried to map their East European regional identities onto the terrain of the new world.

While each organization discussed below made a statement by sharing the name Bialystok, none of these new organizations functioned in the same manner, offered identical services, or envisioned the legacy of Bialystok in the same way. Each was a fluid, organic entity, responding to the evolving needs of its constituents. In New York, the Bialystoker Center demonstrated its "Bialystoker identity" by acting as a model social welfare agency. In contrast, the Bialystoker Farband in Buenos Aires emphasized a class-centered vision of Bialystok's legacy, focusing their institution on working-class politics, education, and Yiddish culture. In Palestine, to be a "Bialystoker" entailed raising money from wealthy Bialystoker Jews around the world to build a new Jewish homeland. In Australia, the performance of one's "Bialystokness" involved participation in the numerous social and charitable activities sponsored by the Bialystoker émigré community there. Despite their divergent foci, each Bialystoker émigré institution through their membership requirements, rhetoric, and activities shaped the complexion of everyday life for the thousands of Jews who participated in them by helping them mediate between their interwoven needs as Jews, immigrants, and members of a new self-proclaimed diaspora community stemming from Eastern Europe.

"Bialystok on East Broadway"; Rebuilding Bialystok in New York, 1877–1939

Long before Sohn's rousing speech in 1919, Jewish immigrants from Bialystok who found themselves in New York City demonstrated a keen desire to develop new organizations to tend both to their economic and their existential needs. Indeed, most who stepped off the boat at Ellis Island, and soon found themselves, like thousands of other East European Jews, on the crowded tip of Manhattan, commonly known today as the Lower East Side, were drawn to these organizations to make sense of their new surroundings. New York, with its towering buildings and tenement houses taller than any building in Bialystok, overwhelmed many who believed they had come from a big city. The sheer density of people, along with the absence of forests or grassy fields in the maze of streets that comprised their new home, made the reality of life in New York quite difficult for many newcomers.[8] Jews from Bialystok who had long heard tales of the easy money to be made in New York's garment industry were equally dismayed by the limited economic options on the Lower East side: there, as Rukhl Rifkin recalled, many toiled long hours, "even on *shabes* [the Sabbath]" for low wages that barely covered the cost of food or housing.[9] Indeed as Max Pogorelsky's relatives warned him after he arrived in 1916, America was not the *goldene medina* (land of gold): New York City's system of ready-made garment production—with small sweatshops, contractors, and piece work—replicated many of the worst elements of Bialystok's exploitative *loynketnik* system.[10]

Despite the initial disillusionment, Jews from Bialystok used their skills and familiarity with industrial production to achieve relative economic security. While many East European Jewish migrants complained in their memoirs of long periods of unemployment, most Jews from Bialystok report securing jobs within weeks, in part because they arrived during a period when the women's ready-to-wear clothing industry was rapidly expanding and tailoring skills were usually in great demand.[11] Two days after B. Rosen, a tailor from Bialystok, arrived in New York, his brother found him a job because all Jewish garment contractors knew that "a good tailor in Bialystok would make a great tailor in New York."[12] Jews from Bialystok understood the intricacies and vagaries of the production system in the New York garment industry: as in Bialystok, low barriers to entrance into entrepreneurial activity in New York's competitive contracting system encouraged many to turn their homes into small workshops with little capital investment.[13] Max Havelin, who arrived in New York in 1904, drew on his experiences in the loynketnik system, concluding it was imperative to establish himself in his own businesses as soon as possible. In Bialystok, after working as an overseer in a textile factory, Havelin had realized that he had to set up his "own shop if he wanted to succeed"; he ran that operation until he left Russia in 1903. Once in America, he borrowed twenty dollars from his friends to set up a cloak shop on Suffolk Street.[14] Similarly, Max Pogorelsky, a weaver in Bialystok who arrived in the United States in 1916, told his New York relatives of his desire to work as a weaver in America. Their reaction was "No way, Max! If you do that, you will remain a *zeidene torbe* [a poor worker]."[15] After working for a short time in a dressmaking shop, he followed their advice; he and his wife opened up their own small dress shop.[16] Combining manufacturing skills with entrepreneurial drive, many émigrés like Havelin and Pogorelsky devoted their energies to establishing small businesses that they hoped would assure their economic prosperity.[17]

As they struggled to establish themselves financially in New York City, Bialystok's Jews turned to one another for support, developing a rich and diverse network of more than thirty-nine organizations.[18] As a brief survey of several of these organizations demonstrate, Bialystoker associations not only provided basic financial assistance to members (and their families) in times of illness, unemployment, or death but also enabled the diverse cross-section of Jews who arrived from Bialystok to find their social niches in America, regardless of their religious beliefs, gender, age, or class loyalty.[19] Economic concerns always took precedence: the first two organizations founded in the United States by Jews from Bialystok—the Bialystoker Unterstitzungs Verein (founded in 1864) and Mesilas Yesharim (founded in 1868)—provided medical care and financial support to ill or indigent émigrés and their families through a system of mutual aid. Shortly thereafter, more pious members of the community addressed religious needs, forming two congregations—Anshei Chesed (1878) and Ahavat Achim (1884)—to provide a place where all Bialystoker Jews, as member Louis Cohen proclaimed, could "pray and congregate in the Bialystoker way."[20] In practice this meant they ran their daily service according to religious customs that had developed in Bialystok.Even though women could not become members of most Bialystoker societies, as was the case with hundreds of landsmanshaft organizations, they played an active role in émigré life from the beginning, maintaining their

The Bialystoker Synagogue, 7 Willett Street, on New York's Lower East Side.
The building was originally erected in 1826 as a Methodist Episcopal Church in
the late Federal style. The building was constructed of Manhattan schist from a
quarry on nearby Pitt Street. One of the only remaining early-nineteenth-century
fieldstone religious buildings from the Federal period in Lower Manhattan, the
synagogue was listed as a New York City Landmark in 1966. *Courtesy of Rachel
Rabhan.*

own social and charitable societies, such as the Daughters of Israel
(founded in 1888) or the Ladies Auxiliary of the Bialystoker Center
(founded in 1923). Younger men who left Russia in response to the
1905 revolution founded the Bialystoker Young Men's Association in
1906. "Americanization" was their goal, and their organization provided "much-needed forward-looking" educational, cultural, and
social activities to introduce its members to American life and culture. Class loyalty prompted émigré socialists to found the Bialystoker
Branch 88 of the Workmen's Circle (1905). This immensely popular

organization, whose ranks doubled the general membership in the larger Workmen's Circle, provided aid to workers in both New York and in Russia and helped organize several clubs based on professional affiliation, such as the Bialystoker Bricklayers Benevolent Association (1905) and the Bialystoker Painters Club (1934).

Before 1919, these numerous groups and other Bialystoker organizations scattered throughout the Lower East Side and Brooklyn rarely coordinated their activities despite their shared struggle to define Bialystoker identity in America and to remain financially solvent, so their members would not have to turn to Christian charities.[21] Did birth in Bialystok make one a Bialystoker? Or did one have to possess certain traits, and act in a particular manner? Or did one have to belong to certain organizations in America? Debates at the first and longest-operating Bialystoker mutual aid society, the Bialystoker Unterstitzungs Verein Somach Noflim (Bialystoker Mutual Aid Society Somach Noflim) demonstrate the difficulty of balancing between immigrants' need for clear self-definition and financial security. Originally founded in 1866 as the Bialystoker Unterstitzungs Verein, this group tied its members together by their love of Bialystok rather than by any religious commitment or class affiliation. However, the organization was forced to close its doors in 1868 because of lack of funds.[22] In 1877, a group of recently arrived émigrés reestablished the society, but found in 1885 that they needed to attract more members to assure their organization's economic viability. By adopting the Hebrew name Somach Noflim (lit., to lift the fallen), one faction argued, their organization would attract more members because of its immediate association with the similarly named, highly regarded charity in Bialystok.[23] Vehemently opposing such a measure, another group argued against the use of a Hebrew name because of its religious connotations. After much debate, the members chose to compromise, reincorporating their organization in 1886 with both a Yiddish (Bialystoker Unterstitzungs Verein) and a Hebrew (Somach Noflim) name, since they agreed that "one may live in his private life as he pleases, as a radical secular or religious Jew, but in Somach Noflim, one must be a one hundred percent Bialystoker *landsman* (compatriot)."[24]

The founding members of this organization inculcated into new members this vision of Bialystok regional unity. They believed that this identification provided the best means to transcend immigrant Jews' growing ideological differences. To gain membership, a man (and only a man, as only men could join) was forced to answer questions about Bialystok posed to him by a special committee: where had he lived in Bialystok? Who owned the city's largest factory? These questions sought to verify whether the applicant was authentically a born and bred "Bialystoker."[25] Then after paying an initiation fee of three dollars, the new member and his family would be eligible, according to the stipulations of this organization's constitution, for "aid if anyone in the family became ill, unemployed, or otherwise distressed."[26] During its first twenty-five years of operation, it dispensed $116,514 to address its constituents' economic needs, paying for their doctors, hospital expenditures, cemetery plots, and funeral expenses.

At the same time that it dispensed money for immigrants' practical needs, Somach Noflim constantly reiterated its strong attachment to Bialystok by depicting its members as part of a larger endeavor in their promotional materials distributed at balls, excursions, and educational programs.[27] Leafing through its numerous anniversary journals, one sees, for example, in 1911, that members saw their organization's primary goal as "to make the name of Bialystok a great and honored name in the New World [just as it was in the Old]."[28] By succeeding in America, argued later journals, the members of Somach Noflim were not only establishing themselves in their new homes, but also glorifying their former home in Eastern Europe. In an article about the history of Somach Noflim, composed in 1926, David Sohn reported that members saw themselves as "pioneers" whose primary task was to build up a new "Bialystok colony" on American shores.[29] Like the "pilgrims" and "other great explorers" who had come to this country as part of other imperial projects, Bialystoker émigrés were "not greenhorns," Sohn asserted, but rather emissaries sent to the United States to "explore and map out new territories" for Bialystok.[30]

If the language of American discovery and exploration provided the prism through which these Jews viewed their endeavors, then Judaism served as their central mission. Founding members of Somach Noflim demanded that fellow members observe basic elements of Jewish religious practice. Somach Noflim's constitution declared that "every unmarried member must bind himself only to a Jewess, in accordance with the tenets of the Jewish religion. If he marries otherwise, he shall automatically forfeit his membership."[31] Circumcision of sons was also required of all members who wanted their families to be eligible for full benefits. But there was a more general emphasis on the importance of ritual observance: social events were never convened on Saturdays. The menu of the annual dinner followed Jewish dietary laws. As a founding member succinctly put it, all were expected to follow "the religious precept [clal] that we all know and follow: A Good [Bialystoker] Landsman is a Good Jew."[32]

Somach Noflim ultimately succeeded because it appealed to émigrés' desire to see themselves as loyal residents of Bialystok, part of America's foundational myths, and traditional Jews. Yet not all Bialystoker organizations achieved this balance with such ease, as illustrated by a thirty-year rift between the Bialystoker Bikur Holim of the Lower East Side (founded in 1896) and the Bialystoker Bikur Holim of Brooklyn (founded in 1897). Even though the organizations shared a name, claimed Bialystok's Lines Hastedek as their model, and strategically employed a language of regional distinctiveness to rally support for their organizations, their members interpreted the meaning of being a "good Bialystoker" with striking variance, depending on whether they lived on the Lower East Side or in Brooklyn.

Originally founded by émigrés who arrived in the 1890s and realized the desperate need of those who were ill and unable to work, both organizations helped pay for doctors' visits, hospital stays, and missed wages. But they offered their services to different constituencies. Bialystoker Bikur Holim of the Lower East Side, boasted one of its founding members in 1908, demonstrates "the Talmudic dictum that all Bialystokers know well: one must care for the poor of your city first."[33] Interpreting the Talmudic command to care for the "poor of your city" as referring only to Bialystok's Jews in New York (and not all poor Jews), the group on the Lower East Side covered the medical needs of numerous impoverished Bialystoker émigrés. The organization's leadership constantly bemoaned how overwhelmed they felt by the needs of indigent Bialystoker Jews, and "only wished it could have done more . . . for our Bialystoker compatriots."[34]

Bikur Holim in Brooklyn, on the other hand, grew out of a shared sense of values, rather than their common origin: their guiding motto was "to take from the Bialystoker but give to everyone."[35] The Brooklyn group did not strive to build an exclusively Bialystoker community as their compatriots had done on the Lower East Side. Instead, their connection to Bialystok was summoned only to raise money. While one founding member of the Brooklyn group claimed that the new institution drew direct inspiration from Bialystok's renowned Lines Hatsedek, the president emphasized that the use of the foreign name "Bialystok" was "not meant to imply an allegiance to the old country but was chosen for the sole purpose of directing Bialystokers to give money to support their causes."[36] The institution's primary goal, as its constitution outlined, was "to work for the good of the entire community, thereby making the name *Bialystok* an important factor in the community life of Brooklyn."[37] The Brooklyn Bikur Holim did not merely provide medical aid but also sponsored weekly "public forums, high-grade concerts, plays, operas, vaudeville shows, and weekly community dances" to which "all were welcome."[38] It also ran a Jewish arbitration court widely used by many immigrants in Brooklyn. Within a short time, the membership of Bialystoker Bikur Holim of Brooklyn grew dramatically; Bialystok became a well-known name throughout Brooklyn. But few outside of Brooklyn celebrated its organizational success, as it had forfeited its ties to Bialystok and other Bialystoker émigré organizations in America.

Nothing demonstrated their lack of commitment to Bialystok more clearly than their refusal to provide funds to the Lower East Side's Bialystoker Bikur Holim in 1901. Overwhelmed by hundreds of ill applicants, Joseph Lipnick, president of Bialystoker Bikur Holim of the Lower East Side, asked his "brothers in Brooklyn" for a contribution of $250 to meet the emergency. He received nothing, even though it was known that the Brooklyn group had just finished a successful capital campaign that had raised $3,000. Lipnick issued an ultimatum that unless the "money was forthcoming in a short time . . . the Brooklyn Bikur Holim would be dismissed" from the greater Bialystoker community.[39] Tensions mounted between the two groups. The Brooklyn faction initiated another massive fundraising drive to help the needy, but still refused to send anything to help

their "compatriots" on the Lower East side. An informal excommuni-
cation of Brooklyn Bikur Holim followed. The leaders of Bikur Holim
of the Lower East Side declined to speak to their counterparts in
Brooklyn for almost two decades until the erection of the Bialystoker
Center forced an icy reconciliation between them.

Why did members of Brooklyn Bialystoker Bikur Holim divorce
themselves from Bialystok while members of Somach Noflim or Bikur
Holim living on the Lower East Side continued to maintain such a
particularistic attachment? The divergent patterns of Russian Jewish
settlement in New York City played an integral (though rarely discussed) role in molding émigrés' vision of themselves and their connection to their former home. On the Lower East Side, as Moses
Rischin notes, Jews from Eastern Europe carved out smaller subcom-
munities that were defined by place of origin.[40] In such an environment, Bialystok's Jews at first felt the need to root their social identity in something more specific than their Russian–Jewish origins
and emphasized their connection to Bialystok.[41] In late nineteenth-
century Brooklyn, however, Jews did not live in such concentrated
areas as they did on the Lower East Side. Scattered throughout their
borough, Jews in Brooklyn did not deem it necessary to transplant
the distinguishing marker from the Old World, namely regional identity, in order to define their social identity. Thus, in Brooklyn, Jews
from Bialystok perhaps felt that they needed to affiliate and support
all Jews as part of their effort to cultivate stronger Jewish communal
institutions in this newly developing area of Jewish settlement.

The Bialystoker Center: Bialystok Transplanted
and Transformed on the Lower East Side

While Bialystoker Jews in Brooklyn were excommunicated as
a result of their symbolic abandonment of their homeland, almost
all Bialystoker organizations on the Lower East Side would soon
follow their example, redirecting their efforts toward serving the
charitable needs of the Jewish community at large. The Bialystoker
Center, known to many as the "new Bialystok," perfectly captured
this tendency. Growing out of Bialystoker Bikur Holim of the Lower

East side founded in 1896 to care exclusively for sick Bialystoker Jews in New York City, the Bialystoker Center officially opened in 1919 to coordinate the fundraising efforts on behalf of war-ravaged Bialystok. In 1927, the success of the Bialystoker Center in raising funds for Poland prompted members to transform this institution once again. This time, it became the Bialystoker Center and Old Age Home, an elderly-care facility open to any Jew in need.

The multiple recasting of this institution would have been shocking to the founding members of Bikur Holim, who in 1896 saw their task as simple and focused: providing aid to sick Bialystoker Jews in New York. Indeed, their institution succeeded in its mission, as a founding member proclaimed: "Our organization provides the most aid in the city to sick Bialystoker mothers and children."[42] Despite its initial success, this organization, like many other landsmanshaft societies, shifted its course as a result of the First World War.[43] One factor was that thousands of immigrants wanted to send money back to Eastern Europe. Many American banks, however, refused to transmit money to this region, as Joseph Lipnick recalled, because of "the general chaos in this part of the world."[44] With no other choice, hundreds of landsmanshaftn combined efforts and chose a member to deliver funds personally: as *Der tog*, the popular New York Yiddish daily, reported, "There is not a single landsmanshaft here in America which has not sent, is sending or will send a delegate with money . . . to the other side of the ocean."[45] This problem prompted David Sohn to lobby the wealthy leaders of Bikur Holim, the Bialystoker organization with the most members in New York, to transform their organization into a center for relief work, or to use his words, a "Bialystoker Center." As an umbrella organization uniting all Bialystoker landsmanshaft groups, Sohn argued, the Bialystoker Center would be able to send delegates and to collect and distribute relief funds more efficiently and speedily than any individual Bialystoker organization.

Sohn's successful campaign to create a Bialystoker Center left a formidable imprint on the entire dispersed community of Bialystok's Jews. The board of trustees of the newly formed Center immediately appointed Sohn, a journalist, its executive director, and Sohn, taking his charge seriously, recast himself as the community's unofficial ambassador, a new type of Jewish *shtadlan* (Jewish communal intermediary).[46] No fabulist would have cast this tall, serious, and at times ornery man as the central character in a transnational drama that would soon engage the attention of tens of thousands of East European Jews and involve the international transfer of millions of dollars. At the time of his arrival in the United States in 1912, few would have ever believed that the youngest son of the pious Rabbi Moshe Sohn would become known as "Mr. Bialystok" less than two decades later.[47] In contrast to the pious rabbis or wealthy Jewish merchants who acted as communal representatives or intermediaries in nineteenth-century Bialystok and throughout Eastern Europe, David Sohn was not wealthy, pious, or learned.[48] He represented a new type of Jewish communal leader, the self-appointed *shtadlan*, whose power derived from the fact that he was a gifted organizer who inspired others to give funds and who earned his livelihood by serving the needs of the Jewish community.

As the first hired professional of the Bialystok émigré community, David Sohn devoted himself to bolstering Jewish life in Bialystok and to perpetuating the legacy of his beloved hometown. Sohn served as the Bialystoker Center's executive director for almost fifty years until his death in 1967, shaping its internal agenda and external activism in countless ways. While the Bialystoker Center regularly held annual elections, the process did not necessarily render this institution democratic, as historian Daniel Soyer argues in his study of landsmanshaft organizations. Rather, despite having elected officers, the institution took on an autocratic character, as Sohn made all of the important decisions concerning the agenda as its executive director. His influence extended beyond the Bialystoker Center as well. In 1938, for example, when the government-sponsored Yiddish Writers' Project compiled its report on landsmanshaftn organizations, David Sohn was considered the leader of half of the Bialystoker organizations in New York City.[49] This autocratic style of leadership extended beyond Sohn, for instance, in the case of the Bialystoker Center's Ladies Auxiliary, where Ida Adack held onto the presidency for more than two decades.[50]

Sohn's domination of the Bialystoker Center and the entire network of Bialystoker émigré organizations in New York did not trouble many, as they believed no one was more dedicated to their former home. In fact, as Joseph Lipnick, the first president of the Bialystoker Center, reminisced, the Bialystoker Center would have never been built without Sohn:

> The transformation of Bialystoker Bikur Holim into the Bialystoker Center can be traced to the arrival on the scene of the well known Bialystoker David Sohn, who in July 1919, as a young man convened a meeting of Bialystokers in the headquarters of Bikur Holim at 246 East Broadway. . . . While I did not at the time entertain any great hopes for the realization of David Sohn's plans, he spoke so imploringly and at the same time so convincingly that I as well as the others present were deeply moved by the plight of our old home town Bialystok.
> . . . He portrayed conditions prevailing then in Bialystok and concluded with a fiery appeal to all to unite in the urgent relief work for the old home.[51]

By July 1919, Sohn's passionate appeals had enticed thirty-five different Bialystoker landsmanshaft organizations to affiliate with the Bialystoker Center.[52] The mission of this institution was to serve both "the interests of the Bialystoker landsmanshaftn in America and the interests of the Jewish population in Bialystok" through its collection and distribution of funds.[53] Hailed as "saviors" by Jews in Bialystok for their relief efforts, representatives of the Bialystoker Center were considered by local Polish officials as powerful emissaries of the American Jewish community. The Bialystoker Center played a pivotal role in rebuilding life in this Polish Jewish community between 1919 and 1932, distributing more than $9 million (equivalent to $107 million at 2008 currency values) in aid to both needy individuals and institutions.[54]

The Bialystoker Center, in the eyes of Bialystok's Jews living in New York, demonstrated the true greatness of Bialystok, for only Bialystoker Jews—through their ingenuity and creativity—were able to transplant the distinctive charitable traditions of their former hometown to America and unite groups divided by deep ideological

Parade marking the convocation of the Bialystoker Center Old Age Home, 1931. *Courtesy of the Goren-Goldstein Center for the Study of Diaspora Jewry, Tel Aviv University.*

differences.[55] Bialystok's Jews from across the United States looked to the center with pride. The center raised the status and prestige of the entire émigré community with its towering height and illustrious address on the Lower East Side's main thoroughfare of East Broadway. Located just blocks away from the famed *Forverts* (Jewish Daily Forward) building and directly in the shadow of the Educational Alliance, two of the most renowned and influential Jewish institutions on the Lower East Side, the center's building demonstrated that Bialystok aspired to be a critical force in American Jewish life.

The sentiment, or in fact hope, that Bialystok would play an instrumental role in American Jewish life like the Forward newspaper or Educational Alliance prodded thousands to line the streets for a public celebration marking the opening of the Bialystoker Center building in 1923.[56] At the opening, a small orchestra played the "Star Spangled Banner" as "a group of Bialystoker girls" carried the center banner. "This is the great time for Bialystoker compatriots throughout the world," proclaimed Jacob Krepliak, a Bialystoker émigré, well-known Yiddish journalist, and editor of the illustrious Yiddish journal *Di Tsukunft* (The Future), a participant in the Center's "truly awe-inspiring" opening ceremonies.[57] "Now Bialystoker Jews have a community building," he continued, "where we can have a spiritual center for the children of the best Jewish city of the old world in the best Jewish city of the new world."[58] Krepliak's description hints that his pride was informed by an Old World mentality of regional competition: Jews from Bialystok were truly exceptional since they had accomplished a feat that no other landsmanshaft group in America could match. Even landsmanshaftn from "larger cities than Bialystok," he emphasized, "have not built for themselves such an institution."[59] Zelig Tigel, a correspondent for the Warsaw Yiddish daily *Der haynt* echoed Krepliak. In his comparison of Warsaw and Bialystok in an article, Tigel argued that the new Bialystoker Center reconfigured the map of Eastern Europe, with an extension of Bialystok now relocated to the Lower East Side, with arms extending to other Bialystoker hubs such as Paterson, New Jersey.[60]

The failed efforts of Bialystoker émigrés in Chicago to organize their own "center" illustrate how U.S. regional divides reinforced regional sensibilities among these East European Jewish immigrants. Nathan Miller, a Bialystoker émigré who settled in Chicago in 1906, described how his pride in Bialystok became entangled with envy as he and others in Chicago looked in awe upon the Bialystoker Center. "The activities of our New York friends," Miller wrote, particularly "the founding of a Bialystoker Center in New York make us [in Chicago] feel jealous, and we had just decided at our last meeting, although there is disagreement if we need it, to get a place of our own."[61] Seeing New York rather than Eastern Europe as their benchmark, Miller concluded his report with the admission that perhaps "we 'farmers' here in Chicago will [not be able to] imitate your achievement in New York" and "build a Bialystoker home in

Chicago."[62] To be sure, "farming" and its demands would not keep the tailors and bakers who comprised this group from erecting a new "center," but as Miller's reflections clearly evoke, regional competition, albeit in relation to a new map, continued to shape East European Jews' understanding of themselves and how to articulate their hopes, dreams, and self-perceptions.

With Bialystok's Jews throughout the country emulating their undertaking, the leaders of the center made a great effort to emphasize its connection to Bialystok. At one of its first board meetings, David Sohn stressed that "the Bialystoker Center's first goal [is to] succeed in organizing a smooth functioning new Bialystok on the shores of America so that the traditions and spirit of Old Bialystok are preserved."[63] Sohn's casting of his institution at the forefront of Bialystok's expansion echoes the rhetoric of other immigrant groups, such as the Japanese who as historian Eiichiro Azuma points out, often "confounded emigration with colonial expansion."[64] The center functioned as a "new Bialystok" by raising money for its namesake in Poland, running events in its honor, and publishing reports about its reconstruction. In its first five years of existence, the Bialystoker Center organized more than one hundred dinners, theater benefits, and concerts to raise millions of dollars to rebuild Bialystok's Jewish communal institutions. At these events, recent American visitors to Bialystok or leaders of that city's Jewish community, whom the center brought to America, spoke at length about the situation there. In 1923, for example, Dr. Synaglowski, the head of the ORT (*Obshtchestvo Remeslenovo Truda* [Society for the Encouragement of Handicrafts]), appeared at a dinner sponsored by the Bialystoker Relief Committee in New York. Synaglowski spoke passionately about the high unemployment rates, inadequate training, and general despair of Jewish workers; the audience was so moved that they raised more than $7,000 in one night to build new vocational and agricultural training schools open only to Jews.[65]

Beyond fortifying the ties between Bialystok and the United States, Sohn dedicated the center's resources to publishing the *Bialystoker Stimme*, a quarterly magazine both explicitly and implicitly dedicated to strengthening the bonds of Bialystok's dispersed Jewish émigrés.

The Bialystoker Center, circa 1931. While the home's cornerstone was laid in
September 1929, the developing financial crisis saw the building only fully com-
pleted twenty-two months later. *Courtesy of the Goren-Goldstein Center for the
Study of Diaspora Jewry, Tel Aviv University.*

Print culture, as Benedict Anderson points out, plays a key role in creating and sustaining group identity, particularly when a group does not share clear territorial cohesiveness.[66] Newspapers and quarterly journals, as exemplified by the *Bialystoker Stimme*, played a pivotal role in defining the collective identity of this increasingly scattered Jewish community. The *Bialystoker Stimme*, first published in 1921, was filled with editorials in which émigrés discussed and debated the contours of their identities, articles about current events in Bialystok, and reports from Bialystoker émigré communities throughout the world.

During its first few decades of publication, the four thousand copies of the *Bialystoker Stimme* brought out quarterly reached tens of thousands of dedicated readers throughout the world.[67] As Anna Gepner recalled, in Melbourne, Australia, everyone gathered together regularly to read the paper when it arrived at her uncle's home.[68] Yehezkel Aran similarly reminisced how he would gather with some friends regularly in a cafe in Tel Aviv to share common woes and to "catch up on all the news conveyed in the *Bialystoker Stimme*."[69] Appreciating the newspapers' wide readership, Sohn solicited contributions from all over the world to report on Bialystoker émigré life. With banner headlines declaring "Bialystok in Crisis," regular columns devoted to "Our One World" and to the tales of émigrés living in Chicago, Berlin, Palestine, and Mexico, as well as feature articles entitled "A New Bialystok in Argentina" or "Bialystok in America and America in Bialystok," the *Bialystoker Stimme* encouraged its readers to see their new communities as extensions of their former home. Editorials emphasized that all Bialystoker émigrés throughout the world were involved in the same task: expanding Bialystok's influence as they endeavored to build for themselves lives in their respective new homes.[70]

As he oversaw the distribution of funds in Bialystok and the forging of a new dispersed Jewish community, Sohn began to appreciate the great power he and his compatriots wielded. Echoing a larger trend similarly identified by historian Daniel Soyer among other landsmanshaft groups, the Bialystoker Center's "involvement in relief efforts drew [it] out of isolation," and prompted Bialystoker émigrés to think about how their "charity could serve the broader Jewish community" and extend their influence in New York's Jewish circles.[71] The leadership of the center began to question the exclusive focus on Bialystok. As David Sohn recalled:[72]

> Soon all active in the Center realized that extending aid to compatriots overseas was not enough. . . . They realized that Bialystoker children, growing up, faced the vexing question: how could they avert the embarrassment of placing 'mother' or 'dad,' advanced in years, into a charity Old Age Home? . . . They hit upon the answer: set up a Bialystoker Home for the Aged in which the Bialystoker old folks would feel at home among their compatriots. The decision in Jan. 1927 to erect a Home for the Aged was greeted with an enthusiastic response.[73]

The desire to recast the Bialystoker Center from a philanthropic institution focused Bialystok into a welfare organization centered on aiding the elderly, reflects the pressures of shifting demographic patterns in New York's Jewish immigrant community. Caring for the elderly, as historian Michael Katz observes, was a major problem for many immigrants groups and members of the urban working class in turn-of-the-century New York. While there was a vast array of public institutions—both religious and government-sponsored—to care for young children (such as the public school system), there were practically no institutions to care for the elderly or infirm. Beginning in the 1920s, the fear that elderly, haggard, and sickly Jews would be forced into poorhouses or Christian institutions prompted several landsmanshaft groups, such as the Warsawer and Mohilever, to erect old age homes.[74] By the 1930s, David Sohn pointed out, the fear was not only that Jews would be forced into Christian institutions, but rather that if the two hundred thousand elderly Jews living in New York City flocked to municipal poorhouses there would be antisemitic and nativist repercussions.[75]

Sohn was particularly invested in this institutional transformation, as it provided him with a vehicle through which to extend his influence beyond the parameters of his particular émigré community. Fashioning himself into a Jewish communal advocate for the elderly, he had always fancied himself as an intellectual and communal activist but had not yet had the opportunity to prove himself.[76] "In New York," Sohn wrote in 1933 in the widely circulated Yiddish magazine *Yom tov bleter,* "there are over 200,000 Jews above the age of sixty . . . who are [constantly faced with the] burning question of where to? . . . since there is no Jewish old age home where they could find themselves a true home."[77] Sohn expanded upon the concerns of the Bialystoker Center's board and sought to transform the Bialystoker Center into a promising Jewish welfare agency. In the coming decade, Sohn wrote other articles in national Yiddish publications to raise awareness of the growing "problem" of the Jewish elderly. He also advanced his innovative and creative solutions, which were embodied in the Bialystoker Center.[78]

While the leadership all embraced the idea of devoting its resources to converting the Bialystoker Center into an old age home, members of the board initially faced severe obstacles when they approached the larger émigré community with their idea. Numerous ads in the *Bialystoker Stimme* pleaded for support with no apparent success. Sohn ascribed these fundraising troubles to the lack of interest among Bialystoker émigrés in addressing the needs of the larger Jewish immigrant community.[79] Bialystok and its destruction, not the elderly, prompted the members of this community to assist financially. With this in mind, Sohn argued that money donated to build the Bialystoker Old Age Home should not be viewed within the context of addressing the needs of the general Jewish community, but as yet another way to glorify Bialystok: by creating a model institution with the Bialystoker name on it, Sohn argued, Bialystok's Jewish émigrés would actually be elevating their city by demonstrating its Jews' unparalleled creativity and strength.[80]

As compelling as this argument may have sounded, few responded. Yet that did not diminish Sohn's desire to see his project through and to expand the Bialystoker Center so that it could became a functioning old age home. In his search for new partners and sources of funding, Sohn turned his attention to Brooklyn and to mending the decades-old rift between Bialystok's Jews in Brooklyn and those on the Lower East Side. The tension was palpable on December 3, 1927, when Sohn arrived in Brooklyn with five other leading members of the Bialystoker Center to meet with the board of the Brooklyn Bialystoker Bikur Holim.[81] The chairman of the Brooklyn board, Chaim [Harry] Yudinsky, offered clear ground rules for the conversation: "no yelling, name calling . . . and the man who brings forth lies [*rekhilus*] will not be allowed to participate."[82] Nonetheless, the conversation degenerated quickly, particularly once the topic of money was raised. While the representatives of Brooklyn Bikur Holim highly valued all the work the center had done for Bialystok and clearly recognized the importance of an old age home, they were reluctant to hand over their assets—$15,000—to finally affiliate themselves with the Bialystoker Center. They wanted to maintain control over their money since they had worked hard to raise it. Representatives of the Bialystoker Center insisted that all money, "one hundred percent of it," be used for its operating budget, dispensed at the discretion of its board. Sohn acted, in the words of Yudinsky, as a "doctor," soothing disgruntled members. His witty remarks urged all to remember that their decision "would help Bialystoker Jews throughout the world." With more funds, Sohn pointed out "the Bialystoker Center could serve more sick Jews throughout the world," indicating that the old age home was only part of his larger plan, and would further glorify the name of Bialystok throughout America. Sohn's vision ultimately won out. A compromise was forged between these two contentious groups; Brooklyn Bikur Holim joined the Bialystoker Center, and over the next three years, funds were raised to add the requisite bathrooms and rooms so that the Center could be officially transformed into an old age home.

The bulk of the funds were fortunately collected by 1930, before the effects of Great Depression were felt throughout New York's Jewish immigrant world. With the proper medical equipment in place, the building was ready to accept its first residents. The Bialystoker Center and Old Age home, as it was officially renamed, was ready to open. Thousands thronged the streets to watch a "parade of 25,000 Bialystokers," as the *Forverts* reported, marching down East Broadway carrying American flags, banners, and ribbons flecked with red, white, and blue. This parade demonstrated "a high degree of collective self-assurance,"[83] indicating that Bialystoker Jews in New York saw the opening of this facility as enhancing their social power in the civic arena. As the engineer of this event, Sohn projected, to use the words of historian Arthur Goren, "a sense of self [that] was increasingly marked by ambiguity."[84] Did he still consider himself first and foremost the leader of Bialystok's Jews in New York? Or was he now truly an American Jewish communal leader who was a leading advocate for the elderly? Such questions plagued Sohn as he strove to construct and sustain a community whose collective identity centered on Bialystok but not focused on serving Bialystok's needs.

At the precise moment when one might question whether the Bialystoker Center was moving away from its "Bialystokness," Sohn argued in a two-page feature story in the *Forverts* that the new old age home he helped erect represented a "new Bialystok," elevating Bialystoker Jews' status in America and Eastern Europe as well. "Bialystok [is] on East Broadway," Sohn trumpeted in his June 21, 1931, article.[85] Tens of thousands of *Forverts* readers understood that Bialystok had not been transplanted from the Second Polish Republic and relocated to the Lower East Side's main thoroughfare. But they appreciated why Sohn would summon the map of Eastern Europe to hail the consecration of a new "edifice that anyone who travels on the bridges between New York and Brooklyn" would easily see, with "its fine architecture" and "towering" presence.[86] This Polish city's crowning achievement was not its role in the development of Zionism or socialism but its erection of an old age home at 226 East Broadway.

While raising funds for Bialystok had given his former home a second life, Sohn observed in the *Forverts* that Bialystok's full potential was only truly realized in America: "Bialystok has no building, like the Bialystoker Center and Old Age Home, [but Bialystok's] legacy inspired émigrés to create such an institution on the other side of the world. This new Bialystok testifies to Bialystok's traditions as well as its continued strength and vitality."[87] To be sure, Sohn was well aware of his own underlying motivations in this transformation, but he made sure to cast the successful erection of the Bialystoker Center and Old Age Home in the *Forverts* as illustrative of Bialystok Jewry's distinctiveness in Europe. "Bialystokers have set the standard for others to go by," David Sohn contended.[88] "Other landsmanshaftn—for example the Kolomayer," whose constituents lacked Bialystoker Jews' drive and enthusiasm, "can [only] dream of having a center such as our Bialystoker Center." Those from "the Warsawer, Odesser societies toil and ceaselessly endeavor to follow in the footsteps of the Bialystoker."[89] Indeed, it was the achievements of the Bialystok's Jewish diaspora that forced all to reconsider this city's legacy and its revered place in Jewish Eastern Europe.

Yet at the same time it aggrandized Bialystok, the new Bialystoker Center and Old Age Home represented a monumental shift in its members' projection of their identities as Bialystok's Jews.[90] Overwhelmed by the financial strains of the Great Depression and familial responsibilities, members of this community no longer saw themselves in the crucible of their foreign regional attachments. Replacing their previous commitment to financially supporting Bialystok with a general commitment to elderly welfare, members of this community radically redefined "Bialystokness." Splashed across the cover of the *Bialystoker Stimme* throughout the 1930s were not portraits of penury and desolation in Bialystok, but rather the elderly inhabitants of the Bialystoker Center Old Age home who required financial assistance. As these portraits insisted, to be a "Bialystoker" had become a question of spirit, conviction, and purpose, not only a matter of birthplace; anyone who joined wholeheartedly in the Bialystoker Center's mission—providing funds for the elderly and creating a vanguard Jewish welfare institution—could proclaim that he or she had successfully helped transplant "Bialystok to East Broadway."

The instant success of the old age home became a major source of pride among Bialystok's Jews in New York. The number of residents in the Bialystoker Old Age Home grew from 75 in 1931 to 250 in 1938. The home gave first priority to Bialystoker Jews, but the vast majority of its residents hailed from other regions in Eastern Europe. As they became intimately involved in serving the needs of the larger Jewish community, Bialystoker émigrés began to envision their center as teaching the American Jewish community the lessons of Bialystok, defined in 1934 in the following way:

The significance of the center's achievement is that it not only united various types of landsmanshaftn groups to build this institution but has also welded together various types of Jews: the religious and radical, the Orthodox and non-Orthodox among its residents.[91]

This description of the Home's ecumenicism reveals not only the centrality of tolerance and unity to émigrés' vision of their former home, but also the degree to which Bialystok's Jews in New York had slowly "Americanized," identifying themselves primarily as part of an American religious group rather than an East European regional group. As sociologist Will Herberg observed in 1955, it was common among turn-of-the-century immigrant groups adapting to life in America to relinquish their regional "immigrant identities" and transform themselves into members of "American religious communities," concerned more about their co-religionists' needs than their former place of origin.[92] As vividly illustrated on the institutional level by the Bialystoker Center, Bialystok's Jews in New York by 1930 no longer applauded themselves for aiding Jews and Jewish institutions in Bialystok, but rather celebrated how their "center" served Jews of different regional backgrounds and varying ideologies. In contrast, however, to Herberg's vision of Americanization, the members of the Bialystoker Center and Old Age Home still relied upon a language of regional distinctiveness to articulate their goals and aspirations despite the shift in their philanthropic focus.

Regardless of whether a Bialystoker organization identified itself with Bialystok because it primarily served a constituency born in that city or because it recreated some putative charitable legacy of the city, the variety of organizations clearly illustrated the malleability of East European regional identity. In many ways, the pliancy of the term *Bialystoker* eased these Jewish immigrants' adaptation to American life by enabling them to preserve some elements of their pre-migration identities. By 1939, most Bialystoker organizations could no longer service an exclusive Bialystoker constituency but rather expanded to concentrate on addressing the welfare needs of the larger Jewish community. Yet these organizations still employed idioms of regional distinctiveness, inculcating in their members the defining role that affiliations from the Old World played in new one. Such a vision of the continued centrality of Bialystok to their lives was shared by many former residents of the city, a significant portion of whom chose not to settle in the United States but in other parts of the world.

The Singing Looms of Villa Lynch: Bialystok's Jews Encounter Argentina

After visiting Bialystok and the surrounding area in the 1890s, itinerant Yiddish preacher Zvi Hirsh Masliansky could not stop talking about "the 'new' movement . . . that engulfed all cities [he visited] . . . making the far-away land of Argentina, a land few Jews had ever heard of, become immediately transformed into 'the land of milk and honey.'"[93] Luring hundreds of Jews from Bialystok among the thousands of East European Jews in the decades before the First World War, Argentina turned out to be far from a biblical land of plenty. Indeed, Argentina's distinctive social, economic, cultural, and political culture, Catholic in nature and passionately devoted to limiting industrial development, presented Jews from manufacturing centers such as Bialystok many unforeseen challenges. The struggles of Bialystok's Jews in Argentina to rebuild their lives and communal institutions at the beginning of the twentieth century highlight the differential communal configurations that emerge when migrants find themselves in a place that does not welcome their industrial skills or their religious beliefs.

The travails and triumphs of Bialystok's Jews in Argentina reflect the larger challenges East European Jews faced as they tried to integrate into Argentine society, a society undergoing rapid political and economic change during the late nineteenth and early twentieth centuries. Argentina, one of the largest colonies of the Spanish Empire, had begun its fight for independence in May 1810. Despite revolutionaries' efforts to overthrow the existing colonial power, the new Argentine government did not abandon the Church. In fact, its first manifesto pledged to make every effort "to preserve our [new nation's] holy faith," Catholicism.[94] The principled antagonism to all non-Catholics grew over the coming decades, culminating in the contentious debate that erupted after President Nicolás Avellaneda passed the Immigration and Colonization Law in 1876. Desperate to find workers to bolster the country's developing economy, the president and his advisers established new branches of government to attract European immigrants. Members of the Constituent Assembly, however, championed an explicitly Catholic national code that would prohibit governmental support for non-Catholic immigrants.[95] In the end, however, economic concerns outweighed religious loyalties, and the Constituent Assembly reluctantly agreed to endorse non-Catholic immigration.

Despite the Argentine government's lukewarm embrace of non-Catholic migrants, rumors began to spread throughout Eastern Europe about the endless economic opportunities Argentina offered those who lived there. Fueling these rumors were new Jewish organizations, most notably Baron Maurice de Hirsch's Jewish Colonization Association (JCA), founded in 1891. Through the establishment of the JCA, Baron de Hirsch sought to facilitate and accelerate the move of 3.5 million Jews out of Russia to new lands, such as Argentina.[96] Hirsch, to use the words of historian Derek Penslar, advanced "a vision of Jewish social engineering no less audacious than Theodore Herzl's *The Jewish State*."[97] Hirsch believed that Russian Jewish migration to Argentina would not only relieve population pressure and destitution in Eastern Europe but would also counter antisemitic claims that Jews were unproductive members of society by demonstrating that Jews could be trained to work as farmers, and could succeed if given the chance to settle on cooperative farms in regions such as the Pampas of Argentina.[98] Between 1891 and 1896, Hirsch contributed the vast sum of $10 million to pursue his goal, purchasing collective farms in Argentina and paying Russian Jews to emigrate to them.[99] In the history of turn-of-the-century Jewish migration, the JCA stands out: in contrast to other Jewish organizations that provided aid to Jewish immigrants only after they arrived at their destination of choice, the JCA actually shaped the migratory path by recruiting tens of thousands of East European Jews to consider settling in rural Argentina and Brazil.[100]

Jews in Bialystok, as the Hebrew newspaper *Ha-melitz* reported in 1889, were particularly taken by the promise of Argentina's rolling mountains and lush fields. Hundreds flocked to the JCA, searching for help in the immigration process.[101] In response to their requests, the JCA paid to settle thousands of Jews from Bialystok, as they did for Jews from all corners of Eastern Europe, in farming communities scattered throughout the Pampas. The first group of Bialystoker Jews who arrived in Argentina landed on a collective farm named Palacios, located in the rural Entre Rios region halfway between Moisesville and Los Palemos (see map 2).[102] Soon, other Jews from Bialystok, wanting to be placed with familiar faces, joined Palacios, bestowing on a large area of this agricultural settlement the nickname "Bialystok."[103]

From the outset, despite the generous funding of Baron de Hirsch, Jews from Bialystok, like most East European Jewish settlers, found their adjustment to agricultural life in Argentina extremely difficult. At first, the green fields of corn that stretched as far as the eye could see were a refreshing change from the urban squalor of Bialystok's muddy streets. But as these immigrant Jews struggled to care for their crops, their straw-walled cottages, and their cattle, they realized that they were really urban laborers who did not possess many of the basic skills necessary for survival in a rural economy. Several Bialystoker Jews reminisced in the 1950s about their first years in Argentina, noting that they felt totally adrift in Moisesville, where the rhythms of life were so different from anything they had earlier experienced.[104] Moreover, many had worked as tailors, not farmers, in Bialystok and the JCA failed to provide classes on farming techniques prior to migration.[105] Isaac Kaplan, for example, who arrived in Argentina from Bialystok with his parents and six brothers in 1895, had never held a farm tool before settling on a farm in the Pampas. He, not surprisingly, became discouraged when all his crops failed and his efforts to be a successful farmer came to nothing.[106]

Floods, locust plagues, and other natural disasters as well as disagreements with the JCA over debt repayment exacerbated the financial situation of Bialystok's Jews in Argentina. By the late 1890s, the Bialystok settlement in Moisesville, like dozens of other Jewish collective settlements, was in dire straits.

Selected Jewish farming colonies in Argentina, circa 1905.

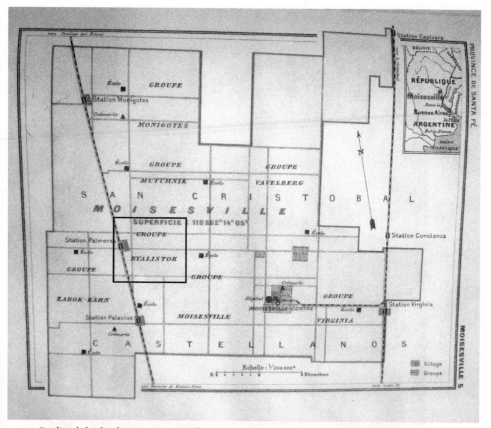

Byalistok [*sic*] colony in Moisesville in a 1913 report of the Baron de Hirsch Fund. *Source:* Atlas des colonies et domaines de la Jewish Colonization Association en République Argentine et au Brésil *(Paris: Jewish Colonization Association, 1914), p. 5.*

Discouraged and disillusioned, many Bialystok émigrés decided to abandon the Moisesville colony shortly after the turn of the century. Their departure was part of a larger mass exodus, as a 1907 JCA report recounts: between 1900 and 1905, one out of every five East European Jewish settlers relocated to new homes, both within Argentina and abroad.[107] While many Jewish agricultural ventures folded, the failure of the Bialystok colony became infamous throughout the Argentine Jewish community. Among Argentine Jewry emerged a saying that "the two things that Bialystoker émigrés brought with them to the distant land of Argentina were the

Farmers at Moisesville. *Courtesy of Fundación IWO, Buenos Aires, Argentina.*

name Bialystok and a bad name for Bialystokers among all the colonists."[108] The consensus in the Argentine Jewish community, according to Moyshe Yakhnuk, was that "when a Bialystoker says 'I want to become a colonist,' everyone must answer him, 'A Bialystoker can never make himself into a colonist.'"[109]

Many former residents of Moisesville left Argentina altogether, either returning to Eastern Europe or venturing to the United States. Others settled in Buenos Aires, a rapidly developing center of East European Jewish life.[110] This densely populated city at first glance was strikingly similar to Bialystok, with its tightly packed three-story buildings and its large commercial squares. To be sure, while the city overall was five times the size of Bialystok, the central area in which the fifty thousand Jews who comprised the bulk of the Jewish community lived in 1914 was a maze of winding streets with open fields. Moreover, the community was, like Bialystok dominated by Jewish migrants: between 1890 and 1930, at least two-thirds of Buenos Aires's Jews were foreign-born.[111]

Bialystok's Jews found life in Buenos Aires refreshingly familiar. Yet, despite their ease with urban life, they faced one major obstacle: in contrast to Bialystok or New York, there were practically no factories for entry-level employment or support for industrial development there. In fact, the landed oligarchy, the most powerful group in Argentine society, only supported the government if it allocated its resources to developing the agricultural sector of the economy and limited industrial development.[112] As a result, Bialystok's Jews who settled in Buenos Aires were forced to create their own textile factories, but many found it difficult to obtain enough money for initial startup costs.[113] Jewish charities, such as the JCA, provided few loans to facilitate such endeavors because they were intent upon settling Jews on farms, not in cities, in accordance with the wishes of Baron de Hirsch.[114] Moreover, with stiff competition from foreign imports, factories had to fight to survive.

Exacerbating these difficult economic conditions was the less than welcoming Catholic population with whom all Jews in Buenos Aires had to contend.[115] The legal status of Jews was at times precarious, and many in Buenos Aires openly questioned whether Jews could ever be incorporated into the Catholic nation.[116] In 1919, a week of antisemitic violence following labor unrest, infamously known as *la semana trágica* (the tragic week), reminded Jews that although Argentina's government may have officially claimed to embrace religious toleration in its constitution, many understood that concept only in relation to Christianity: Catholicism remained the national faith, Protestantism would be tolerated, but Jews, often referred to as Rusos, were suspect.[117] Indeed the accepted maxim at the turn of the century was that "Argentina was a Catholic nation by virtue of its history, national identity, and population."[118] As historian Judith Elkin notes, the rejection of the values of cultural and ethnic pluralism in Argentine society created a social milieu that expected conformity and placed many obstacles in the way of Jewish integration.[119] Elkin concludes that "despite demands that immigrants assimilate, the latter's efforts to integrate themselves met with suspicion, if not outright rejection . . . [because Argentina was] still grounded in the pre-Enlightenment past . . . [causing] the Jews of the Latin American republics [to still be associated with] the hateful religious and political stigmata [of the Old World]."[120]

The relative absence of government-sponsored or existing private Jewish institutions to aid in Jewish urban workers' adaptation to Buenos Aires forced émigrés to devote their time and energy to developing their own organizations.[121] Yet their dire economic need often complicated these efforts.[122] As one émigré reminisced, "Who had time to worry about supporting a Bialystoker [organization] when one's family did not have anything to eat?"[123] As a result, the first attempt to establish a Bialystoker organization in Argentina failed miserably; the Bialystoker landsmanshaft, founded in 1923, was forced to close in 1924 because, as a founding member recalled, "no one had any time or money to spare."[124] It was not until 1930, after a new influx of émigrés arrived in Buenos Aires from Bialystok that the Bialystoker Jewish émigré community had a quorum to support their own organization, which they named the Bialistoker Farband un Credit Cooperativ La Textil (Bialystoker Organization and Credit Union for Textiles, hereafter referred to as the Bialystoker Farband).[125] Responding to the lack of government support for industrial development and the JCA's lack of interest in the endeavors of urban Jewish settlers, this organization's primary function was to provide financial support to struggling Bialystoker émigré entrepreneurs by granting them loans to "maintain themselves, acquire property and [achieve] general [economic] progress."[126]

The Bialystoker Farband played an integral role in the economic advancement of Bialystok's Jews in Buenos Aires by offering loans to families to help them establish their own businesses. As with East European Jewish loan associations in the United States, the Farband expedited the process of upward mobility by supplying the necessary capital to networks of family entrepreneurs so that they could expand their businesses.[127] The success of this tactic is vividly narrated by the Ovsejevich brothers, who arrived in Argentina between 1927 and 1941.[128] Building on their experiences working with their father, Yoel Owsiejewicz, in Bialystok's textile industry, Bernardo (Berl), Jose (Yishai), and Teodoro (Tanjun) Ovsejevich founded Ovsejevich Hermanos Negocio Corbatas (Ovsejevich Brothers Business, Inc.) in 1930 to produce raw fabrics. Their immediate success prodded the brothers to establish Textiseda Villa Lynch Tejeduria, a textile factory in Villa Lynch, a rapidly developing Jewish industrial area on the outskirts of Buenos Aires. Aided by the high demand for cheaper, nonimported clothing, the Ovsejevich brothers soon opened two additional factories. They soon had enough money to devote themselves to running the Bialystoker Farband, the organization that initially provided the loan to launch their first factory, and to helping procure visas for their brother and others still living in Bialystok.

The Ovsejevich brothers, while wildly successful, were far from exceptional: dozens of East European Jews in Argentina also established small factories in Buenos Aires. Bialystok's Jews, however, concentrated their efforts in one neighborhood, Villa Lynch, which soon emerged as the backbone of Buenos Aires's cheap, ready-to-wear garment industry.[129] Zóras, Solomon, Owsey, and Abraham Ponieman, four brothers from Bialystok, founded small spinning and weaving factories in the Villa Lynch neighborhood.[130] These prosperous factories provided employment for waves of Bialystoker Jewish émigrés who arrived in the late 1930s. As Pedro Linkowski recalled, both his father and his uncle, who left Bialystok in 1935 due to mounting antisemitism, worked for years, often thirteen hours a day, in the Ponieman Brothers' factory. When he was old enough, he too worked at that factory. His job pattern seemed natural in Villa Lynch, where by the late 1930s there was a dense settlement of Bialystok's Jews, with factories and homes existing side-by-side.[131]

The structure of Villa Lynch and its success earned it the nickname "the Manchester of Argentina," a moniker that evoked the well-known nickname of Bialystok—commonly called the "Manchester of Lithuania."[132] As the Bialystok-born and New York-based Yiddish journalist Hayim Shoshkes remarked after visiting Villa Lynch in 1946, "the singing of the machines" and the "beating of the weaving looms" makes one think one has stumbled into Bialystok, "where the symphony of textile manufacturing always filled the air."[133] By binding émigrés together as employees and employers, buyers and sellers, lenders and borrowers, the Bialystoker Farband not only helped émigrés alleviate their financial stress, but also reinforced their cultural and ethnic ties.[134] Thus, Shoshkes concluded, the Bialystoker Farband must be acknowledged for helping spread Bialystok throughout the world, enabling émigrés to create a replica of "Bialystok's textile industry in Villa Lynch."[135]

As it reinforced its constituents' ties to each other, the Farband addressed the larger ideological question of what it meant to identify as a Bialystoker in Argentina. From its inception, the organization's focus on acquiring capital linked the self-perception of its members to economic issues and the politics of the working class. The leaders of the Bialystoker Farband stressed that "in order to be a true Bialystoker," one had to know how "to improve oneself, through hard tireless work."[136] The Bialystoker Farband's concept of self-help became enshrined in its members' memories of the city itself. As Moyshe Reisman, founding member of the Bialystoker Farband, noted, "Bialystok's historical past teaches all the benefit of hard work . . . [and] that Jewish workers can achieve success despite daunting obstacles."[137] Their experiences in their hometown, Reisman continued, led to the foundation of the Bialystoker Farband and other charitable and welfare organizations such as cooperative banks, illustrating the ways in which "people must aid themselves."[138]

With its actions and rhetoric, the Bialystoker Farband tried to inculcate in its members the values of "tireless work" and self-improvement—ostensibly central attributes of Bialystoker identity. Soon émigrés in Buenos Aires began to see themselves as more authentically "Bialystoker" than the *"allrightniks"* (the Yiddish term for parvenu) who had left Bialystok to settle in the United States.[139] In contrast to their American compatriots, who were "quick successes" and forgot the lessons of life in Bialystok, supporting a wide array of Jewish religious institutions that served constituencies far beyond the Bialystoker community, émigrés in Buenos Aires continued the traditions "of the working-class city of Bialystok" by concerning themselves with the immediate problems of the laborer.[140]

The proletarian vision of Bialystoker identity marked a turning point in this dispersed migrant community: no longer was Bialystok the primary point of reference to which émigrés turned to define themselves; rather, the United States was an equally central touchstone for their self-perceptions. As they struggled to articulate the distinct boundaries of their identities, these émigrés, who saw themselves as part of a large Bialystok diasporic community, could not explain what it meant to be a "Bialystoker" only by looking back to Eastern Europe; they also now defined themselves against the perceived class status and achievements of their former compatriots living thousands of miles away. Contrasting their faithfulness to Bialystok with the questionable loyalty of Bialystok's Jews who had settled in the United States, the members of the Farband saw the centrality of their common birth in Bialystok as less important than their shared experiences of migration.

Even though they denigrated émigrés in the United States for their abandonment of a particularistic "Bialystoker heritage," émigrés in Argentina also dedicated their energy to developing nonexclusive Bialystoker institutions, particularly Jewish schools that benefited the wider Jewish community. As a result of the dominant role played by Catholicism in Argentine culture, there were few truly secular schools to which East European Jews felt comfortable sending their children.[141] To fill this void, Bialystoker émigrés decided to dedicate their resources to founding and maintaining educational institutions devoted to teaching the Yiddish language, the lingua franca of

Jewish Buenos Aires.[142] By the late 1930s, the Bialystoker Farband was supporting a Yiddish library, a Yiddish reading room, a Yiddish women's reading circle, and Yiddish evening courses that were open to young and old.[143] Their experiences establishing institutions devoted to Yiddish language and culture inspired a few Bialystoker émigrés to participate in the founding of the YIVO Yiddish library in Buenos Aires, a Yiddish Folks-Library in the Villa Alsina area of the city, as well as a Yiddish school and library in the Campamore textile factory.[144]

The Y. L. Peretz Folkshule, a Yiddish-language elementary school named after the legendary Yiddish writer, exemplified the Farband's understanding of Bialystok's legacy as centered on a commitment to Yiddish education.[145] The Bialystoker Farband fully supported the Peretz Folkshule, founded in 1943 in the "Bialystoker" suburb of Villa Lynch. At the groundbreaking for the school's new building in 1949, Bialystoker émigrés took full credit for the school, which they claimed "embodied the traditions of our home city . . . by treasuring Yiddish culture."[146]

The school brought together the values that émigrés identified as "Bialystoker": education, the value of hard work, and Yiddish culture. Isaac Munaker, the president of the Farband, saw it as one of his organization's greatest achievements:

> The former industrial workers, wage workers, and weavers were truly authentic Jews who were imbued with the Bialystoker tradition of culture and creativity. After the success of their economic endeavors . . . [they] understood that they must devote themselves and their creativity to cultural work. . . . Therefore, they founded the Peretz School where children study in their own building and they have a youth club, which conducts itself in the Bialystoker way and which is the center of all cultural and social work in the Bialystoker community of Villa Lynch, a strong and proud Jewish settlement in Argentina . . . that bears the stamp of Bialystoker creativity.[147]

While the Peretz Folkshule was not founded or maintained as an exclusive organization of the Bialystoker community, members of the Farband hailed it as a truly "Bialystoker" institution in contrast to the Bialystoker Center in New York with its focus on care for the elderly. How did members of the Bialystoker Farband explain their actions or reconcile them with their criticisms of their American counterparts? Were they not following in their footsteps by also supporting an institution that benefited that larger Jewish community? Their answer to this question pivoted around the link between Yiddish education and literacy with working-class politics.[148] As did hundreds of other East European Jews who had been involved with the Bund in Europe and had settled throughout the world in this period, these Jews from Bialystok identified themselves with organizations of the Jewish working class and saw it as their duty to build up and sustain institutions devoted to Yiddish cultural life in their new homes.[149] They understood their emphasis on Yiddish education as a continuation of the efforts undertaken by Jewish workers in Bialystok who had embraced Yiddish as they strove to inculcate in its members the need to overthrow the tsar.[150] Thus, in their eyes, there was a sea of difference between an old age home and a Yiddish educational institution that cultivated among its students self-reliance and a deep appreciation for the values of the Jewish working class—the true lessons to be learned from the city of Bialystok.

The events of the Second World War deepened the Bialystoker Farband's devotion to Yiddish literary and educational concerns, particularly after Hershel Ovsejevich, who arrived in Buenos Aires in 1941, confirmed rumors that much of Jewish Bialystok had been destroyed that same year. Aside from creating schools that "reflected Bialystoker character," the Bialystoker Farband sponsored the publication of a magazine, *Bialystoker vegn* (The Ways of Bialystok), whose overt goal was to "preserve Yiddish culture."[151] The cover of this sixty-page magazine evocatively conveyed how Bialystoker Jews in Argentina understood their efforts: in the top left corner appeared a visual representation of a group of factories from which a long winding road emerged. This road then curved and meandered past a representation of the destroyed Bialystoker Synagogue and Bialystoker clock tower; the road then ended at the name "Bialystoker Farband" emblazoned under a picture of a quill in an ink jar. The image conveyed how émigrés in Argentina understood their endeavors: the road from (or legacy of) Bialystok maintained itself in the writings and cultural productions of Bialystoker Jews in Argentina. Its title page reiterated this message in the editorial which stated that Bialystoker Jews were charged with a mission "to nurture Yiddish culture in all their new homes."[152] *Bialistoker vegn* published reports, poetry, and stories written by Bialystok's Jews scattered throughout South America, and encouraged émigrés to link their Bialystoker identity to their devotion to Yiddish.

By the 1940s, émigrés argued that the Bialystoker Farband, Villa Lynch, and the Peretz Folkshule all demonstrated that the "gift Bialystoker Jews brought with them from Bialystok to Argentina was their flair for creating and spinning all that is beautiful in Jewish life."[153] In fact, some contended that the development of the Bialystoker émigré community in Argentina mirrored the rapid expansion of Bialystok itself: by the Second World War, both Buenos Aires and Bialystok had grown from small provincial towns in the early nineteenth century into major industrial centers. By bringing Bialystok's distinct legacy to Argentina, Isaac Munaker, editor of *Bialistoker vegn,* argued, Jews were able to rebuild Bialystok in Argentina:

> Ingrained in the hearts of every Bialystok Jew is the famed Bialystoker particularistic Jewish culture infused with an impulse to create . . . dense networks of schools, fine philanthropic organizations, and exemplary trade unions. It was Bialystoker Jews' inexhaustible energy that enabled them to build up by themselves a complex textile industry [in Bialystok], and this energy ingrained in the heart of every Bialystoker Jew the desire to spread their creative entrepreneurial spirit throughout the four corners of the world [as evidenced by] . . . the establishment of the textile industry in Villa Lynch—the "Manchester of Argentina."[154]

Bialystoker émigrés in Argentina, Munaker claimed, provided the best example of this city-specific "impulse to create."

Despite Munaker's claims of uniqueness, Bialystoker Jews who settled in Buenos Aires had in fact acted as did thousands of other East European Jews throughout the world, establishing organizations to address their pressing needs and in the process conjuring up

Cover Page of *Bialistoker vegn* (1949). Author's private collection.

a new identity. Their divergent needs from those Bialystoker Jews who settled in New York ultimately pushed the larger organization to stress émigrés' ties to Bialystok's working-class history. As their constant comparison to the *"allrightnik"* Bialystoker Jews in the United States sought to highlight, Bialystoker Jews in Argentina still defined their Jewish identities in regional terms. Yet they did not envision themselves in juxtaposition to other residents in their new country of settlement but rather in contradistinction to Bialystoker Jews scattered throughout the world. Those who arrived in Argentina had entered a new Jewish diasporic mentality.

Palestine

Pursuing the dream of rebuilding the Jews' historic homeland drove thousands of Jews to leave Bialystok in the early twentieth century to settle in Palestine. At least 20,000 Jews from Bialystok were among the approximately 400,000 Jews who settled in Palestine between 1881 and 1933. The first group arrived in 1883, and as lore contends, they helped to save Petach Tivka, Palestine's first Jewish agricultural settlement, from extinction. Whether this group did play an integral role in attracting the attention of several philanthropists, who provided the necessary funds to maintain the colony, remains unclear, but they clearly did boost the settlement's waning morale.[155] By the beginning of the twentieth century, more groups arrived, inspired in part by the teachings of Bialystok's chief rabbi, Samuel Mohilever, who advocated settlement in the land of Israel as the only answer to the Jewish problem in Russia.[156]

As in Argentina, economic conditions in Palestine made financial success elusive for Jewish immigrants who were skilled as urban laborers. Palestine's indigenous economy revolved around agricultural production based on a semi-feudal land tenure system. For Jews from Bialystok, the agricultural settlements of early twentieth-century Palestine, with their arid fields, primitive dwellings, and mosquito-infested swamps were unlike any setting they had ever encountered. Moreover, the scarcity of natural resources, especially water, and the inexperience of the settlers, made even farming most difficult. If not for Baron Edmond de Rothschild's generous philanthropy, most of the early agricultural settlements in Palestine would have eventually all been forced to disperse.

But economic success was far from the main motivating factor drawing Bialystoker Jews along with other East European Jews to Palestine. Rather, their desire to construct a new Jewish national homeland —whose eventual nature was by no means assured—pushed them to cross the Mediterranean. After the violence of the 1905 revolution, a significant wave of émigrés, comprising what scholars call the Second

Aliyah, arrived in Palestine imbued with both radical socialist ideals and Zionist beliefs. Inspired by thinkers such as Nahum Syrkin and A. D. Gordon, this group stressed the importance of personal participation in the rebuilding of the Jewish national homeland, holding up the self-reliant *halutz* or "pioneer" as their heroic model.[157] They emphatically asserted that agriculture and self-reliance belonged at the center of the new Jewish national identity.

Like other agricultural settlers, this highly ideological and motivated group of Jewish pioneers ultimately became dependent on overseas philanthropy for survival. One of the greatest paradoxes of Zionist Jewish settlement prior to the First World War was that while it celebrated the self-made and self-sustaining pioneer as its national icon, the difficult economic and political circumstances forced them to depend upon European and American Jewish generosity to address their daily needs. To be sure, East European Jewish émigrés who arrived in Palestine after 1905 were more self-reliant than their predecessors, as evident in their success in setting up collective farms and working the land. Yet Arab violence, malaria, drought, and the generally harsh conditions of the region severely complicated their efforts. By 1914, most Jews working the land in Palestine depended on financial subsidies supplied from abroad and channeled through institutions such as the Jewish National Fund (a branch of the World Zionist Organization).

The tension between the need for philanthropy and the pioneer ethos shaped the organizations formed by Bialystoker Jews who immigrated to Palestine. In contrast to their counterparts in the United States and Argentina, they did not tend to their constituents' economic needs by providing mutual aid or loans. Rather, they launched fundraising appeals outside Palestine to further a variety of economic and ideological goals. The first such organization, the Bialystok Association for Land Purchases, was formed in Bialystok in 1912 with the goal of collecting money to buy land for Bialystok's Jews to settle in Palestine. It allocated, however, no funds to help these émigrés once they had settled.[158] Thus, Jewish settlers from Bialystok had to found another organization in Tel Aviv to address their immediate needs. Naming another new organization Club Bialystok, in 1923 a

group of Bialystok's Jews explained their mission in a letter to David
Sohn of the Bialystoker Center:

> We have founded a Bialystoker Club in Eretz Yisrael:
>
> 1] To give aid to a new settler immediately from the minute
> he descends from the boat. Because of the dire economic
> situation in Poland, almost all of the settlers sell all their
> belongings on the way and come to the land empty-handed.
> Because of this we have founded a charitable fund . . . [that]
> is supported by different local sources and by different
> volunteers.
>
> 2] . . . to help settlers establish a base for support and tie
> them to the land because they spend much time wandering
> around looking for work and do not become rooted to the
> land. Therefore, they would not hesitate to pick up their
> things again and find a new country.[159]

Although economic viability had concerned Bialystoker organizations in other regions of the world, the ideological component under-
pinning Bialystoker migration to Palestine gave their enterprise
greater significance in the minds of the founders of Club Bialystok.
From the vantage point of these émigrés, the failure of Bialystok's
Jews to succeed in Palestine had ramifications far beyond individual
disappointment. As Zionists, the founders of Club Bialystok believed
their efforts were linked to the fate of all other Jews, and the failure
of even a single émigré could impede the rebuilding of the Jewish
homeland and the rejuvenation of the Jewish people. Addressing
the problem of unemployment, the result of the lack of industrial
development in Palestine took on more weight than the need to alleviate poverty in the émigré community. As the founders of Club
Bialystok poignantly described to Sohn, they felt obliged to ensure
that Bialystoker Jews forged a tie to their new homeland. Creating
this connection to the land proved particularly problematic for the
founders of Club Bialystok, who argued that Jews from Bialystok,
who were "craftsmen or workmen," found it particularly difficult
to feel at home in Palestine where "they were unemployed . . . [and]
there were so few factories."[160] Many settlers fell into "a state of
despair and apathy" that, as the founders of Club Bialystok empha-

Meeting of Club Bialystok in Tel Aviv, 1922. *Courtesy of the Merhavia Collection, Jewish National Library, Jerusalem.*

sized, "marked a great tragedy for the worker's family, the land and the whole [Jewish] nation."[161]

Their solution to saving Bialystoker émigrés from fiscal and emotional depression, interestingly, had nothing to do with fostering industrial development in Palestine. In contrast to the Bialystoker Farband in Argentina that provided loans to help unemployed workers establish their own factories, Club Bialystok's founders in Tel Aviv encouraged Bialystok's Jews to develop their agricultural skills by providing them with land to farm. Such a strategy reflected not only the central ideal of the Zionist movement—to resettle the land—but also the pragmatic concern of feeding a growing unemployed population. In the words of Club Bialystok's founders:

> In order to prevent despair among Bialystoker émigrés, we must give the worker's family a plot of land, not far from the city. The family, upon receipt of this small plot, around 5 dunams, will have enough room for their apartment, to raise some chickens,

and an animal to milk, grow vegetables for their house and possibly some extra to sell. And all this farm work is done by the members of the family: the wife, the small children and the workers themselves. . . . Unfortunately, to our sorrow, our resources which we have at our disposal right now cannot accommodate such a goal. For every family we need 100 Egyptian liras. . . . Therefore, we now respectfully turn to you, our dear brothers, to loan us 1000 Egyptian liras so that we can set up 10 families in such a way.[162]

Two points stand out in Club Bialystok's program: first, the goals clearly diverged from other Bialystoker organizations in its advocacy for an agricultural solution to the economic quandary of its constituents. Second, and more important, this was the first Bialystoker organization that sought to achieve its goals by raising funds from fraternal organizations abroad. Indeed, the founders of Club Bialystok outlined their vision not in a mission statement, but in a fundraising letter to David Sohn, executive director of the Bialystoker Center in New York. The letter suggests that the desire to raise money for operational costs and to provide effective leadership to help Bialystok's Jews adapt to life in Palestine drove the creation of this new Bialystoker organization.

The founding of an émigré organization in the dispersed Bialystok community to raise money from other émigrés marked a watershed moment in the history of this dispersed community. Bialystoker émigré organizations in both the United States and Argentina faced times of severe economic crisis during which some were even forced to close their doors. Prior to the establishment of Club Bialystok, however, no other Bialystoker émigré organization had ever asked for money from other members of the transnational Bialystoker Jewish community. Yet this did not seem so revolutionary to the members of Club Bialystok who resided in a society in which large numbers of Jewish immigrants depended on financial aid from abroad to cover many of their basic needs.

The concluding lines of this letter emphasize the centrality of fundraising to Bialystoker Jews' understanding of why they needed their own organization in Palestine:

> We think it is superfluous to explain to you the great need for
> a lot of help for the Land of Israel and for the entire nation and
> that you will give the opportunity for A FAMILY to settle on the
> land, and to adjust and find a way to support themselves. . . .
> We are sure that you can feel the great suffering of each fam-
> ily, and of each halutz who has come to this new land, which
> is still quite desolate, to build and to plant with the sweat of
> their brow and the blood of their heart driving them, because
> you were also pioneers to a new land.
>
> We hope that your duty to your birth land will [speedily]
> cause you to help the people of your town and you will fulfill
> our request.[163]

As the closing line of this heavy-handed appeal demonstrates, émigrés in Palestine strategically summoned up Bialystoker loyalty to
solicit money from their wealthier former compatriots now living
in the United States. The absence of any reference to maintaining
Bialystoker Jews' distinctive culture reflected the Zionist emphasis
on creating an unprecedented type of Jew. Zionist thinkers across
the ideological spectrum urged Jewish émigrés in Palestine to forget their origins and instead transform themselves into "new Jews"
by learning and speaking Hebrew.[164] Accordingly, it is no surprise
that the founders of Club Bialystok would not articulate a desire to
rebuild Bialystok; nonetheless, the constant correspondence of the
Palestinian settlers with their former compatriots scattered throughout the world suggests they felt that they, too, belonged to another
diaspora whose members they could rely upon in times of trouble.

The invocation of Bialystok for fundraising purposes is evident again in an article in the February 1923 issue of the *Bialystoker
Stimme*. Yehuda Zar, a Bialystoker émigré living in Petach Tikva,
emphasized his connection to Bialystok in trying to raise funds in
the United States:

> During the last two years, the landsmanshaftn have collected
> the . . . colossal sum of one million dollars [for individual
> Jewish relief in Bialystok]! . . . That saved the Jewish institu-
> tions which were doomed! . . . There are many halutzim in
> Bialystok who wish to help build up the Yishuv [Jewish settle-
> ment in Palestine] . . .

You must give them the resources!

For only $70 you can help healthy, sturdy hard-working Jews go to Israel. . . . Bialystokers in America must help support a group of Bialystoker Halutzim. Your help will be a monument to your brotherly support and love for Bialystok! Many colonies can flourish with your help—an everlasting memorial to Bialystok! . . . Can you find a more constructive way to help your fellow Jews?[165]

Zar's innovative argument—that people could show their love and devotion to Bialystok by sending money to Palestine—did not win many converts in New York. In the months that followed, Bialystoker Jews in Palestine received only enough money to support a few pioneer families.[166] Nonetheless, his efforts are noteworthy because they represented the first of many attempts by Bialystok's Jews in Palestine to build Jewish national consciousness among the members of the Bialystok diaspora by summoning up icons of East European Jewish life. With little financial support, however, Club Bialystok appears to have produced few lasting results.[167] Bialystok's Jews who moved to Palestine in the 1920s and 1930s do not recall the existence of any formal Bialystoker organization.[168] Any aid they did receive came from established networks of earlier settlers from Bialystok.[169] Without any sustained support, many Jews from Bialystok returned to Poland, like hundreds of other Jewish settlers, unable to endure the hardships of life in the Middle East.[170] For those who remained, the ideological component motivating their migration and settlement made any attachment to Bialystok pale beside the desire to make themselves into Zionist pioneers.[171]

The early 1930s witnessed the arrival of hundreds of new Bialystoker émigrés as part of the 350,000 Jews who sought refuge from deteriorating economic conditions in Poland and rising Polish antisemitism. Deploying their skills to develop new industries in Palestine, one group of seventy Bialystoker Jews, for example, "spent $150,000" to purchase "7,500 dunams of land in the town of Je'da near Haifa upon which they erected a textile plant equipped with weaving machines and diesel motors."[172] Despite the high costs, these Jews from Bialystok remained committed to developing this settlement in order to fulfill the "desire to establish a Jewish community in the Holy Land," one that combined the legacy of Bialystok—textile production—with the Zionist dream of "deriving sustenance from agriculture."[173] So in 1933, recalled Mordechai Greenstein, his parents, grandparents, and uncle, along with ten other families arrived in Je'da and immediately started working in a factory they named Hanol, after the Hebrew word used for yarn in weaving. The factory produced fine linen cloth that was exported to Europe.[174] But their success was short-lived as recession and political instability, in particularly the Arab revolt of 1929, prodded many to return to Bialystok.[175]Those who remained were ultimately forced to leave Je'da in 1936 after the settlement's main factory burned down during the Arab revolt.[176] As Mordechai Greenstein recalled, after the Hanol Factory closed, his family was forced into penury; they moved to Tel Aviv where they sold used furniture to survive.[177]

The failures of Club Bialystok and the demise of the Je'da experiment did not dull Palestine's luster, as Polish economic boycotts of Jewish businesses pushed many Jews to see Zionism as their only prospect for the future.[178] As one young Polish Jew summed up in his memoir, "If anyone asked me what I would do after finishing school, I would not have known how to answer. In this terrible situation, I took to Zionism like a drowning person to a board."[179] For Jews in Bialystok, the situation was particularly dire, as the Polish Jewish economist Menakhem Linder demonstrated in his study of the precipitous decline of Jewish-owned shops in the Bialystok region.[180] As he concluded, the Great Depression, coupled with antisemitic campaigns and competition with the growing number of Polish and Ukrainian workers in the city, pauperized Bialystok's Jewish community. Those who were able to gather the funds to move to Palestine still had pressing financial needs, which they hoped to address by forming a new "Bialystoker" institution in 1937. Through a new organization named the Bialystoker Centre of Palestine, these struggling immigrants sought to convey to their compatriots in New York that they saw the New York Bialystoker Center as a model for successful adaptation. It was their beacon in the Bialystok diaspora. Crafting a letter in Yiddish to request aid from a representative of the Bialystoker Center of New York who was visiting Israel, they wrote:

> . . . for the past two and a half years we have been dealing with a difficult crisis which has hit families particularly hard and particularly those from Bialystok . . . because of the difficult economic situation in Poland which has seen most of the industry in Bialystok collapse. [Immigrants] now come with few resources, making their situation here immediately very dire. . . . The Bialystokers in the Land of Israel need IMMEDIATE CONSTRUCTIVE AND PRODUCTIVE HELP . . . We are not just lazy beggars [*schnorers*] who do not want to work . . . but we need moral help . . . and for you to give us productive help so that we can become self-supporting which would not only be a blessing for us but also for the land. We need practical help to build up workshops and industry like there were in Bialystok.[181]

Underscoring that they were not *schnorers* (beggars) merely seeking to exploit a connection to Bialystok, these Jews who had suffered greatly in Bialystok did not shy away from hard work. Rather, they begged for aid so that they could become financially independent as well as constructive and productive members of their new society. Accordingly, they suggested an adaptive strategy that diverged in striking ways from those offered up by Club Bialystok a decade earlier: they did not seek to help Bialystoker émigrés adapt by settling them on the land, but rather by helping them to create workshops reminiscent of those so prevalent in Bialystok. Realizing, as did leaders of the Zionist movement during the interwar period, that a return to the land was not enough to sustain a Jewish state, the Bialystoker Centre of Palestine stressed the importance of loans to develop industry in Palestine. Their letter not only conveys a shift in how Bialystok's Jews in Palestine sought to address their problems, but also contains a substantive change in tone:

> If you want your Bialystoker brothers in Israel to be able to become as productive as you, you must help your dear beloved brothers with their request for help to build up . . . a bank . . . which would support small businesses . . .
> . . . Help your Bialystoker brothers . . . who are in great need and who are now working with the greater Jewish people

for respect. . . . BROTHERS, HELP YOUR BIALYSTOKER LANDSLAYT
IN ISRAEL. You can determine our fate. . . . we need your help
to become self-sufficient . . . Create a drive in America for the
Bialystoker residents of Israel.[182]

Many elements of this letter reflect the earlier appeal of Club Bialystok,
particularly the final plea that Bialystoker émigrés in America launch
a fundraising drive on behalf of their former neighbors now Jews living in Palestine; however, the most notably different aspect lies in the
manner in which the members of the Bialystoker Centre emphasized
their desire to refashion Bialystoker émigrés in Palestine not after the
image of the paradigmatic Zionist Jew who works the land but on the
model of successful émigrés already settled in America.

Once again, the diasporic mentality of Bialystoker émigrés compelled them to look to Bialystokers scattered around the world, and
not just back to Bialystok, as they searched for a way to adapt their
regional identity to their new homes. In contrast to Bialystoker émigrés in Argentina who viewed those who settled in New York as cor-
rupting the legacy of Bialystok, émigrés in Palestine rather saw the
New York community as a model of a successful Bialystoker, intrin-
sically linked to being a "producer." Their request suggests a clear
paradigm shift: rather than plead for aid to build a new type of self-
sufficient "pioneer" Jew, Bialystoker émigrés in Palestine begged for
help to transform themselves into economically successful individuals like their compatriots in the United States.

The new emphasis on economic success rather than on the value
of working the land was exemplified by Zalman Yerushalmi, who
became known as the "father of the Bialystokers" in Palestine.[183]
Yerushalmi immigrated to Palestine in 1925, where he founded and
ran two successful textile factories and a cement plant.[184] Initially,
he offered jobs or loans to newly arrived Bialystoker émigrés to help
them "land with their feet on the ground."[185] Then, in the early
1940s, Yerushalmi decided to form an institution to provide similar
services to a wider émigré population. The organization, Irgun Yotzei
Bialistok (Organization of Bialystoker Émigrés), remained obscure
until November 23, 1944, when it formed the Va'ad le-'ezrat Yehudei
Bialistok (Organization for the Aid of Bialystoker Jewry). This new
organization had two primary goals: to obtain more information

about Jewish life in Bialystok, and to raise money to help Jews who would return after the war.[186] By 1945, this organization had successfully located several hundred survivors and sent them care packages. Using the information they gathered from survivors, the members of Va'ad le-'ezrat Yehudei Bialistok composed a history of Jewish life in Bialystok under the Nazi regime; they distributed this work throughout the world.[187]

A flood of Bialystoker Jews arrived in Israel following the founding of the State of Israel. These post-1948 arrivals possessed little except for the clothes on their backs, overwhelming the struggling Bialystoker émigré community who had been living in Palestine since the 1920s. With few monetary funds, the community quickly exhausted its resources and could not provide the needy newcomers with the little help they demanded. Yerushalmi lobbied David Sohn to transfer all the money that had originally been collected to erect a memorial in Bialystok; instead, the community would fund a new enterprise: the creation of "a new Bialystok" in Israel, where all Bialystoker refugees would be able to have a home.[188]

The funding and erection of Kiryat Bialystok (lit., the village of Bialystok), a "new Bialystok" near the town of Yehud in central Israel, represents the crowning achievement of the Bialystoker émigré community in the new state of Israel. On April 24, 1951, Kiryat Bialystok opened to the public amid great fanfare, greeting Bialystoker visitors from around the world.[189] The 208 new homes, the kindergarten, the medical infirmary, the synagogue, and the cultural center there addressed the pressing needs of newly arrived Bialystoker émigrés by providing them with housing, schooling, and jobs.[190] Although Bialystoker émigrés in Israel considered Kiryat Bialystok "the greatest achievement of Bialystoker Jews in Israel," this settlement would never have been built without the tireless efforts of Jews in the United States.[191] Kiryat Bialystok may have been physically located in Israel but all critical decisions were made by a retired Bialystoker émigré industrialist named Ralph Wein who ran the Kiryat Bialystok Foundation out of New York.

Thus, although Zalman Yerushalmi and other Bialystoker Jews in Israel may have played a central role in the daily maintenance and administration of Kiryat Bialystok, in the end, the great achievement of the Bialystokers in Israel came about because of the tireless efforts of their compatriots living overseas. Kiryat Bialystok, like its predecessors, highlights that in Palestine, in contrast to the United States and Argentina, Bialystoker Jews employed their connection to Bialystok not to preserve the memory of their former home but to appeal for financial assistance. By deploying the language of regional distinctiveness, Jews living in Palestine, the mythic Jewish diaspora homeland, capitalized upon Bialystoker Jews' feelings of nostalgia for what they considered a paradigmatic Jewish polity. Indeed, as the papers of Club Bialystok, the Bialystoker Centre of Palestine, and Kiryat Bialystok suggest, Zionist rhetoric diverged markedly in practice: rather than creating a new type of Jew, Jews from Bialystok turned to overseas philanthropists to define the agenda and shape where Bialystok fit into the new Jewish state.

Socializing in the New Bialystok: The Bialystoker Centre of Melbourne

Australia—the most distant outpost of the dispersed Bialystok émigré community—became a popular destination for Polish Jews in the late 1920s, when immigration restriction laws closed off most other options.[192] Because of the great distance and the fact that the journey from Eastern Europe was long, hazardous, and expensive, only a few thousand Jews from Bialystok settled there. Australia, like Argentina, was primarily an exporter of raw materials and had few well-developed industries. In contrast to Argentina, however, the Australian government promoted the development of a manufacturing sector through indigenous capital investment because Australia's geographic isolation made importing prohibitively expensive.[193] Moreover, Australia's imperial ties to England nurtured in this society a deep appreciation of religious toleration as well as a firm belief in ethnic pluralism. This tolerance facilitated social integration and secularization among Jews in Australia prior to the Second World War.[194]

When Bialystok's Jews began arriving in Australia, they found that their manufacturing skills gave them an advantage: Australian society embraced their economic acumen, presuming it promoted social success as it had for Jews who had come to Australia from

England.[195] Since "passage costs were so high compared with those to the Americas," sociologist Charles Price notes, most Jewish immigrants from Eastern Europe from the outset were dependent on friends and relatives already established in Australia."[196] The experiences of Leo Fink vividly illustrate the central role family networks played in the life of Australia's Bialystok Jewish community:[197] Fink arrived in Melbourne from Bialystok in 1928. With a small loan from an uncle and the skills he had acquired in Bialystok, he built a successful textile business, known as the United Woolen Mills, devoted to the manufacture of men's knitwear. Within a year, his factory had doubled in size. Fink's success was attributed to the fact that he "knew how to make a cheap suit, which every working man could afford," which was desperately needed in Australia where import taxes made suits too expensive for most working-class men.[198] His success helped him set up his brother, Jack Fink, in a mill that specialized in spinning and weaving wool in 1929. When the Waks family, cousins of the Fink brothers, arrived in the 1940s, their cousins' success helped them to establish Waks Brothers Carpets, another prosperous business.[199]

These Jewish settlers, along with other East European Jews, dramatically reshaped the small Australian Jewish community that had numbered only 21,615 in 1921. Until then, most Jewish immigrants arrived in Australia via England and settled in Sydney in the New South Wales region, where various religious organizations helped them to confront the challenges they faced.[200] The leaders of the Jewish community in Sydney, highly secular, antagonistic to Jewish immigration, and ambivalent toward Zionism, saw the parameters of their community totally redefined by the twenty thousand East European Jews who began settling in Melbourne in the 1920s.[201] Melbourne, where only five thousand Jews had lived prior to the war, was unlike any city in Eastern Europe. Even in the working-class St. Kilda neighborhood where most of the new arrivals settled, there were few densely packed buildings; most poor Jews resided in one-story cottages surrounded by small gardens. This massive influx of Jewish immigrants doubled the size of the Melbourne Jewish community, enabling it to quickly surpass Sydney as the main Jewish population center in Australia.[202]

Approximately five hundred Bialystoker families settled in Melbourne, where the total Jewish population was just over 10,000 in 1939.[203] As Anna Gepner, who arrived in Melbourne in 1937, has described, the perception among the growing Jewish community in Melbourne was that "Bialystok was the largest city in Poland since almost every Polish Jew in Melbourne came from Bialystok."[204] To be sure, Bialystoker Jews represented only one of many groups to settle in this city, yet their dominance—perhaps rooted in their quick economic success and concentration—allowed them to shape the larger Jewish communal organizations in ways unparalleled in cities such as New York or Buenos Aires. With few Jewish newspapers, charities, or social organizations, new arrivals from Bialystok found themselves forced to channel their energies into a wide array of communal institutions serving the larger Jewish community. With great enthusiasm, they developed a network of institutions that molded this evolving Jewish community and articulated a new vision of what it meant to be a Bialystoker.

Exemplifying the ways in which Bialystok's Jews used institutions of Australia's larger Jewish community to serve their needs was Melbourne's weekly Yiddish newspaper *Oystralisher idishe lebn* (Australian Jewish Life). Prior to 1933, every attempt to publish a weekly Yiddish newspaper in Melbourne failed as a result of opposition from local rabbis who wanted Jewish East European émigrés to learn English. But in that year, in response to the demands of the growing East European Jewish immigrant community, *The Jewish News,* an English-language weekly, sponsored the immigration of Eliezer Rubinstein, a Bialystoker journalist. His mission was to found and edit a Yiddish section of *The Jewish News.* Rubinstein, who had worked as a newspaper editor at Bialystok's Yiddish daily *Unzer lebn* (Our Life), modeled many aspects of *Oystralisher idishe lebn,* such as its name and front-page format, on the popular Yiddish newspaper he had helped shape in Bialystok.[205] Soon, this weekly became the most widely read and distributed Yiddish newspaper in Australia.[206]

Although it served the entire Yiddish-speaking community by providing both international and communal news in Yiddish, *Oystralisher idishe lebn* was also the unofficial newsletter of the

Bialystoker émigré community. In addition to weekly updates on the activities of the Bialystoker landsmanshaft in Australia (and publishing a few updates for other landsmanshaft groups), the newspaper also featured on its front page the annual balance sheet of the Bialystoker society, called the Bialystoker Lay Kassa, as well as solicitations for charities in Bialystok, which it constantly designated as "our home."[207] Finally, it regularly presented reports on Jewish life in Bialystok, along with debates over how best to provide for Jews there during the interwar period.[208] Eliezer Rubinstein did not hide his fierce loyalty to his former home; on the front page of his newspaper, he emphasized the importance of maintaining a financial connection to Bialystok, stressing that "even the editor of *Oystralisher idishe lebn* will send 50 pounds to Bialystok, and urges all" to send money to this worthy cause."[209] In this former outpost of the British Empire, Rubinstein saw financial ties, and the act of sending money to Bialystok, as defining what it meant to be a "Bialystoker."

Bialystoker Jewish émigrés in Melbourne also founded the Bialystoker Lay Kassa. From its inception in 1927, its main goal was to "aid Bialystoker Jews in their adjustment to life in Australia" by providing them with financial support and organizing social events to integrate them into the community.[210] Newcomers were granted loans to start their own businesses. In 1934, for example, the Kassa gave out almost 170 pounds in interest-free loans.[211] Like the Bialystoker Farband in Argentina, it sought to accelerate the process of upward mobility in this émigré enclave.[212]

The critical financial services of the Bialystoker Lay Kassa paled beside its intense efforts to facilitate its members' social integration into the Melbourne Jewish community. This was no simple task, since many of the cultural practices in Australia perplexed Jews from interwar Bialystok. As Isaac Kipen, who arrived in the late 1930s summed up, "the mores of Australian society are peculiar: for instance, it is fully acceptable to begin a conversation with a stranger [by making] reference to the weather or the sport then in its season [but no one would] discuss politics or religion with strangers [as was common in Poland] since it is considered in bad taste, for it could potentially offend the other's sensibilities."[213] Pinhas Goldhar echoed Kipen's amazement in *Oystralisher idishe lebn,* noting that most Australians only get excited when discussing local sports teams and would never raise their voices if they disagreed with someone over political debates taking place in the House of Commons.[214]

Helping Bialystoker Jews learn to navigate such cultural hurdles became a major focus of the Bialystoker Lay Kassa. As Michael Pitt, its founding president, believed, the most important factor in successful immigrant adjustment was "creating a socialization group, so a new émigré would not feel isolated."[215] Pitt helped many newcomers find employment in textile factories or mills.[216] Throughout the 1930s, the Bialystoker Lay Kassa used its connections to find jobs for recent arrivals in places where other Jews from Bialystok were working, such as at Leo Fink's United Woolen Mills in Melbourne.[217] The Bialystoker Lay Kassa also helped families forge ties with the larger Jewish community. According to Anna Gepner, "We arrived in Melbourne on Monday night and on Tuesday night, Michael and Esther Pitt hosted my entire family along with several other families from Bialystok, so that I immediately had friends to play with, my brothers and sisters would know people at school and my parents would immediately know people at work."[218] The Kassa also sponsored informal social events, such as barbeques or tennis parties, so that families could meet the entire Bialystoker émigré community. As Ada Kanyzyski Kagan recalled, "I have read a lot of books about how lonely immigrants are when they arrive in a new country but I have no memories like that because [at the events of the Kassa] we met so many warm people who helped us learn the English language, showed us around our new hometown and aided our efforts to find new jobs.[219] Ada Kanyzyski Kagan even met her husband, Leon, a future vice president of the Bialystoker Centre, while playing tennis at one of these events.[220]

With its focus on social integration, it is not surprising that the Kassa's annual banquet dinner soon became an important fixture in the social calendar of the Jewish immigrant community in Melbourne. The overt goal of the ball was to integrate "newly arrived émigrés from Poland" into the Melbourne Jewish community.[221] By all accounts, beginning with the first ball held in 1930, the Kassa achieved its goal: not only did it bring more established members of the community together with newer arrivals, but it also was celebrated by all for its "good music and delicious food," which in the words of *Oystralisher idishe lebn* was "the maximum any ball could offer."[222] The whole Jewish immigrant community attended this event, as a report in the *Oystralisher idishe lebn* described it in 1935. There "the young danced, and older people joked and played cards in a room which was filled with the most delightful music."[223] In addition to offering a wide array of entertainment for adults, the ball also included activities for children and distributed toys. With music, dancing, and games for both young and old, the Bialystoker Ball emerged as Melbourne Jewry's social event of the year, an event *Oystralisher idishe lebn* emphasized, should not by missed by anyone.[224]

The members of the Bilaystok émigré community prided themselves on their ability to run the most celebrated social event in the Melbourne Jewish community. After the Bialystoker Lay Kassa opened its own building in 1945, which it named the Bialystoker Centre after its model in New York, it pursued a mission of "developing and strengthening" the East European Jewish organizational networks of the Melbourne Jewish community. It did so by offering its space, as one of the few landsmanshaft associations with its own house, to other groups for celebrations, memorials, and political meetings. The Bialystoker Centre's 1947 Annual report boasted its rich and varied schedule of social events:

> The Bialystoker Centre has become a real communal centre which was willingly loaned for lectures, artistic performances and entertainments. Many Jewish institutions and organizations . . . like the Yiddish school, Talmud Torah, Poele Zion [sic], the Bund, National Council for Jewish Women, "landsmanshafts," made use of our rooms. . . . The Committee was always of the opinion that, apart from its varied activities of assistance to Bialystoker here and elsewhere, it had a duty toward the Melbourne Jewish community and ought to help strengthen and develop it [by acting as a Jewish community center].[225]

As this report forcefully suggests, Bialystok's Jews in Melbourne saw their mission no longer exclusively in terms of serving Bialystoker

Jewry but rather as having obligations to Australian Jewry as well. Leaders emphasized that even if their new center provided "a cultural home for the settled [Australian Jew,] it still stood as a symbol of the past hospitality and friendliness of Bialystok—that is [what makes] the Bialystoker Centre [truly Bialystoker]."[226]

Throughout the 1920s and 1930s, as the Bialystoker Lay Kassa carved out a central place for itself in Melbourne's Jewish community, Michael Pitt played a critical role in shaping the institution. Echoing in many ways David Sohn's instrumental role in defining the agenda of the Bialystoker Center in New York, Pitt's tireless involvement led him to define many aspects of the Bialystoker community in Melbourne. Arriving in Melbourne in 1927, Pitt immediately founded the Bialystoker Lay Kassa even though he was personally still struggling to find a job. In Bialystok, Pitt had worked as an accountant. His initial linguistic limitations provoked few large companies or factories to see him as a potential asset, forcing Pitt to reluctantly take a job in a hosiery factory. But as a result of his background in accounting and knowledge of the textile industry from his days in Bialystok, he was able to buy out the entire company after a few years of hard work.

The same tireless energy that helped Pitt succeed in business was also evident in his activities on behalf of Bialystok's Jews in Australia. He was a "community-oriented man," recalled his daughter, Paula Pitt Hansky. He enjoyed socializing and saw all Bialystokers as his extended family, in essence replacing the family he had left behind in Poland.[227] Pitt and his wife, Esther, personally met every newly arrived Bialystoker at the train station and entertained them in their home. Pitt also hosted a wide array of social activities such as dinners, dances, tennis tournaments, and weekly "card parties" at his own home in the years before the Bialystoker Lay Kassa acquired its Bialystoker Centre building. The weekly "card parties" raised large sums for both Bialystok and Palestine and reflected Pitt's love of gambling, which he firmly believed encouraged group social integration.

The structure of the Bialystoker Lay Kassa also reflected Pitt's familial approach to the Bialystoker community. In contrast to the formal bureaucracy of the Bialystoker Center in New York, which held annual elections, Michael Pitt, who acted as president of the Kassa and later the Bialystoker Centre for over two decades, was "never formally elected," Leon Kagan recalled. "He just always acted as president and no one challenged him," Anna Gepner explained, "because he was like the father of our family—and no one would challenge a father's decisions." Pitt handpicked the "officers of the Centre and they all worked tirelessly together," as Gepner recalled, "to keep the Centre running with Pitt himself often going there in the middle of the night to fix a broken pipe or leaky window."[228]

As news of the situation in Europe trickled into Australia in the 1940s, social action replaced socializing as the defining focus of the community. As the devastation of the Jewish community in Bialystok became apparent, the Bialystoker Lay Kassa shifted its mission from sending money to aid Jews in Poland to providing funds to assist those who wished to immigrate to Australia.[229] Leo Fink, a successful textile industrialist, exemplified the ways in which "being a Bialystoker" in Australia became interlaced with social action. He strongly believed that "emigration was the only answer to the devastating situation in Europe."[230] When the war officially ended in 1945, he negotiated with Arthur Caldwell, the Australian Minister of Immigration, for entry visas for six hundred Polish Jews.[231] This was no small achievement, as the Australian government officially opposed Jewish migration to Australia. Fink acquired the visas by claiming that the refugees were relatives, enabling them to enter Australia under a family reunion program. Caldwell was impressed by Fink's persistence, remarking that "he never knew a man who had so many cousins."[232] Since Fink maintained that "all Jews were family," he stood by all "his cousins," personally helping them find jobs and places to live.

Conclusion

By 1939, more than seventy Bialystoker organizations operated throughout the world, provoking David Sohn to declare: "Bialystoker Jews have won wide repute everywhere for their innate ability [to] build and create organizations."[233] Serving the estimated seventy-five thousand Jews who emigrated from Bialystok and settled in the United States, Argentina, Palestine, and Australia, these organizations, as Joseph Chaikan, a reporter working for the American Jewish Committee, proclaimed, both "transplanted and transformed Bialystok."[234] Whether or not they actually transplanted tangible attributes of Bialystok, the history of Bialystok's émigré organizations complicate the central assumption of both popular Jewish folklore and scholarship that unlike other immigrants groups, Jews "generally considered their migration permanent, the past forever behind them," retaining few fond memories of the Old Country.[235] While many summon up this lack of attachment to explain Jews' rapid and successful adaptation to life in the New World, in fact success was often elusive and Bialystok's Jews remained passionately committed to their place of origin in Eastern Europe.[236] To be sure, while Bialystok's Jews claimed that their new institutions supported and perpetuated the true legacy of Bialystok, all recognized that, in fact, each organization fundamentally recast what it meant to be a Bialystoker. Even when Bialystoker landsmanshaft organizations shifted away from serving an exclusive constituency, idioms of regional distinctiveness continued to galvanize their members. In short, these organizations underscored that the only way many East European Jews could envision building new lives was through establishing institutions that transplanted imagined elements of Eastern Europe to their new homes.

These organizations enmeshed East European Jews throughout the world in the trans-Oceanic debate over the "authentic" legacy of Eastern Europe. The divergent social, cultural, and economic environments of the United States, Argentina, Palestine, and Australia demanded these organizations provide dramatically different services, which each organization saw as representing the "true legacy" of Bialystok. The elasticity of the term "Bialystoker" enabled Bialystoker Jews throughout the world to see their respective organizations as both perpetuating the past and rooting them in the present. While the Bialystoker Center in New York claimed that it was "Bialystok on East Broadway" because of its dedication to caring for the Jewish elderly, the Bialystoker Farband in Argentina saw itself as "Bialystok rebuilt" because it supported Yiddish education. In the end, the strongest link that these organizations shared was their common use of the Bialystok name to legitimate their adaptive efforts. Mirroring the quandary faced by Jews for centuries after their ancestors' dispersal from the biblical land of Israel, the organizations grappled with how to define and maintain a Bialystoker identity when Bialystok was thousands of miles away. Whereas other solutions created by Jews in the past appeared to be more enduring, the efforts of Bialystoker Jewish émigrés, and other East European Jewish émigrés as well, deserve attention for both their successes and failures.

The cross-cultural comparison of Bialystoker landsmanshaft institutional life highlights the complex dynamics that came into play as immigrant Jews forged a new Jewish diaspora community. Bialystoker émigrés articulated their visions of themselves by looking to Bialystok for inspiration, but also by contrasting themselves to Bialystoker émigrés in other parts of the world. Such a comparativist approach to Jewish identity was not revolutionary: East European Jewry had long mapped their identities by comparing themselves to Jews from other regions. However, migration saw this comparative lens of Jewish identity projected onto a new map that encompassed the entire world. Landsmanshaft organizations promoted the idea that East European regional affiliation was still instrumental to the definition of Jewish identity. As we shall see in the next chapter, the shaky foundations of this transnational polity were solidified following the First World War through new philanthropic organizations that provided a common goal around which all members of Bialystok's Jewish diaspora could rally.

CHAPTER 3

"Buying Bricks for Bialystok": Philanthropy and the Bonds of the New Jewish Diaspora

A striking image appeared on the December 1926 cover of the *Bialystoker Stimme,* the Yiddish quarterly distributed worldwide by the Bialystoker Center in New York.[1] At first glance, it appears as though the viewer is gazing at a single cityscape: on the right looms a three-story tower, overshadowing all the buildings around it. While the clock face on the tower is difficult to see, for all those who have ever lived in Bialystok, this edifice is immediately identifiable as Bialystok's clock tower, erected in 1742 and located at the center of the city's main commercial square.[2]

To the immediate left, mirroring the stature of the clock tower, appears a rendering of a six-story building with the words "Bialystoker Center and Bikur Holim" carved on its front in Yiddish. While the American flag flying high above the Bialystoker Center reminds the viewer of the thousands of miles dividing these two imagined beacons, the illustration actually casts these buildings as if they were down the street from each another, with only a column between them.[3] Testifying to these immigrant Jews' view of their connection to their former home, the column has engraved on its top the word *kultur* (culture), while on its base appears the word *hilf* (aid). Charity not only served as the nexus through which the immigrants interacted with their former home, but more importantly, it provided the foundation for Bialystoker culture in the years following the First World War. The Decalogue-shaped frame encasing these two structures—a regular image on the *Bialystoker Stimme*'s cover and masthead—reminds the viewer of the moral imperative of charity[4] and conveys the idea that to be a Bialystoker meant to be charitable and to send money back to Bialystok.[5]

Cover, *Bialystoker Stimme*, December 1926 (New York).

Masthead of the *Bialystoker Stimme* 1928–1950.

Postcard of Bialystok's central market square, circa 1925. The clock tower appears in the upper right corner. *Courtesy of Merhavia Collection, Jewish National Library, Jerusalem.*

Indeed, philanthropy enmeshed Jews in Bialystok and Jews from Bialystok in a trans-Atlantic drama, transforming all members of this dispersed Jewish community. Throughout independent Poland, the devastation of the First World War, the Russian civil war, and the Russo–Polish war created an unprecedented Jewish welfare crisis.[6] With national borders in flux, drained Jewish communal resources, and an unresponsive Polish government, Jews throughout Poland turned to compatriots abroad for aid. Bialystoker Jewish émigrés, along with other East European Jewish émigrés, responded enthusiastically to their calls, collecting and distributing millions of dollars between the outbreak of the First World War and the German invasion of Poland in 1939.[7] The Bialystoker Center alone sent more than $9 million to Bialystok (equivalent to more than $112 million in 2008 values), intended to relieve the acute famine and poverty affecting Jews in the region while simultaneously furthering émigrés' underlying political agenda: to help their former neighbors, relatives, and friends reestablish Bialystok as a vital center for Jewish life in the Second Polish Republic.[8]

How did the collection and distribution of these vast funds transform the ways in which Bialystok's Jews who were scattered throughout the world community related to one another? How far did émigré philanthropy mold the redevelopment of Jewish life in interwar Bialystok? How did it change the ways in which these East European émigré Jews envisioned their identities as Diaspora Jews living apart from their country of origin? As scholars of contemporary "diasporas" often point out, philanthropy can be critical for the construction of a migrant diasporic identity by helping émigrés maintain ties to their former homes and by financing organizations that create transnational spaces through which they can engage one another and their respective nation-states.[9] As members of the Bialystoker Center in New York sent money to their distressed compatriots living in the Second Polish Republic, they made possible the survival of numerous innovative organizations and Yiddish newspapers that transcended narrow nationalist categories and subtly pushed Jews to challenge the authority of the new and less-than-friendly Polish nation-state.[10] As émigrés became increasingly aware of the political power of their dollars, they became more invested in collecting money because it enabled them both to gain social prestige and to reinvent themselves as powerful leaders rather than struggling newcomers.

Charity had always played a central role in organized Jewish life, but during the 1920s, a period of unprecedented economic prosperity in the American Jewish immigrant community and one of desperate need for Jews in Bialystok, it defined almost every dimension and interaction in this transnational Jewish community. The growing centrality of philanthropy to the Bialystok diaspora community reflects a broader trend in twentieth-century Jewish life in which the giving of charity became a major vehicle through which Jews demonstrated their political, religious, and social commitments.[11] To be sure, the tradition of giving charity, known in Hebrew as *tzedakah,* represents a pillar of Jewish law and communal life; but mass fundraising drives, which produced and relied upon new myths and symbols, linked the giving of money to distinctly twentieth-century modes of cultural transmission, such as postcard production, elaborate parades, and shows.[12] As East European Jews in America faced rising anti-immigrant sentiment as well as social antisemitism, they also witnessed the power their vast sums wielded in their former homes, inverting their sense of marginality as relatively poor immigrants in an increasingly hostile nation; their distribution of money in Eastern Europe allowed them to see themselves as influential figures.[13] Money, immigrants learned quite quickly, meant power.

Employing a discourse laden with marketplace images, immigrant activists began to link their philanthropic work with an ethos of consumption. Imploring its constituents to "buy bricks," "invest in cornerstones," or "purchase certificates," the Bialystoker Center not only raised vast sums but also pushed émigrés to see philanthropy as linked to the acquisition of status, enabling them to fuse their commitment to their former home with a distinctly American sense of status that revolved around consumption through the "purchasing" of certificates, bricks, and cornerstones—objects that bespoke their beneficence.[14] Thus the collection and distribution of money in this dispersed community served the needs of both donors and recipients, by helping Jews in Bialystok survive the economic devastation of the war, enabling Jews in America to earn status and prestige, and cementing the ties of this dispersed Jewish community.

Creating the Bialystok Welfare Crisis: The First World War and Its Aftermath

The memory of the total eradication of Jewish life in the Holocaust overshadows the history of destruction along the Eastern Front during the First World War. Devastation from what was called the Great War was particularly extensive in borderland cities such as Bialystok. Despite the prevailing expectations of a short war, the absence of any decisive victory forced the war to drag on. For the first time in Russian history, civilians endured as much hardship as common soldiers on the frontlines.[15] Located near the Russian–German border, Bialystok found itself at the center of heavy fighting at different points during the war. Invading German forces in 1915 bombarded the city, uprooted thousands, set fire to hundreds of homes, and dismantled local factories. The scorched-earth tactics decimated the city's Jewish community: the Jewish population plummeted from 70,000 in 1913 to only 37,186 in 1921.[16]

Jews from the surrounding countryside flooded into Bialystok in 1915, despite the heavy fighting, with hope that the city would offer greater safety.[17] A horrified Paul Nathan, founder of *Hilfsverein der Deutschen Juden* (Relief Organization of German Jews) visited the city in the winter of 1916. Overwhelmed by the thousands of Jewish refugees he saw inundating Jewish soup kitchens and welfare organizations, Nathan immediately forwarded $200,000 to help the Jewish community form new soup kitchens.[18] Recognizing the acute refugee problem left in the wake of the German retreat in 1917, tsarist authorities established the *Liga pomoshi golodaiwshchim Evreiam v Zaniatykh nepriatelem mestnostiakh* (League to Aid Starving Jews in Enemy-Occupied Territories), which was to aid Jewish refugees in Poland.[19] The League dispensed more than 50,000 rubles to support several Jewish welfare agencies in Bialystok between 1917 and 1919.[20] Charitable efforts kept thousands from starving, but failed to address the long-term consequences of the war, most notably the destruction of Bialystok's economic infrastructure, whose vibrancy was essential for the long-term sustenance of the community.[21]

Bialystok Jewry greeted the end of the war with high hopes for political stability and renewed economic prosperity.[22] The first elections for the 70-member Bialystok kehilla (Jewish community council) in December 1918 attracted over 13,000 members of the community to vote. The socialist block of parties won the majority (25 seats) with the Zionist (19 seats) and the Orthodox (18 seats) parties trailing slightly behind. Aside from sponsoring elections for Jewish communal self-governance, Jews were particularly encouraged by the political transformations taking place around them: with the collapse of the tsarist, Ottoman and Austro-Hungarian Empires, Jews found themselves no longer subjects of empires but were fragmented into a myriad of new nation-states and republics. Even though the Second Polish Republic failed to discuss its eastern borders at the Versailles Conference, Jews in Bialystok assumed their city would fall under Polish sovereignty even though some hoped it would become

Unemployed workers on the corner of Rynek Koscuszki in Bialystok, circa 1920. Alter Kacyzne, the *Jewish Daily Forward*'s renowned photographer, captioned this image, "Standing on the corner, looking for a little work." *From the Archives of the YIVO Institute for Jewish Research, New York.*

part of the new Lithuanian state that openly involved its Jewish population in deliberations. The Minority Rights Treaty signed by Poland in 1919, Jews in Bialystok believed, guaranteed them like all minority groups in Poland, a limited measure of autonomy in their own school systems, and the use of their vernacular, Yiddish for official purposes.[23]

Despite the auspicious terms of the Minority Rights Treaty, the severe economic depression that followed the war placed the Jewish population of the Second Polish Republic at economic and political risk. The cessation of the Russian civil war saw the Soviet Union close the Russian market in 1920 to all "foreign" trade with Poland, dashing many Jews' hopes for a rapid economic recovery. The lack of government support for Bialystok's industrial revival left most members of Bialystok's Jewish community unemployed and poverty-stricken. Furthermore, the rapid growth of the city's population as a result of migration from the hinterlands made competition fierce for the few available jobs.[24] In 1921, 40 percent of local workers were unemployed; even those with jobs often only worked three days a week.[25] Hyperinflation in Poland caused food prices to rise beyond the reach of most Jewish workers and forced the collapse of the few remaining large textile manufactures in the city.[26]

These economic quandaries, as difficult as they were, paled in comparison to the political dilemmas that Jews faced in Bialystok as their city became part of the Second Polish Republic. The subject of Polish–Jewish relations is a long and complex one that cannot be fully treated here.[27] Relations between the groups in Bialystok, as in many cities in Poland, deteriorated steadily during the First World War, reaching crisis proportions by 1919. Polish nationalists not only accused the Jewish population of cooperation with the German occupation forces, but were also totally enraged by many Jews' refusal to embrace or even recognize the authority of the Polish state.

Many of Bialystok's Jews remained hostile to the Second Polish Republic, fearing the fate of the ethnic self-determination clauses of the Polish constitution, a sentiment often expressed in the pages of the Jewish press. Since Jews continued to comprise a majority of Bialystok's population, the editors of the Russian-language newspaper *Golos Belostoka* (The Voice of Bialystok), the first Jewish-sponsored newspaper published after the war, demanded a plebiscite to decide whether Bialystok, a city with a Jewish majority, should be annexed by the Soviet Union or become part of Lithuania or perhaps its own special zone.[28] Yiddish newspapers also argued unswervingly against Poland, claiming the annexation of Bialystok was illegal, given that less than one-third of the city's residents were Polish.[29] Another Yiddish editorialist asserted that Bialystok, with its large number of Jewish residents originally from Lithuanian provinces, should not have been given to Poland at the Versailles Conference; it belonged in the new Lithuanian state.[30]

Leaders of Bialystok's kehilla also voiced opposition to Polish authority. The kehilla in interwar Poland, unlike its predecessor in Late Imperial Russia, operated as a democratic institution under the aegis of the new Polish government.[31] Hoping to receive financial and administrative support from the Polish authorities, the kehilla defined its mission in terms of Jewish cultural autonomy while simultaneously facilitating the integration of Jews into a new multinational Polish state. Despite the affiliation with the new Polish government, kehilla leaders from the outset opposed overtly nationalist legislation, such as the 1920 policy requiring all shop and street signs to be written in Polish. Such laws, they claimed, violated the fundamental tenets of the Minorities Treaty that promised all minority groups the use of their own languages for official state purposes. Kehilla leaders urged all Jews not to comply, and also proposed that Jews resist the Polish draft board, encouraging Jewish men to provide the draft registration board with false identification papers.[32]

The new kehilla-sponsored initiatives further ignited the ire of local Poles who saw this Jewish entity as openly indifferent to the future of the Polish nation. The first major kehilla conference in June 1919, funded by the Polish government was, in fact, devoted to discussing the "types of emigration projects" Jews ought to "undertake to remedy Polish Jewry's dire situation."[33] Speaking to the pressing economic problems facing Jewish workers, "ninety-five percent of whom want to immigrate to the United States," the delegates concluded that they should not invest money in Bialystok's economic redevelopment but rather devote their energies to finding new places for Jewish settlement. With few funds available, however, the conferees' conclusions had few substantive effects. But the symbolic value of the proceedings—with emphasis on emigration as the best solution to the problem of the Jewish community—exacerbated interethnic tensions, providing evidence to local Poles of the reluctance of Jews in Bialystok to join the Polish republic.[34]

In response, the Polish press unleashed a litany of antisemitic rhetoric. Polish newspapers regularly began referring to local Jews as "foreigners," "traitors" or "Jewish-Communists," who did not deserve to live on Polish soil.[35] Outraged by calls in Jewish circles for a plebiscite to decide Bialystok's political future, *Dziennk Białostocki* (Bialystok

Daily News) emphatically asserted that Bialystok was "clearly a Polish city."[36] Local Poles, as another *Dziennk Białostocki* editorial urged, must fight hard to make sure that the Jewish vote would not cause Bialystok to become part of "Jewish-Communist Russia."[37] While antisemitic rhetoric was prevalent in newspapers throughout Poland during the interwar period, *Dziennk Białostocki* constantly deployed the image of the "Jew-Communist," despite the fact that few Jews in Bialystok belonged to the Communist Party (as the local party apparatus often secretly complained to Moscow).[38] The Jews were portrayed as a devious, subversive entity, dangerous to the stability of the new Polish nation, and lethal to Polish Catholic society.

The newly established Polish municipality used both legal and political means to combat Jewish antagonism to Polish authority. Fearing the election of few Poles to local government in 1919 (and the subsequent challenges of minority groups to Poland's claims on Bialystok), the Polish government made one municipal unit out of the city of Bialystok and the surrounding Polish countryside. In the end, this gerrymandering of Bialystok's electoral districts proved unnecessary, since the city's Jewish population boycotted the 1919 municipal elections after it was decreed on July 7, 1919, that only Polish could be used by elected officials.[39] Every member of the new municipal government, declared the new legislation, would have to speak and write in Polish. Such a decree, local Jewish leaders argued, marked a clear violation of the Minorities Rights Treaty.[40] Jews were urged by kehilla leaders to continue using Yiddish in official correspondences. As a result, the Polish government barred all Jews from serving in Bialystok's municipal government in September 1919.[41]

This exclusion rendered the kehilla the sole legislative body through which Jews could exercise control over their collective future; however, as in other cities scattered throughout Poland, political divisions and corruption among Bialystok's Jewish communal leaders defeated all attempts at unified action.[42] In Bialystok, as in other cities, the new kehilla oversaw a complex and fragmented set of institutions. While the Jewish community enthusiastically embraced its newfound freedom after the demise of the tsarist empire, and as Sonia Mazny recalled, "we established a new Jewish organization every day," many expressed despair over the lack of ideological and institutional consensus, questioning whether one organizational entity would ever be able to claim to speak for all of the city's Jews.[43] Their fears were well-founded: after Bialystok's large Jewish working class elected predominately socialist representatives in the 1918 election, prominent Jewish industrialists withheld their financial support. Kehilla leaders refused to welcome the American diplomat Henry Morgenthau on his 1919 visit to Bialystok on the grounds that he represented the capitalist, imperialistic United States.[44] Wealthy Jews demanded that the Polish government dissolve the kehilla.[45] Compounding the internal crisis, several elected kehilla officials absconded with communal funds during the war with the Soviet Union in 1920, using the money to pay for their summer vacation in the countryside. This kind of corruption damaged the kehilla's standing as a legislative body. The Red Cross consequently refused to give the kehilla funds, prompting the American Joint Distribution Committee and the Bialystoker Center to set up their own philanthropic offices in the city in 1920 to make sure that donations sent from the United States served the community's needs.[46]

Answering the Call of Distress: Émigré Philanthropy and the Redevelopment of Jewish Organizational Life

It was against this backdrop of interethnic strain and Jewish communal corruption that the Bialystoker Relief Committee sent representatives to dispense the $5 million in aid they collected between 1919 and 1932. Bialystoker Jews were far from exceptional in their efforts: in 1920, Hugh Gibson, the American ambassador in Poland, reported there were more than 290 landsmanshaft delegates registered with the embassy, wandering throughout the country distributing funds.[47]

American dollars transformed Jewish life on the local level, enabling Jewish welfare and cultural organizations to expand services, and accentuating the divide between the economic fate of local Poles and Jews.[48] With industrial workers' real wages equal to only 52 percent of the pre-1914 figure and the American dollar equivalent to approximately 4,550 Polish marks in 1921, the money brought by the representatives of organizations such as the Bialystoker Center translated into millions of Polish marks, and even small grants had an immense impact.[49]

The activities of David Sohn, the first Bialystoker Center representative to reach Bialystok, illustrate the larger role that émigré philanthropy played in the economic and political upheaval. Sohn distributed $128,532 in cash, worth more than 18 million Polish marks, to 1,800 Jewish families in Bialystok.[50] With few employment prospects, these funds kept many families from starving. Sohn then divided up the remaining $80,000, worth approximately 11 million Polish marks, among the city's impoverished Jewish communal institutions: the Jewish educational board received a grant of 1 million marks to help pay for the establishment of three new schools; the Jewish hospital, the Jewish orphanage, and the Jewish old age home received grants totaling more than half a million Polish marks to rebuild their structures destroyed in the war and to serve the growing ranks of orphans and invalids produced by the war; the kehilla received a grant of 2.5 million Polish marks to help maintain the numerous soup kitchens and welfare organizations it had founded; and several other smaller organizations received grants to extend the types of services they offered.[51] For example, as a result of the grant it received from émigré funds, Lines Hatsedek was able to extend its services beyond caring for the ill, and began distributing food, new shoes and clothing to Jews in Bialystok.[52] Malka A., a woman who received clothes and shoes from that organization in 1921, remembered that when she showed up for her first day of school at the local Polish grade school, she was immediately identified as being Jewish and teased about her "new Jew shoes." As she explained, "Only a Jewish child in Bialystok would have new shoes in 1921."[53]

The economic gap noted by schoolchildren was also apparent to adults, as an analysis of Bialystok's annual municipal budgets vividly illustrates. Poland's depressed economy throughout the interwar period left few municipal funds to support the city's welfare and cultural organizations; consequently, many Polish welfare institutions struggled for survival.[54] Even the local Red Cross was forced to drastically pare down its services.[55] Jewish organizations, on the other

Linas Hatsedek ambulances purchased with donations from the United States, circa, 1928. The photograph, taken by B. Loznicki, shows five members of this volunteer medical aid association in front of Lines Hatsedek's headquarters. *From the Archives of the YIVO Institute for Jewish Research, New York.*

hand, with the generous help of émigrés, continued to serve their constituencies and actually expanded, despite diminished municipal funding. The Sholem Aleichem library, for example, founded in 1919 with émigré funds, watched its municipal funding slowly evaporate over the course of the interwar period: while it received a grant of 2,000 zlotys in 1927, by 1935, it was allotted only 400 zlotys by the local government to buy books for its collection and to run educational programs.[56] Despite this precipitous drop in funding, the library actually expanded its collection, purchasing a total of 789 books, and began running educational programs, supported by the large grants it had received from Bialystok's Jews living overseas.[57]

The gulf between Jewish and non-Jewish welfare and cultural institutions became more evident as leaders of Bialystok's Jewish community began personally soliciting funds from American donors to pursue new goals.[58] In 1923, Dr. Synaglowski, the head of the ORT (*Obshchestvo Remeslennojo Truda;* Society for the Encouragement of Handicrafts) appeared at a dinner in New York sponsored by the Bialystoker Relief Committee. Synaglowski spoke passionately about Jewish workers' high unemployment rates, inadequate training, and general despair. The audience was so moved by his story that they raised more than $7,000 in one night to build new vocational and agricultural training schools open only to Jews.[59] A similar event took place in 1925, when Eugene Lifshitz, an elected representative of Bialystok's kehilla, came to New York to raise money for a "cooperative bank" that could grant loans to businessman to stimulate the economy. Responding to his appeal, the members of the Bialystoker Center raised $40,000 to establish an interest-free loan society for Jews (Yidisher payen bank in Bialistok) to encourage (and support) private entrepreneurship in the Jewish community.[60]

Aside from financial support, émigrés also offered advice on ways to rebuild the community, encouraging Jewish leaders to incorporate "American" standards of organization in their institutions.[61] Charitable groups were encouraged to become more organized, keep strict records, and publish balance sheets and annual reports.[62] In 1923, for example, Rochelle Rachmanowitz, the director of the largest Jewish orphanage in Bialystok, obtained a large grant from several donors in New York to care for the city's growing ranks of orphans. Rachmanowitz, who had been caring for the city's Jewish orphans informally for decades, suddenly divided all her charges by age, purchased uniforms, and set up a curriculum for each age group.[63] She also modernized the format of her institution's annual report, which she then sent around the world to illustrate that her orphanage was an efficient charity worthy of greater support. Such transformations were replicated throughout Bialystok.[64] Bialystok's local rabbinical school, Beys Midrash Beys Yosef, also recast itself in an effort to acquire more funding from abroad. Not only did it begin to keep strict records, but it also started issuing textbooks and publishing balance sheets and annual reports.[65] Realizing the possibilities, the Jewish hospital in Bialystok reorganized its accounting system and reformed

Ezras Yesomim Governing Board, circa 1925. Seated in the front row in the center in a white dress is Rochelle Rachmanowitz, the orphanage's director. *Courtesy of the Merhavia Collection, Jewish National Library, Jerusalem.*

the structure of care in order to attract more overseas donations.[66] To be sure, this period also witnessed the increased involvement of Polish officials in Jewish organizational life. However, as the letters and annual reports of these organizations suggest, the lure of émigré funding and the perceived demands of American philanthropists played a pivotal role in molding the ways in which Jewish institutions represented themselves and organized their operations.

Émigré Philanthropy and Bialystok's Subversive Yiddish Press

The formative impact of émigré philanthropy was most vividly evident in the blossoming of a subversive Jewish press during the interwar period. After the establishment of the Second Polish Republic and the expulsion of Jews from municipal government, Jewish newspapers became the main vehicle through which Jews in Bialystok voiced their opinions about the region's shifting political boundaries.[67] The content of *Dos naye lebn*, the most popular and widely circulated Yiddish newspaper in interwar Bialystok, clearly demonstrates the central role that émigré funds played in maintaining this Jewish forum of political debate. In 1919, its editorial staff advanced the idea that since Poland had never clearly defined its eastern borders at the Versailles Conference, the inclusion of Bialystok in the Second Polish Republic must be viewed as illegal.[68] Needless to say, such claims angered local Polish officials, who brought a libel suit against *Dos naye lebn*.[69] Mounting legal costs strained the newspaper's finances, prompting *Dos naye lebn*'s editor, Pesach Kaplan, to write to David Sohn for help. Sohn immediately sent Kaplan money to defray legal expenses but also contributed articles to *Dos naye lebn* about current events in America so that the newspaper would not have to support correspondents abroad. As Sohn became aware of the pressures and issues facing Jewish newspaper editors, he began sending dozens of grants—ranging from $50 to $300—and maintaining extensive correspondence with every major Jewish newspaper editor.[70] Sohn demanded to know how his funds were utilized and offered advice that fundamentally altered how Jewish editors approached issues such as marketing, budget management, and staffing.[71]

Emboldened by the absolute support of émigré philanthropists, the Yiddish press in Bialystok continued to question Polish sovereignty and cultivated a new vision of Bialystok as an international city shaped by events taking place not only within Poland's geographic borders but even far beyond. Contributors continually sparred over where to locate themselves within the region's new political order, but almost all agreed that Bialystok did not constitute a Polish city. Many editors continued to publish inflammatory editorials, under titles such as "The Lithuanian Question" or "The Beginning of the End," that argued unceasingly against the inclusion of Bialystok in the Second Polish Republic.[72] At the same time, editorialists enthusiastically embraced and even solicited American Jews' involvement, in pieces sensationally entitled "We Need America's Help!"[73] Reporting on events in the United States as urgent items of "news" and apportioning a central space to these articles, Jewish newspapers located America at the center of current events in Bialystok.[74] In regularly featured columns entitled "What Have You Heard in Bialystok" and "What Have You Heard in America?" published side-by-side on the newspaper's second page, the editorial staff disseminated the idea that Bialystoker Jews throughout the world belonged to one political entity. The government's attempt to censure and control the city's Jewish press failed miserably. Less concerned with government approval because of financial support from abroad, editors of Jewish newspapers continued to express their controversial opinions freely.

Polish Responses to American Jewish Philanthropy

Jewish émigré philanthropists were far from nonpartisan welfare workers. Polish government officials began to monitor all visiting émigrés who distributed funds, and recorded information about them in secret weekly "situation reports" (*Tygodniowe sprawozdania sytuacyjne*) produced by the police. In a March 1928 report, for example, the police commissar discussed the "revolutionary meetings" of agitating Belorussians in the region, and in the same context mentioned the "subversive" visit of "Daniel Persky from America," who distributed money and "talked about Jews in America."[75] Government officials, along with the local Polish press, kept careful watch over the amount of money that each Jewish communal organization received from overseas philanthropy. Meetings sponsored by organizations receiving major grants from American Jewish philanthropists were also closely watched.

Aside from drawing the attention of Polish authorities to the intricate workings of Jewish communal life, émigré philanthropy also provoked the proliferation of antisemitic rhetoric in Bialystok's Polish press. In contrast to commonly deployed tropes about Jews, Bialystok's local weekly *Chata Polska* (Polish Hut) argued that the Jewish "international conspiracy" did not only involve the spread of Bolshevism but also the desire of the Jewish "foreign element" to involve overseas bodies in local politics.[76] As one article argued, Jews were seeking to instigate anti-Jewish violence in the city so that they "could shout to the whole world that they were harmed in Poland" and thus gain "the necessary support they needed from foreign countries."[77] In rallying calls to strengthen "Polish industry for the Polish nation" or to support "Polish workers," the daily newspaper *Dziennik Białostocki* always emphasized that Jews were a "foreign element" who were not inclined to work hard but found ways to make "easy money."[78] Such a caricature of the Jew as an idle exploiter was not revolutionary in Polish folk culture, but the depiction took on new resonance in Bialystok in light of Jews' reliance on overseas philanthropy.[79] A 1919 exposé of crime in Bialystok emphasized Jews' disproportionate involvement in illegal profiteering and smuggling as proof of their proclivity for idleness and laziness.[80] As a report on Jewish immigration to Palestine in that newspaper noted, "Life in Palestine is not as [Jewish] immigrants imagined." They cannot support themselves through philanthropy or by "trading, earning easy money or profiteering," continued the article, but only through "hard physical labor . . . [that] Jews from Poland do not welcome since they are lazy and do not like hard work."[81]

American Jewish philanthropists did not fare much better in the Polish press. While the emissaries of the Bialystoker Center were painted in messianic hues by the Yiddish press, which called them "saviors," *Dziennik Białostocki* referred to them as Jewish "big-shot" activists from America (*działacz Żydowski w Ameryce*) or delegates of the "American Jewish mission" (*delegat amerykańskiej zydowskiej misji*). Such phrases clearly indicate that local Poles did not envision American Jewish philanthropists as altruistic charity workers but as suspicious political agents.[82] In its regular column "Help for the Jews," *Dzienniki Białostocki* disdainfully chronicled the "meddling" of Bialystoker Relief Committee representatives.[83] *Prożektor,* a local Polish weekly magazine, even featured portraits of American Jewish philanthropists along with other celebrities who visited the community. One article accompanying a portrait of Louis Markus and his wife, "the exceptional American philanthropist," described how, unlike other Jews from the United States, these "generous and nice visitors from America" provided philanthropic aid to institutions and individuals "regardless of their confession or nationality."[84]

Fueling the Bialystoker Philanthropist: Political and Economic Empowerment

The attention lavished upon representatives of the Bialystoker Center by journalists in the local press, the police, and leaders of Bialystok's Jewish community made an impression on the American visitors. While they had initially embraced their philanthropic endeavors as loyal "Bialystoker Jews," they soon saw that their money changed not only the lives of their impoverished compatriots but their own status as well. It provided them with a vehicle through which they could gain prestige and recognition. They were not merely generous immigrant donors, but because their philanthropy extended beyond the financial realm into the arena of politics, they could imagine they had become important and powerful international figures.

A wealth of images produced by the Bialystoker Relief Committee in the early 1920s bespeaks this new understanding of the link between philanthropy and political power. From the turn of the century on, Jewish philanthropic organizations deployed visual images to project their new understandings of Jewish identity.[85] As many Jewish groups did in the interwar period, the Bialystoker Center sponsored the production of postcards to be sent to the émigré community to project a new image of themselves and to raise more funds. The image on one postcard—commemorating the visit to Bialystok of Morris Sunshine, who owned a dry cleaning business on the Lower East Side—evocatively illustrates how philanthropy was reshaping Bialystok's Jewish émigrés' vision of themselves. While from the perspective of other Americans they were still struggling immigrant small businessmen, once they landed on Polish soil, the vast sums they collected transformed them into rich, powerful ambassadors.[86]

The postcard image combined two photographs: one of a group of eight men assembled in front of the mausoleum of Chaim Hertz Halpern, the former chief rabbi of Bialystok; the other of a far taller man superimposed onto the postcard's lower left corner. The left-hand figure was Morris Sunshine, vice president of the Bialystoker

Synagogue in New York and a member of the Bialystoker Relief Committee, who arrived in Bialystok in 1921 to distribute funds. As in other portraits of American Jews visiting Eastern Europe in this period, a display of anonymous groups of slovenly, crowded, and ragged men was often sought out as the photographer strove to accentuate the prosperous attire of American visitors, pictured in this case in splendid isolation.[87] Elegantly dressed in a formal three-piece suit, with a cane in his hand and a bowler hat on his head, Sunshine served as an icon of upper-class respectability. While no other pictures exist from Sunshine's visit, other portraits of him from the period, along with his own description of the peril he faced as he tried to reach Bialystok, indicate that he did not regularly don such a costume nor would he have dressed in such ostentatious attire on his trip to Poland, out of fear of attracting attention to himself while traveling with large sums of money.[88]

So why did Sunshine present himself on this fundraising post-card in such attire? In this highly self-conscious image, he conveyed to future donors the ways in which philanthropic donations would enhance their status in American society, where philanthropic commitments had long been markers of ascent into the upper class.[89] In Bialystok they could reinvent themselves, enacting the part of their imagined identities. Sunshine's stature, posture, and lack of engagement with the group emphatically asserts his understanding that in bringing funds to Bialystok, he had transformed himself from a beleaguered immigrant into a powerful patron of Bialystok. Like West European Jewish philanthropists in the nineteenth century, East European Jews in the United States sought to enter into the middle class, and they, as Derek Penslar argues, "internalized liberal concepts of self-reliance and diligence," and hoped that their economic accomplishments might place them in a position of power over their impoverished former compatriots.[90] Sunshine's attire clearly conveyed his understanding of his newfound political power: his elegant formal wear resembled the uniform of British diplomats, underscoring his appreciation of the imperial dimensions of his philanthropic endeavors in Bialystok.[91] Far from seeing himself as a dry cleaner who was carrying checks to Bialystok, Sunshine envisioned himself as a powerful ambassador of the Wilsonian mission to Europe.

Postcard commemorating Morris Sunshine's 1921 visit to Bialystok, circa 1921.
Courtesy of the Goren-Goldstein Center for the Study of Diaspora Jewry, Tel Aviv University.

Image of Morris Sunshine, vice president of the Bialystoker Synagogue, from another postcard he created to advertise his dry cleaning business. *Reproduced from* Bialystoker Stimme *10:1 (1926).*

The intoxicating empowerment that Bialystoker émigrés felt as a result of their philanthropic endeavors was echoed in many articles published in the *Bialystoker Stimme*. For example, Muttel Dovesh, living in New York, summoned up the idiom of empire to describe the new community he saw created through Bialystoker Jewish émigrés' charity. In contrast to other empires, Dovesh noted, Bialystok interestingly derived it strength and "became a great empire not through armies or diplomats, but through a more original method: the charity box."[92] Equating charity with diplomacy and military victory, Dovesh not only illuminated the relationship between money and power in this dispersed community but also argued that the center of the Bialystok empire was not necessarily located in Bialystok. Rather, the colony's success at supporting the motherland helped establish New York, Dovesh argued, as "the central driving force of this gigantic Bialystok empire . . . as the official residence of the Bialystoker *pushke* [charity box]."[93]

Dovesh's argument that émigrés' ability to collect and distribute vast sums of money had transformed Bialystok into an imperial power demonstrates how philanthropy bestowed a sense of authority on Bialystoker émigrés. While some of their prestige was imagined, the Bialystoker Center's vast financial resources did, in fact, increase its stature and power in the transnational Bialystok Jewish community. As the sole arbiter deciding which Bialystoker Jewish organizations to fund, the Bialystoker Center's Relief Committee held in its hand the fate of many organizations. A letter in 1925 from the prospective editorial staff of a new Bialystok weekly paper entitled *Naye byalistoker shtime* (The New Voice of Bialystok) underscored the power of the Bialystoker Center: the letter pleaded with David Sohn, the center's executive director, to "influence the Bialystoker *landslayt* [countrymen] in America . . . so that we can get the funds necessary to start such an important newspaper." While "all cultural leaders and journalists in Bialystok agree such a publication is essential," the editors continued, no such newspaper had yet appeared because of a lack of funds.[94] Other Jewish leaders in Bialystok admitted that émigrés in the United States were the true decision makers in Bialystok's Jewish communal affairs since they decided which Jewish organizations to fund.[95]

As news of its generosity became known throughout the Bialystoker émigré community, the Bialystoker Center's Relief Committee became inundated with requests for funds from Bialystoker Jews throughout the world, reinforcing its perception that the vast funds it collected reshaped the balance of power in this transnational Jewish community.[96] One such request, by Yehuda Zar in Palestine, stressed how Bialystoker émigrés had single-handedly "rebuilt Bialystok" and "saved thousands from hardship and starvation" with "the colossal sums" they had collected.[97] Zar saw New York as the center of the Bialystoker empire because Bialystoker émigrés in New York had the resources to support other "Bialystoker colonies." Only with the support of "Bialystokers in America," Zar argued, would "the thousands of [Bialystoker] brothers who are now languishing in different European centers" be able to settle in Palestine, the ironically reversed diaspora homeland of "our grandfathers." The future of the Zionist dream, Zar concluded, lay in the hands of the Bialystoker Center, which had the funds to "build an everlasting memorial to Bialystok [in Palestine]."[98]

While Zar's pleas were unsuccessful (the Bialystoker Center sent him only two hundred dollars), his letter provides one example of the critical role the allocation of funds played in cementing the links of Bialystok's Jewish diaspora community.[99] Interestingly, while many scholars of other dispersed migrant groups comment how the money sent by émigrés back to their homelands strengthened a group's collective diasporic identity, few pay adequate attention to the critical role played by philanthropic grants sent *between* different émigré communities in shaping a diasporic community's vision of itself.[100] In the dispersed Bialystok Jewish community, for example, the Bialystoker Center in New York forged links with other émigré communities scattered throughout Europe by sending donations and demanding that recipient communities keep the center updated on how its philanthropic largesse was spent. Correspondence became regular between the Bialystoker Center and Bialystoker Jews living in Berlin after members of the Bialystoker Relief Committee sent $1,300 in 1921 to help defray the costs of immigration to America for several Jews in the community. The hope of procuring more funds encouraged other Jews in Berlin originally from Bialystok to better organize their community. A dozen gathered together to form the Bialystoker Farband in Berlin, an association that regularly sent reports and letters to the Bialystoker Center chronicling its activities and reporting on the economic challenges its members faced.[101] Clearly aware of the power dynamics and how their fellow émigrés in New York saw themselves, members of the Bialystoker Farband described themselves as "a Bialystoker colony," and constantly bemoaned their escalating debts due to German hyperinflation. Their numerous appeals for greater sums of money were embedded in almost every report, reports that often concluded with extensive praise of the generosity of the Bialystoker Center.[102] Communities of Bialystoker Jews in Kovno kept in similar contact with the Bialystoker Center after receiving philanthropic grants.[103]

Philanthropic activities transformed the Bialystoker Center from an insular, émigré organization aiding Bialystoker Jews' adjustment to life in New York City into an international institution. Michael Arye's description of the annual board of directors meeting in 1926 reflected the imperial vision that members of the Bialystoker Center saw their institution assuming:

> First, the representative of the Ladies' Auxiliary, now seen as the strongest arm of the Bialystoker Center spoke. . . . Then the secretary begins reading the mail [there are letters from Detroit, Chicago, Newark, Palestine, and Havana]. Many of the letters asked for aid. A letter from Bialystok, telling about the troubles and suffering there, thanks the center for all its help and requests more help. . . . Hearing all this, it seems to me that I am in a House of Parliament and that the correspondence is being read from the various colonies of a mother country. . . . I believe that Dr. Frank's article on "Bialystok as a Colonial Power," in the *Bialystoker Stimme* no. 8 states a true fact indeed.[104]

Although the main item on the agenda was the Bialystoker Center's expenditures, which in 1926 totaled more than $139,651.69, Arye did not even mention the sum, as he was far more impressed by the constant solicitation of the Bialystoker Center from all the corners of Bialystok's Jewish diaspora.[105] Depicting the Bialystoker Center as a "House of Parliament," Arye not only rendered the Bialystoker Center's philanthropic accomplishments as political acts but also shifted the center of the Bialystoker empire from Bialystok to New York. The power of the dollar enabled Jews in America to keep Bialystok's Jews throughout the world tied together and to remake themselves into the unspoken leaders of this dispersed East European Jewish community.

Gender and Interwar Philanthropy in the Bialystok Diaspora

While far from the focus of Arye's report, the minutes of the 1926 board meeting highlight that the early 1920s also witnessed a power shift *within* the New York Bialystoker community: the record indicates the growing involvement of women in the central organs of the Bialystoker Center. The demands of raising large sums to fund the trips of emissaries and to address the needs of its members in the United States placed the Bialystoker Center under incredible financial pressure. In 1926 alone, for example, the Bialystoker Center distributed $92,416 to Jews in Bialystok and $107,599 to needy members in the United States.[106] Women, who proved to be phenomenal fundraisers, answered the distressed call of the Bialystoker Center, establishing themselves as "the new arm of the center," and transforming how this community approached the collection of funds.

The growth of the Bialystoker Center's Ladies' Auxiliary, founded in 1923, clearly illustrates that the need for more funds fundamentally changed the role women played in the Jewish immigrant community. While there had existed a dense array of separate female organizations in the Bialystoker émigré community since the 1880s, male leaders of the Bialystoker Center initially vehemently opposed even the founding of a Ladies' Auxiliary in the Bialystoker Center since they saw women's groups as social outlets rather than activist organizations.[107] Thus, when female members of the émigré community approached the Bialystoker Center's board of directors to form their own group, their request was denied. As Anna Alpert, secretary of the Ladies' Auxiliary, recalled, the "unwarranted intrusion of a group of women in a field that had been dominated exclusively by men was looked upon unfavorably by a great number of male Bialystokers."[108] Even though the male board of directors considered women vital for the functioning of the community, they accorded them only a circumscribed role in the solution of social problems.[109] Soon, however, the demands of fundraising forced the male members of the Bialystoker Center to reconsider their decision. This army of unpaid workers could not be disregarded in times of crisis.[110] Thus, on February 12, 1923, the Ladies' Auxiliary of the Bialystoker Center issued its charter.

Within a decade the Ladies' Auxiliary had surpassed everyone's wildest expectations. In its first three years, it had raised more than $100,000 for the center.[111] Beyond garnering phenomenal sums, the Ladies' Auxiliary also attracted hundreds to join its ranks, enabling the entire Bialystoker Center to grow significantly in both stature and size. David Sohn noted in the *Bialystoker Stimme* that in the first three years after the Ladies' Auxiliary had been established,

"Bialystoker countrywomen gave generous and warmhearted aid to many sick and needy fellow Bialystokers" throughout the community.[112] As they "made rounds in Bialystoker homes," Sohn elaborated, they "provided needy families with firewood for the winter or rent . . . and several spinsters with dowries." Their activism soon attracted dozens of women to join their cause. During its first three years, membership in the Ladies' Auxiliary grew from 27 to 400.[113] By 1933, the Bialystoker Center's Ladies' Auxiliary had more than 1,200 members, making it the largest women's landsmanshaft organization in New York City.

To be sure, much of the Ladies' Auxiliary's initial success was directly related to the Great Depression which placed enormous financial strain on this struggling immigrant community. First and foremost, the Ladies' Auxiliary spared the greater Bialystoker community great embarrassment during the Depression by "helping families, who because of financial difficulties were unable to help themselves and who otherwise would be forced to seek aid at a public charity."[114]As the economy weakened and male lay leaders donated less money and had less time to spare for Bialystoker organizational life, the Ladies' Auxiliary stepped in, filling the void so that the dream of the Bialystoker Center Old Age Home could be realized. Under the best of circumstances, the construction of this expensive building would have placed some strain on the finances of the Bialystoker Center, but the stock market crash filled this institution's leadership with a deep fear for the project's viability or even the general stability of their institution. As the *Byalistoker froyen zhurnal* reported, women not only raised thousands of dollars but also volunteered their time to run the Bialystoker Old Age home. Aside from sponsoring "grocery and linen showers" several times a year to provide the home with all basic food and bedding necessities,[115] the Ladies' Auxiliary also donated $50,000, establishing the Ladies' Auxiliary as one of the main providers of income for the Bialystoker Center and Old Age Home.[116] Moreover, the Ladies' Auxiliary provided one of the most valuable commodities: their time. They volunteered to care for the two hundred residents of the home when the Bialystoker Center could not afford to employ sufficient staff.

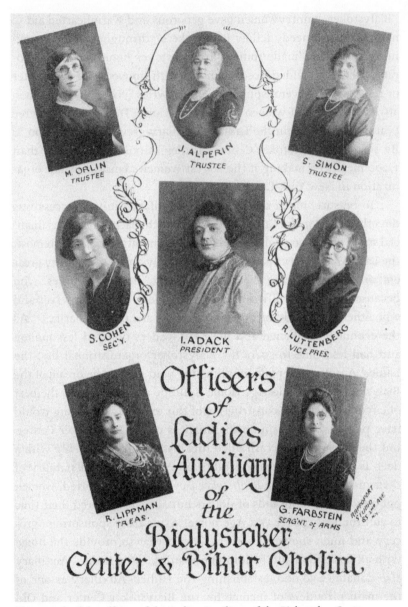

M. ORLIN
TRUSTEE

J. ALPERIN
TRUSTEE

S. SIMON
TRUSTEE

S. COHEN
SEC'Y.

I. ADACK
PRESIDENT

R. LUTTENBERG
VICE PRES.

R. LIPPMAN
TREAS.

G. FARBSTEIN
SERG'NT of ARMS

Officers
of
Ladies
Auxiliary
of
the
Bialystoker
Center & Bikur Cholim.

Photograph of the officers of the Ladies Auxiliary of the Bialystoker Center
and Bikur Cholim that appeared in the Ladies Auxiliary Jubilee Issue of the
Bialystoker Stimme (January 1928), 4.

As a result of the pivotal role they played in maintaining the old age home, Sohn argued that the founding of the Ladies' Auxiliary "marked a glorious chapter in the history of Bialystoker Jewry."[117] As he and other members of the community celebrated the women, they searched and found different explanations for their success. Sohn, for example, saw it rooted in the fact that the Ladies' Auxiliary embraced "young and elderly ladies, religious and nonreligious, American and foreign, [who were all] attracted to their very holy and sacred work and found spiritual satisfaction in promoting their great cause."[118] Others claimed that the women achieved so much and attracted so many new members because "they rendered their noble deeds . . . in a quiet, modest manner so as not to cause embarrassment to those who were compelled to apply for aid."[119]

Ida Adack, the first president of the Ladies' Auxiliary, gave a practical explanation for the Ladies' Auxiliary's success: the women were able to raise vast sums and attract new members because they linked their activities and fundraising efforts to public social events. Running numerous events each month, the Ladies' Auxiliary organized picnics, luncheons, stage shows, theater benefits, and masquerade balls, raising tens of thousands of dollars. These events attracted hundreds of people because, as Adack explained, "the greater part of Bialystoker women love socializing . . . [and through the Ladies' Auxiliary] they can do that and help those in need . . . [thereby] bridging . . . these [two types] of noble work."[120] By 1931, the funds raised by events run by the Ladies' Auxiliary comprised almost half of the Bialystoker Center and Old Age Home's annual operating budget and earned Adack a place on the Bialystoker Center's board of directors.[121]

Linking philanthropy to social events, the Ladies' Auxiliary forced its members to regard giving charity not only as donating money privately but as an act that required the donor to participate publicly in a group event. David Sohn recalled that the success of a Ladies' Auxiliary banquet in 1924 lay in the fact that it "gave the women a strong additional impulse to [organize] more activities [for] the Auxiliary," because so many offered impressive sums while attending the event.[122] By redefining *how* philanthropy was collected in this émigré community, the Ladies' Auxiliary gave greater prominence to public performance, altering not only how Bialystok's Jews in New York City experienced the act of giving charity but also how they understood how one could project a "Bialystoker" identity to the larger world.

The Ladies' Auxiliary became central to the newly projected Bialystoker identity in America not only because of the many events they hosted, but more essentially because their success demonstrated their community's entrance into the middle class. As members of the New York Jewish community, the Bialystoker émigré community continued to embrace and idealize middle-class values, most notably maintaining the notion that the middle-class family did not allow women to work, even in times of economic need.[123] Since the mid-nineteenth century, a woman's involvement in philanthropic endeavors was seen as an indicator of her family's class status.[124] Reflecting the vision that the Ladies' Auxiliary demonstrated the Bialystoker community's class status was David Sohn's tribute to this organization on the cover of the 1933 *Bialystoker Stimme*. There he claimed that "the idea of creating a Ladies' Auxiliary . . . was indeed a prophetical vision . . . since the women of Bialystok, are intelligent and intellectual" and their fine upbringing and refined "manners" drove them to "zealously and willingly sacrifice much of their time to bring every measure of happiness and comfort to the old folks."[125] Sohn concluded that the members of the Ladies' Auxiliary were like "the mothers of [the Home's] old men and women."[126]

Emphasizing their good manners and intellect, Sohn portrayed the members of the Ladies' Auxiliary as possessing the attributes of upper-class women. By describing them as "mothers" to the elderly, Sohn celebrated their active public role in the maintenance of the Bialystoker Center and Old Age Home, while simultaneously stressing the unpaid nature of their work. His community was clearly middle class because its women could afford not to work. Such a rendering of the Ladies' Auxiliary was further developed by Theodore Storch in an article entitled "Women of Tomorrow," in which he argued that the achievements of the Ladies' Auxiliary were directly akin to the "contributions to society" made by illustrious women such as Florence Nightingale, Susan B. Anthony, and Lillian Wald.[127]

Public Performance and Émigré Philanthropy

To be sure, the Ladies' Auxiliary pioneered many new fundraising techniques. Yet they could not take sole credit for many of their innovations, such as linking philanthropy to public performance. In fact, this innovation was part of a much larger phenomenon sweeping the interwar Jewish world. As Jeffrey Shandler observes, it became commonplace for Jewish philanthropists to see their endeavors as "entailing not simply an ideological or financial commitment, but also the public demonstration of this commitment."[128] As fundraising pageants, balls, and theatrical performances arranged by Zionists illuminate, many Jewish donors measured their success "not merely in financial terms" but also by their ability to rouse the public to appreciate their cause's "merit—on aesthetic, political and moral grounds."[129] The links between fundraising for Jewish collectives in Eastern Europe and Palestine, while discussed by few contemporary scholars, were abundantly clear to most Jews during the interwar years.[130] First, fundraising drives for both of these locales centered on urging donors to help build new Jewish utopias. Moreover, both utilized revolutionary new techniques: in contrast to traditional models of Jewish charity that stressed the importance of anonymity, discretion, and secrecy, interwar fundraising appeals emphasized that the giving of charity was a public endeavor through which donors demonstrated their ideological beliefs, their newly achieved class status, and their continued sense of obligation to their coreligionists. For Bialystoker Jewish émigrés, the public performances demanded by Bialystoker philanthropic organizations merged émigrés' commitment to Bialystok with their understanding of the privileges of their newly attained economic position. Through fundraising concerts, meetings, and parades, the Bialystoker Center made philanthropy the main realm in which Bialystoker Jewish émigrés expressed their identities, articulated their loyalties, and exercised their rights as members of a new Jewish middle class.

From its founding in 1919, the Bialystoker Center relied on public events and passionate performances to raise funds for the former home. These events often stressed form over content. In 1932, Joseph Lipnick recalled the first meeting of the Bialystok Relief Committee in 1919: "I was chairman of that conference and I remember how many of the audience were enthused by the way David Sohn spoke."[131] Although Lipnick could not recall *what* Sohn had said, he did remember how he said it: such passion we "were not accustomed to hearing at society meetings."[132] When a representative returned from Bialystok, a dramatic and theatrical meeting would be convened in the main auditorium. As the emissaries spoke about the situation in their former home, they tried to create as much dramatic tension as possible. Ralph Wein, president of the Bialystoker Center, for example, was overcome with emotion as he spoke to a crowd about the "tragedy of Bialystok" after his sojourn in Poland in 1923.[133] The spectacle continued as Wein went on to describe how those who were the wealthy patrons of the community before the war were now dependent on philanthropy and how thousands of former compatriots were waiting anxiously for their visas.[134] The audience responded to such melodramatic reports by standing up and making spontaneous public announcements of their donations, a practice that became prevalent at luncheons and dinners sponsored by the Bialystoker Center.

Highly publicized musical performances were also used to raise money for the Bialystoker Center. An informational brochure titled "What does the Bialystok Relief Committee Do?" not only enumerated the amount of money sent to Bialystok by relief organizations in New York, Chicago, Detroit, Cleveland, and Paterson, New Jersey, but also elaborated on the wonderful "concerts and balls" sponsored by the Bialystoker Center that showcased "the best musicians" in the city.[135] Appreciating its constituents' desire for leisure activities, the Bialystoker Center stressed in its promotional literature that by giving money to Bialystok through the purchase of a ticket, an individual, who probably was a struggling émigré with fewer resources, could show his or her support for Bialystok while simultaneously enjoying a night on the town.[136]

Nothing better illustrates the centrality of public musical performances to Bialystoker philanthropic culture than the benefit concerts of opera singer Rosa Raisa. According to the *Bialystoker Stimme*, no woman did more for Bialystok than Raisa, "[who] displayed endless devotion and loyalty to her old home and to her compatriots."[137] Born and raised in Bialystok and trained in Italy, Raisa had immigrated to the United States shortly before the First World War. Although based in Chicago, she spent most of her time touring throughout the United States and Europe. In 1919, upon hearing of the devastation of her home city during the war, Raisa canceled all her engagements so that she could give a large benefit concert in New York to raise money for relief efforts in Bialystok.[138] This act, according to a feature article in the 1926 *Bialystoker Stimme*, established Raisa as "the beloved daughter of Bialystok."[139]

Raisa's concert for Bialystok, held in New York's renowned Hippodrome Theatre on May 20, 1920, was the first major event run by the Bialystoker Center, and served to kick off its fundraising drive. An astonishing four thousand people crowded into the concert where Raisa demonstrated her versatility as an opera singer, as well as her continued commitment to her roots in Eastern Europe. In a carefully arranged program, she sang selected arias from several operas such as *La Tosca* as well as renditions of traditional Hebrew and Yiddish songs, such as "Eli, Eli."[140]

Raisa lived up to her reputation: her impressive performance, as the Bialystoker Center's press releases reported, raised more than $10,000. More importantly, as reporters for both the *Bialystoker Stimme* and the *Forverts* pointed out, Raisa attracted a most impressive audience, most notably President Wilson's daughter,[141] whose presence not only gave greater legitimacy to the Bialystok cause but also helped the Bialystoker Center advance the idea that their philanthropic events were major social events that demanded everyone's personal participation. Who would pass up "a chance to see people like President Wilson's daughter?" asked an advertisement for a fundraising concert in 1924.[142] It was not enough just to buy a ticket to show one's support of Bialystok: one had to attend the concert, so that one could see and be seen by others in the audience. This focus on seeing and being seen at a Bialystoker fundraising event, though not necessarily helping their impoverished brethren, became a major motivating factor behind émigrés' participation in future fundraising performances.[143] By 1926, revenues from concerts and other public social events, such as masquerade balls and theater benefits, constituted more than one-third of the Bialystoker Center's annual budget, which was used to fund programs both in the United States and throughout the Bialystoker diaspora.[144]

Raisa's performance also provided Bialystoker Jewish émigrés in the United States another way to link philanthropy to an expression of their aspired material identity. More than just a devoted Bialystoker *landsman,* she was a successful artist and wealthy woman who bore all the markings of the upper class. Accompanying articles or advertisements about her were portraits of her bare-shouldered and bejeweled appearance, illustrating her immodest American wardrobe along with her material success.[145] The *Bialystoker Stimme* took pride in Raisa's material achievements but emphasized that her greatest accomplishment was in achieving economic success without forgetting her past. In sharp contrast to other Jewish artists in the United States, Raisa "openly and with pride [continued to] demonstrate her commitment . . . to the Jewish people and to her compatriots."[146]

Public display and public recognition soon became central to how Bialystoker émigrés practiced the act of giving charity. In a 1926 plea for funds, the Bialystoker Relief Committee announced that "the suffering of the unfortunates in Bialystok requires our immediate and whole-hearted assistance. . . . Pity your fellow Bialystoker on the other side of the ocean."[147] If pity was not enough, the Bialystoker Relief Committee promised, "the names of all the people who have sent in their contributions will be made public through the press."[148] Such an overt inversion of the traditional Jewish paradigm to give charity anonymously allowed Bialystoker émigrés to demonstrate publicly both their commitment to their former home and the extent to which they had succeeded financially.

Philanthropy, Consumption, and Fundraising Appeals for the Bialystoker Center's Old Age Home

Boosted by its success in raising funds for Bialystok, the Bialystoker Center expanded its horizons to address the needs of

Rosa Raisa, world-renowned opera singer, born in Bialystok. She was considered the "quintessential Bialystoker." The photograph appeared in *Bialystoker Stimme* 10:1 (March 1926), 24.

Jews living on the Lower East Side. The center deployed the public fundraising strategies it had honed to address a pressing local need: tending to the aging Jewish population in New York.[149] At its annual meeting in 1927, the Bialystoker Center executive committee declared its intention to build an old-age home on the premises of the Bialystoker Center. This was a major financial undertaking, requiring the raising of extensive funds, but David Sohn, executive director of the Bialystoker Center, was sure that it would "not be necessary to appeal repeatedly to our Bialystoker compatriots to help maintain our home in America, as all know about the great necessity of such an institution."[150] Playing on his knowledge of his constituents' desire to demonstrate their wealth, Sohn emphasized that this new campaign to raise money for the Bialystoker Center would exhibit the affluence and achievements of its donors even more than donations sent to Bialystok. Since all members of the Bialystoker Center "had done so much in helping our brothers and sisters overseas in their time of great need," Sohn argued, "now you must respond to our great need here, and give more than your pocket allows," so that all on the Lower East Side could appreciate the great wealth and generosity of those Jews from Bialystok in New York. Bialystok Jewry's needs, while still compelling, could not compete with immigrants' desire to display their financial success closer to home where they could more immediately enjoy the prestige and intoxicating sense of empowerment experienced by their compatriot philanthropists overseas. Thus, Sohn concluded, "buy a brick for the Bialystoker Old Age Home," and build for your community a much needed institution and yourself a great reputation.[151]

By urging his constituents not just to give donations but also to "buy bricks," Sohn not only played to his constituents' desire to display their wealth but, more significantly, embedded his appeals in a commercial discourse. Over the next few years, Sohn would continue to summon commercial discourse as he tried to link Bialystoker philanthropic endeavors with an American marketplace ethos, emphasizing that one *gives* charity to show that one *can afford* to give money away. By clearly demonstrating one's financial success, this ethos would play a central role in American Bialystoker philanthropic fundraising appeals during the late 1920s and early 1930s. The mantra to "buy bricks" became prominently displayed in advertisements in several editions of the *Bialystoker Stimme* as well as on the cover of a new magazine edited by Sohn called the *Bialystoker heym* (Bialystoker Home), which reported on the fundraising drive for the Bialystoker Old Age Home.[152] By publicly donating money to Bialystoker causes, or "buying bricks for Bialystok," Sohn tried to convince the Bialystoker émigré community that donations of charity, like public consumption of goods, could demonstrate wealth and status.

Public recognition of charitable donations reached new heights in a newly created special section of the *Bialystoker Stimme* that listed the amounts contributed by every individual donor to both local and international Bialystoker causes. These pages appeared in the center of the publication, where the Bialystoker Center's annual financial report had been printed between 1923 and 1925. The importance of public acknowledgement of philanthropic donations in the Bialystoker émigré community is further evidenced by the fact that during the Great Depression, when the Bialystoker Center was forced to pare down the length of the *Bialystoker Stimme* for economic reasons, the editorial staff of this magazine limited only the number of articles published but maintained the numerous pages announcing members' donations.

The commercial discourse in the Bialystoker Center's fundraising campaigns created some unintended squabbles. For example, a heated controversy erupted around the name to appear on the center's cornerstone. Two respected families in the community—the Lutenbergs and the Marcuses—each responded to Sohn's plea to "buy bricks" by contributing a large sum to the Bialystoker Center. Each family was convinced that their munificent donation would be eternally recognized and celebrated by the community through an inscription on the cornerstone. Both families, however, became irate upon hearing that they would have to share the coveted honor; one family even threatened to renege on their commitment. To avoid conflict with the families and assure that they would give the money they had pledged, David Sohn then decided to lay two cornerstones to publicly recognize each family's generosity. The Marcus family's name was inscribed on the eastern cornerstone while the Lutenberg family's name was placed on the western one. Unfortunately, this dual recognition did not resolve the conflict but instead encouraged a rivalry between the two families, each of which wanted to be given the sole credit for the successful completion of the Bialystoker Center Old Age Home. Ultimately, the center's board planted shrubbery to conceal the names on both cornerstones so that neither family would feel the other had received greater recognition.[153]

Despite the cornerstone fiasco, the Bialystoker Center continued its use of commercial discourse to raise money: donors were still encouraged to "buy" items instead of making charitable "donations."

Through the constant deployment of such language, members of the Bialystoker Center began to believe that they were not merely offering financial support, but were acquiring pieces, or actual bricks, of the Bialystoker Center. This emphasis on buying and ownership rather than on altruistic financial support, appealed to many members of the community in the early 1930s. Most Jewish immigrants had seen their economic situation improve in the 1920s, but the Depression then raised serious concerns about their future in America.[154] With the dream of entrenching themselves in the middle class fading quickly, such fundraising rhetoric allowed émigrés to see themselves as homeowners through their "ownership" of the Bialystoker Center. Appreciating the centrality of economic achievement to Bialystoker émigrés' view of themselves, the philanthropic efforts of the Bialystoker Center stressed that while on the individual level, few Bialystoker émigrés might ever own a home, on a collective communal level, the émigrés could achieve such a dream through their connection to and support of the Bialystoker Center.

In addition to selling "bricks," the Bialystoker Center began in 1931 to raise funds by imploring its members to "purchase certificates" that proclaimed their lifetime membership in the Bialystoker Center and Old Age Home.[155] With each donation of ten dollars, donors would receive an ornately embellished certificate to hang on their wall so that they could demonstrate to any visitor that they were "life-time member[s] of the Bialystoker Old Age home."[156] Understanding the harsh economic times, the Bialystoker Center allowed its donors to pay for their certificates in five installments, employing a strategy increasingly used by retailers among shoppers who aspired to own items such as washing machines but could not afford to do so. Echoing the bargain rhetoric prevalent in American advertising of the period, Sohn also stressed how the certificates were such a bargain that everyone was "so anxious to get a certificate [that they] are rushing to procure them."[157] Like any shrewd marketer selling a product, Sohn realized that not everyone would be attracted to "purchasing" a bargain, so he concluded by stressing that the certificates were really a necessity for any self-respecting Bialystoker home and that "within a few weeks, there will be no house . . . in

[any] Bialystoker colony where the walls will lack the decoration of an honorary certificate."[158]

Building on their success in "selling" certificates, in the 1930s the Bialystoker Center began "selling" memorial tablets to individuals or families who gave large donations. Families "purchased" tablets as memorials and then had them installed in the Bialystoker Old Age Home at large ceremonies, a process that linked philanthropy once again to public performance.[159] The tablets came in three different colors—gold, silver, or bronze—providing another easily identifiable way for Bialystoker émigrés to display their material achievements as well as their commitment to their imagined heritage as a Jew from Bialystok.

It is no coincidence that these fundraising techniques became prevalent exactly at the moment when most Bialystokers were most insecure about their future economic status. The Great Depression produced deep anxieties among many East European Jewish émigrés in New York.[160] While larger Jewish philanthropic agencies, such as the United Jewish Appeal, shifted their focus from welfare relief to the maintenance of ethnic identity, smaller Jewish philanthropic institutions, such as the Bialystoker Center, cemented a link between philanthropy and material achievement. In 1932, economic strain forced the Bialystoker Center to close the Bialystoker Relief Committee and to cease sending money overseas where few of the donor's neighbors could see evidence of generosity and wealth.[161] At the same time, the Bialystoker Center began representing its Old Age Home as the epitome of American upper-class taste and values. In promotional pictures taken of the home, residents were featured alongside chandeliers and pianos. Portraits of the lobby of the old age home focused on the Bialystoker Center's doorman in uniform, cap, and tie, standing at attention and ready to serve all those who entered (see figure on page 171).[162] The décor reassured Bialystoker émigré "owners" that their money had been well spent and that the Home clearly demonstrated taste, class, and material security.

The celebration held after the Bialystoker Center paid off its mortgage illustrates the extent to which the Home served as a symbol of its donors' economic well-being. At the event, where hundreds

Certificate marking a donor's charitable gift to the Bialystoker Center, circa 1932.
Courtesy of the Merhavia Collection, Jewish National Library, Jerusalem.

crammed into the home's main auditorium, speakers delivered passionate orations praising the Bialystoker community's great economic
achievement in raising the money to build such an exemplary residence. As they lauded the donors, they expounded on the ways in
which their efforts entrenched the legacy of Bialystok in America.
The high point of the evening occurred when David Sohn tore up the
Bialystoker Center's mortgage and set it on fire amid the wild cheer-
ing of hundreds. Then, amid this wild frenzy, everyone who had
made a donation to the Bialystoker Center was given a small slip of
paper representing a part of the Bialystoker Center, and each person
set their "personal mortgage" on fire.[163]

By the late 1930s, it did not even matter if one came from
Bialystok to be considered a loyal Bialystoker. Donors just had to
participate in the community's rich philanthropic culture. As Tilly

Doorman at the Bialystoker Center, circa 1930. *Courtesy of the Goren-Goldstein Center for the Study of Diaspora Jewry, Tel Aviv University.*

Raskin explained: "if a man is a rabbi, his wife is a rebbetzin; so too, if a man considers himself a Bialystoker, his wife regardless of where she was born . . . [must give money and be] a member of the Ladies' Auxiliary."[164] Many women in the Ladies' Auxiliary were not originally from Bialystok but considered themselves loyal, committed Bialystokers because they were active members of the Ladies' Auxiliary; philanthropy transformed people into "Bialystokers." Such a transformative power was celebrated in the Bialystoker émigré community in the United States, where over the course of the interwar period Bialystoker émigrés had used philanthropic endeavors to convert Bialystok from an impoverished East European industrial city into an "imperial center" and themselves from struggling immigrants into esteemed patrons.

American Philanthropy and Bialystok Jewry on the Eve of the Second World War

With limited funds, Bialystoker émigrés could not sustain both the doorman and chandeliers of the Bialystoker Center and the numerous needy communal organizations in their former home. In 1932, the Bialystok Relief Committee closed its doors. While individuals continued to send assistance to their families abroad, little money was sent to support Bialystok's Jewish communal institutions. The cessation of institutional funding left a deep imprint on Bialystok Jewry. Between 1932 and the Russian invasion of Poland in 1939, fifteen regularly published newspapers, weekly magazines, and monthly periodicals were forced to cease publication because of insufficient funding.[165] While the American Joint Distribution Committee continued to offer basic health-care support to the poor, Jewish welfare institutions were forced to cut services.[166] The newfound poverty of the Jewish community exacerbated tensions between Jews and Poles as their respective welfare institutions were forced into fierce competition with one another. In 1937 Polish–Jewish relations reached their nadir. A Polish boycott of Jewish businesses, as economist Menakhem Linder observed, devastated the local Jewish economy and forced many into penury.[167]

Despite the reduction of funding, the image of the American Jewish philanthropist persisted, as Jews in Bialystok continued to imagine their community as inextricably linked to their compatriots in America. Sektor Film's 1939 Bialystok travelogue reflected this mentality. The film company, owned by Shaul and Yitzhak Goskind, handled work for the major American studios in Poland, including MGM, Fox, and Warner Brothers. With an eye toward the American Yiddish-speaking audience, they embarked on a project to encourage Jewish tourism to Poland.[168] Collaborating with local communities, Sektor Films produced promotional films about Warsaw, Vilna, Lodz, Lvov, and Bialystok. In each film, the narrator takes the visitor on a journey through the sites of the city: first the visitor is introduced to municipal sites, then to its Jewish sites and industry. The film ends with a view of the Jewish population's cultural activities in the city's public spaces. In Vilna and Warsaw, for example, Goskind focused on Jewish sporting events and political debates. In Bialystok, by contrast, the closing segment showed a group of young Jewish women strolling along in the gardens surrounding the old Brancki palace. America, not politics, occupied their thoughts, as Sektor narrated in Yiddish: "Bialystok girls stroll among the flowers, dreaming of wealthy American husbands, for American boys are the most desirable." With the closing shot of one of these young women smiling seductively at the camera to lure in a rich American husband, Goskind concluded, "Come visit Bialystok—you will not regret it!"[169] While the film's overt goal was to attract Jews to visit the city, the fascination with America in contrast to the promotional films on other cities suggests that the passionate commitment of Bialystok's Jews particularly in the United States prompted Jews in Bialystok to see their salvation in America, not in political debates at the Sejm, the Second Polish Republic's House of Parliament.

Conclusion

Philanthropy—both its collection and distribution—transformed every node of the Bialystoker Jewish community between 1919 and 1939. Bialystoker émigré philanthropic organizations may have been parochial, but their impact went far beyond the interwar period and indeed beyond Bialystok. The transatlantic drama involving the Bialystok diaspora was far from exceptional: between the outbreak of the First World War and the German invasion of Poland in 1939, hundreds of small landsmanshaftn collected more than $100,000,000 to rebuild Jewish life in Eastern Europe.[170] The metamorphosis of East European and American Jewry during the interwar period, a topic explored by many scholars, can be fully appreciated only in light of these transatlantic links.[171]

While the coalitions formed and constituencies served by philanthropic work spanned national boundaries, they were nevertheless shaped by the specific needs of both donors and recipients, who were

struggling to come to terms with radically new political and economic situations. In Eastern Europe, the political and economic chaos
of the postwar years placed immense strain on communal resources.
With Jewish migrants in search of work streaming into Bialystok
from the surrounding countryside, and with corrupt Jewish leaders
and an unresponsive Polish government, Jews in Bialystok were in
desperate need of help. Their cries were heard by Bialystoker Jewish
émigrés living in the United States who were struggling to establish
themselves in their new homeland. As these émigrés distributed vast
sums to rebuild their former home, they not only emboldened Jewish
leaders in Bialystok to challenge the authority of the Polish government but also transformed the ways in which they saw themselves
and understood their power and place in the world.[172] Local needs
became intricately intertwined with international concerns.

The transformation of this dispersed community was equally
shaped by the collection of funds. Bialystoker Jewish émigrés created
a distinct culture through their philanthropic organizations, parallel
to the work of American Zionists who "were cast [into a distinctive
role] during the years between the two World Wars, by others as well
as by themselves, as impresarios of Zionism." "Like theatrical producers," scholar Jeffrey Shandler describes, "American Zionists' activities
centered on making financial and other material arrangements for an
enterprise realized by others . . . their power is at some remove from
the ultimate result of their efforts yet is vitally linked to it."[173] As was
the case with American Zionists, Bialystoker Jews cast themselves
as producers whose task was to reshape Jewish Bialystok. If raising
money for Palestine became akin to "producing the future," fundraising for Bialystok, like the rest of Eastern Europe, was a way to "produce the past." Like interwar Yiddish filmmakers, who were "looking
over their shoulders [at their audiences] as well as at the screen,"
image-conscious Bialystoker émigrés used philanthropy to project
a new image of themselves and their pasts.[174] Philanthropy allowed
them to convey their newfound sense of power as they became economically successful in their new homes. The centrality of a commercial discourse in Bialystoker émigré fundraising appeals reinforced
the growing importance of demonstrating wealth and illuminates the

ways in which a larger discourse on Jewish economics, charity, and power that had permeated European Jewish culture in the late nineteenth and early twentieth centuries shaped Jewish life in America. Fundraising for Eastern Europe served, in some ways (as chapter five will explore), as a dress rehearsal for fundraising for Israel.

Philanthropy enabled Bialystoker Jewish émigrés not only to demonstrate their success, wealth, and self-reliance, but also to cement the links tying together this dispersed migrant community. While scholars of contemporary immigrant diasporas have claimed that Jews irrevocably divided themselves from their former homes, in fact, as Bialystok's Jews spread throughout the world, their economic involvements, philanthropic networks, and cultural identities linked their new homes to their places of origin in diverse multilayered patterns, forcing concerns of local, national, and transnational communities into collision with one another. The metaphors Bialystoker émigrés used to describe the international scope of their philanthropy in the interwar period, as a parliament, or as akin to diplomacy, must be seen as a foil to the devastating situation narrated by the letters of their coreligionists still living in Bialystok. While for some sending money served to convey a connection to their diasporic center in Poland, for others writing about Bialystok expressed this undying commitment to their former home. As in other "dispersed nations," Bialystoker émigrés developed their own dense array of publications that they also used to recreate their former world that was rapidly changing before their eyes. As they published narratives about Bialystok, they sought to make sense of their new lives while inverting the sense of powerlessness they felt as they witnessed what was happening to Jews in Poland. Through the creation of numerous magazines and newspapers that were distributed internationally, Bialystok's Jews articulated their understanding of their shared communal identity, which, along with money, strengthened the ties of their dispersed community struggling to remain united in the age of mass migration.

CHAPTER 4

Rewriting the Jewish Diaspora:
Images of Bialystok in the Transnational
Bialystoker Jewish Press, 1921–1949

Celebrating the success of the first issue of the *Bialystoker Stimme* in 1922, David Sohn commended Bialystok's Jews around the world for not "lapsing into 'an ocean of forgetfulness.'"[1] As an outpouring of letters from readers in the United States, South America, and Europe illustrated, Bialystok provided "materials of interest to those in America as well as those in Bialystok." Moreover, Sohn continued, the *Bialystoker Stimme* marked a milestone in Yiddish literary history, as it was "a truly revolutionary publication" that printed articles by any member of "the various Bialystoker colonies throughout the world" who chose to write about Bialystok, whether he or she was a "common person" or a professional writer. Overwhelmed by the interest in this publication, Sohn invited any "writers among our compatriots to take a turn editing this journal," as he sought to craft a truly populist publication, filled with the thoughts, poems, and reminiscences of every former resident of Jewish Bialystok. By doing so, he hoped that the "the voice of Bialystok" would be heard through its people, who could be found not only in Poland, but were scattered throughout the world. Filling the journal with lyrical devotions to Bialystok, Sohn believed his publication would provide the liturgy to bind together this new dispersed Jewish community, serving as a new type of communal prayer book.

The response to Sohn's clarion call over the next seventy years suggests that the act of writing about Eastern Europe filled a vacuum left in the lives of hundreds of Jewish immigrants from Bialystok. They turned to writing about their former home in the *Bialystoker*

Stimme as well as in dozens of other newspapers, magazines, and journals sponsored by various organizations that comprised the backbone of this dispersed Jewish community. Scholars of modern diasporas have observed that exilic communities sustain themselves across vast distances through the press, in which they constantly tell and retell the story of their shared past and dispersal.[2] The newspapers of the transnational Bialystoker Jewish community redefined the vision of Jewish diasporic identity by creating a sphere for reflection on longings for a former home as well as on nostalgia for a lost time.

Drawing upon not only traditional Jewish liturgy but also upon a long-standing tradition in Russian Jewish society, Bialystok's Jews used print culture to debate, police, and grapple with the shifting boundaries of their communal lives.[3] Beginning in the 1860s, Jewish newspapers in the Russian, Yiddish, and Hebrew languages appeared throughout the empire, enabling Jewish contributors to express conflicting views of cultural change. These newspapers not only offered up revolutionary new visions of the Jewish future and the Jewish past, but also inculcated in their readers the notion that the press was the vehicle for disaffected Jews to discuss the shifting contours of the surrounding political, cultural, and economic landscapes.

Whether they settled in new cities in Europe, North America, or South America, Bialystok's Jews all toyed with fresh images of their former home, viewing it as a motherland, diasporic homeland, or imperial center. Whimsical visions of Bialystok redefined how its Jews viewed themselves, their connection to their region of origin, and their relationships to one another.[4] As the newspapers of the transnational Bialystok Jewish community discussed in this chapter suggest, migration projected the vexing question of Jews' relationship to the nation-state—a constant subject of debate in the pages of the Russian Jewish press—onto a new stage. In their publications, Bialystoker Jewish authors on both sides of the Atlantic wrestled with questions of regional distinctiveness and the relationship between place and peoplehood. Mobilizing striking idioms and metaphors to describe Bialystok, these ingénue émigré writers used their literary recreations of Bialystok to protest current conditions in Eastern Europe and to comment on circumstances in their new homes.

This chapter surveys the subtle shifts in the projected image of Bialystok between 1921 and 1949 as a means to recover the inner world of Jewish Bialystok's diaspora: not merely émigrés' experiences but also their worldview through which they interpreted and made sense of their experiences.[5] At the beginning of the interwar period, ingénue immigrant writers focused on the physical qualities of their former home; by the 1930s, however, the attributes of its residents became the focal point of their portrayals. A ubiquitous theme throughout the period, repeated with liturgical regularity, is that Bialystok was a Jewish homeland; its tender compassion nurtured Jewish life and culture. Arguing that their former home was more than a source of nostalgia, immigrant writers directly engaged the complex debates raging in the Jewish world about the relationship between writing and place in the construction of modern Jewish identity.[6] In discussions about the ways in which Zionist ideologues, Jewish socialists, and proponents of Diaspora Nationalism clashed over whether Eastern Europe or Palestine provided the best environment for Jewish cultural renewal, few scholars have considered the voices of East European Jewish émigrés who advanced the notion in their newspapers that the "promised land" was the Eastern Europe of their memory. Migration had placed them in a new symbolic Jewish diaspora, which, as they knew from two thousand years of Jewish lore, depended on the pen for vital sustenance. Thus, while the image of exile could shift, a need to write about their former home, even after it was totally obliterated in the Second World War, would never change.

Giving Voice to Bialystok in the Wake of Its Destruction: The Creation of *Der Bialystoker Stimme*

As news of the devastation of Bialystok made its way to America in 1920, Bialystoker Jewish immigrants came together to publish the *Bialystoker Stimme,* a magazine whose stated goal was to provide a forum for "Bialystoker Jews throughout the world" to "voice" their concerns.[7] From its inception in 1921, the journal nurtured a network of regular contributors and readers seeking new ways to navigate their relationship to Eastern Europe and to other East European Jews scattered throughout the world. According to available circulation figures, the *Bialystoker Stimme* was read by tens of thousands of Jews in the United States and several thousand living elsewhere. When issues of the journal arrived at Anna Gepner's parents' home in Australia, she recalled, "everyone would flock to my living room, anxiously awaiting my father's return from work so that they could hear the news of the world."[8] The world, in her eyes, meant Bialystok's dispersed Jewish émigré community.

The world conveyed in the pages of the *Bialystoker Stimme* was defined by headlines such as "Bialystok: A Colonial Power." The publication also featured stories such as "The American Red Cross in Bialystok," or "The Two Threads Connecting Bialystok and New York." A regular column entitled "Our One World" related the experiences of Bialystoker Jews living in Chicago, Berlin, Palestine, and Mexico in strikingly similar terms.[9] From the outset, the *Bialystoker Stimme* located its readers in an ideological universe whose very center was Eastern Europe. The journal's emphasis was reflected in its front-page devotion to current events in Bialystok, its focus upon the Bialystoker Jewish émigré enclave as the locus of its world news, and its regular features on Bialystok Jewry's history and literature.

The resolute focus on Eastern Europe differentiated the *Bialystoker Stimme* from the mainstream Yiddish immigrant press in New York, where it was published. Newspapers such as the *Forverts* concentrated on America and its readership's new identity as Americans. The other publications summoned portraits of the Old Country mostly to demonstrate how life in America was so much better.[10] At the same time as the mainstream Yiddish press used portraits of the Old World to celebrate the New World and trumpet a narrative of integration, the *Bialystoker Stimme* presented a counter-narrative of alienation, mourning the world left behind and drawing on feelings of ambivalence toward the processes of migration and resettlement.[11] In its celebration of the Old World, the *Bialystoker Stimme* acted much as the non-Jewish Slavic immigrant presses did by creating a sense of historical continuity between Eastern Europe and the United States.[12] To be sure, the *Forverts* was not geared exclusively to one local regional group, as was the *Bialystoker Stimme,* and it thus played down regional identifications as part of its effort to Americanize its readership and to create a sense of an East European, Jewish American community; nonetheless, its fundamentally negative portraits of Eastern Europe were strikingly divergent from those presented by *Bialystoker Stimme,* where the common values shared by Bialystoker Jews abroad and at home were continually stressed.[13]

Visions of Bialystok as a Nurturing Motherland in the 1920s

The most dramatic illustrations of the different visions of Eastern Europe presented by the *Bialystoker Stimme* and the mainstream Yiddish press are seen in the actual language used by contributors to describe Eastern Europe. Writers in the *Bialystoker Stimme* rarely referred to Bialystok as their *alte heym* (old home), as it was commonly called in the *Forverts;* rather, they referred to Bialystok as their *muter shtot* (mother city) or, in some cases, their *muterland* (motherland).[14] While nostalgia can explain why East European Jewish immigrants summoned maternal imagery, contributors to the *Bialystoker Stimme* did not indicate a desire to withdraw from the present and return to an imagined past—a central goal of nostalgia, in contrast to homesickness.[15] Historian Susan Matt contrasts homesickness with nostalgia, noting than nostalgia is defined "by the longing for a particular home, that may carry within it a yearning for home, a home faraway in time rather than space."[16] This yearning, while not an exclusive product of "the social, political, and economic changes of the last two or three centuries," continues Matt, is always shaped by a specific historic context. For Bialystok's Jews, the context was the radical political shifts wreaking havoc on Eastern Europe's borders during the interwar period.[17] By rewriting Bialystok, they hoped to demonstrate that their former home was not merely an economically depressed Polish city but a nurturing, inspirational homeland that stirred its former residents in the ways that other national homelands did throughout the world.

Jacob Krepliak's ode to his home-city (*heymish shtot*) in the 1926 *Bialystoker Stimme* evokes a common vision of Bialystok as a bucolic

Eden. Krepliak, who immigrated in 1912, was a successful journalist, well-known socialist leader and editor of the Yiddish political and literary journal *Tsukunft*. Despite his success and adaptability to life in America, he claimed he still did not feel at home in the United States.[18] As he bemoaned:

> I have been away for many years. . . . But I have not once been able to forget my dear city . . . I constantly contemplate your mountains . . . when my feet carry me to the sea, [all I can] think about is your river . . . under the greatest waterfall in the world, all I could hear was the sound of your water running in my ears. . . . My spirit has been hurt, my ideas are raging: WHEN THE TIME COMES AT LEAST I SHOULD NOT REMAIN IN THIS STRANGE LAND. . . . I left many years ago, but my feelings have yet to diminish. Indeed, the miraculous power of my intimate—beloved—mother-land [*heymish-lieber-muter-erd*] prevents this from happening.[19]

Krepliak's emphasis signals his desire to leave his new home, but he never actually does. His dilemma thus illustrates Matthew Frye Jacobson's apt description that the "diasporic imagination often has more to do with how one sees and thinks about the world than with where one ultimately chooses to live in it."[20] The tone of Krepliak's piece, with its emphasis on the imagined overpowering natural beauty of Bialystok (which had vanished even before Krepliak's birth due to the city's rapid industrial expansion), vividly conveys the ways in which Bialystok stood in his mind as a goading reminder of the new world's inadequacies. Moreover, he borrows directly from early twentieth-century European nationalist rhetoric, which often deployed feminine and naturalistic symbols to convey the central-ity of the land to the formation of the nation. Krepliak thus imparts a new vision of Bialystok: far from being just another small city in Poland, it acted as a nation in the way that it shaped its former resi-dents' approach to the world and their adaptation to new homes.[21] Krepliak's redolent use of the Yiddish word *erd*, meaning soil, in his depiction of Bialystok as a beloved motherland (*heymish-lieber-muter-erd*) further underlines the author's primal attachment to the city's natural landscape and locates his vision of his former home in the cultural orbit of other early twentieth-century nationalist movements in which overpowering landscape was a common motif.[22]

Like Krepliak, Mordechai Babitsh also felt that Bialystok's natural landscape provided the universal language to which all Bialystoker émigrés could relate and understand in their shared exile.[23] Babitsh, a Yiddish journalist in Bialystok who immigrated to New York in 1920, exclaimed in the 1921 *Bialystoker Stimme* that "everywhere in the world pales in comparison to the fantastic Bialystok forest. The unique Bialystok forest awakens so much longing and love," he continued, "that everyone craves to see it daily as they crave for a beloved glimpse of their own mother."[24] He maintained that as a nation molds its residents' souls wherever they may wander, so did Bialystok shape its former residents' engagement with the world. Thus, "wherever the Bialystoker finds himself," he intoned, "whether it is in New York, or the heavenly California, Mexico . . . the tip of Africa or Argentina. . . . Wherever in the whole wide world, his eyes will never be able to see more beautiful sunsets, finer waterfalls, more wonderful mountains, or more magnificent forests."[25] Drawing again on landscape imagery to convey the primacy of his attachment, Babitsh emphasized that even "heavenly" locales in the new world could not replace the nurturing presence of Bialystok. Rather than a memory, Bialystok remained a constant unresolved presence that cast a dark shadow on everything in the new world.

Gendered imagery was constantly being appropriated by Bialystoker émigré writers to express their emotional relationship to Bialystok.[26] For example, the Yiddish writer Zalman Segelowitz composed the poem "Bialystok" in 1923 to portray his deep sense of loneliness after leaving his city for Warsaw. In this poem, Segelowitz draws upon female imagery to convey his sense of displacement as well as his confusion. He remains puzzled about why he is still so enamored of his birthplace and has not begun to love his new home:

> Nothing forces me to love you
> any more as my city
> Yet I remain to you loyal
> [for I am] your man, and I am your poet.[27]

Drawing yet again on female imagery, Segelowitz clearly demonstrates the depth of his love for, and loyalty to, the feminine—though not maternal—Bialystok. Segelowitz adds an erotic dimension to his devotion to Bialystok, by depicting it as a lover who enraptures him for reasons he cannot understand, leaving him unsatisfied and drawn to writing. Though many had left Bialystok long ago, its presence still exerted a powerful, almost mystical hold on those who traced their origins there, and always would, whether they lived in nearby Warsaw, as did Segelowitz, or settled in far more distant capitals, like Babitsh, who in New York would summon feminine imagery to express the primacy of his attachment. To be a Bialystoker Jew outside of Bialystok, as Segelowitz conveys, implied neither a simple nor straightforward attachment. The relationship was complex and demanding, best understood as a tortured love affair. Segelowitz's stress on his continued devotion resonated with Bialystoker Jews throughout the world. In fact, the sheer frequency with which this poem was printed and reprinted in Jewish newspapers read by members of the Bialystok diaspora both in Poland and in the new world, leads to the conclusion that this paean to Bialystok became the defining expression of their attachment to their former home in this dispersed Jewish community.[28]

Female imagery was also summoned in the Bialystok press to convey not only émigrés' confusion but also their overwhelming sense of guilt as they watched contemporary political dilemmas transform life in their former home. In 1922, Nathan Kaplan mourned in the poem "O' Bialystok" for his "mother whose name was once boasted in every city in the land."[29] While "once upon a time you shined as a result of your good fortune" and "you were loved by all Jews and Christians," now "you have been dealt a hard hand" with the destruction of the city's "radiance and magnificence" by war. Despite this turns of events in Bialystok, Kaplan concludes:

> Still you comfort us, O' Bialystok, our dear mother,
> But there is coming a new time
> since your children will not sit quietly
> and they will not stay far away forever.[30]

With galvanizing poetics, Kaplan turned to the press to prod his compatriots to take up arms for their eternally nurturing motherland, "enslaved" both by political circumstances and the abandonment of her children. He emphasized not only that Bialystok still served as a touchstone to which its former residents turned for comfort, but also that many members of Bialystok's Jewish diaspora viewed the radical changes unfolding in Eastern Europe as entwined with their own personal transformations: why had they failed to adequately help their "mother" in her hour of great need? Had migration made them inherently selfish? As he reflected on the poverty, violence, and politics of ethnic nationalism tearing Eastern Europe apart, Kaplan also implicitly questioned the price of migration. His noble and courageous effort to build a new life also entailed a selfish abandonment of Eastern Europe. Did he and his compatriots not respond to their "mother" in her time of need because they had been fundamentally changed by the process of migration? While their radical transformation may not be evident to themselves, Kaplan argued, it was immeasurably clear to all in Bialystok.

The Shtetlization of the City: Bialystok as Holy Jewish Polity and Migration as Exile

Kaplan's questioning of the price of migration by highlighting the ways in which it made Bialystok's Jews more selfish was echoed on the pages of the transnational Bialystoker press. Articles portrayed this city as akin to a small *shtetl* (semi-urban village), the mythic Jewish polis of East European lore. As Dan Miron and David Roskies have shown, the ruptures of the nineteenth century, including rapid urbanization, prompted prominent Yiddish writers to depict the shtetl in their search for a "usable past" upon which they could root their identities.[31] While the shtetl engaged literary elites, such as Sholem Aleichem and Y. L. Peretz, the city captivated the attention of writers who contributed to the *Bialystoker Stimme*, running the gamut from respected Yiddish journalists to unknown émigré ingénues, who also found solace in portraying their former home as a Jewish polity, despite its actual political status.[32]

This vision of Bialystok as an organic Jewish community defined by close personal relations and family closeness is clearly conveyed in the premier issue of the *Bialystoker Stimme*. In an anonymous article succinctly titled "Bialystok," the writer declares, "I am thankful to have once been linked with the narrow and dirty streets of Bialystok." And although Jews in Bialystok "have not yet overcome the troubles of the last eight years," he continues, they are still better off than their compatriots who reside in New York. While a "New York East Side Jew" may think that Jews in Bialystok suffer because they possess only "very small buildings and stark rooms," they are in fact better off than those living in New York because "they are not as lonely as we are."[33] Implicitly contrasting the cold, dirty, and "stark" physical appearance of Bialystok with the warmth of its people, the author emphasizes the disjunction between the tender familial social life in Bialystok and the harshness of life in New York City. While recognizing the terrible economic situation in Bialystok, he chooses its troubles over those faced by people living in New York where few Jews, he claims, enjoy such close personal relationships.

The stress on the nurturing intimacy of Bialystok points to the "shtetlization" of the East European city in the literary culture of East European Jews adjusting to life in America.[34] By recasting East European cities undergoing rapid industrialization as small semi-urban towns, immigrant authors, not only from Bialystok, communicated their deep sense of isolation and ambivalence about the process of migration. Had they made the right decision in leaving Eastern Europe? Would America, or New York in particular, prove to be the "promised land," or had they in fact left it behind? These questions plagued many Yiddish immigrant writers: Binyamin Bialostocki, a poet who arrived in America in 1911, similarly pondered this conundrum in his discussion of the virtues of Vilna, a city with almost 200,000 residents that he called "a shtetl by a highway."[35] In his paean to Pinsk, a city of more than 30,000 residents in Byelorussia, Morris Aizenberg-Brodsky declared his deep love for "Pinsk, my shtetl."[36] Rendering their former urban homes as small Jewish polities endowed with an enveloping tenderness, these authors downplayed their urban pasts to underscore the great achievements in New York.

Jacob Eskolosky, rabbi of New York City's Bes Kneses Anshey Bialistok (Synagogue of the People of Bialystok), conjured up a comparable vision of Bialystok in his congregation's fiftieth anniversary journal. This congregation, located on Willet Street on the Lower East Side, was originally founded in 1878. Marking its fiftieth anniversary in 1928, the synagogue sponsored the publication of a special journal to which Eskolosky contributed the following description of Bialystok and Bialystoker Jewish immigrants:

> Since we all came from . . . [such] an *ir va-'em bi-yisroel* [literally, a city and mother in Israel], a city well-known for its institutions, and its great, wise, learned men, *maskilim* . . . all Bialystokers know how to adapt themselves and better their economic situation . . . [while at the same time] maintaining the traditions we brought with us from Bialystok, the holy inheritance we received from our parents . . . [in contrast to] other Jews who settled in America.[37]

While he does not use the term *shtetl*, Eskolosky centers his description of Bialystok on the phrase "a city and mother in Israel" [*ir va-'em bi-yisroel*], a biblical idiom, traditionally reserved for places renowned for their great piety.[38] In contrast to other descriptions of Bialystok, such as that of Zvi Hirsch Masliansky, famed rabbi and orator of the Lower East Side's Educational Alliance who proclaimed that Bialystok is not "a city and mother in Israel" but rather "a daughter in Israel" since it possessed no "learned Jewish scholars or thinkers," Eskolosky precisely described his former home as a holy space, to distinguish it from materialist and godless America.[39] Echoing literary scholar Dan Miron's point that when an author paints his former home as a center of Jewish piety and learning, he seeks to convey his deep sense of insecurity, Eskolosky's description of Bialystok and its "holy inheritance" highlighted his concern about the bitter struggle between maintaining one's religious commitments and achieving material success.[40] Even the vast sums that Bialystoker Jewish immigrants donated to keep Bes Kneses Anshey Bialystok solvent could not alleviate the rabbi's anxieties about the future of Jewish piety in his new home, where the desire for financial success provoked many to jettison the traditional Jewish observances he cherished.

While the language of piety may be seen to come naturally to rabbis, laymen also invoked Bialystok as a holy Jewish polity in the newspapers of the Bialystok diaspora. Contributors to *Der bialistoker fraynd* [The Bialystoker Comrade], a quarterly published by the Bialystoker Branch 88 of the Workmen's Circle, enshrined the image of Jerusalem—the archetypal Jewish holy city—in depictions of their former home. Bialystok, the "Jerusalem of the Bund," was a sacred place because of its socialist legacy. It inculcated in its residents a distinct "holy" brand of socialist piety that shaped their affiliations and commitments in America, exemplified by the establishment of a Bialystoker branch of the Workmen's Circle. Striving to keep the legacy of "holy" Bialystok alive, these Bialystok socialists hoped to inoculate their readers against the greatest peril facing them in America: the lure of money that pushed many to abandon their deeply held commitments.[41] Combating the perils of the new world was not only achieved in socialist venues, argued Jacob Krepliak, but also by members of the Bialystoker Center.[42] "When one hears the phrase '*hanukas ha-bayes* [lit., dedication of the sanctuary]," observed Krepliak at the 1923 dedication of the Bialystoker Center building, "one thinks immediately of the dedication of the Holy Temple that after much war, destruction, death, and exile was rebuilt and became a spiritual center for the Jewish people." Lending biblical dimensions to the opening of the Bialystoker Center building, Krepliak compared the rebuilding of the Temple with the erection of the Bialystoker Center. As yearning for Zion and Jerusalem had inspired Jewish devotion for centuries, so, too, did Bialystok now exert a powerful ethical hold on its former residents, Krepliak concluded, pushing them to build a similarly holy institution greater than that of any "other landsmanshaftn organization" in the world.[43]

Bialystok as Imperial Power and Migration as Colonial Mission

The vision of Bialystok as Jerusalem acquired a political cast in the lead story of the February 1924 *Bialystoker Stimme:* "Bialystok: A Colonial Power." There, Dr. Herman Frank, a Bialystok-born,

German-trained sociologist who had immigrated to America in 1923, compared Bialystok to a great colonial empire:

> In the political terminology, the words "colonial power" connote a certain concept very clearly—England with its large array of colonies throughout the world . . . it would seem as though the concept of "colonial power" and Bialystok seem to have little in common. However, over the past few years in front of our eyes has occurred a communal phenomenon [so that now] one can correctly speak about a new colonial power—Bialystok.
>
> . . . Following the catastrophe of 1914 . . . the mutual dependence and strong connection between the colony and the motherland first became apparent . . . and from that moment when blood was first displayed, a special bond predominated between the two parts of our people, like the familial bond of a daughter and an old mother, like the bond of a colony and her motherland.[44]

The notion that England—the largest imperial power in the interwar world—and Bialystok—a small, war-ravaged industrial city in northeastern Poland—were comparable colonial powers is evidently preposterous. By imagining Bialystok in such a "style," to use the words of Benedict Anderson,[45] Frank conveyed a new understanding of empire as transcending nation-states and military power.[46] Attuned to the irony of his claims, Frank sought to capture the intensity of the bond Bialystoker Jews felt for their former home as well as the political impact this connection had on life back in Bialystok. Reimagining Bialystok as an imperial center with Jews at its helm, Frank metaphorically empowered Bialystok Jewry, portraying them not as disenfranchised Polish citizens but rather as members of an international empire.

But Frank did not only offer up a new empowering vision of Jews in Bialystok; he also articulated a fresh understanding of migration. By portraying himself and other Bialystoker Jews as "colonists" working on behalf of their motherland, Frank recast his emigration as a colonial mission. This vision of migration spoke directly to the acute sense of guilt and frustration many immigrants felt during the interwar period as they watched the disintegration of Eastern Europe. Viewing migration through an imperialist lens enabled immigrants to see their move as not motivated by selfish desires but rather as the expression of an intense devotion to their former home. Émigrés' sense of ambivalence over having left their beloved homeland in Eastern Europe caused this image of Bialystok as an "empire of charity" to gain currency throughout the émigré community. Muttel Dovesh, a Bialystoker living in New York, thundered in the July 1924 issue of the *Bialystoker Stimme:*

> It is now evident that our Bialystok is truly a colonial power, a true empire, which is spread throughout the entire world with a central kingdom at the head in Eastern Europe.
>
> Is that not something truly we should all admire!?! [Bialystok] overcame all adversity to become a colonial power. And what is more interesting is the fact that Bialystok has emerged as a colonial power not by diplomats, armies or violence but by a more original method: the charity box.[47]

According to Dovesh, the laudable efforts of émigrés, rather than those of the inhabitants of Bialystok itself, transformed the city into a "great kingdom." All Bialystoker Jews throughout the world must recognize, he concluded, that New York is the "central force driving the gigantic Bialystok empire since it was the official residence of the Bialystoker charity box [*pushke*]."[48] Far from abandoning their former home, immigrants enacted their inexorable commitment to it by collecting money for Bialystok and talking about it within an imperial framework. In their own eyes, immigrant activism expanded Bialystok beyond the geographic borders of Poland.

The colonial vision of migration—marking the expansion rather than the abandonment of Eastern Europe—became prevalent among many members of Bialystok's Jewish diaspora. With this in mind, Zelig Tigel juxtaposed Bialystok onto Warsaw. Tigel, a correspondent for Warsaw's *Tageblat,* maintained that Bialystoker Jews' migration not only expanded Bialystok beyond the boundaries of the Polish nation-state, but even elevated the status of the city within Polish Jewish society. While Warsaw's Jewish community plays a leading role in defining Jewish political culture in Poland, he observed, in America, "Bialystokers . . . are clearly the leaders [of the Jewish community]," with "Warsaw's émigrés trail[ing] far behind."[49]

"Bialystoker immigrants should be very proud" of their impressive accomplishments, Tigel maintained, because their activism transformed how Jews in Eastern Europe think about Bialystok. While still considered "secondary to Warsaw in the old home," Bialystok had become "a clear leader of Jewish life" with the extraordinary Bialystok Center guiding Jews "in the new home."[50] Although geographically limited by the borders of the Second Polish Republic, Bialystok and Warsaw were, in his mind, both part of a larger Jewish "empire."[51]

New Visions of Bialystok within Bialystok Itself

The new map of Jewish Eastern Europe transformed the way Jews living in Bialystok envisioned their home, and led them to rethink their place in the Second Polish Republic. The correspondence between David Sohn, executive director of the Bialystoker Center and editor of the *Bialystoker Stimme,* and Pesach Kaplan, editor of *Dos naye lebn* (The New Life), the most widely circulated newspaper in interwar Bialystok, shows that Jews in Bialystok remained extremely interested in reading what their fellow compatriots living abroad thought about their former home.[52] Anna Gepner, whose uncle Eliezer Rubinstein edited Australia's Yiddish weekly *Oystralisher idishe lebn,* recalled the deluge of requests her uncle received to write for *Dos naye lebn* about life in Australia.[53] Sohn sent numerous contributions that recounted stories about Bialystokers in America as well as other articles on political developments in America, earning him the title of "special New York correspondent."[54]

Such a transatlantic dialogue was by no means particular to Bialystoker Jews. The dense literary entanglements of Yiddish journalists in the United States and Poland—rarely addressed in contemporary scholarship but abundantly clear to most Jews between the wars—gave the interwar Yiddish press a distinctly international flavor. With correspondents scattered throughout the world, the internationalism of the Yiddish press and its readership fostered cultural innovation on both sides of the Atlantic and created a new set of international celebrities who redefined Jewish popular culture through cartoons, satire, the Yiddish theater, and film.[55]

In Bialystok's three most popular Yiddish newspapers, *Dos naye lebn, Unzer lebn,* and *Naye byalistoker shtime,* journalists constantly tried to locate themselves within the region's new political order. With its frequent front-page coverage of American activism on behalf of their former home, and regular columns that queried "What have you heard in America?" or "Notes from Bialystoker Jews in Russia?," the Yiddish press in Bialystok played a critical role in spreading the idea that Bialystoker Jews throughout the world belonged to a single political entity. The most widely circulated Yiddish newspaper in interwar Bialystok, *Dos naye lebn,* was particularly important in this effort. In its front-page reporting on events in the United States, Russia, and Palestine, as well as in its regular feature columns concerning Bialystokers around the world, the paper forged "an imagined community" among its readers, who saw themselves as positioned at the center of a worldwide dispersion.[56] As this newspaper emphasized the international connections of Bialystok Jewry, it also questioned the limits of Polish authority, in editorials that argued persistently against Bialystok's inclusion in the Second Polish Republic.[57] With editorials entitled "We Need America's Help!" and "An American Aid Bank for Jews in Bialystok," *Dos naye lebn* enthusiastically embraced Americans' involvement in Bialystok's financial rebuilding.[58] In these editorials, reprints of articles from the New York *Bialystoker Stimme* and *Dos naye lebn* cultivated among its readers a vision of Bialystok as an international city, its destiny tied to the outcome of debates in the Polish Sejm (Poland's Lower House of Parliament) and to political developments beyond Poland's geographic borders.[59]

An understanding of Bialystok as an international political entity surfaced vividly in the writings of Pesach Kaplan, editor of *Dos naye lebn,* who proclaimed in 1931 that "Bialystok's unique character" was evident not only in "the boundless untiring energies of its populace" but in the fact that "wherever there are a few Bialystoker Jews, regardless of their number, they immediately organize themselves into a colony, in order to support their motherland and [to keep] in touch with other Bialystoker colonies scattered throughout the world."[60] His use of the term *colony* suggests that he had not only read the writings of his former compatriots now living in America but had also internalized the vision they had sculpted of their former home and their relationship to it. Clearly inspired by the imagery contained in newspapers such as the *Bialystoker Stimme,* Kaplan consciously distanced it from the surrounding Polish countryside. Considering the antagonism he and other Jews were facing from their Polish neighbors, such rhetoric was quite comforting: despite the fact that their home was geographically located in the Second Polish Republic, they were part of a larger political entity whose loyal subjects were scattered throughout the world.

Embracing the Great Colonial Mission: Images of Bialystok, the People of Bialystok, and Migration in the 1930s

Few imagined Bialystok as a Jewish polity during the 1930s, a period marked by anxiety and uncertainty for all members of this dispersed community.[61] Rising antisemitism, along with extensive unemployment, prompted Jewish immigrants throughout the United States to question their previously rosy view of their futures in America. But the news from Poland—where antisemitic legislation and unemployment prompted severe economic decline—intensified émigrés' anxiety. Despite the problems they found in their new home, as well as the challenges faced there, these newcomers came to understand that the United States offered them the best options for an economically secure future.[62] A special photo-journalist series in the New York *Forverts* highlighted the penury of Bialystok Jewry and the ways in which rising unemployment and antisemitism threatened their former home's very existence.[63]

The poetry of Rosa Nevodovska, a Yiddish poet who had emigrated from Bialystok in 1928 at the age of twenty-nine, suggests that émigrés addressed their growing anxiety about their own personal vulnerability as well as their growing despair over the situation of their former compatriots in Poland by describing Bialystok as a still-beloved home, yet one to view from afar. In her poem "Homesickness," written in 1933, she stated:

> My beloved home, gentle and thoughtful
> My distant home, between the forest and the valley
> like the sun at dawn, growing anew with me. . . .

> Throughout the world, I still carry you with me
> Throughout new lands, which are mild and beautiful
> I must make myself forget that which I loved from birth
> But what can replace the tones of your beloved voice?[64]

Nevodovska, who taught Yiddish language and literature in New York, echoed in her poems the loneliness and alienation of earlier émigré contributors to the *Bialystoker Stimme*.[65] Like her predecessors, she drew on nature motifs to convey the beauty of Bialystok, yet she did not just refer to it as her "beloved home." It was now also a "distant home." Her added emphasis on fear and distance reflected the tense circumstances of the 1930s that forced émigrés to realize that despite their grievances with life in America, their present home was more secure than Poland. Thus, in contrast to earlier émigré writers, Nevodovska felt compelled to acknowledge the difficulty she faced in forgetting the primal love she felt for Bialystok, a love that nothing seemed to replace.

Nevodovska reiterated these themes in her much celebrated paean to Bialystok, "To My Home-City," a poem that clearly illustrates how the events of the 1930s re-tinted émigrés' nostalgic view of their former home:

> I love my home city
> the streets, the alleys
> the forests, the rolling fields
> . . . the river from which many times, I have drunk
>
> I see our cemetery
> . . . graves after graves
> of our martyrs [of the 1906 Pogrom]—
> in sorrow
> the dark pillar which calls,
> to the West, East, North, and South[66]
>
> I love my home-city
> the people, the close friends
> the streets, the forest and the river—
> of all the cities in the world—
> none are as closely dear to me—
> My city! I look to you from afar![67]

Despite beginning and ending her poem about her longings for her "home-city" with its beautiful streets and forests, the core of the poem stresses the central role antisemitism played in shaping life in Bialystok. At its center, the lengthy description of Bialystok's Jewish cemetery, with its memorial to the martyrs of the 1906 pogrom that "calls out" to all in the West, East, North, and South, evocatively demonstrates why the poet views Bialystok "from afar" rather than living in the city so "dear to her." Far from reflecting on the price of migration or expressing a desire to return to Bialystok as writers had done a decade earlier, Nevodovska incorporates the terrifying new realities facing her former home. As the Jewish community of Bialystok was slowly being strangled by economic recession and Polish antisemitism, Nevodovska could not entertain the hopeful vision of Bialystok that had endured throughout the 1920s. She understood—along with so many of her compatriots—that America, for better or worse, would remain home.

The pages of the 1930s transnational Bialystok press are filled with similar views of Bialystok, suggesting that as the city grew to be a more distant memory and its political situation more dire, immigrants' nostalgic desire to return diminished. To be sure, it was a long and difficult process to fully divest themselves of their former home. Many still harbored yearnings for their utopian vision of life in pre-1917 Bialystok. As David Sohn noted in his description of Bialystok in the anniversary souvenir journal of Bialystoker Unterstitzungs Verein Somach Noflim in 1931, "Bialystok has indeed a peculiar charm of its own and a particular pride."[68] Yet, as he watched antisemitic economic boycotts threaten the very existence of Bialystok's Jewish community, Sohn was forced to acknowledge the pessimistic reality of life there that "neither failed nor faltered in the midst of its numerous difficulties and hardships."[69] These depressing realities prompted him to develop a newfound acceptance of America that dovetailed with a new vision of migration: "The spirit and spunk of Bialystok, a cosmopolitan city," wrote Sohn, "is remarkably preserved . . . within its sons and daughters, in all points and places, times and climes." Migration, far from representing an act of abandonment, Sohn argued, in fact assured that Bialystok's legacy would never disappear. Émigrés' success in the new world proved essential to preserving their former home's "spirit and spunk."

This vision of migration as mission was further developed by Sohn in other writings, in which he often compared Bialystoker immigrants in America to "pioneers," "pilgrims," and other "great American explorers." By arguing that his compatriots had ventured to the United States to "explore and to map out new territories" for their motherland, Sohn simultaneously reiterated a vision of Bialystok as an inspirational homeland while he embedded Bialystoker Jewish émigrés' experience into the defining narrative of American national identity.[70] Their intense bond to their former home reinforced their strong ties to America. Émigrés embraced Sohn's vision and began to constantly deploy such terms as *colonist, pioneer,* and *pilgrim* throughout the 1930s, thereby advancing the idea that Bialystoker Jews, or "Bialystoker colonists," could be both passionate Bialystoker patriots and loyal Americans. To further illustrate the compatibility of these two homelands, Sohn turned to using more transliterated English in his descriptions of Bialystok and throughout the *Bialystoker Stimme*. Moreover, echoing trends in the larger Yiddish press in America, the *Bialystoker Stimme* began, in 1936, to include English pages, with both original articles and translated pieces from the Yiddish section of the magazine. This linguistic shift and summoning of colonialist imagery conveyed how members of this diaspora community began to acclimate to their new homeland in America. While America could not compare to Bialystok, it became less of an exile and more of a permanent home.

As the "colonial" image of migration resurfaced once again on the pages of the Bialystoker press, a corollary idea also gained currency: far from marking an abandonment of a beloved motherland, migration came to represent the quintessential Bialystok experience. In other words, Bialystoker Jews enacted the central component of their regional identity by leaving their former home.[71] Writing in 1933 to celebrate the tenth anniversary of the Bialystoker Center's Ladies' Auxiliary, its president Ida Adack described Bialystok as "a magnetic force" as evidenced not by its forests or waterfalls but by the fact that it had filled all Bialystoker "souls with pride throughout the world," provoking them to spread "throughout the world [their] fine tastes and beautiful feelings." Building on Adack's emphasis on the people and not the city, David Sohn claimed in 1933 that the grandeur of his former home was illustrated by the "men and women of culture, learning, wisdom, manners and refinement" who have built up "the Bialystoker Colony in America," not the city's natural attributes.[72]

This radical shift away from celebrating the physical Bialystok to lauding its people highlights the increasingly important role a sense of peoplehood played in this dispersed community as its members reconfigured their East European diasporic identity in response to events in Eastern Europe and in America.[73] Since poverty and Polish antisemitism transformed Bialystok into a place few émigrés recognized, and their memories of their former lives were fading, the only raw and vivid memories they all shared concerned the act of migration. Through the constant retelling of their common origin in Bialystok and their shared experience of dispersal, members of the diaspora community articulated a new vision of their identity that revolved around the act of moving and the sense of camaraderie it engendered. A 1940 article by Solomon Kahan, a musician and Yiddish educator who settled in Mexico, best exemplifies this shift in emphasis:[74]

> If someone would ask me: What special characteristics differenti-
> ate a Bialystoker from all other immigrants? It would not take me
> long to answer: spiritual strength, dynamism, a lust for creation,
> and a strong desire to be close to other Bialystokers . . . [for] once
> you are a Bialystoker—you are always a Bialystoker. . . .
>
> Last but certainly not least, I have been among many differ-
> ent Eastern European Jewish immigrants, but with none do I
> feel such a close affinity as I do with the Bialystokers . . . When
> a Bialystoker meets with another Bialystoker while emigrating,
> they soon enter a warm, spiritual context. . . . and together they
> soon feel like they are in their eternal birth city.[75]

Here, Kahan clearly illustrates that the strong links binding this scattered community were not its members' shared link with their physical birthplace but their common experience of dispersal. Echoing metaphors used in the nineteenth-century Yiddish literary portrayal of the shtetl, Kahan contends that central to being a Bialystoker was the phenomenon of leaving Bialystok.[76] Migration became the defining trait of Bialystok Jewry. Still articulating an eternal loyalty to his former home, Kahan argues that only through migration could Bialystok Jews appreciate their unique legacy. Arguing that people, rather than locale or landscape, create (and recreate) Bialystok, Kahan foretold the mood of the 1940s, when writing about Bialystok became entwined with the treatment of the as yet unknown effects of the Second World War. With his new emphasis on Bialystoker "warm" spirituality, Kahan formulated a rationale for Bialystoker Jews to remain linked together even in the possible absence of a physical Bialystok. Such an understanding of communal identity, dependent on a shared sense of peoplehood and not a specific place, would be expanded upon during the 1940s, particularly as the viability of Jewish Bialystok became more threatened.

"Bialystok Transplanted and Transformed": Images of Bialystok in the 1940s

The ominous sense of foreboding that is hinted at in Kahan's writing became even more pronounced in the Bialystok émigré press as the war progressed. The Nazi invasion of Poland in 1941 definitively divided Bialystok Jewish émigrés from their former home. All publication of Jewish newspapers in Bialystok ceased. Most immigrants lost contact with their loved ones who had remained in Bialystok.[77] This total separation, along with the knowledge of the Nazi menace, engendered great fear in the transnational Bialystoker émigré community. In September 1940, David Sohn summoned the metaphor of *goles* (exile) to convey how the ancient expulsion was being reenacted in Bialystok, as thousands of Jews were being forced from their homes by the invading Russian army.[78] The Bialystoker refugee crisis was depicted as an archetypal exile scene with cosmic overtones, locating the experience of Bialystok Jewry within the larger chain of Jewish history. Such an invoking of sacred Jewish texts was prevalent in the early twentieth century, when after the First World War many Russian Jews invoked metaphors from traditional Jewish texts to express the depths of their despair over the war's devastation.[79] As they had done in the wake of the war, Bialystok's émigrés again began to sacralize Bialystok by using idioms traditionally associated with the destruction of Jerusalem. As in depictions of the shtetl in the nineteenth century, Bialystok came to represent a tiny exiled Jerusalem, a destroyed Jewish polity par excellence. Depicting Bialystok as consumed "by the flames of war," Sohn turned to idioms and metaphors reminiscent of texts such as the Book of Lamentations that described Jerusalem's burning. These tropes allowed him to impart his personal anguish at the realization that he could no longer consider himself a Bialystoker pioneer but was now a permanently homeless Bialystoker exile.[80]

In 1943, reflecting Sohn's and many Bialystoker émigrés' fears and deep despair over the fate of Jewish Bialystok, Abraham Shevach, an émigré living in Buenos Aires, wrote the following tribute to the memory of his former home, entitled "Bialystok My Home." Since memory often leads to an unpredictable process of construction, Shevach's piece reinvents Bialystok as an abandoned utopia, suggesting the ways in which the Nazi invasion provoked members of the Bialystok diaspora once again to envision their former home and to question the price of migration. Shevach wrote:

> How can I forget my old dear home?
> How can I forget from where I stem?
> How can I pull out the roots of a tree which has already
>   grown for generations?
>
> I recall Bialystok, before I had deserted you,
> happy, sincere, no one could hate you
> The houses, the streets, the people,
> a divine presence was all around them . . .
>
> Bialystok—my home!
> Bialystok—my dream! . . .
>
> Bialystok of today
> How can I now be silent or act indifferent?
> How can I forget my home, even for a minute?

How can I remain far away. . . .
when I see my brothers there bathed in blood?!

. . . Bialystok—my home!
Bialystok—my dream!
After the death you will become born anew;
have courage and have faith—
victory will come
and the whole world will no longer be enslaved.[81]

Articulating the inability to fill the void left by Bialystok that many of Bialystok's émigré writers before him expressed, Shevach conveyed his deep sense of despair and hopelessness over the fate of Bialystok. Far from trying to invert his despair by rendering his former home as the powerful center of an empire, Shevach depicted it as a place that only existed in his mind. As he questioned his behavior and wondered why he "remained so far away" and had "deserted" his beloved former home, Shevach still described his "dear old home," as a dreamlike or imaginary place engulfed by a "divine presence." While he retained some hope for Bialystok's future as a center for Jewish life—a time when "the whole world will no longer be enslaved"—Shevach's invocation of the Divine and use of the word *dream* illustrates how fundamentally the Nazi menace changed Bialystoker Jews' perception and depiction of Bialystok.[82] His deep belief in the perseverance of Bialystok, however, could not overshadow his realization that Bialystok probably no longer existed in the real world. While he shared the pain articulated by earlier generations of émigré writers, Shevach feared he was permanently cut off from his past.

As the news that the Bialystok ghetto had been liquidated reached America, members of Bialystok's diaspora turned to the press to console themselves over their loss. Embracing once again several of the images presented by David Sohn in earlier decades, most notably that Bialystok remained eternally alive in its diaspora. As Joseph Chaikan's 1944 feature article, "Bialystok: Transplanted and Transformed," argued, even though the physical Bialystok may have been destroyed, no elegies should be written for it, for the city was still alive, as evidenced by the numerous Bialystoker organizational activities throughout the world.[83] Bialystoker émigrés had "saved" their hometown by rebuilding it on new shores. Chaikan's notion that Bialystoker émigré communities kept Bialystok alive ultimately led him to conclude that now the United States, the place with the strongest and most active Bialystoker émigré community, was truly a "second Bialystok."

Arguing that Bialystok was "transplanted" to the United States, Chaikan downplayed the devastating loss of the city as a means to console himself and other Bialystoker émigrés. As historian Deborah Lipstadt points out, such a lack of engagement with the complete destruction of Bialystok and rupture with the past reflects the general incredulity that many Jews and American leaders expressed toward the destruction of Jewish Eastern Europe in 1944.[84] By suggesting that Bialystok was alive, though transplanted and transformed, Chaikan emphasized continuity above rupture, reassuring Bialystoker émigrés that they had made the right choices. Through migration, they had not abandoned their compatriots or acted indifferently toward their plight, as Abraham Shevach claimed. Rather, their migration had saved Bialystok.

David Sohn and other readers of the *Bialystoker Stimme* echoed Chaikan's vision of émigré institutions and publications keeping Bialystok alive. In 1944, Sohn wrote a new history of Bialystok in honor of the Bialystoker Center's twenty-fifth anniversary: opening his narrative with a discussion of notable "Bialystoker personalities of the past," such as Rabbi Samuel Mohilever and Dr. Ludwig Zamenhof. Sohn drew a direct line between these leaders and the achievements of émigrés who dedicated their energy to running the Bialystoker Center in the United States. "The peak" of Bialystoker activism, Sohn argued, was reached "not in Bialystok," but rather in New York when "Bialystok landsmenshaftn in 1919 establish[ed] their first Federation of Bialystoker Organizations known as the Bialystoker Center" whose leaders epitomized "the great chain of Bialystoker achievement."[85] Volf Garber, who lived in Montreal, Canada, and had never seen the Bialystoker Center, maintained that its publication, the *Bialystoker Stimme,* filled the void left by the Holocaust, helping him grapple with the loss of Bialystok. As he eloquently described, "When I come from work and find the *Stimme,* it is as though as I am being grabbed by my best friend, with greetings from my Bialystoker family, that is scattered and dispersed throughout all the land."[86] Garber might not have been able to return to Bialystok, but by reading the *Stimme*, he argued, he could lead "a full [Bialystoker] life." In short, Bialystok's Jews in North America wrote about their own community as a way to avoid directly confronting the devastating loss of Bialystok itself.[87]

Such a denial of Bialystok's "death," and their view that Bialystok was resurrected in the Bialystoker émigré communal organizations in the United States, was not, however, accepted by Bialystoker émigrés throughout the world. In South America, members of the Bialystok émigré community would not deny the enormity of their loss and turned to writing about Bialystok to "bear witness" to the world that had been lost, to use the words of literary scholar Terrence Des Pres.[88] A poignant refutation of Bialystok's resurrection in America can be seen in the writings of Sonia Rapalovsky, a Bialystoker émigré living in Santiago, Chile, who vehemently attacked the idea that Bialystok could ever be transplanted to another place. The character of the city could never be replicated, she intoned:

> [Bialystok] was a name that demanded love and respect from all who heard it. Why specifically Bialystok? There were many cities in Poland which were bigger in size or had richer populations. Bialystoker was even a proletariat city, so what was the great merit? Why was there such a "local patriotism?" . . . [It is because] Bialystok always was a fortress of Jewishness and Jewish culture. Bialystok was a true barrier against assimilation like no other city in the world.[89]

In Rapalovsky's eyes, the only way Bialystoker émigrés could repay their debt to their destroyed former home was not by claiming that they had rebuilt it but by accepting its total loss. Trying to explain why Bialystok yielded such "local patriotism," Rapalovsky constructed Bialystok as the ultimate bulwark against assimilation, a model Jewish city. Being a Bialystoker, in Rapalovsky's eyes, demanded a class (proletariat) consciousness as well as a religious or ethnic affiliation. More than simply reflecting her despair over Bialystok's destruction, Rapalovsky's description suggests the

never-ending pain she experienced as a result of her family's acculturation to their new home. The prevention of assimilation emerges
as Bialystok's greatest achievement in her portrayal, highlighting
her greatest disappointment with her new life in Chile: in contrast
to other Latin American countries, East European Jewish émigrés
quickly integrated into Chilean culture, often intermarrying, as they
were celebrated for expanding the economy and modernizing the
country.[90] The pain Rapalovsky expresses entwines her feelings of
the loss for her former homeland with her despondency over "losing" her children to another cultural world. Envisioning Bialystok as
an organic Jewish community that provided "a true barrier against
assimilation," Rapalovsky reflected anew on the painful sacrifices
demanded by the processes of migration and acculturation.

The rendering of Bialystok as a model Jewish polity was most
striking among those who found themselves in Palestine in the 1940s;
their vision did not diminish following the establishment of the state
of Israel. Reflecting a larger trend in the dispersed East European
Jewish community, Jews from Bialystok could only write about
the creation of Israel as entwined with the destruction of Jewish
Eastern Europe. Conjoining images of Israel and Bialystok, writers
such as Zalman Segelowitz discussed these two watershed events as
they struggled to incorporate Israel into their collective identities.
Segelowitz, famed for his paean to his "lover" Bialystok that became
the anthem of his international community, escaped to Palestine in
1940. Although he often wrote about his cultural alienation from
the Hebrew-dominated culture in Tel Aviv, he also felt comfort in
Tel Aviv, a city he saw as cut from the same cloth as Bialystok. In his
eyes Tel Aviv, like Bialystok, emerged from the dust thanks to the
tireless efforts of East European Jews.

The strong links between Bialystok, the model Jewish city, and
Tel Aviv, the Jewish city of the future, to use the words of Barbara
Mann, are summed up in a 1943 article penned by Segelowitz about
his old home and his new one. While "everything . . . was all white
sand three years ago," Segelowitz begins, now "when I gaze out my
window," I see "the streets from the north," lined with houses possessing a unique "symmetry of half-round, shallow façades." How
did men build up [Tel Aviv] in such a short time? he rhetorically

queried. The answer lay far from the Mediterranean, in the forests of northeastern Poland, as he elaborated:

> And how had my city of Bialystok been built? Two hundred years ago it was only the Branicki Palace . . . and a few houses. Then came the Germans, and they founded a textile factory. Then a Jew came, and he founded a second factory. Two hundred years later, my city is home to one hundred thousand people. And all of this change occurred so quickly. Legendary speed, the transformation happened in secret, just like things have been built up here [in Tel Aviv.][91]

Finding the answer to his query about Tel Aviv's rapid expansion in Bialystok's historical past, Segelowitz presents these two cities as mirror images. Acknowledging that Germans and Poles were present in the city's past, Segelowitz nonetheless constructs Bialystok as a Jewish polity, transformed overnight from a small Polish village into a large industrial city through Jewish efforts. By asserting that the construction of Tel Aviv continued the legacy of Bialystok, Segelowitz directly challenged the Zionist narrative that constantly strove to distance the new Jewish state from previous Jewish life in Eastern Europe. Segelowitz, like many Bialystoker émigrés, could not accept the Zionist ideology's negation of the vitality of Jewish life in the Diaspora; Bialystok's Jews saw Bialystok as a vital Jewish cultural center. In fact, as Yisroel Prenski, a Bialystoker Jew who immigrated to Palestine in the 1920s once remarked, "Bialystok was just like Tel Aviv. You get the same feeling in both of being in a Jewish city, but in fact, Bialystok felt even more Jewish than Tel Aviv."[92]

Echoing Prenski's sentiments, other Bialystoker Jewish émigrés in Palestine, and after 1948, Israel, would diverge markedly from Zionist discourse, arguing through their portrayal of Bialystok that their former home in Eastern Europe provided a model for the new Jewish state. As members of the Irgun Yotzei Bialystok (Organization of Bialystoker Émigrés) articulated in their charter:

> Bialystok, our city, a large city with a large Jewish community, a city of Torah and education, love of fellow Jews, justice and charity. Jews founded it, built it and perfected it and spread the reputation of its products and commerce to the far corners

of the earth and to distant isles. It was at the forefront of many
movements of national and social liberation. . . . Jewish culture
in its numerous facets flourished in it. . . . [93]

Bialystok is not only described as a Jewish space, devoid of non-Jews,
but it also represents a "perfect" Jewish polity. Employing terms used
often by nineteenth and twentieth-century Zionist thinkers to depict
their utopian dreams for the new Jewish state, these émigrés living in
Israel cast Bialystok as a prototype of a Jewish nation-state, spreading its products and ideals of liberation throughout the world.[94] If
American Zionists, as historian Jonathan Sarna argues, saw Israel in
the image of the "model" American state, Bialystoker Jewish émigrés
identified Bialystok as the blueprint for the state of Israel.[95] By reinventing Bialystok in such a way, they inserted themselves directly
into the Zionist narrative, which was slowly redefining the contours
of Jewish diasporic discourse and identity throughout the world.

"The triumph of Zionism," Matthew Jacobson notes, "created a
peculiar position for Jews who voluntarily remained in the 'exile' of
the Diaspora." Some of these Jews became consumed by writing to
explain their new diasporic identities to themselves and others.[96] Such
a peculiar position was quite familiar to Bialystoker Jewish émigrés,
who had long felt themselves to be displaced exiles but never returned
to Bialystok except in their imaginations and writings. Their feelings
of dislocation engendered by migration were now compounded by
the devastation of the Second World War and the triumph of Zionism,
discussed in more detail in the coming chapter.

Conclusion

Despite external manifestations of successful adaptation as illustrated by their social institutions and philanthropic organizations,
many members of the dispersed Bialystok Jewish migrant community
found their feelings of dislocation too intense to put behind them.
Hence, they established newspapers to reflect upon their concerns as
they searched for strength to build new lives. To be sure, the process
of acculturation was at work during the interwar period, as Jews
in the new world and Eastern Europe adapted to life in their new

homes. Yet, as the pages of the transnational Bialystok Jewish press suggest, East European Jews held tenaciously to earlier attachments and orientations, most notably to their regional identities, and still portrayed themselves as belonging to a distinct community rooted in Eastern Europe.[97] As they looked to the map of that region to define the boundaries of their identities in their new homes, these Jewish immigrants saw the void left by Eastern Europe eclipsing the promise of the new world. For many immigrants, the creative process of adaptation became entwined with, and in some cases even aided by, that void.[98] As Paul Novick, a Jew from Brisk [Brest-Litovsk], summed up, "Just what is Brisk? The truth is Brisk is what we want it to be."[99]

Between 1921 and 1949, the *Bialystoker Stimme, Der bialistoker fraynd, Bialistoker vegn,* and a host of other publications sponsored by this far-flung-community offered many different visions of Eastern Europe through which its contributors protested current conditions there, commented on circumstances in their new homes, and policed the boundaries of their communal identities. In their search for a way to assuage the separation of migration and find a way to be a "Bialystoker Jew" outside of Bialystok, some émigrés echoed the literary reconstruction of the shtetl, while others employed imperial and biblical idioms to describe Bialystok.[100] Regardless of the different visions they presented of their former home, all contributors gave voice to feelings that transformed the ways in which Bialystok's Jews on both sides of the Atlantic viewed themselves, the process of migration, and their relationships with one another and to the nation-states in which they lived. In short, the transnational Bialystok Jewish press not only reflected upon communal change, but actually served as the motor for change.

Bialystoker Jewish émigrés were not the only Jewish émigrés who engaged in such an endeavor. Thousands of East European Jews constantly reinvented their former homes on the pages of the landsmanshaft press in ways that belie the common view that East European Jews believed they were "stateless" or "deterritorialized." As the depictions of Bialystok in various publications produced by its former residents suggest, the larger political debates concerning the relationship between place and Jewish identity and the eternally vexing question of the relationship of Jews to the East European state—dominated by Zionist thinkers and Diaspora Nationalists in Eastern Europe—did not vanish as a result of migration. Rather, they were projected onto a new terrain. More attention must be paid to the voices of East European Jewish émigrés in these debates, who advanced a fresh vision of both Jewish identity and Eastern Europe when they represented the cities and towns of Eastern Europe as quintessential Jewish homelands. In crafting such a vision, they repeated the trend that had long preceded them: writing about Zion to reflect upon their visions of themselves, their feelings of longings for former homes, and their own displacement.

If migration separated Jews from Eastern Europe, the Second World War irreparably severed them from it. With the loss of Jewish Eastern Europe, their reflections began to dance around several pressing questions: how would they sustain their diasporic identity without a "homeland"? Could Bialystok once again serve as a center of Jewish life? Or they asked the quintessential question Jews faced for centuries, albeit now focused on Bialystok: how would émigrés be able to cultivate a diasporic community without any clear territorial cohesiveness? As we shall see in the following chapter, these questions would intensify and become more complex as this community turned to rebuild and reshape itself in the years following the Second World War.

CHAPTER 5

Shifting Centers, Conflicting Philanthropists: Rebuilding, Resettling, and Remembering Jewish Bialystok in the Post-Holocaust Era

The mood was both jubilant and apprehensive as fifty-five representatives of Bialystok's Jews from around the world gathered on August 20, 1949, in New York for the third World Bialystoker Convention. Their task was to formulate new strategies to address the grim plight of those Jews who survived the war, returned to Bialystok, and wished to begin life anew. Vacillating between disbelief and horror, this international group scrambled to salvage what was left of the world they once knew. But they also sought to address a deeper existential question: what did it mean to be a "Bialystoker" if no Jewish Bialystok existed? As conferees struggled with the realities of postwar Poland, the "whole conference," recalled one participant, "took on the semblance of one large splendid and spirited demonstration of Bialystoker stubbornness (*bialistoker akshones*) . . . [and] courage."[1] Despite the astounding formation of a new Jewish state in the mythical homeland of the Jews, some members of this dispersed Jewish migrant community could not imagine expressing loyalties to any homeland other than their former home in Poland.

Conferees' initial jubilation and sense of shared purpose was rapidly forgotten as they wrestled with and argued over the quagmire of emotional, existential and geopolitical issues raised by the total destruction of the Second World War and the practically concurrent founding of the State of Israel. While scholars and popular writers continually examine diasporic groups' relationship to their former homes and remain fascinated by the issue of Holocaust memory, few have paid close attention to the painful debates that raged among many East European Jewish regional groups in the aftermath of the Second World War.[2] Mourning the fate of Jewish Bialystok, Bialystok's dispersed Jews immediately sent money to rebuild their former home, a common response among East European Jews rarely discussed by scholars of the post-war era.[3] The shift to support Israel in the 1950s must be viewed as part of a complex international matrix of events that took place when persistent Polish antisemitism quashed hopes for the renewal of Jewish life in Poland. By the 1950s, creating spaces—both physical and literary—to "bear witness" to the great legacy of Jewish Bialystok became the unspoken mission that knitted together this dispersed community. But the growing rifts among Bialystok's Jews about how adequately to project to the world their former home's legacy ultimately tore apart the bonds of this transnational Jewish community.[4]

In contrast to other diasporic groups, Bialystok's Jewish diaspora saw its bonds irreparably weakened rather than solidified by the trauma of the war, as vividly illustrated by the concluding compromise of the 1949 World Bialystoker Convention. Unable to rally all attendees around one project, the conference committed itself to raising money to erect a "town of Bialystok" in Israel and to producing literary projects that would "pass on the golden Bialystok heritage" to "their children and children's children" for generations to come (sof kol ha-doyres)."[5] The continued persistent loyalty of this one small slice of the East European Jewish diaspora to its region of origin was echoed throughout the larger Jewish world, illustrating up close why the entrenchment of Israel, to use the words of Deborah Dash Moore, as "an affirmed and celebrated component of Jewish identity" during the postwar period "was far from inevitable."[6] As the coming pages narrate, the failure of Jewish communal life to take root again in Bialystok was likely the result of postwar antisemitic violence, the domination of Polish Jewish life by Zionist leaders, and the savvy negotiations of Jews in Australia, who acquired visas for their former compatriots, setting in motion a mass wave of emigration.[7] Indeed, even adamant "patriots" in Bialystok's dispersed Jewish immigrant community could no longer summon apocalyptic and prophetical language to urge all to rebuild Bialystok when most Jewish residents of Bialystok preferred to live in Australia or Israel.

As Bialystok's Jews shifted their philanthropic allegiances from Poland to Israel, they began replacing Eastern Europe with Israel to provide the content and expression of their Jewish identities. Readers of the *Bialystoker Stimme* were bombarded with advertisements to buy bricks and bonds for Israel. To be sure, some members of this dispersed community displayed an approach to their former home that seemed less concerned with its long-term legacy than with their own personal acquisition of power and prestige through philanthropy. In the many discussions over "the most valuable way" to spend "Bialystoker" philanthropic dollars, one can see vividly how behaviors developed during the interwar period with regard to rebuilding Bialystok shaped the ways in which members of Bialystok's Jewish diaspora viewed their relationship to the new state of Israel and their philanthropic endeavors upon its behalf. As they and their children doled out money for Israel, a self-proclaimed "homeland" few would venture to live in, Bialystok's Jews' actions and rhetoric clearly suggest the ways in which Jews' dispersal from and efforts to remain connected to Eastern Europe in the first half of the twentieth century formatively molded their and their descendants' (who would comprise the vast majority of Jews in the West) understanding, performance, and practice of their historic diasporic attachments to the Jewish state.

The Destruction of Jewish Bialystok, 1939–1943

The shift away from identifying Bialystok as a Jewish homeland would not have taken place if not for its total destruction in the Second World War. Like many cities in eastern Poland, Bialystok did not immediately fall into Nazi hands; it was annexed by the Soviet Union in September 1939 as part of the Soviet–German Nonaggression Pact.[8] With Soviet rule seen as less threatening than Nazi Germany, Bialystok became a haven for Jewish refugees fleeing Nazi-occupied Lodz and Warsaw. The city's Malkinia railway station, the main artery on the Warsaw–Vilna lines, saw thousands of Jews pass through its doors daily. Flooding the small hotels by the station, many stayed several days as they plotted the best route to cities and relatives outside the clutches of Nazi terror.[9] Unable to complete their trips, some remained in Bialystok, causing the city's Jewish population to swell from 107,000 in 1938 to more than 250,000 by December 1939.[10]

Considering the world was at war, Bialystok fared quite well under Soviet rule. It became the capital of the Soviet's western Belorussia region, held up by high-ranking party officials as a showpiece of the annexed regions. Soviet authorities implemented policies crafted in the 1920s to integrate Jews into Soviet life: banning Jewish youth groups, closing Jewish schools, and outlawing Jewish political parties. Independent Jewish institutions ceased to function unless they became part of the Communist Party matrix. Jewish-owned factories were ordered to aid in the war effort.[11] But Jewish industrialists were able to keep control by quickly adapting, pushing their factories to operate with additional shifts. Unemployment fell as new jobs were created within the textile industry and the new local Communist Party and municipal authority. Some Jewish youths relished the additional educational and social opportunities open to them under the communist regime.[12] In short, the local Jewish population continued to support themselves, and some even remained in contact with their compatriots abroad from whom they also received support.[13]

Tragically, the thousands of Jews who moved to Bialystok to escape the clutches of the Nazis did not fare well. Many were deported to work camps in the Soviet Union. Initial attempts by Soviet forces to recruit Jewish refugees to work in the Soviet Union had failed, provoking the Soviet army to seize and deport Jewish refugees under the pretext of accusing Jews of subversion. Hundreds of Jews, who were desperately trying to remain in contact with their families in western Poland, were accused of espionage and soon found themselves living in Gulag-style camps in Siberia or in cities such as Baku in Central Asia.[14]

As dire as the situation of these deported Jews seemed at the time, it spared them from the Nazi invasion: on June 27, 1941, the Nazi army entered Bialystok and set aflame the city's largest synagogue, with two thousand Jews inside. As Chaika Grossman recalled, "The fire spread from the synagogue to the wooden houses in the alleys of the surrounding Jewish neighborhood. All went up in smoke like

Remnants of Bialystok's Main Synagogue, 1946. The synagogue, with more than two thousand Jews inside, was destroyed in a fire set by the invading Nazi army on June 27, 1941. *From the Archives of the YIVO Institute for Jewish Research, New York.*

matchboxes."[15] Over the following several days, another five thousand Jews were rounded up, taken to the forest, and shot. These events made it abundantly clear to the remaining Jewish residents of Bialystok that even those who worked or cooperated would not be spared Nazi terror. After a ghetto was established in August 1941, some fled to the surrounding forest to fight as partisans, while others formed an underground movement.[16] Approximately fifteen thousand Jews remained in the ghetto until August 15, 1943, when Nazi forces began rounding up Jews for deportation to the Treblinka extermination camp. Painfully aware of their fates and inspired by events in Warsaw, several hundred Jews, led by Mordechaj Tanenbaum and Daniel Moszkowicz, launched an attack against the Nazi battalion in the city on August 17, 1943. Armed with only one machine gun, several dozen pistols, and Molotov cocktails, the Jewish fighters managed to kill or wound more than one hundred Nazi soldiers. Yet this victory was short-lived: on August 21, 1943, the Bialystok ghetto was liquidated; all its inhabitants, except those who fled to the forest to fight with the partisans, were sent to their deaths at Treblinka. When the Russians liberated Bialystok in July 1944, only 114 Jews, who had hidden during the war, survived out of the thousands who had lived there prior to 1939.

The Diaspora Responds to Its Homeland's Destruction

Cut off from Bialystok by war, members of its dispersed Jewish community were eager for news. The first reports from Bialystok were hard to believe: David Bigelman, who had returned to Bialystok from Russia's interior with hundreds of other Jews, claimed that the city he left in 1939 "filled with over 100,000 Jews" had "become practically overnight a city of 100,000 Poles."[17] No longer was there a bustling central square with Jewish merchants and artisans chatting and trading in Yiddish in the shadow of the city's clock tower.[18] "Our Jewish Bialystok," Bigelman explained to his shocked former neighbors who voraciously read the *Bialystoker Stimme,* now has "a Polish face (*a polisher poynim*)."[19] He grieved that the great Jewish city of Bialystok, like many cities in Eastern Europe, now resembled a Jewish ghost town.

Surprisingly, even such horrifying reports did not quash Bialystok's Jewish émigrés' commitment to rebuilding their former home. The philanthropic efforts of this group underscore how for a short period, members of world Jewry did not see the devastation of the war as marking the final chapter of Jewish life in Poland. At the beginning of the war, the Bialystoker Center claimed that as a result of the ongoing economic depression, "its limited funds [dedicated to] taking care of 300 elderly charges" left only several hundred dollars for their former compatriots in Soviet-occupied Poland.[20] As the American economy improved and the situation grew worse in Poland between 1940 and 1941, the Bialystoker Center was able to collect and send more than $6,000 to Bialystok through the American Joint Distribution Committee to aid Bialystok's Jews who were "refugees stranded in various countries" by the war.[21] With the German invasion of eastern Poland and America's entrance into the war, the leaders of the Bialystoker Center became totally cut off from Eastern Europe, scrambling but failing to make contact with those still in Bialystok. Convincing themselves that aiding the American war effort was the best way to help Bialystok, the Bialystoker Center urged its members to buy American war bonds and to support soldiers on the front. Unable to ship its newspaper abroad and appreciating its members' growing identification with America, the Bialystoker Center debuted a new feature in the *Bialystoker Stimme* that showcased "a gallery" of photographs of young men in uniform alongside advertisements commanding readers: "For Victory: Buy United States War Bonds and Stamps."[22] The news from sons, husbands, and brothers on the front led Bialystok's Jews in America to identify more strongly as Americans, perhaps out of fear that even with a victory there might no longer be a Jewish Bialystok to which they could cleave.[23]

As rumors of the liquidation of Bialystok's ghetto began to spread, members of this international community began organizing themselves as they had in 1919, to rebuild their former home. Despite horrific tales of massacres, many of Bialystok's Jews living abroad could not believe that the devastation was really fundamentally different from what they had encountered after the First World War. They firmly believed that Bialystok and Jewish Eastern Europe writ large could be rebuilt. A headline in a 1944 issue of the *Bialystoker Stimme* declared: "Bialystok, We Shall Come." The ensuing article by Daniel Charney explained that Bialystok's Jews would return to rescue and rebuild it, "as we have done in the past."[24] Or as Yakov Eyskolsky of Paterson, New Jersey, summed up, "When," not if, "the time comes to rebuild Bialystok," he would be the first in line "to help our mother Bialystok [*mame-bialistok*]."[25] Restoring Bialystok to its former stature, mused another editorialist that year, represented how "we shall take revenge for [the loss of] our holy martyrs [*kedoshim*]."[26] Joseph Chaikan's tribute to the Bialystoker Center and its successful transplantation of Bialystok to America ended by noting that the "new Bialystok agenda" would be dominated "in the near future" by the immense need to reconstruct Bialystok."[27]

The community in the United States, seeing itself as ensnared in war, did not spearhead or direct the rebuilding effort as it had after the First World War, forcing Bialystok's Jews in Palestine, who indeed were also enmeshed in the war, to lead the way. In 1944 in Tel Aviv, former residents of Bialystok created the Irgun le-Ezrat Yehude Bialistok (Organization for the Aid of Bialystoker Jewry) to investigate the viability of Jewish life in Bialystok and to raise funds for survivors.[28] By the end of 1944, this organization had compiled a full list of Jewish survivors in Bialystok and composed the first complete historical account of Bialystok's ghetto.[29] Furthermore, this organization collected substantial sums to finance the shipping of care packages to Bialystok, realizing that money, particularly amid the chaos of postwar Poland where there would be virtually no commercial infrastructure, was less useful than items for barter or trade.[30] By November 1944, they had raised money from Bialystok's Jews living scattered throughout the world to send more than 2,500 packages of medicine, food, and clothes to Bialystok.[31] However, as a result of the war, the packages never reached their destination. Learning from the experiences of their compatriots in Palestine, the Bialystoker Farband in Argentina collected 204,000 pesos, which they sent to Bialystok via the American Joint Distribution Committee to buy food, clothing, and medicine in Poland.[32]

Despite the reports issued by Bialystok's "colonies" in Palestine and Argentina, members of the Bialystoker Center in New York were not consumed with addressing the plight of Jews in Bialystok, but focused solely on the American war effort and the needs of New York's Jewish elderly. The Bialystoker Center became the focal point of their concern. The *Bialystoker Stimme* pleaded with its readers to support its elderly residents: "Help us," cried out the cover story of the July 1943 issue, "in these difficult summer months."[33] The "big tragedy," according to a headline in February 1944, was not the murder of Bialystok Jewry, which had been confirmed several months earlier by compatriots in Tel Aviv but America's failure to care for its elderly.[34] Honoring the center's successes in addressing the "tragic" situation of the elderly in America, the March 1944 *Bialystoker Stimme* featured a portrait of an elderly female resident of the home on its the cover; buried on page twenty-five was a call to attend a memorial service on April 16th to honor those "martyrs" who perished in Bialystok.[35]

Shortly after the end of the war, Bialystok reclaimed its central position in the Bialystoker Center's debates. Hayim Shoshkes, a leading member of the center who worked for the Hebrew Immigrant Aid Society, joined dozens of representatives of other organizations, including the American Federation of Polish Jews and the American Jewish Committee, on a 1945 mission to Poland.[36] As Shoskes reported after visiting Bialystok with Jacob Pat, executive director of the Jewish Worker's Committee and a past resident of Bialystok, "the city, as all its former residents remember it, is no more."[37] "Eighty percent of the city lay in ruins," he elaborated, with "Poles now the residents [of the homes], where Jews once freely lived." The devastation, in short, was fundamentally different from the destruction this dispersed community had confronted after the First World War. While Shoskes pessimistically noted that "the tremendous hatred of the Polish population for the Jews . . . can be felt at every turn and in every step one takes," he did not totally discount the possibility of Jewish Bialystok rising again. Distributing three million zlotys to stimulate Jewish communal renewal, he noted that there were some signs indicating that rebirth was at least possible in 1945 once those who had been detained in Russia returned.[38]

The Failed Renaissance: Jewish Bialystok and the Postwar Polish Jewish Experiment

Bialystok's dispersed Jews were far from alone in harboring high hopes for the reconstitution of Jewish life in Poland. The reestablishment of Jewish organizations there in 1944 and the worldwide fundraising drives undertaken to support them underscored the belief many Jews shared that a Jewish community could take root and blossom again in Eastern Europe. Hopes for renewal intensified as hundreds of Jews who had survived the war in the Asiatic region of Russia or in Siberia came back to Poland starting in 1944.[39] With thousands more expected to return, Jews in Lublin formed the Centralny Komitet Żydów w Polsce (Central Committee for Jews in Poland; CKZP), an organization dedicated to resurrecting the *kehillot* (Jewish community councils) as centers of Jewish economic, cultural, and religious activity; rebuilding Jewish schools, cultural institutions and the Jewish press; organizing special programs for the needy; establishing connections with Jewish organizations abroad; and helping Jews seeking to recover property confiscated during the war. The immediate postwar Polish government enthusiastically supported these endeavors. Within a few months, the CKZP established several kehillot, Jewish schools and religious congregations, along with an extensive network of charity organizations for Jewish orphans and the homeless. Moreover, the CKZP supported the publication of more than twenty periodicals in Yiddish, Polish, and Hebrew. Other cultural activities, such as the reestablishment of the Jewish Historical Institute and a Jewish Institute of Art, made some Jews believe that there could be a Jewish renaissance in Poland despite the devastation of the war years.[40]

Bialystok's brief rebirth as a center of Jewish life provides some vivid examples of the extent of this Polish Jewish renaissance as well as the reasons for its failure.[41] While at its Soviet liberation, Bialystok was home to only 114 Jews, by 1945, close to 1,000 Jews lived there; they convened a conference for Jews in the region, at which Dr. Shimon Datner, a former teacher at Bialystok's Hebrew Gymnasium, was elected president of the revitalized Bialystok Jewish Regional Committee. The Committee's first program—a Passover seder— attracted several hundred Jews. Dressed in their finest, whether a Russian military uniform or a new dress, all celebrated their "freedom" against the backdrop of Zionist placards proclaiming "the land of Israel for the people of Israel." Zionism, as it had been before the war, remained central to Bialystok Jewish life, but in the context of 1945 Poland, the concept had different implications.[42]

Shimon Datner, a staunch Zionist, firmly believed in Bialystok's renewal and the potential riches Poland offered its Jews. As he argued in a caustic editorial published in New York's Yiddish daily

Seder at the Jewish group home on the corner of Surazer and Minsk streets in
Bialystok, circa 1946. In the background are Hebrew placards welcoming those
who returned and proclaiming "The Land of Israel for the Jewish people." *From
the Archives of the YIVO Institute for Jewish Research, New York.*

Yidishe tageblat, "the land of Israel [*Erets-Yisroel*] question," or more
precisely the belief that only Palestine, and not Eastern Europe,
could provide an answer to the Jewish refugee problem, deserved
more careful attention.[43] Acknowledging the devastation—"only
130 Jews survived in my city of Bialystok out of the 200,000 who
lived there in 1939"—Datner celebrated Bialystok's growing community, to which dozens arrived daily "from Soviet Russia where
they had escaped during the war." Datner boasted of the success of
Bialystok's new Jewish school, its reading circles, library, and coop-
eratives for Jewish bakers, cobblers, and tailors. While he acknowledged the grim tasks the community was also forced to address, such
as setting grave markers along mass graves where many residents of
Jewish Bialystok had met their end in 1941, the mood of Datner's
editorial was triumphant, culminating with an inspiring description
of the regional Jewish leadership conference at which thirty-eight

Photograph of the Centralny Komitet Żydów w Polsce [Central Committee for Jews in Poland] Regional Conference, Bialystok, 1949. Seated from left to right are Y. Bialistotski, M. Bitter, H. Hokmaier, and M. Wenslik. *From the Archives of the YIVO Institute for Jewish Research, New York.*

delegates democratically elected their representative to the Polish government.

Bialystok's inspiring rebirth stemmed from Datner's foresight in acquiring a Jewish "group home" at the corner of Surazer and Minsk streets, the city's main intersection. There, the returning Jews could tend to their practical needs, getting assistance in finding housing, employment, healthcare, and education. Housing posed the greatest problem for most Jews returning to Bialystok because in postwar Poland, as historian Jan Gross points out, Polish inhabitants of Jewish homes and apartments, commonly referred to as "formerly Jewish property [*mienie pożydowskie*]," often refused to cede their new homes to their rightful Jewish owners.[44] Ewa Kracowski recalled when she returned to her family home from fighting with the partisans in 1944, she was forced to sleep in her front yard with her two friends, because the family who took over her home refused to return it to her. After a few days, their taunts prodded her to leave

Bialystok for Grodno, where she heard there was a safe place for Jews to live.[45] Purchasing a "formerly Jewish" warehouse with funds provided by the CKZP and the Bialystoker Center, Datner followed in the footsteps of Bialystok's interwar Jewish leaders by constantly writing to David Sohn for funds; Sohn, as Bigelman recalled, sent "help quickly," since he appreciated the precarious situation and did not want Jews to become dependent on charity.[46]

Healthcare and education garnered the lion's share of Datner's attention in the immediate postwar period. Responding to the growing fear that the situation in Poland could be worse than it had been after the First World War, when typhus and the great influenza epidemic claimed millions of lives worldwide, Datner worked tirelessly to reestablish the Bialystok branch of OZE (abbreviated name of *Obshchestvo Zdravookhraneniia Evreev;* Society for the Protection of the Health of the Jews]), an organization that before 1939 had run 368 medical and public health institutions and had employed approximately 1,000 doctors, nurses, dentists, and medical assistants in Bialystok and its environs.[47] By 1947, the new Bialystok branch helped more than 700 patients, expending over 1,143,000 zlotys for doctors, midwives, medicine, and nursing care.[48] The high birth rate among the returning Jewish population forced Datner and the Jewish Committee in Bialystok to found a new school, where children studied subjects ranging from Polish literature to mathematics. In July 1946 alone, the committee spent 114,665 zlotys on its 134 students.[49] Instruction took place in the Yiddish language, which combined with the school's curriculum imparted to its students the implicit message that Poland could provide a secure future for the remnants of Polish Jewry.[50]

The terrifying resurgence of violent antisemitism in 1946 marked a turning point in Bialystok's renewal, as it did for Jewish rebuilding efforts throughout Poland, forcing Jews to rethink about the future of Jewish life there. As Jan Gross points out, returning Jews were often "welcomed home" with violence by Poles who wished to keep the materials the latter had purloined during the war.[51] In Bialystok, smaller violent outbursts claimed the lives of eleven Jews in 1946 but failed to spark any mass exodus, in contrast to the aftermath of

Student body of the Jewish school founded in Bialystok in 1946, circa 1949. *From the Archives of the YIVO Institute for Jewish Research, New York.*

ferocious violence in Kielce more than one hundred miles away on July 4, 1946.[52] The Kielce pogrom, as it came to be known, began in response to a rumor that the local militia arrested a Jew who supposedly had killed a Ukrainian boy and then drank his blood. A group of 150 men gathered around Kielce's Jewish group home to "retaliate." As local police searched the house for the alleged victim, a shot was fired and a riot ensued. Within four hours, forty-two Jews were killed, beaten to death with stones, bayonets, and bricks. Shockingly, the victims even included a pregnant woman in her eighth month, whose stomach was pierced by a bayonet.[53] The violence soon spread to the train station, where several Jewish passengers were dragged off trains and beaten to death. The new Polish government tried to indict the perpetrators and make them stand trial, but it was too late: the Kielce pogrom had already prompted a massive wave of Jewish emigration from Poland. The Polish Jewish community's new leaders, who overwhelming shared Datner's Zionist political orientation, embraced an ideology of emigration (particularly to Palestine) as the only solution to the Jewish quandary in Poland.[54]

Datner and other leaders of the Bialystok Jewish Committee in 1947 dramatically altered their request: no longer did they require financial aid for communal redevelopment; rather they needed help in obtaining visas. Resettlement abroad took on the utmost urgency.[55] As Datner argued, why was a memorial necessary in Bialystok if no Jews would be there to mourn at its feet? Penning a letter of protest to the editor of the *Bialystoker Stimme,* members of Bialystok's Jewish Committee railed against the vast sums sent to Bialystok to build a memorial for those who died.[56] Instead, the leaders of the committee urged supporters to collect funds to build a village of Bialystok in Palestine where Bialystoker Jews could resettle and build a memorial that all could visit.[57] As the pleas of Datner, the once-hopeful future leader of Bialystok Jewry, made abundantly clear, Bialystok would never again serve as a vital center of Jewish life.

Australia's Bialystoker Centre and the Effort to Resettle Jewish Bialystok

Bialystok's Jews in Australia were the first to take action in response to the pleas emerging from Poland, steering the larger Bialystok diaspora to embrace emigration as the answer to the dilemmas of their day. Agreeing with the Polish Jewish leaders' program, Leo Fink, Michael Pitt, and Abraham Zbar, leaders of the Bialystok émigré community in Melbourne, began actively lobbying the Australian government for visas and their American "cousins" for funds. Their pursuit of their goals through both political and philanthropic channels laid bare the extensive difficulties involved in East European Jewish migration in the postwar world shaped by an anti-refugee hysteria: not only were visas extremely difficult to procure but governments offered no financial support for absorbing immigrants. In Australia, sponsors of the refugees were responsible for reception and integration, meaning in practice that the Jewish community would have to pay not only for refugees' passage, but their accommodations as well.

Ignoring the financial obstacles, Leo Fink, who had arrived in Australia in 1928, successfully negotiated with Arthur Caldwell, the Australian Minister of Immigration, to acquire six hundred visas for Polish Jews in 1946.[58] Despite the Australian government's open opposition to Jewish migration, Fink succeeded with a creative claim that all Jewish refugees were part of his family, enabling them to enter under a family reunion program.[59] But Fink's negotiations with Caldwell made Fink painfully aware of governmental concerns and its latent antisemitism. Fearful that these haggard survivors would become dependants of the state, Fink founded the United Jewish Relief Fund, an organization almost totally funded by the New York–based Joint Distribution Committee (JDC) that provided support to newly arrived Jewish immigrants in Australia.[60]

Fink's joint venture with the JDC highlights the rarely discussed role American Jewry played in Jewish refugee settlement in Australia in the postwar era.[61] Realistic about the dim prospects for mass Jewish refugee resettlement in the United States as debates over the Displaced Persons Act raged in Congress, American Jewish philanthropic organizations such as the JDC and the Hebrew Immigration Aid Society secretly joined forces with Australian Jewish leaders to develop what became known as the "Australian Immigration Project." This program not only paid for the transport and absorption of more than 25,000 Polish Jews but also set in motion a demographic revolution: Australian Jewry doubled in size, from 27,000 Jews in 1936 to more than 54,000 by 1954.

The creation and growth of the Bialystoker Centre in Melbourne perfectly illustrates the integral role American Jews and their money played in Australian Jewry's demographic and institutional expansion. To insure that Jewish refugees from Bialystok succeeded in their new home, Michael Pitt and Abraham Zbar, leaders of Melbourne's Bialystoker Lay Kassa, founded the Bialystoker Centre in 1945. Inspired by New York's Bialystoker Center, hailed as an icon of successful transplantation of Bialystok to foreign soil and revered for its tireless efforts to rebuild interwar Bialystok, Pitt and Zbar hoped their new institution would implant Bialystok in Australia. By 1947 it had succeeded in collecting visas for several dozen families from

Bialystok to settle in Melbourne.[62] Then Zbar pushed the officers of the Bialystoker Centre to acquire a group home for these refugees, where they could stay for free while learning English and receiving vocational training.[63] "Not only was the cost of transport astronomical," wrote Abraham Zbar to David Sohn, but maintaining the group home placed the Bialystoker Centre under constant economic stress.[64] Michael Pitt, recalled his daughter, devoted his weekends to fixing the group home's broken windows and toilets. By November 1947, the Bialystoker Centre owed 22,500 Australian dollars for the ship tickets and 12,000 Australian dollars for the home.[65] Having exhausted the resources of its members and the larger Jewish community in Australia, Zbar begged Sohn to raise money from his constituents in New York.[66]

But Zbar's pleas from Australia fell on deaf ears. Sohn, who had devoted himself tirelessly to nurturing Bialystok since 1919, was distracted, tending to the Bialystoker Center's Old Age Home, and his ailing eldest daughter, Sylvia Sohn, who worked at the Bialystoker Center and was being groomed to take it over.[67] Suffering from a debilitating kidney disease, Sylvia Sohn would pass away in January 1946.[68] Fueled by the loss of his daughter, Sohn became consumed with the desire to financially endow the Bialystoker Center and Old Age Home. His endless fundraising drives ultimately succeeded, culminating in a "mortgage burning ceremony" on January 12, 1947. But few were as emotional as David Sohn, who was overcome with "a feeling of sacredness," as he realized that his "life's work" of establishing a new Bialystok in New York on East Broadway was "never-to-be-forgotten."[69] Sohn then turned his attention to "rebuilding our demolished hometown" and to "replacing outmoded philanthropic methods with new, modern approaches," so that the center could quickly "dispatch relief. . . . and establish contact with our landsmanshaftn the world over."[70]

The Australian Bialystoker Centre's pleas were first addressed through the launching of a "Bialystoker Immigration Fund" in February 1947. Sohn requested that all generously donate so that $100,000 could be sent to Australia to "help our brothers and sisters [in Bialystok] find a new, secure home in the free Australia where

Bialystoker Centre in Melbourne. *Author's private collection.*

they can rebuild their destroyed lives."[71] Jews living in Los Angeles, Chicago, Montreal, Milwaukee, Boston, and Detroit responded immediately, sending almost $50,000 in less than two months to aid the Australian resettlement program.[72] After Sohn wired this sum to Zbar, he closely monitored how all the funds were spent, as he had with the interwar leaders of the Bialystok Jewish community, enmeshing himself in weekly correspondence with Zbar. Thoroughly impressed with Zbar, who obtained a visa for one of his nieces who had survived in Bialystok, Sohn sent to Australia thousands of dollars from the Bialystoker Center's discretionary fund.[73] By the end of 1947, overseas donations from America in fact constituted the bulk of the Australian Bialystoker Centre's budget, enabling this institution to resettle close to two thousand former Jewish residents of Bialystok in Melbourne.[74] In addition to cash, Sohn convinced the New York Bialystoker Center's Board of Trustees to send Zbar a most coveted prize: an American car. Sohn argued to the board that Zbar "would make good use of it and drive it on the highways of humanitarian service for our unfortunate brethren in need."[75]

The reports of this great success convinced others that migration provided the best programmatic course of action to address Jewish Bialystok's post-war dilemmas. But after 1947, obtaining visas became increasingly complex for the United States, South America, or Australia for anyone other than a direct relative. So the internationally circulated *Bialystoker Stimme* assumed the responsibility of helping survivors find their relatives. Launching a column called "Relatives Sought [*Keruvim gezukht*]," the publication used its smallest typeface to reprint every letter it received. The March 1947 column is illustrative: spanning over six pages, the column contains reprints of ninety-five letters from former residents of Bialystok in the American-occupied zone of Germany. Chaim Rosenblum's posting was typical: "Rosenblum, Chaim from Legenove Street in Bialystok is now in Camp Fuhrenwald in American-Occupied Germany. I am looking for my Bialystoker family, named Luria, Weinreich, Gebel, and Polanky who migrated to America in the 1930s. Please write me with your addresses at C. Rosenblum, Camp Fuhrenwald, Florida 10/3, Post Wolfrathausen, Bavaria Germany, US Zone."[76] Such short missives predominated in this column, as survivors sought to locate their transient relatives, who as one David Solomon complained "used to reside at 1192 East Tremont in New York" but now were nowhere to be found. Others looked far beyond the United States, as did Dora Veynshel in Ansbach, Germany, who asked for help finding her relative, Lazar Sharf, in Uruguay and Minna Feinsod, who sought relatives in Peru.[77]

In some way, the efforts of this dispersed émigré community to address the plight of the wandering, homeless and persecuted postwar Jewish refugee was familiar in a mythic sense—a seemingly recurring drama for Jews since their dispersal from their ancient homeland millennia earlier. But on another level, the figure of the Jewish refugee, displaced from his home, separated from his family and in search of a homeland, was all to familiar to these émigrés in an immediate concrete sense as well. The poignancy and immediacy of this crisis was reflected on the cover of the March 1948 *Bialystoker Stimme.*

Echoing the image presented on the 1920s cover of this periodical, the 1948 cover also portrays the two beacons of Jewish Bialystok —the Bialystok clock tower in Poland and the Bialystoker Center in New York—engulfed in a dark haze. A man appears striding across the center of the page, clutching a staff in one hand and a book with a bag emblazoned with the Star of David in the other. This man—the iconographic representation of a wandering Jew—appears lost, staring toward some unknown destination.[78] Unclear whether he is looking to America, Palestine, or Australia, the figure clearly conveys that the future of Bialystok Jewry depended upon migration. Reinforcing the cover's visual argument, the issue's articles stressed that all readers must devote time and energy to helping Jews in Bialystok realize their dream of immigration and resettlement, which in the context of postwar Poland was truly a necessity. But where this dream would be fulfilled remained on open question.

Rebuilding Bialystok in the New Jewish State

The ambiguity of the March 1948 cover portended the larger ideological debate that followed the declaration of Israel's statehood on May 14, 1948. Would the new state offer the solution to the larger dilemma of Jewish homelessness? In fact, the achievement of political independence did provide an answer to the mounting Jewish refugee crisis, but it simultaneously raised new questions that would embroil the dispersed Bialystok Jewish community, along with many others in the larger East European Jewish diaspora, in turf wars for over a decade. To be sure, while some Jews were not staunch Zionists, members of this dispersed Jewish community were generally not anti-

Cover page, *Bialystoker Stimme* 250 (March-April 1948).

Zionist; nor were they reluctant to support the State of Israel due to the specter of dual loyalty.[79] Rather, it was far from clear whether migration to the besieged new Jewish state, as William Kavee recalled discussing with his father-in-law David Sohn, "could address the needs of the haggard survivors," who comprised the remnants of

Jewish Bialystok.[80] How should members of the Bialystok diaspora allocate their limited resources? Would this new state, bent on creating a new Jew and not perpetuating aspects of Eastern Europe, be able to pay tribute to Jewish Bialystok and its legacy?

Jews from Bialystok were far from the only East European Jews befuddled by the events taking place around them. As sociologist Hannah Kliger points out, the concurrent founding of Israel along with the harsh realization of the situation in Eastern Europe raised difficult dilemmas for East European Jews throughout the world: "Should they help the Jews of Israel? Or should they still help their landslayt in the Old Home?"[81] Samuel Rabinowitch argued in a letter to David Sohn in September 1946 that while the Bialystoker Relief Committee "after the last war may have helped hundreds of Bialystoker Jews by rebuilding their home-city in Eastern Europe," the complete devastation caused by this war demanded a different reaction from the Bialystoker Center: "All the American dollars," he maintained, "cannot rebuild Bialystok because there is no one to rebuild it and those survivors [karbonos] of the war would find the best help in the land of Israel."[82] Perhaps if the Bialystoker Center "supported the erection of a colony [koylonia] named Bialystok in the Land of Israel, the legacy of this great Jewish city would not disappear."

Zalman Yerushalmi, head of Irgun Yotzei Bialystok in Tel Aviv, set in motion the campaign to mobilize the international Bialystok community to financially support Israel. In a letter to the Bialystoker Stimme, he called on all Bialystoker Jews to unite and "build Bialystok in the Jewish homeland so that Bialystok could live again."[83] There was much ambivalence about financially abandoning Bialystok, sparking interest in convening an international conference to discuss these matters. On August 21, 1949, delegates arrived at the New York Bialystoker Center from Argentina, Canada, Mexico, France, South Africa, Australia, and Israel for the World Bialystoker Convention. Eclipsing the situation in both Poland and Israel for some conferees was the presence of "Bialystokers" from at least twelve countries, a gathering seen as "representing a true miracle—like the ingathering of the exiles" from the Bialystok "diaspora."[84] These Jews still saw themselves primarily through the lens of their attachment to and dispersal from Bialystok.

Appreciating the vast sums at stake, the National Committee of Labor in Israel sent a telegram to the 1949 World Bialystoker Convention, promising "gladly to help the project of building an everlasting memorial to your great Jewish community."[85] Through the intervention of Zalman Yerushalmi, who argued that the new circumstances of world Jewry demanded they support Bialystoker Jews living in Israel, conferees voted to shift the focus of its philanthropic drives from Eastern Europe to Israel. But resisters, who deployed biblical imagery to describe the fate of Bialystok, were not swept up in the historical moment of Zionism's triumph and insisted that funds be used only to construct a "*pintele Bialistok*," literally, the essence of Bialystok in the new Jewish state.[86] As one conferee summed it up, "How could the state of Israel be a successful Jewish polity [*melukha*] without incorporating the legacy of the greatest Jewish city of Poland?"[87]

What would "a new Bialystok" look like in the new state of Israel? Would it have replicas of its landmarks such as the clock tower or great synagogue? How would it recreate the essence of this city? The conferees resolved that the "new Bialystok" would first and foremost contain 250 homes for the remnants of Bialystok Jewry that had found their way to Israel. Eloquently illustrating the overwhelming sense of loss and death pervading this renewal project, no clock tower or synagogue stood at the center of the new Bialystok; rather it would be built around the graves of Samuel Mohiliver, chief rabbi of Bialystok and founder of Hibbat Zion, and Yosef Chazanowich, founder of the Jewish National Library in Jerusalem. So that it would resemble other new settlements in the state, conferees also resolved to support the construction of "a community center [*beys 'am*], a synagogue, a house of study [*beys midrash*] and a school." Most important, the convention agreed to erect a textile factory to stimulate the village's industrial development. Some of the village's intersections and streets would bear the names of Bialystok's famed boulevards, while others would possess the monikers of large donors who would "buy" the honor to have their names inscribed in the landscape of the new Bialystok directly alongside those of illustrious personalities who had shaped this city in the past.[88]

The World Bialystoker Convention established the Kiryat Bialystok Foundation and appointed Ralph Wein, a successful New York businessman who had been involved in the Bialystoker Center since the 1920s, as its president.[89] The convention charged the Kiryat Bialystok Foundation with a threefold mission: to raise $1 million, to erect a new Bialystok in Israel that would "perpetuate on Israel's soil the legacy of Bialystok, and to educate youth in Israel about Bialystok."[90] The fundraising goal consumed most of the foundation's attention. Drawing upon techniques developed by the Bialystoker Center to raise money for Bialystok and the Bialystoker Old Age Home in the 1920s, Wein contacted Leon Sourasky and Herbert Smith in Mexico, wealthy textile manufacturers, who each directed special "businessmen's" campaigns that drew upon their social networks to raise money.[91] The foundation also launched a "Brick Campaign" for which donors were encouraged to "buy bricks for Kiryat Bialystok."[92] "A dollar [is all that is needed] for a brick," urged the Bialystoker Center's Ladies' Auxiliary, as it deployed bargain rhetoric in its fund-raising drive.[93] The foundation also ran a widely advertised "certificate campaign" that promised to grant donors eternal recognition. Each certificate entitled the donor to the right of having his or her "name . . . inscribed on a plaque to be erected in the Kiryat Bialystok Hall of Fame."[94] Finally, the foundation rewarded generous donors by promiscuously handing out titles: by 1952 the foundation boasted seven vice presidents, five "directors," and two secretaries working under Wein, with no clear, discernible tasks.

If not for conflicts that arose in 1952, these targeted international campaigns, allocations of prestigious posts, and promises of eternal recognition would have enabled the Kiryat Bialystok Foundation, which collected over $107,000 in less than a year, to succeed in its task.[95] But it did not succeed, as a result of an exposé article appearing in a 1952 issue of the *Bialystoker Stimme* alleging deep corruption in the Rasco Corporation, the building company contracted in Israel to build Kiryat Bialystok. Wolf Onin, the reporter, claimed to have uncovered the shocking "truth about Kiryat Bialystok": the

Kiryat Bialystok, 1999. *Author's private collection.*

Rasco Corporation failed to erect half of the homes in the village despite being paid to do so; moreover, houses already erected were of such low quality that they had already fallen into disrepair. Most outrageous, he argued, was that occupying some of these few finished homes were survivors with no direct links to Bialystok! Onin gave voice to many donors' frustrations; with so many officers in the foundation, it was unclear who was responsible for managing the distribution of money.[96] Outraged, Onin critiqued the foundation not only out of his heartfelt concern to help those survivors of Jewish Bialystok who had made their way to Israel, but also out of his deep sense of injustice that "he [and other donors] had been cheated."[97] The marriage of a consumerist rhetoric to fundraising during the interwar era made Onin believe that he and other donors were entitled to see immediate results from their donations.

This critique and the ensuing resignation of Wolf Abrahamson, the foundation's executive director, sparked worldwide debate about the larger project of "rebuilding" Bialystok in Israel. American donors condemned leaders in Israel for not properly overseeing the project, and threatened to cease all payments.[98] This troubled many Bialystoker Jews in Israel, as Michael Flicker recalled, because it seemed as though the "Americans were reneging on their commitments because of their inability to accept that there was no future for Jews in Poland. For those of us who arrived in Israel with nothing, it was difficult to understand what our American cousins were trying to achieve."[99] Lev Koppel, a member of Kiryat Bialystok's *va'ad* (governing board), grew exasperated with "the American donors who did not appreciate that withholding funds would not remedy the situation. The new state of Israel was not like America—homes could not be built overnight from high-grade materials like they are in New York."[100] But a consumerist ethos fueled the indignation of many donors, particularly in the United States, who believed that they (and the residents of Kiryat Bialystok) had not received the goods that they had "purchased" through their philanthropic dollars.

To be sure, Rasco Corporation did fail to fulfill its contractual obligations. "Homes remained uninhabitable," complained a letter sent by Kiryat Bialystok's governing board to David Sohn. "The communal kindergarten still had no roof and there was no playground for children or even a tree for shade. Our health clinic still cannot operate."[101] Moreover, it was unclear whether these issues would be resolved, as no one was pressuring the builder to remedy the situation: "Ralph Wein and his advisor in Israel, Louis Bernstein," continued the letter to Sohn, "failed to meet regularly with the builders to oversee the construction." An appeal by the governing board of the residents of Kiryat Bialystok to "all their Bialystoker compatriots [landslayt] in America" pleaded with the American donors "to intervene" on behalf of those in Israel because "organizational funds are being distributed without any control."[102] Indeed, many residents of Kiryat Bialystok felt that the general support for Israel in the Bialystok diaspora was being exploited by the Bialystoker Center to raise funds for its own projects.[103]

Embarrassed by the letters and articles, the leadership of the Kiryat Bialystok Foundation lashed out at Sohn, questioning his decades of leadership at the Bialystoker Center. In an anonymous front-page article, a writer rhetorically queried and answered: "Do you really believe that the *Bialystoker Stimme* is the voice of Bialystok? The truth is that the *Bialystoker Stimme* is no longer the voice of Bialystoker compatriots throughout the world but is rather just the vehicle for David Sohn's "views."[104] As Sohn's son-in-law recalled, this "stab in the back deeply pained Sohn," who had dedicated his life to the cause of Bialystok and to the pursuit of truth through journalism.[105] The writer went on to question whether it was "valuable" for the Bialystoker émigré community to spend thousands of dollars each year supporting a newspaper that rarely reported the "facts."[106] Responding to this personal attack, Sohn condemned the "shameful [Kiryat Bialystok] *Bulletin*" for "bringing into our landsmanshaft hatred and quarrels" for the first time in its history.[107]

An irreparable rift grew between the Bialystoker Center and the Kiryat Bialystok Foundation.[108] Sohn urged members of the Bialystoker Center to give money to the new state of Israel but not to the foundation. Often campaigning on the pages of the *Bialystoker Stimme* to drum up support for Israel bonds, Sohn made sure that his readers remained committed to seeing Israel as Bialystok Jewry's best option for the future; the paper featured pictures of important figures in the Bialystoker Center visiting sites in the new state and celebrating those who donated ambulances to struggling communities there.[109] The Kiryat Bialystok Foundation, tainted by controversy, failed to raise any more funds and was forced to close its doors before completing its "new Bialystok." Without the support of the Bialystoker Center, few opened their wallets to fund a settlement dedicated to embedding in Israel "the lessons and legacy of Bialystok," as the World Bialystoker Convention had originally intended.[110]

Rewriting Bialystok

As the effort to resurrect Bialystok in Israel slowly unraveled, the attempt to recreate Bialystok on the printed page progressed more

Kiryat Bialystok, 1999. *Author's private collection.*

successfully, providing some much needed glue to this frayed community. Reflecting the larger literary craze that swept through the East European Jewish world in which thousands put their pens to paper to produce books known as *yizker bikher* (memorial books; sing., *yizker bukh*), members of Jewish Bialystok's diaspora sought to bestow on their former home an "eternal life." As scholars Jack Kugelmass and Jonathan Boyarin note, "memorial books emerged as a genuinely collective response" in the wake of the realization of all the destruction.[111] Seeking "to bear witness" to what happened, to use the words of Terrence des Pres, and to create a metaphoric gravestone, East European Jews culled data from their personal photographic collections, communal records, synagogue journals, city directories, and newspapers to chronicle the life and death of Jews in their former homes.[112] While clearly deriving inspiration from traditional chronicles of Jewish mourning, these publications differed primarily in the fact that they were composed by international groups of nonprofessional writers rather than individuals. As a result, these volumes often became mired in disputes as writers and editors in different locales debated their former home's legacy to the world.[113]

Immediately following the war, there was an outpouring of writing about Bialystok by members of its diaspora living in Buenos Aires, Johannesburg, London, Melbourne, Montreal, Poland, and Tel Aviv. The *Bialystoker Stimme* expanded to include all the submissions it received, debuting a new feature, "Hurban Bialistok [Bialystok's Destruction]," written by Bialystok's Jewish communal leader Shimon Datner, which chronicled in utmost detail every last moment of Jewish life in the city as well as its renewal.[114] Stitched into Datner's narrative was the underlying question of what would become of Bialystok Jewry's heritage. Were Jews in New York and the Bialystoker Center able and willing to assume a dominant role in spreading its legacy? This query is representative of a larger self-reflective questioning that consumed the Jewish world in the aftermath of the war as religious figures, writers, and educators grappled with whether American Jews—the wealthiest remnant of the East European Jewish diaspora whom many saw lacking intellectual rigor and passion—could assume the responsibility of creating and spreading East European Jewish culture.

At first, the Bialystoker Center illustrated that American Jews were not ready to assume the mantle of nurturing Bialystoker culture. In 1946, Rafa'el Rayzner (1894–1953) arrived on the doorstep of the Bialystoker Center in New York—what he considered "the largest organization of Bialystokers in the world"—with his handwritten manuscript, *Der umkum fun Byalistoker yidntum, 1939–1945* (The Annihilation of Bialystok Jewry), which he had hidden in Bialystok's rubble. Rayzner, a celebrated journalist and editor in interwar Bialystok, was shocked that the manuscript sat untouched for almost a year. In his critical assessment, this "Center" for Bialystok "felt a greater sense of responsibility towards the three hundred residents of its old age home" than to help aspiring authors publish works about

Bialystok.[115] Ultimately, Rayzner and his manuscript made their way to Australia. There he was welcomed by family and by the leaders of the Bialystoker Centre, who dedicated themselves to bringing his manuscript to a larger reading public.

Rayzner's work—an instant sensation in the Yiddish book world —raised larger questions about language and the transmission of Bialystok's legacy across time and space. Introducing this chronicle of Bialystok Jewry, Yehoshua Rapaport (1895–1971), editor of *Oystralisher idishe lebn* hailed Rayzner's "simple Yiddish" that encapsulated the beauty and diversity of Jewish Bialystok.[116] Because Rayzner wrote as "a man of the people [*folks-mentsh*]" without any literary flourishes, Rapaport pointed out, his work would be easily understood by members of the Bialystok diaspora and easily translated for their children, poignantly underscoring the linguistic challenge of educating future generations about Bialystok. As Samuel Rabinowitch warned in a letter to David Sohn concerning the publication of a *yovel bukh* (anniversary book) to celebrate the achievements, rather than the destruction of Bialystok Jewry, if such a volume was not "accessible," it would just be bought by thousands out of commitment to their parents but would never be read.[117] As he remarked about his own family: "while I know German, English, Yiddish, and a bit of Russian," my wife and son, for whom this book would serve a most important educative purpose, "only know English and some German. Neither can read Yiddish."[118] Rabinowitch feared his family epitomized many in the Bialystok diaspora, where the processes of assimilation and linguistic acculturation divided generations.

Like many Jewish intellectuals, Sohn had been pessimistic about the future of Yiddish culture in America even before the war.[119] Wrestling with such questions became more acute and painful for all East European Jews in the post-Holocaust era. Sohn asked himself as he set out to create a volume to commemorate Jewish Bialystok: what could he do to keep Bialystok as a meaningful part of the lives of Bialystok's Jews and their children in America, Australia, or Argentina? Why would the next generation, who could barely identify Bialystok's landmarks and struggled to speak Yiddish, be interested in keeping Jewish Bialystok's cultural legacy alive? Indeed, could Bialystoker or East European Jewish culture writ large survive, let alone thrive outside Eastern Europe?

In 1952, the publication of *Bialystok: Photo Album of a Renowned City and Its Jews the World Over* addressed these questions through the reproduction of 1,200 photographs that strove to capture Jewish Bialystok's complexity, density, and sheer cacophony of voices. Heeding Rabinowitch's warning, Sohn furiously collected hundreds of family portraits of Bialystok's religious leaders, wealthy philanthropists, and industrialists, as well as group photographs of Jewish sports clubs, theater groups, political organizations, and welfare societies, so that he could narrate with precision Jewish Bialystok's contribution to the world. The photographs were sent to Sohn by readers of *Bialystoker Stimme* in response to his numerous requests to erect a visual "monument to Bialystok" that would stand as a testament "to the interesting" diversity of Jews both in "our famous city and all over the world."[120] Firmly believing that photographs possessed the kind of authority that the printed word enjoyed in the past, and acknowledging the limited shelf life of Yiddish books, Sohn urged all members of the dispersed Bialystok community to help him write the "true" history "of Bialystok's plain folk," and to search through their collections for pictures that captured "a world that is no more," and could convey, Sohn argued, "the epic drama of Eastern European Jewry, in which Jewish Bialystok played such a prominent role through its spiritual and social creativity, its textile industry and scores of other economic and financial undertakings."[121]

The album's cover vividly captures Sohn's understanding of Jews' place in Bialystok's history as well as America's role in maintaining the legacies of Jewish Bialystok. At the bottom center of the page appears a rendering of the New York Bialystoker Center and Old Age Home, precariously perched atop a globe surrounded by three pictures of Bialystok's renowned landmarks: the central market's clock tower, Bialystok's textile mills, and the city's Branicki Palace. The rays of sunshine emanating from the Bialystoker Center and connecting it to the historic icons of Bialystok's past demonstrates Sohn's contention: New York served in the aftermath of the war as the new Bialystok, a pointed counternarrative to supporters of Kiryat Bialystok who

Cover of David Sohn's *Bialystok: Photo Album of a Renowned City and its Jews the World Over (Byalistok: bilder album fun a barimter shtot un ire iden iber der velt)*, 1952. Courtesy of the Goren-Goldstein Center for the Study of Diaspora Jewry, Tel Aviv University.

sought to convince members of this dispersed community that their East European regional loyalties should be rechanneled and remapped onto Israel. To further illustrate his belief that America had become the new site defining Bialystokness for the world, Sohn encased these images in a frame that was actually the façade at the entrance to the Bialystoker Center on the Lower East Side. With "Bialystoker" emblazoned above representations of the twelve tribes of Israel, this book sought to replicate the entrance to the Bialystoker Center where Bialystok appeared as the defining identification of Jewish life. Just as the twelve tribes of Israel molded the parameters of life in ancient Israel, so did regional loyalties shape the complexion of Jewish life in the new world: one was not just a Jew but a Jew from Bialystok.

Sohn's clarion call for photographs to tell Bialystok's tale was prescient: visual images became the main medium through which the Holocaust and Jewish Eastern Europe became entrenched in postwar historical memory. Images, and specifically photographs, as scholar Barbie Zelizer points out, "helped stabilize and anchor collective memory's transient and fluctuating nature."[122] Arguing that "one picture is worth a thousand words," Sohn stressed to his readers, many of whom could not read one word of Yiddish, his hope that the images of Jewish Bialystok would "remain burned in their memory longer than any printed word."[123] Sohn's emphasis in the volume on capturing the lives of Bialystok's "plain folk" followed in the footsteps of other publications on Eastern Europe that were written both during and in the immediate aftermath of the war. Beginning in 1943, numerous books openly sought to bring back to life the "world" of East European Jewry: Maurice Samuel's *The World of Sholem Aleichem* (published in 1943) sought to expose alienated American Jews to the "world" of their grandfathers;[124] Abraham Joshua Heschel's *The Earth Is the Lord's* (based on Heschel's stirring lecture delivered at YIVO in 1945) mourned the irreversible loss of the rich "inner world" of East European Jewry.[125] Through the "vividness and immediacy of their accounts," these works, as scholar Barbara Kirshenblatt-Gimblett points out, sought to "make readers feel that they could step through [their] pages and onto the streets of the Jewish town mapped out in [the] text."[126] By 1947, artists sought to mimic these evocative literary texts with the publication of encyclopedic compendiums of photographs similar to Sohn's volume; among these were Rafa'el Abramovitsh's *Di farshvundene velt* (The Vanished World)[127] and Roman Vishniac's *Polish Jews: A Pictorial Record*.[128] Sohn admired Vishniac's effort to capture "real life unposed," so that non-Yiddish speakers could have an unparalleled, authentic window through which to see "the intense religious quality of East European Jewish life."[129]

With the goal of creating a volume akin to these celebrated works that would serve as a model to the landsmanshaft world, Sohn sat down to write an introduction to Bialystok's history that he knew would uphold a definitive vision of the city and its uniqueness for his readers. He conveyed immigrants' visions of themselves as the central figures in Bialystok's development both while they lived there and even after they had left. Sohn surrounded each photograph with a cryptic caption, which, as scholar Barbara Kirshenblatt-Gimblett points out, gave the reader the impression that the people, places, and scenes captured were "typical, rather than particular."[130] But in his effort to create a timeless vision of Jewish Bialystok, Sohn ironically accentuated the radical transformation his work wrought on these photographs: a photograph that had originally been intended to validate and mark a celebratory anniversary of an organization's success in 1905 only bespoke of the tragedy and loss of the war when published in 1952. While the photos survived, their unknown subjects and the stories surrounding each image vanished into oblivion during the war.

Thus, Sohn's narrative and the pictures he included told not only stories of triumph, but also shared tales of ambivalence about life in Eastern Europe and the new world. As his edition displayed celebratory pictures of annual dinners of the Bialystoker Farband in Argentina, the mortgage-burning ceremony at the Bialystoker Center in New York, or picnics at the Australian Bialystoker Centre, what lurked beneath the surface was a set of troubling questions confronting all East European Jews: would Jewish Bialystok's diaspora ever be able to nurture teachers, leaders and writers like those who lived in Europe? Ultimately, did the new world's materialism and individualist focus make it impossible to replicate the intense collective Jewish identity that had existed in Europe?

Despite the underlying tragedy and troubling questions raised by Sohn's photographic monument to his former home, this work was immediately celebrated and bought by thousands around the world. To be sure, circulation figures for memorial books are notoriously scant: Hasia Diner conjectures that the issue of language kept number of copies actually sold down to rarely beyond the several hundred members of a dying landsmanshaft group.[131] But the media-savvy Sohn not only sold books to members of the Bialystoker Center in New York, the Bialystoker Farband in Argentina, and the Bialystoker Centre in Australia; he also sent his album to numerous reviewers so that his work would receive a wider reading public. Reviews (all incredibly favorable) appeared in newspapers spanning from *Der tog*, to the *Forverts*, to *Novoye Ruskoye Slovo* in New York, to the *Idishen zhurnal* in Toronto. All reviewers were impressed, as *Forverts* writer J. M. Kersht summed up with what he called a "spectacular and unique monument to the city of Bialystok and its Jews the world over!"[132] The renowned Jewish demographer and scholar Jacob Letchinsky wrote adoringly in the *Forverts* of his experience "turning it leaf by leaf so that [he could] read it time and again" and noted in appreciation how "very thoughtful it was of the author to portray not only the Bialystok in dust and ashes but also the living Bialystok in New York, Buenos Aires, Jerusalem, and Tel Aviv that continues and carries on the blessing of immortality."[133] Indeed, Sohn's decision to end Jewish Bialystok's narrative in its diaspora prodded famous Yiddish playwright Osip Dimov to declare in his review in Buenos Aires's Yiddish *Di presse* that "This album is more than a book; it is an epoch, a history, an idyll, a great human drama" that captures the scope and power of migration in transforming not only Bialystok but the entire world of Jewish Eastern Europe.[134]

By ending his narrative of Bialystok's story not in Poland but in places as distant as Melbourne, Paris, and New York, Sohn not only sought rave reviews but also to address the pressing question haunting most postwar Yiddish writers: How can one represent such unimaginable destruction and still give Jews hope for the future? Indeed, Sohn argued, as he looked at his own life's work and the thousands of photographs he was sent by Bialystok's Jews now living throughout the world, all hope should not be lost. While Bialystok might never again serve as a center for Jewish life, its legacies would be kept alive in its diaspora.

Conclusion

The virtual erasure of Eastern Europe from the map of the Jewish world, followed by the formation of a new Jewish state as the self-proclaimed center of the Jewish universe, set in motion a historic shift in how East European Jews thought about the building blocks of Jewish life—namely, exile, diaspora, and home. As the postwar debates and efforts of Bialystok's dispersed Jews illustrate, this historic shift away from viewing Eastern Europe as a quintessential Jewish homeland to Israel was far from simple or straightforward. For far too long, "Jewish life, thought and scholarship," as David Shneer and Caryn Aviv point out, "has revolved around the idea that Israel is, has been and always will be at the center of the Jewish universe."[135] But East European Jewish immigrants' steadfast commitment to Eastern Europe in the immediate postwar period suggests they harbored an alternate vision of this Jewish universe and its gravitational center.

The ultimate failure to erect Kiryat Bialystok in its original design suggests that even though it was apparent that Eastern Europe could no longer serve as a nurturing Jewish home, Bialystok's Jews did not unequivocally embrace Israel as *the* Jewish homeland. The marrying of consumption to philanthropy in the interwar period laid the foundations for the rift between Sohn and the leaders of Kiryat Bialystok. But it also raised troubling questions: how did America's ethos of consumption, individualism, and materialism reshape the powerful collective regionalist identity Bialystok had cultivated among its former inhabitants? Whereas at the beginning of the interwar period, fundraising drives urged émigrés to demonstrate their "Bialystoker" identity by giving money to Bialystok, by 1952, the search for the greatest value drove philanthropic drives on Bialystok's behalf. Indeed, the dispersed Bialystok community is far from exceptional and provides an interesting lens through which to view the ever-shifting late twentieth-century relationship of American Jews to Israel.[136] To be sure, the "divergent cultures" of Israeli and American Jewry are direct products of late twentieth-century political developments—such as the Six Day War, the growing affluence of American Jewry, Israel's rising wealth, and the erosion of the American Jewish liberal coalition—but these cultural divides also have long historic roots related to each Jewish immigrant community's understanding of homeland, diaspora, and the role Eastern Europe played in shaping the modern Jewish world. In many ways, American Jewry's critiques of Israel that surfaced at the end of the twentieth century only appear surprising if one operates under the assumption that their embrace of Zionism was instantaneous, wholehearted, and without debate in the middle of that century.

Bialystok offers a concrete example of the East European Jewish effort to explain the legacy of their former home without reference to Israel. Beginning its narratives with photographs of nineteenth-century Bialystok and concluding with photographs of landsmanshaft groups in New York, Paris, Argentina, Australia, and Israel, this illustrated volume captured how Bialystok's Jews still saw their community as concurrently representing a new diaspora and an expansive empire. Ignoring traditional nation-state borders as colonial entities often do, Sohn captured in pictures the cacophony of Jewish voices, institutions, clubs, and political organizations that made Bialystok renowned both in Europe and around the world. But the book also demonstrated how Bialystok's dispersed Jews were not a powerful empire as Sohn argued in 1921 but rather a vulnerable diaspora. The book was in essence "a rite of return," to use the words of Barbara Kirshenblatt-Gimblett, which highlighted the impossibility of return for this vulnerable dispersed group of Jewish migrants. The many photographs may have visually recreated the vitality of life in prewar Bialystok, but the irony—that the photos taken originally to mark a milestone in a person's life now served as memorials or virtual gravestones—was lost on no member of this dispersed Jewish community which during the war realized it could not save Bialystok, the place that nurtured it but whose fate it could not control.

Diaspora and the Politics of East European Jewish Identity in the Age of Mass Migration

Ten in the morning, and already the hot, May sun beat down on the main bus terminal in Yehud, a small municipality on the edge of Israel's Ben Gurion International Airport. The deafening noise of landing planes rang in my ears as I got onto a local bus and told the drive the address at which I was expected in Kiryat Bialystok. Fifteen minutes later, after a circuitous, bumpy ride, the bus shuddered to a stop, and the bus driver shouted to the back of the bus, "*Giveret, heganu li-Bialistok: Terdi*" (Lady, we've arrived in Bialystok. Get off the bus). Waiting for me on the palm-tree lined street in front of a large domed-edifice made from Jerusalem stone was Michael Flicker, leader of the Irgun Yotzei Bialystok, the organization for Bialystok's Jews in Israel. And although it was as late as 1998, Flicker proudly led me into the synagogue created to evoke the memory of Bialystok's great synagogue (and designed by the grandson of its former chief rabbi, Samuel Mohilever). The synagogue represented one part of his lifelong struggle to recreate the world he had known in Poland. His success, he argued, was evident in the fact that only in Israel were there celebrations of the intellectual and political contributions made to the world by Bialystok's children, or commemorations of this city's tragic losses during the wars of the early twentieth century.

With a group of half a dozen Jews born in Bialystok he had gathered for my visit, Flicker devoted the afternoon to constructing for me a monumental elegy to Jewish Bialystok. The lively group discussion not only laid bare the ways in which Bialystok, as a construct, continued to shape these Jews' intellectual, cultural and social lives, but also revealed their perceptions of themselves as historical actors, participants in the final chapter of the saga of Bialystok and its Jews, a tale they imagined ended in Israel, but which they appreciated had significance beyond their personal lives.[1]

While elderly residents of Kiryat Bialystok may end the story of *Jewish Bialystok and Its Diaspora* with the notion, imaginary but nonetheless powerful, of a geographic relocation of the original Jewish Bialystok to Israel, in truth, it is more thematically appropriate to close with the example of another postwar Polish Jewish émigré, Eva Hoffman. She argued that for herself and other migrants from Poland, "dislocation is the norm rather than the aberration."[2] Her numerous sojourns in Poland, Western Europe, Canada, and the United States made her entire life seem like a "never-ending process of passage and arrival."[3] Hoffman, of course, rarely identified herself primarily as a Jew. But her persistent feelings of displacement, passage, and resettlement echo the experiences of thousands of East European Jews who time and again over the course of the nineteenth and twentieth centuries left their homes in search of economic opportunities, more stable living conditions, education, or the hope of achieving greater social integration.[4] Moving first to cities within the Russian Empire, such as Bialystok, Kiev, or Minsk, and later overseas, these Jews on the move created new types of political, welfare, and cultural organizations that challenged traditional authorities and crafted a new vision of Jewish identity, linked both to larger ideological movements and to local regions.[5] Indeed, as several recent studies of other cities in late Imperial Russia illuminate, migrating Jews' efforts to address their pressing economic and existential needs reinforced revolutionary ideologies, setting in motion deep cultural, social, and institutional shifts in fin-de-siècle Russia.[6]

The sweeping changes brought about by the demands of Jewish migrants in tsarist Russia soon spread beyond Russia's borders, as thousands of Jews saw migration to cities in North America, South America, South Africa, Palestine, and Australia as their best option to cope with Russia's deteriorating industrial economy and increasing political instability.[7] Like other turn-of-the-century migrants, East European Jews experienced their overseas journey as part of a longer series of migrations. Drawing upon their previous "experi-

היכל
ביליסטוק

Hekhal Bialystok, the cultural center and town hall of Kiryat Bialystok. Originally completed in 1954 with the support of American funds, the building was renovated and expanded in the 1960s to accommodate a library and archive. *Author's private collection.*

ences of sojourning," to use a phrase coined by Madeline Hsu to describe Chinese migrants, they were able to succeed economically (to varying degrees) in the different countries in which they settled.[8] For far too long, the tale of East European Jewish migration has virtually ignored the migratory experience in Eastern Europe. The consensus, to quote Hasia Diner, is that "immigration abroad proved to be more transformative" than any prior relocation. Such a limited vision obscures the critical skills and survival strategies Jews developed in Eastern Europe—such as negotiating opportunities in rapidly industrializing markets, taking entrepreneurial risks, and forming new organizations—that continued to inform and enhance East European Jews' lives long after they had left the region.[9]

The most exciting insights afforded by the comparative study of Bialystok's Jews, and studies of Jews from other cities as diverse as Vilna and Salonika, are the ways in which these communities, to use the words of Sara Stein, "unravel certain inherited dichotomies" that have long defined the field of Jewish history. Both Ashkenazic and Sephardic Jews, even when they emerge from one city, belie the existence of a "single, unified Jewish people or culture."[10] Past narrations of Jewish migration rarely contrast the divergent Jewish immigrant experiences in America, Argentina, Australia, or Palestine, impoverishing our broader understanding of the wider economic, political, and cultural trends that shaped the processes of Jewish migration, adaptation, and acculturation over the last century.

The network of Bialystok's Jews' associations that remained devoted to advancing its members' economic well-being as well as remapping their regional loyalties onto the terrain of the New World provides one example of how a renewed engagement with Jewish regionalism—an engagement sensitive to both its local and global dimensions—can productively destabilize our narration of modern Jewish history. Historians writing about Jews, for the most part, continue to operate in dichotomous frameworks dictated by nationalist paradigms, privileging the boundaries imposed by nation-states. While a significant number of twentieth-century Jews articulated their identities along regional lines and millions migrated, living in several empires or nation-states over the course of their lifetimes, the writing of Jewish history still bears the imprint of an old, nineteenth-century ideology about the nation being the natural carrier of historical meaning. Scholars of Jewish life need to pay heed to Salo Baron's clarion call forty-five years ago for "Jewish historians [to] realize the historic interdependence of various Jewish groups and the impossibility of comprehending any particular territorial evolution without reference to their totality."[11] To be sure, conceptualizing, theorizing, and writing such history involves its fair share of linguistic obstacles, but as the transnational Bialystok Jewish community—tied to a local region but operating on a global plane—brings into sharp focus, state borders rarely coincided neatly with the boundaries of Jews' cultural identities. The historical experiences of Jews in the long century of mass migration, to use the words of Thomas Bender, "cannot be properly written as if they were self-contained."[12]

By looking at the history of Jewish Eastern Europe through the lens of its migrant dispersal, the chapters in this book strive to provide a fresh lens to view the relationship between Eastern Europe and Jewish identity that has long been obscured by the destruction of the Holocaust and the political triumph of Zionism. Prior to the upheavals of the twentieth century, segments of East European Jewry imagined Poland as representing not only a Jewish homeland, but a holy land akin to the ancient Jewish homeland. Sholem Asch eloquently conveyed this sentiment in his rendition of the famous Yiddish folktale explaining the name *Poland:*

> God took a piece of *Eretz yisroel* [the Land of Israel], which he had hidden away in the heavens at the time when the Temple was destroyed and sent it down upon the earth and said: "Be My resting place for my children in their exile." That is why it is called Poland *(Polin)* from the Hebrew *po lin,* which means: "Here shall thou lodge" in the exile. . . . And in the great future, when the Messiah will come, God will certainly transport Poland with all its settlements, synagogues and yeshivas to *Eretz yisroel.* How else could it be?[13]

The notion that Poland, the geographic home of Auschwitz, represents a divinely selected place of refuge for the Jewish people in exile has been virtually erased from both Jewish collective memory and contemporary popular narratives of twentieth-century East European Jewish history. But before the Second World War, it was this widely shared idea that made many Jews from Poland experience immigration not as a journey to a promised land but rather as an excruciating launch into a new exile. As Jonathan Boyarin observes, Polish Jews in Paris thought of themselves "as exiles from Poland rather than as exiles from the biblical Land of Israel."[14] Indeed, Bialystok's dispersed Jews and millions of other Jewish immigrants saw their pieces of Poland as "home," expressing a sense of entitlement and acting like an archetypal migrant diaspora—according to the accepted definition of "diaspora" in contemporary scholarly literature—as they shared collective memories of these former "homes," sent remittances there, and established institutions to carry on its traditions.[15] The repertoire of cultural strategies developed by early twentieth-century migrant Jews, such as a literary recreation of Eastern Europe as the archetypal Jewish homeland, not only altered the lives of those who migrated but also molded their children's lives as well, as future generations would imaginatively recreate "homes" in Israel or on the Lower East Side as they searched for "Jewish spaces" in which to root their identities.[16] Moreover, the immigrant generation's philanthropic commitment to their inspirational home in Eastern Europe, a land few would contemplate living in, anticipates many aspects of Western Jewry's relationship to Israel in the second half of the twentieth century.

The rhetoric that Bialystok's Jews deployed to imagine their dispersed community challenges accepted views of Jewish diasporic identity in the twentieth century. In crafting a vision of themselves as living in *goles bialistok* (Bialystok's exile), these East European Jews belied the standard, static view of the Jewish Diaspora. Indeed, many early twentieth-century East European immigrant Jews saw the pain of exile not only in relation to ancient Zion but in reference to Eastern Europe. Diaspora, in their eyes, was a highly contested and dynamic category through which they could reinterpret their experiences and ponder their place in the world. While the articles in the *Bialystoker Stimme* were far from ideological treatises, the playful style in which these immigrant writers deployed biblical diasporic idiom echoes parts of Daniel and Jonathan Boyarin's arguments about the nature of a Jewish diasporic identity that never was beholden to the power of one nation-state.[17] Jews often felt deep connections to lands without having any dominion over them. Yet, the ways in which most scholars use the concept of *diaspora* in modern Jewish historical studies, as Jon Stratton notes, remains "fundamentally bound up with the politics of the [Jewish] nation-state," masking that fact that Jews have always harbored a complex web of longings for many real and imagined homelands.[18] Bialystok's Jews force us to appreciate the multi-diasporic nature of modern Jewish life. Migration transformed Eastern Europe, a land considered the traditional periphery of the Jewish diaspora, into its imagined center. If scholars relinquish a narrow definition of diaspora, they will come to more fully appreciate the ways the process of migration—whether to Babylonia in the fifth century or from Spain in the fifteenth—profoundly reoriented the ways in which Jews thought about their connections and loyalties, and expressed their identities as a dispersed people.[19]

The tale of Bialystok's Jews also offers a powerful lesson to those interested in contemporary migrant communities: not all dispersals constitute a diaspora. In certain respects, the above tale may not benefit from the current scholarly infatuation with the concept of diaspora, since the ever-expanding field of "Diaspora studies" dissociates Jewish migrants from its discussions of contemporary migrant diasporas. However, I did not deploy this concept with the goal of reinserting Jews into a larger scholarly discourse and demonstrating how scholars of modern Jewries can contribute to this theoretical field. Rather, I did so because my subjects chose to explain their inner worlds through this conceptual framework. While I do believe scholars of modern Jewries need to engage more directly with this growing field, which often resists contemplating the modern Jewish experience, I do not believe it is beneficial to cast all Jews who dispersed in pursuit of economic opportunity, colonial enterprises, or civic integration as forming new Jewish diasporas. Indeed, in recent years, it has become increasingly popular to call dispersed communities of Jews who maintain literary links in the British Empire an "Anglophone Jewish diaspora," or Jews in the United States living below the Mason-Dixon line as constituting a "Dixie Diaspora."[20] Scholars of Jewish history must not be lured into promiscuously applying the term *diaspora* to any Jewish dispersal (as scholars of other migrant groups often do), because it renders this rich and evocative term meaningless. Diaspora has been deployed by Jews for the past two thousand years not merely to depict their dispersals, but also to convey their deeper sense of alienation rooted in their loss of not only a physical home but a spiritual one as well. The thousands of migrants—Jews, Chinese, or South Asians—who dispersed in pursuit of trade or colonial enterprises over the last two centuries did not always cast themselves as forming a new type of exile; many, in fact, embraced their new situations. Thus, what scholars of modern

Jewish migration can offer the student of contemporary migration is a renewed appreciation that "diaspora" is not, as anthropologist Sandhya Shukla argues, the "dominant way of being in the world"; rather, some dispersals may become diasporas, but many do not.[21]

Regardless of the framework in which one chooses to cast migrant dispersal, most migrants echo Eva Hoffman, who noted that on the boat to North America, she was not filled with joy, hope, or anticipation, traditional emotions ascribed to East European Jewish migrants, but rather with *tęskonta*—homesickness—that forced her to confront "a whole new geography of emotions" centered on the pain of "absence."[22] The political triumph of Zionism and the destruction of Jewish Eastern Europe in the Second World War should not obscure the *tęskonta* experienced by East European Jews in the last century, many of whom felt, like Hoffman, that there were many "geographic centers pulling the world together . . . New York, Warsaw—all made claims on [their] imagination[s]."[23] Through innovative organizations, philanthropies, and modes of literary expression, Jewish immigrants confronted the pain of migration and exile by creating new ways in which they could remain connected to one another, a phenomenon that shaped generations of Jews. Membership numbers in landsmanshaft organizations may have dwindled, but as Deborah Dash Moore's study of postwar American Jews in Los Angeles and Miami illustrates, when Jews settled in new regions in the United States, regional affiliation continued to be a defining feature of Jewish communal life, albeit now in terms of New York or Chicago rather than Bialystok or Warsaw.[24] Moreover, few contemporary Jews give money to Eastern Europe, but many donate millions of dollars to Israel, illustrating that the behaviors developed by dispersed East European Jewish migrant communities to express their attachment to their homeland made a deep imprint on late twentieth-century Jewry's understanding of the performance of their Jewish diasporic identity. Recent studies of contemporary Jewry highlight the continued centrality of literary reinvention to modern Jewish identity.[25] Thus, the simple decision of millions of Jews to uproot themselves from their places of birth in Eastern Europe and move to new homes transformed much more than the demographics of East European

Jewry; it also radically redefined how East European Jews and their descendants (by 1945 the vast majority of Western Jewry) understood the meaning of exile, the power of dispersal, and the practice of being a diaspora Jew.

As migration continues to redefine the nation and the world, we must think anew about the multiplicity of descriptions we ascribe to the experience of migrant dispersal. Like Jews at the dawn of the twentieth century, contemporary migrant groups, spanning regions as diverse as South Asia, Mexico, and the Dominican Republic, articulate a sense of alienation from their new homes. At the same time, they enjoy, to some extent, its economic resources, often deploying their newfound economic might to reshape the political landscapes and cultural dialogues in their former homes. While the speed and frequency of these encounters has increased as a result of advances in technology, the underlying realities of existence have not shifted as much as may be expected. As the World Bank reported in 2009, migrant remittances serve as "lifesavers," contributing in developing countries anywhere from 2–6 percent of the gross domestic products. While most see the experiences and imaginative engagements of these new exiles in our "globalized" world as revolutionary, they truly are not strikingly different from those exhibited by the three million immigrant Jews who left Eastern Europe over the course of the nineteenth and early twentieth centuries, who sent millions of dollars back to their former hometowns and were seen by many in Eastern Europe as possessing formidable power.[26] Thus, while it is undeniable that many contemporary immigrants rightfully see themselves as politically disenfranchised, they too, at times, wield power when they use the funds at their disposal to alter local elections in Mexico, or to provide funds to the micro-finance industry in India. Indeed, these contemporary migrants are also caught, as East European Jews were in the first half of the twentieth century, between the dilemmas of political exile and the joys of economic empowerment.

NOTES

Introduction

1. Daniel Soyer estimates that "one million Jews" were "at one time connected directly or indirectly with the 3,000 landsmanshaft associations active in New York City in this era. See Daniel Soyer, *Jewish Immigrant Associations and American Identity in New York, 1880–1939*, 1–2. Isaac Ronch, head of the WPA Yiddish writers' group, contended that these Jewish immigrant associations and their publications served as the "backbone" of Jewish immigrant life. See his "The Present State of the Landsmanschaften," 360–78. The role these publications played in the Yiddish public sphere is further discussed in Yosef Chaikin, *Yidishe bleter in Amerike* and in Arthur Goren's "The Jewish Press," in *The Ethnic Press in the United States: A Historical Analysis and Handbook*, 203–228.

2. Khaym Horowitz, "Mir bialistoker (gedanken un gefiln)," *Bialystoker Stimme* 1 (November 1921): 2.

3. The triumphant vision of Jewish immigrants' encounter with America, where they were able to synthesize a new vision of Jewish identity as well as help forge a new America, is one of the most prevalent themes in American Jewish history. There are too many works that advance this vision, but defining works on this topic include Moses Rischin, *The Promised City: New York Jews, 1870–1914;* Abraham Karp, ed., *Golden Door to America: The Jewish Immigrant Experience;* Deborah Dash Moore, *At Home in America;* Hasia Diner, *A Time for Gathering: The Second Migration, 1821–1880;* Jenna Weisman Joselit, *The Wonders of America: Reinventing Jewish Culture, 1880–1950.* The general "uncritical triumphalism" prevalent in American Jewish history, and in particular in its analysis of Jewish migrant adaptation, is adeptly discussed by Tony Michels in his *A Fire in Their Hearts: Yiddish Socialists in New York* (Cambridge, Mass., 2005), 16–25.

4. Such articulations of ambivalence over leaving Europe were not the creation of Horowitz but are prevalent in the larger oeuvre of American Yiddish literature. See Mikhail Krutikov, *Yiddish Fiction and the Crisis of Modernity*, 150–55; Leah Garrett, "Shipping the Self to America: The Perils of Assimilation in Glatshteyn's and Shapiro's Immigration Novels," 203–230; and Matthew Frye Jacobson, "The Quintessence of the Jew: Polemics of Nationalism and Peoplehood in Turn-of-the-Century Yiddish Fiction," 103–122.

5. Dovid Sohn, "Redaktsianele notitsen," *Bialystoker Stimme* 2 (1922): 15.

6. Ibid.

7. For more on the critical role imperialism plays in shaping America's interface with nations and groups around the world as well as its own domestic culture see Amy Kaplan, *The Anarchy of Empire in the Making of U.S. Culture*, 1–4. Kaplan and other wonderful studies that have pushed scholars to embrace seeing America

and American culture in an imperial framework rarely address how America's immigrants have contributed to America's place in the world.

8. Benedict Anderson, *Imagined Communities: Reflections on the Origin and Spread of Nationalism*, 6.

9. For more on the conceptualization of East European Jewish migration as a silent revolution see Rebecca Kobrin, "The 1905 Revolution Abroad: Mass Migration, Russian Jewish Liberalism and American Jewry, 1903–1914," in *The 1905 Revolution: A Turning Point in Jewish History?*, 227–46; and Gur Alroey, *ha-Mahpekhah ha-sheḳeṭah: ha-Hagirah ha-Yehudit meha-Imperyah ha-Rusit 1875–1924*.

10. Moses Rischin's pioneering *The Promised City: New York's Jews, 1870–1914* and the works he inspired on Jewish immigrant New York rarely acknowledge that New York was one of several destinations pursued by East European Jewish immigrants.

11. The mass migration of East European Jewry marks the largest voluntary demographic shift in modern Jewish history. Jacob Lestchinsky, "Jewish Migrations, 1840–1956," in Louis Finkelstein, ed., *The Jews: Their History, Culture and Religion*, 1536–96; "Migrations," *Encyclopedia Judaica*, Vol. 16: 1518–22; Shaul Stampfer, "Patterns of Internal Jewish Migration in the Russian Empire," in Yaakov Roi, ed., *Jews and Jewish Life in Russia and the Soviet Union*, 28–47.

12. Joseph Telushkin's *The Golden Land: The Story of Jewish Immigration to America: An Interactive History with Removable Documents and Artifacts*, exemplifies how popular writers narrate East European Jewish migration to America. Oscar Handlin, a pioneering scholar in both the fields of American Jewish history and American immigration history also wrote extensively on this point. He often used the East European Jewish example to argue that America is not just comprised of immigrants, but that its very goodness (i.e., liberalism and opportunity for all) depends upon their influx. See Oscar Handlin, "The American Jewish Pattern, after 300 Years"; "We Need More Immigrants"; "America Recognizes Diverse Loyalties"; "A Twenty-Year Retrospect of American Jewish Historiography"; "Democracy Needs the Open Door"; "New Paths in American Jewish History"; and "American Views of the Jew at the Opening of the Twentieth Century."

13. On the larger migratory shifts of the late-nineteenth and early-twentieth century see Adam McKeown, "World Migrations."

14. These articulations of discontent are rarely discussed, particularly in the American context, as a result of reigning paradigms in American history concerning immigrants' embrace of America as well as the paucity of scholars who work in immigrant languages. Indeed, many immigrant groups at times saw the price of migration eclipsing the promise of America. For a discussion of Polish and Irish immigrants similar expressions of ambivalence at the beginning of the twentieth century, see Matthew Jacobson, *Special Sorrows* and Kerby Miller, *Emigrants and Exile: Ireland and the Irish Exodus to North America*.

15. The journal *Diaspora* has played a pivotal role in the development of the field of Diaspora Studies. Scholars in Jewish studies, however have contributed noticeably little to these debates with the exception of Daniel and Jonathan Boyarin, *The Powers of Diaspora*; Jonathan Stratton, "(Dis)placing the Jews:

Historicizing the Idea of Diaspora"; Arnold Band, "The New Diasporism and the Old Diaspora"; Michael Galchinsky, "Scattered Seeds: A Dialogue of Diasporas," in David Biale, Michael Galchinsky and Susannah Heschel, eds., *Insider/Outsider: American Jews and Multiculturalism;* and Caryn Aviv and David Shneer, *New Jews: The End of the Jewish Diaspora.*

16. Yehezkel Kaufmann's magisterial *Golah ve-Nekhar: Meḥkar hisṭori-sot-syologi bi-she'elat goralo shel 'am Yiśra'el mi-yeme ḳedem ve-'ad ha-zeman ha-zeh* provides the most comprehensive treatment of this topic to date.

17. Over a decade ago, Arnold Band analyzed how the concept of diaspora has been used and reformulated by the field of Diaspora Studies. See Band, "The New Diasporism and the Old Diaspora." Other useful discussions are Jonathan Stratton's "(Dis)placing the Jews: Historicizing the Idea of Diaspora" and Michael Galichinsky, "Scattered Seeds: A Dialogue of Diasporas," in David Biale, Michael Galchinsky, and Susannah Heschel, eds., *Insider/Outsider: American Jews and Multiculturalism.*

18. In the past few decades, there has been renewed interest in exploring Jews' ties to multiple homelands primarily by scholars interested in the ancient world and the Spanish expulsion. See Erich Gruen, *Diaspora;* Yosef Yerushalmi, "Exile and Expulsion in Jewish History," in Bernard Gampel, ed., *Crisis and Creativity in the Sephardic World,* 16; Yitzhak Baer, *A History of the Jews in Christian Spain* and his *Galut,* which explore directly how Spanish Jewish migrants used diasporic rhetoric to express their longings for their former lives in Spain; Miriam Bodian, *Hebrews of the Portuguese Nation: Conversos and Community in Early Modern Amsterdam;* Yosef Kaplan, "The Travels of Portuguese Jews from Amsterdam to the 'Lands of Idolatry' (1644–1724)," in Yosef Kaplan, ed., *Jews and Conversos: Studies in Society and the Inquisition.* On more contemporary Jewish migrants there has been relatively little written. For an exception, see Alvin Rosenfeld, "Promised Land[s]: Zion, America and American Jewish Writers."

19. Indeed, the way in which Sohn uses empire—to describe the power immigrants possessed as they engaged with their former home—rarely if ever surfaces in the rich literature on the expanding uses (and abuses) of empire as a conceptual framework. There are too many critical studies on the term and phenomenon of empire to be comprehensive, but several landmark studies shed light not only on the shifting meanings of this term over time, but also provide suggestive insights into why it was so attractive to immigrant Jews in the United States as they made sense of their new economic power, their relationship with Eastern Europe and their place in the world. See Michael W. Doyle, *Empires;* J. A. Hobson, *Imperialism: A Study;* Kenneth Pomeranz, "Empire and Civilizing Missions Past and Present"; Ashley Dawson and Malini Johar Schueller, *Exceptional State: Contemporary U.S. Culture and the New Imperialism;* Victoria De Grazia, *Irresistible Empire: America's Advance through Twentieth-Century Europe;* and Charles S. Maier, *Among Empires: American Ascendancy and Its Predecessors.*

20. Andrew Thompson, "The Language of Imperialism and the Meanings of Empire: Imperial Discourse in British Politics," 147. The term *empire* was constantly being redefined during the interwar period. See R. Koebner and H. D.

Schmidt, *Imperialism: The Story and Significance of a Political Word, 1840–1960*, xiii–xiv.

21. Pioneering work on the American "empire" from the vantage point of Europe include Frank Ninkovich, *The United States and Imperialism*; Geir Mimdestaad's *"Empire" by Integration: The United States and European Integration* as well as his *The United States and Western Europe Since 1945: From Empire by Invitation to Transatlantic Drift*; and Victoria de Grazia's *Irresistible Empire*. For an introduction to the ways these overseas involvements shaped American cultural life see Amy Kaplan, *The Anarchy of Empire in the Making of U.S. Culture;* Amy Kaplan and Donald Pease, eds., *Cultures of United States Imperialism;* Thomas Bender, *A Nation Among Nations;* and Robert W. Rydell and Rob Kroes, *Buffalo Bill in Bologna: The Americanization of the World, 1869–1922*.

22. For discussions of contemporary transnationalism, see Robin Cohen's *Global Diasporas: An Introduction;* Jana Evans Braziel and Anita Mannur's *Theorizing Diaspora*, and the works of Nina Glick Schiller, Linda Basch, and Cristina Szanton Blanc, including *Towards a Transnational Perspective on Migration: Race, Class, Ethnicity and Nationalism Reconsidered; Nations Unbound: Transnational Projects, Postcolonial Predicaments, and Deterritorialized Nation States;* and "From Immigrant to Transmigrant: Theorizing Transnational Migration." For the impact of transnationalism on U.S. literature, see Inderpal Grewal, *Transnational America: Feminisms, Diasporas, Neoliberalism;* and Coleen Glenney Boggs, *Transnationalism and American Literature*.

23. Oscar Handlin, the recognized "father" of both the fields of American immigration history and American Jewish history, is part of the reason why Jews became seen as a model American immigrant group. His monographs entwined his twin interests in Jewish immigration and the larger narrative of American immigrant history as evidenced by closely reading his classic work, *The Uprooted* as well as his works in American Jewish history such as *American Jews: Their Story; Adventures in Freedom: Three Hundred Years of Jewish Life in America;* and *The Dimensions of Liberty*.

24. David Gutiérrez, *Walls and Mirrors: Mexican Americans, Mexican Immigrants, and the Politics of Ethnicity;* Douglas Monroy, *Rebirth: Mexican Los Angeles from the Great Migration to the Great Depression;* and George J. Sanchez, *Becoming Mexican American: Ethnicity, Culture, and Identity in Chicano Los Angeles, 1900–1945*. A more general overview of recent trends in the field can be found in Marc S. Rodriguez, ed., *Repositioning North American Migration History: New Directions in Modern Continental Migration, Citizenship, and Community;* Sandhya Shukla, *India Abroad: Diasporic Cultures of Postwar America and England;* and Robert W. Rydell and Rob Kroes, *Buffalo Bill in Bologna*.

25. Ewa Morawska makes this exact point in her "Immigrants, Transnationalism, and Ethnicization: A Comparison of This Great Wave and the Last," in *E pluribus unum? Contemporary and Historical Perspectives on Immigrant Political Incorporation*.

26. Nina Glick Schiller, Linda Basch, and Cristina Szanton Blanc, *Nations Unbound: Transnational Projects, Postcolonial Predicaments, and Deterritorialized Nation States*, 22. Schiller, Basch, and Blanc have worked collaboratively on theorizing transnationalism, producing several excellent overviews of this con-

cept. See in addition *Towards a Transnational Perspective on Migration: Race, Class, Ethnicity and Nationalism Reconsidered;* "From Immigrant to Transmigrant: Theorizing Transnational Migration." Schiller provides a useful discussion of her various views of the concept of transnationalism in her article, "Transmigrants and Nation-States: Something Old and Something New in the U.S. Immigrant Experience." Other useful works on the utility of this concept for migration to the United States are Roger Rouse, "Mexican Migration and the Social Space of Post-Modernism" and his "Thinking through Transnationalism: Notes on the Cultural Politics of Class Relations in the Contemporary United States"; and Ewa Morawska, "Immigrants, Transnationalism, and Ethnicization: A Comparison of This Great Wave and the Last."

27. Ira Glazier, ed., *Migration from the Russian Empire*.

28. There are relatively few monographs on the growth of small cities (whose populations failed to surpass 100,000 by 1910), but Michael Hamm, ed., *The City in Late Imperial Russia* provides a comparative framework through which to view Bialystok's urbanization in this period. The critical role Jewish migration played in Bialystok's development was far from exceptional. See Steven Zipperstein, *The Jews of Odessa,* 152–53; Natan Meir, "The Jews in Kiev, 1859–1914: Community and Charity in an Imperial Russian City"; Elissa Bemporad, "Red Star on the Jewish Street: The Reshaping of Jewish Life in Soviet Minsk, 1917–1939."

29. Ezra Mendelsohn, *Class Struggle in the Pale,* 4–5; Arcadius Kahan, *Essays in Jewish Social and Economic History*, 29–30; and Yuri Slezkine, *The Jewish Century,* 117.

30. Joseph Chaikan, "Bialystok Transplanted and Transformed," *Bialystoker Stimme* 233 (1944), 41, 45. David Sohn, head of the Bialystoker Center in New York, claimed that 40,000 Bialystoker Jews lived in America. See David Sohn, "Bialystok," *Bialistoker Bilder Album: bilder album fun a barimter shtot on ire iden iber der velt,* 16. Michael Flicker, president of Irgun Yotzei Bialystok in Israel, claims that a survey conducted during the war (1944) found 15,000 Bialystoker Jews residing in Palestine. Although no surveys were conducted in Argentina, memoir materials and landsmanshaftn membership figures suggest that between 8,000 and 10,000 Jews from the Bialystok region settled in Argentina. L. Zhitnitski, "Landsmanshaftn in argentina," *Argentiner yivo shriftn* 3 (1945), 156–59. It is estimated there were approximately 3,000 Bialystokers living in Melbourne by 1939. See Yakov Pat, "Bialistoker yidn in oystralia," quoted in Howard Rubinstein, *The Jews in Victoria, 1835–1985,* 190–91; Anna Gepner, Oral Interview, August 17, 1998. To appreciate these organizations in their larger context, see P. Wald's "Di landslayt fereynen," *Der Avangard* , November 1916, 31–35; and Zosa Szajkowski, "Dos yidishe gezelshaftlekhe lebn in Pariz tsum yor 1939," in E. Tcherikower, ed., *Yidn in Frankraykh*.

31. For statistics on Jews and other migrant groups in this period of mass migration, see Glazier, *Migration from the Russian Empire;* Jacob Lestchinsky, "Jewish Migrations, 1840–1956," 1536–56; Mary Kritz and Hania Zlotnick, *International Migration Systems: A Global Approach;* Mary Kritz, *Global Trends in Migration: Theory and Research on International Population Movements;* Adam McKeown, "Global Migration, 1846–1940," 151–90. Despite the striking parallels between Bialystok and other cities, I must note that Bialystok did have

proportionally one of the largest Jewish migrant populations of any city in Eastern Europe. According to the 1897 Russian census, Warsaw, for example, was home to 210,526 Jews and they comprised 34 percent of the city's population. In contrast, while only 41,905 Jews lived in Bialystok, they constituted over 60 percent of the population and consequently, their needs left a substantial imprint on this city's economic and civic life. See Corrsin, *Warsaw before the First World War*, 145; Tomasz Wisniewski, *Jewish Bialystok: A Guide for Yesterday and Today*, Appendix III.

32. Nancy Green and François Weil, "Introduction" in Nancy Green and François Weil, eds., *Citizenship and Those Who Leave*, 1.

33. A list of monographs focusing on East European Jewish immigration is too long to provide but ever since Moses Rischin's pioneering *The Promised City*, almost all scholarship on East European Jewish migration has approached its subjects from the vantage point of arrival and settlement. Even migration studies dealing with places outside the United States also focus on settlement and arrival. See, for example, Lloyd Gartner, *The Jewish Immigrant in England, 1870–1914*; Nancy Green, *The Pletzl of Paris: Jewish Immigrant Workers in the Belle Epoque*; Suzanne Rutland, *Edge of the Diaspora: Two Centuries of Jewish Settlements in Australia*; Victor Mirelman, *Jewish Buenos Aires, 1890–1930*; Haim Avni, *Argentina and the Jews*.

34. One of the seminal works in Jewish immigrant history to use the converging migration method is Thomas Kessner's *The Golden Door: Italian and Jewish Immigrant Mobility in New York City, 1880–1915*. Another work which uses the converging migration model to structure its analysis is Judith Smith's *Family Connections: A History of Italian and Jewish Immigrant Lives in Providence, Rhode Island, 1900–1940*. Also see Thomas Kessner and Betty Caroli's "New Immigrant Women at Work: Italians and Jews in New York City, 1880–1915," as well as Corianne Krause's "Urbanization Without Breakdown: Italian, Jewish and Slavic Immigrant Women in Pittsburgh, 1900–1945." For more on African Americans and white immigrants, see Olivier Zunz, *The Changing Face of Inequality: Urbanization, Industrial Development and Immigrants in Detroit, 1880–1920*; Stanley Lieberson, *A Piece of the Pie: Blacks and White Immigrants Since 1880*.

35. On this point, see Nancy Green, "The Comparative Method and Poststructural Structuralism—New Perspectives for Migration Studies" and her "L' Histoire comparative et le champ des etudes migratoires." Max Weinreich's pioneering *Geshikhte fun der yidisher shprakh: bagrifn, faktn, metodn* suggests just how useful such a transnational lens could be for the study of East European Jewry. Jonathan Frankel's pioneering study of Jewish socialism illustrated the intricate links between all migrant centers of Russian Jewish life and Russia, spanning New York, London, Paris, and South America: see Jonathan Frankel, *Prophecy and Politics*. Recent scholarship on Sephardic Jewry provides suggestive examples of how illuminating this methodology could be. See Aron Rodrigue and Esther Benbassa, *The Jews of the Balkans: The Judeo Spanish Community, 15th to 20th Centuries*; and Sarah Abrevaya Stein, *Making Jews Modern: The Yiddish and Ladino Press in the Russian and Ottoman Empires*.

36. Even though Nancy Green argued for such comparative work over fifteen years ago, few studies of Jewish migration has yet to be written using a divergent model. Green did inspire exemplary work using the divergent comparative model concerning Italian and Irish immigration. This work illuminates that region of origin also played a fundamental role in shaping divergent immigrant experiences and influenced even choice of destination country. See Donna Gabaccia, "Is Everywhere Nowhere? Nomads, Nations and the Immigrant Paradigm of United States History," 399; John Briggs, *An Italian Passage: Immigrants to Three American Cities, 1890–1930;* Samuel L. Baily, *Immigrants in the Lands of Promise: Italians in Buenos Aires and New York City, 1870–1914;* Donna R. Gabaccia, *Italy's Many Diasporas;* Donna R. Gabaccia and Fraser M. Ottanelli, eds., *Italian Workers of the World: Labor Migration and the Formation of Multiethnic States;* and Malcolm Campell, "The Other Immigrants: Comparing the Irish in Australia and the United States."

37. To be sure, the intricate links between the writing of modern Jewish history and of the modern nation-state is not particular to Jewish studies, as Celia Applegate notes, as the historical profession emerged within the context of the formation of the nation-state. See Celia Applegate, "A Europe of Regions: Reflections on the Historiography of Sub-National Places in Modern Times," 1162.

38. Regional identity provided a cornerstone for Jewish identity in Eastern Europe; it played a similar role in identity definition throughout Europe. See Eli Lederhendler, "Did Russian Jewry Exist Prior to 1917?" in Yaakov Roi, ed., *Jews and Jewish Life in Russia and the Soviet Union,* 15–22. For the role of regional identity in the larger European context, see Celia Applegate's "A Europe of Regions: Reflections on the Historiography of Sub-National places in Modern Times." Also see Appelgate's *A Nation of Provincials: The German Idea of Heimat,* and Alon Confino's *The Nation as a Local Metaphor: Württemberg, Imperial Germany, and National Memory, 1871–1918.*

39. Israel Beker, *Di bine fun mayn lebn,* 3. Also see Tomasz Wisniewski, *Jewish Bialystok and Surroundings in Eastern Poland: A Guide for Yesterday and Today,* back cover.

40. These popular characterizations are discussed in several sources. Benjamin Nathans, *Beyond the Pale: The Jewish Encounter with Late Imperial Russia,* 124; Israel Cohen, *Vilna,* 105; and Zipperstein, *The Jews of Odessa,* 2.

41. This is not a phenomenon exclusive to Jews or Eastern Europe, as Peter Sahlins discusses in his work on peasants living in the Pyrenees region of France. See Peter Sahlins, *Boundaries: The Making of France and Spain in the Pyrenees,* 270–73.

42. In American immigration history, religion has always been an important distinguishing characteristic. Since Will Herberg's classic *Protestant, Catholic, Jew: An Essay in American Religious Sociology,* many scholars have examined in detail the interrelationship between religious identifications and ethnic identifications, most notably, Robert Orsi's *The Madonna of 115th Street: Faith and Community in Italian Harlem, 1880–1950.* Recent literature has begun to reevaluate the political and social role that religion played in immigrant life but

more in reference to issues of race than of ethnicity. See John McGreevy, *Parish Boundaries: The Catholic Encounter with Race in Twentieth-Century America;* Brian Hayashi, *For the Sake of Our Japanese Brethren: Assimilation, Nationalism and Protestantism among the Japanese of Los Angeles;* and George Sanchez, *Becoming Mexican American: Ethnicity, Culture and Identity in Chicano Los Angeles, 1900–1945.*

43. Itsak Rontch, "Der itstiger matsev fun di landsmanshaftn," in *Di yidishe landsmanshaftn fun nyu york [Jewish Hometown Associations in New York],* 9.

44. Robin Cohen, *Global Diasporas: An Introduction;* Smadar Lavie and Ted Swedenberg, "Introduction," in Smadar Lavie and Ted Swedenberg, eds., *Displacement, Diaspora and the Geographies of Identity,* 1–17; Matthew Jacobson, *Special Sorrows: The Diasporic Imagination of Irish, Poland and Jewish Immigrants in the United States.*

45. Khaching Toloyan, "Introduction," *Diaspora* 10 (2000), 1.

46. Yosef Yerushalmi, "Exile and Expulsion in Jewish History," 3.

47. Daniel and Jonathan Boyarin, *The Power of Diaspora.*

48. "Diaspora" [Gr. *diaspora*, a dispersion from: *dia-*, through, and *spierein*, to scatter] 1] the dispersion of the Jews after the Babylonian exile. See *Webster's Unabridged Dictionary,* 504. William Safran, "Diasporas in Modern Societies: Myths of Homeland and Return," 83.

49. Yerushalmi, 12, 16.

50. My concept of "lived diaspora" is inspired by the category of "lived religion" used by historians of religion to capture the perspectives and attitudes of the historical actors themselves. For an excellent example of how this category is utilized in the scholarly literature, see Robert Orsi's pioneering *The Madonna of 115th Street.*

51. Isaiah Gafni, *Land Center and Diaspora: Jewish Constructs in Late Antiquity,* 12.

52. Ibid., 35–56.

53. Ibid., 96–117.

54. Yerushalmi, "Exile and Expulsion in Jewish History," 16.

55. Ibid., 15–18.

56. Miriam Bodian, *Hebrews of the Portuguese Nation: Conversos and Community in Early Modern Amsterdam,* ix, 6–7. Yosef Kaplan, "The Travels of Portuguese Jews from Amsterdam to the 'Lands of Idolatry' (1644–1724)," 197–211.

57. Eisen, *Galut,* 88.

58. Ahad Ha'am was significantly less negative about the potential for Jewish life in the diaspora than many of his contemporaries, but he still emphasized this theme. See Steven Zipperstein, *Elusive Prophet: Ahad Ha'am and the Origins of Zionism.* In general, on the role "negation of the diaspora" played in the writings of these Zionist thinkers see Ehud Luz, *Parallels Meet: Religion and Nationalism in the Early Zionist Movement, 1882–1904;* and Shlomo Avineri, *The Making of Modern Zionism: Intellectual Origins of the Jewish State.* For the writings of Zionist thinkers who argued for "a negation of the diaspora," see Arthur Hertzberg, ed., *The Zionist Idea,* 200–223, 248–70, 314–25.

59. Simon Dubnow argued for Jewish "autonomism," a socio-political system allowing Jews to contribute to political and civil life in their host societies while retaining the freedom of self-determination. See Sophie Dubnov-Erlich, *The Life and Work of S. M. Dubnov: Diaspora Nationalism and Jewish History.*

60. Eisen, *Galut*, xi.

61. An excellent example of a "crisis" model approach to Jewish migration is David Berger, ed., *The Legacy of Jewish Migration: 1881 and Its Impact.* Scholars have written extensively on Jewish migration but the limits of space allow me to mention only several of the more important works in the field. Beginning in the 1920s, Jewish social scientists began seriously examining Jewish migration, and some of the most important work was done by the scholar Jacob Lestchinsky. For example, see Jacob Lestchinsky, "Die Zahl der Juden auf der Erde," *Zeitschrift für Demographie und Statistik der Juden;* Jacob Lestchinsky, *Prezesledlenie i przewarstowienie Żydów ostatniem stuleciu,* which he expanded upon in his *Jewish Migration for the Past Hundred Years.* Liebmann Hersch's "International Migration of the Jews" in I. Ferenczei and W. Wilcox, eds., *International Migrations* all were pioneering works on Jewish migration. Moses Rischin's *The Promised City: New York's Jews, 1870–1914* is a comprehensive work which set the stage for much of the scholarly interest in East European Jewish immigrant life from the vantage point of arrival and settlement. Irving Howe followed in his footsteps with his *World of Our Fathers* and he inspired others to consider specific group's adaptation as illustrated by Gerald Sorin, *American Jewish Immigrant Radicals, 1880– 1920;* Sydney Weinberg, *World of Our Mothers: The Lives of Jewish Immigrant Women;* and Susan Glenn, *Daughters of the Shtetl: Life and Labor in the Immigrant Generation.* Jewish migration studies dealing with places outside the United States also focus on settlement and arrival. See, for example, Haim Avni, *Argentina and the Jews: A History of Jewish Immigration;* Judith Elkin, *The Jews of Latin America;* and Nancy Green, *The Pletzl of Paris.*

62. Corrsin, *Warsaw before the First World War,* 145.

63. This is reflective of the general world of Jewish philanthropy in the early twentieth century. See Jonathan Woocher, *Sacred Survival: The Civil Religion of American Jews,* 24.

64. Woocher, *Sacred Survival.*

65. Much has been written on the changing image of Eastern Europe in immigrant writings and how that relates to Jewish adaptation. See David Roskies, *The Jewish Search for a Usable Past,* 41–66; Dan Miron, "Literary Image of the Shtetl"; Ewa Morawska, "Changing Images of the Old Country in the Development of Ethnic Identity among East European Immigrants, 1880s–1930s: A Comparison of Jewish and Slavic Representations."

66. My study was greatly influenced by several exemplary models of this type of examination such as Ewa Morawska's *For Bread with Butter: Lifeworlds of East Central European Immigrants in Johnstown, Pennsylvania, 1890–1940;* and Robert Orsi's *The Madonna of 115th Street: Faith and Community in Italian Harlem, 1880–1950.*

67. Matthew Jacobson, *Special Sorrows;* Paul Gilroy, *The Black Atlantic: Modernity and Double Consciousness;* James Clifford, "Diasporas," in *Routes: Travel and Translation in the Late Twentieth Century,* 244–78.

1. The Dispersal Within

1. Nikolai Leskov, "Iz odnogo dorozhnogo dnevnika" [From a Travel Diary], *Polnoe sobranie sochinenii*, vol. 3, 44–46. For more on Leskov, see Gabriella Safran, *Rewriting the Jew: Assimilation Narratives in the Russian Empire*, 108–146. I would like to thank Gabriella Safran for directing me to Leskov's reflections on Bialystok.

2. *Pervaia vseobshchaia perepis' naseleniia Rossiiskoi imperii, 1897 goda*, vol. 11, 46–50.

3. Y. B. RG102, Box 15, Autobiography 178, p. 25. YIVO Autobiography Collection, 1939 Contest. YIVO Institute for Jewish Research.

4. Zvi Hirsh Masliansky, *Zikhroynes: firtsik yor lebn un kemfn*, 66.

5. Ibid.

6. Olga Litvak, *Conscription and the Search for Modern Russian Jewry*, 171–203.

7. Józef Ignacy Kraszewski, considered the guiding father of nineteenth-century Polish nationalism, evocatively captures in his writings the crisis Jewish migration to Poland's cities caused for the nascent Polish nationalist movement. Not only did Krasweski rhetorically ask and answer: "And do you know what makes every Polish town Polish? The Jews," but he also predicted that "If ever the Jews are gone, we will enter into a completely alien country and feel, accustomed as we are to their good sense, as though we ourselves were lost." "A wiecie, co każde miasto polskim czyni? Żydzi. Jak już zabraknie Żydów, wjeżdzamy w kraj obcy zupełnie i czujemy, nawykli do ich przytomności, jakby nam czegoś nie stawało." See Jozef Ignacy Kraszewski, *Latarnia Czarnoksięska*, 261. I would like to thank Tim Snyder and John Micgiel for pointing me to this quotation. For a detailed treatment of Kraszewski's writings and their influence on nineteenth-century Polish nationalist thought, see Wincenty Danek, *Józef Ignacy Kraszewski: Zarys biograficzny*.

8. The vision of Jews as a Russifying agent that would provide a buffer against Polish nationalist agitation became widespread in the tsarist government after 1863. See John Klier, *Imperial Russia's Jewish Question*, chapter 7.

9. Eli Lederhendler, "Classless: On the Social Status of Jews in Russian and Eastern Europe in the Late Nineteenth Century," 509, 522.

10. Jacob Lestchinsky, "Yidn in di gresere shtet fun poyln," 25. Also see Georges Weill, "Lodz," *Encyclopedia Judaica*, vol. XI, 425.

11. For comparative information on other cities, see Zipperstein, *The Jews of Odessa*, 12–40; Elissa Bemporad, "Red Star on the Jewish Street: The Reshaping of Jewish Life in Soviet Minsk, 1917–1939, chapter 1; Natan Meir, "The Jews in Kiev, 1859–1914: Community and Charity in an Imperial Russian City"; and Robert Shapiro, "Jewish Self-Government in Poland: Lodz, 1914–1930."

12. In general, historians of late imperial Russia argue, as does Peter Gatrell, that there were "in peacetime, relatively few non-Russian minorities engaging in widespread migration within the boundaries of the Russian empire"; Peter Gattrell, *A Whole Empire Walking: Refugees in Russia during the First World War*, 5. This overlooks, as Ted Weeks has discussed, the movements of thousands of

Jews to cities in Congress Poland, a population shift that totally reconfigured Polish urban society; see Theodore Weeks, *Nation and State in Late Imperial Russia: Nationalism and Russification on the Western Frontier 1863–1914*, 110–30.

13. Ibid.

14. Natan Meir, "The Jews in Kiev, 1859–1914"; Bemporad, "Red Star on the Jewish Street"; Scott Ury, "Red Banner, Blue Star: Radical Politics, Democratic Institutions and Collective Identity amongst Jews in Warsaw, 1904–1907."

15. Benjamin Nathans, *Beyond the Pale*, 10.

16. Eliyahu Oran and Yisroel Prenski, Oral Interview, June 22, 1997, Tel Aviv. Such a phenomenon was not peculiar to Bialystok, as Steven Zipperstein illustrates in his study of Odessa, where Jews also developed new organizations to respond to the changing context, and these organizations in turn engendered Jewish cultural transformation. See Zipperstein, *The Jews of Odessa*, 70–94, 151–54.

17. Lederhendler, "Did Russian Jewry Exist prior to 1917." See Jozef Chlebowczyk, *On Small and Young Nations of Europe: Nation Forming Processes in the Ethnic Borderlands in East-Central Europe*; Andrzej Walicki, *The Enlightenment and the Birth of Modern Nationhood: Polish Political Thought from Noble Republicanism to Tadeusz Kosciuszko*.

18. For the regional variables shaping Jewish identity in these different locales see Zipperstein, *Jews of Odessa*; and Nathans, *Beyond the Pale*.

19. For more on the political transformation of Bialystok see Juliusz Łukasiewicz, "Białystok w XIX Wieku."

20. Ezra Mendelsohn does not clearly define how he is using the terms *assimilation* or *acculturation*, but he appears to see linguistic assimilation as acculturation and anyone committed to Poland's independence as "assimilated." See Ezra Mendelsohn, "A Note on Jewish Assimilation in the Polish Lands," in Bela Vago, ed., *Jewish Assimilation in Modern Times*, 141–45; Moshe Mishkinsky, "Regional Factors in the Formation of the Jewish Labor Movement in Czarist Russia," 47–49; and Zimmerman, "Poles, Jews and the Politics of Nationality," 115–40.

21. A general overview of Bialystok's demographic growth can be found in Herschberg, *Pinkes Bialystok*, 30–33; Tomasz Wisniewski, *Jewish Bialystok*, 120; and Yerucham Bachrach, *Demografiye fun der idisher befalkerung in Bialystok*, 1–38.

22. Ariusz Małek, "Żydzi w Nowych Prusach Wschodnich," 133–35; Łukasiewicz, "Białystok w XIX Wieku," 59–62; Sara Bender, *The Jews of Białystok during World War II and the Holocaust*, 2–3; and Herschberg, *Pinkes Bialistok* I: 67–83.

23. Małek, "Żydzi w Nowych Prusach Wschodnich," 139–40.

24. Herschberg, *Pinkes Bialistok* I, 67–84; Norman Davies, *God's Playground: A History of Poland*, 112. For more on the haskalah in Western Europe, see Michael Meyer's excellent overview in *Jewish Identity in the Modern World*; and David Sorkin, *The Transformation of German Jewry*. In Eastern Europe, the haskalah followed different patterns. See Immanuel Etkes, ed., *ha-Dat veha-Ḥayim: tenu'at ha-Haskalah ha-Yehudit be-Mizrach Eropah*; Shmuel Feiner, *Haskalah ve-Historyah: toldoteha shel hakarat-'avar Yehudit modernit*; and Mordechai

Zalkin, *Ba'alot ha-shaḥar: ha-Haskaah ha-Yehudit ba-Imperyah ha-Rusit ba-me'ah ha-tesha'esreh.* For more on the haskalah in Western and Eastern Europe, see Shmuel Feiner and David Sorkin, eds., *New Perspectives on the Haskalah.*

25. For an appreciation of the long-term impact of the haskalah on life in Bialystok see Herschberg, *Pinkes Bialistok* I, 214–68.

26. Ibid., 214–20.

27. Yehezkel Kotik, *Mayne zikhroynes,* vol. I, 376, quoted in Herschberg, *Pinkes Bialistok* I, 215.

28. Edward Thadden, *Russia's Western Borderlands,* 59–75.

29. Adam Dobroński, "Z dziejow Żydow na Białostocczyznie w XIX wieku," *Studia Podlaskie* 2 (1989).

30. Edward Thadden, *Russia's Western Borderlands,* 63–70.

31. Łukasiewicz, "Białystok w XIX Wieku," 72–84.

32. For more on the perception of Jews as a "Russifying" agent, see Weeks, *Nation and State in Late Imperial Russia,* 116–17.

33. Stephanie Schuler-Springorum, "Assimilation and Community Reconsidered: The Jewish Community in Konigsberg: 1871–1914."

34. The Jewish birth, death, and marriage records for Bialystok in the nineteenth century are far from complete. The places of birth are mentioned for either mother or father in approximately three-quarters of the entries. Unless otherwise noted, all statistics are drawn from my analysis of *Pervaia vseobshchaia perepis' naseleniia Rossiiskoi imperii, 1897 goda,* vol. 11; Akta Stanu Cywilnego Okręgu Bożniczego w Białymstoku, 1835–1899 nr. zespol 264, Archiwun Państwowe w Białymstoku. I would also like to thank JRI-Poland for access to their database. Oral Interview, Michael Flicker, 5/10/97.

35. Unfortunately, the 1897 Imperial Census only noted residents who were born outside of the Grodno *gubernia* in which Bialystok was situated, thus making it difficult to ascertain how many residents hailed from the surrounding small towns. See *Pervaia vseobshchaia perepis' naseleniia Rossiiskoi imperii, 1897 goda,* vol. 11, 46–50.

36. Y. B. RG102, Box 15, Autobiography 178, p. 25. YIVO Autobiography Collection, 1939 Contest. YIVO Institute for Jewish Research.

37. Weeks, *Nation and State in Late Imperial Russia,* 63; 101–103. Thadden, *Russia's Western Borderlands,* 120–22.

38. All the information about the birthplaces of the residents of Bialystok are derived from *Pervaia vseobshchaia perepis' naseleniia Rossiiskoi imperii, 1897 goda,* vol. 11, 46–54.

39. *Pervaia vseobshchaia perepis' naseleniia Rossiiskoi imperii, 1897 goda,* vol. 11, 54.

40. Paweł Korzec, "Rzemiosło Żydowskie w Białymstoku na Przełomie XIX i XX Stulecia," 23–35.

41. Herschberg, *Pinkes Bialistok* II, 49–53. For more on industrialization in this period in Russia, see Susan McCaffray, *The Politics of Industrialization in Tsarist Russia: The Association of Southern Coal and Steel Producers.*

42. Particularly concerning industrial development in the textile industry, see M. Gately, "The Development of the Russian Cotton Textile Industry, 1861–1913";

Prokhorovy: materialy k istorii Prokhorovskoi Trekhgornoi manafaktury I torgovo-promyshlennoi deiatel'nosti sem'I Prokhorovykh, 1799–1915. With regard to Białystok, see Herschberg, *Pinkes Bialistok*, 45–47; Stanisław Kalabiński, *Pierwszy okres przemysłu i klasy robotniczej Białostocczyzny 1807–1870.*

43. Herschberg, *Pinkes Bialistok*, II, 46–53.

44. Just as Lodz had developed into a center of woolen textile production because of its location on the Polish–Prussian frontier, so did Bialystok, located on the new Russian tariff border, after 1831 also emerge as a center of the textile industry in this area. Needless to say, the shift in tariff borders was a blow to the woolen industries of Lodz, whose owners moved many of their factories across the border to Bialystok. See Davies, *God's Playground*, 172–74; and Piotr Wandycz, *The Lands of Partitioned Poland, 1795–1918*, 122–23.

45. Herschberg, II, 44–45.

46. Ibid., 46–47.

47. Ibid., 45–47.

48. Ibid., 28–38.

49. Max Havelin, YIVO Autobiography Collection, 1939. RG102, #21, YIVO Institute for Jewish Research.

50. Max Pogorelsky, "Why I Left the Old Country and What I Achieved in the U.S.," YIVO Autobiography Collection, 1939. RG102, Box 16, Autobiography #194. YIVO Institute for Jewish Research.

51. Herman Frank, "Der biterer kamf tsvishen de loynketniks un vebers," 368.

52. Herschberg, *Pinkes Bialistok* II, 85.

53. Unlike most other strikes in the Pale that protested factory condition, in Bialystok, strikes targeted the system of production. See Ezra Mendelsohn, *Class Struggle in the Pale*, 19–24. For more on the 1887 strike, see Frank, "Der biterer kamf tsvishen de loynketniks un vebers," 369.

54. Herschberg, *Pinkes Bialistok* II, 81–84.

55. Stanisław Kalabiński, "Stan zatrudnienia w przemyśle Białostocczyzny w latach 1870–1914," 82–85.

56. Ibid., 89–90.

57. Ibid., 90–91. See also Ezra Mendelsohn, *Class Struggle in the Pale*, 23; Max Havelin, Autobiography, #21; Yosef Winiecki, Autobiography #28; Max Pogorelsky, Autobiography #194; Autobiography Collection, YIVO Institute for Jewish Research. One of the largest waves of Jewish emigration from Bialystok occurred between the years 1904 and 1909, when a severe depression left more than half of Bialystok's workers unemployed; see Kalabiński, "Stan zatrudnienia w przemyśle Białostocczyzny w latach 1870–1914," 103–104. For a personal account of the mass migration from Bialystok in this period, see the autobiography of Yosef Winiecki, YIVO Archives, #28

58. For a description of Jewish entrepreneurs' role in the development of the Białystok textile industry (as well as a list of Jews who owned major textile factories), see Herschberg, *Pinkes Bialistok* II, 55–70, and Mendelsohn, *Class Struggle in the Pale*, 18. This pattern continued into the interwar period; see Piotr Wróbel, "Na równi pochyłej. Żydzi Białegostoku w latach 1918–1939," 167–68; Jerzy Joka, "Z dziejów walk klasowych proletariatu Białegostoku w latach 1918, 1939,"

285–352. This is reflective of the general situation of Jewish workers in the Pale. See Mendelsohn, *Class Struggle in the Pale,* 10.

59. For more on the complex relationship between non-Jewish and Jewish workers in Bialystok, see Moshe Mishkinsky, *Reshit tenuat ha-poalim ha-yehudit bi-rusiya,* 180; and Stanislaw Kalabiński, "Początki ruchu robotinczego w białostockim okręgu przemysłowym w latach," 143–94.

60. Herschberg, *Pinkes Bialistok* II, 49–53.

61. Mendelsohn, *Class Struggle in the Pale,* 19–21.

62. Herschberg, *Pinkes Bialistok* II, 81.

63. Ibid., 81–82.

64. Mendelsohn, *Class Struggle in the Pale,* 19–22.

65. For more on the strikes of the 1880s see Frank, "Der biterer kamf tsvishen de loynketniks un vebers," 368–69.

66. Herschberg, *Pinkes Bialistok* II, 81–84; and Frank, "Der biterer kamf tsvishen de loynketniks un vebers," 344–46.

67. Other Bialystoker Jews also note in their reminiscences how the recession in Bialystok in the late 1880s encouraged them to immigrate to the United States. See Zelig Victor, "My First Years in America," 18.

68. Adele Lindenmeyr, *Poverty Is Not a Vice,* 99; and Natan Meir, "The Jewish Community of Kiev: Community and Charity in an Imperial Russian City," 164–99.

69. Herschberg, *Pinkes Bialistok* I, 269–314.

70. Y. B. RG102, Box 15, Autobiography 178, p. 13, YIVO Autobiography Collection, 1939 Contest, YIVO Institute for Jewish Research.

71. Michael Stanislawski, *Tsar Nicholas I and the Jews: The Transformation of Jewish Society in Russia, 1825–1855,* 123–25; 185–86. Eli Lederhendler has argued, building on Max Weber's definition of the state as the legitimate arbiter of violence, that the kahal's monopoly on access and recourse to the state was the central defining characteristic of power in "pre-modern" Jewish politics. See Lederhendler, *The Road to Modern Jewish Politics,* 3–13.

72. On the dense network of new charitable institutions established in Bialystok in this period, see Herschberg, *Pinkes Bialistok* I, 315–41. Benjamin Nathans provides a detailed analysis of this contest for power in his discussion of the mercantile elite in St. Petersburg and their access to government officials, arguing that this contest for power between old and new elites defined Russian Jewish history for much of the next century. See Nathans, *Beyond the Pale,* 38–69. For a general overview of the kehilla see Stanislawski, *Tsar Nicholas I and the Jews,* 123–25; 185–86; and Jacob Katz, *Tradition and Crisis: Jewish Society at the End of the Middle Ages.*

73. Lindenmeyr, *Poverty Is Not a Vice,* provides an excellent overview of this entire movement.

74. RGIA f. 821, d. 108, ll. 143–47.

75. S. Ia. Ianovskii, *Evreiskaia blagotvoritel'nost',* 16–19.

76. *Khronika Voskhoda* No. 39, September 19, 1899, 1194–97.

77. Ianovskii, *Evreiskaia blagotvoritel'nost,'* 19. On the korobka, which Michael Stanislawski has termed "the basic internal tax of the Jewish community," see Stanislawski, *Tsar Nicholas I and the Jews,* 40.

78. Discussions of Jewish philanthropic agencies in St. Petersburg and Kiev illustrate how members of this new Jewish elite throughout the empire used philanthropy for similar goals. See Nathans, *Beyond the Pale,* 123–64; Meir, "The Jewish Community of Kiev," 164–99. Such was the case in Western Europe as well. See Rainer Liedtke, *Jewish Welfare in Hamburg and Manchester, c. 1850–1914,* 10–12.

79. The development of Bialystok's Jewish health care system is similar to other cities in the empire. See Ryszard Zabłotniak, "Niektóre Wiadomości O Żydowskiej Służbie Zdrowia w Białymstoku," 111–15. For a larger perspective, see Lisa Epstein, "Caring for the Soul's House: The Jews of Russia and Health Care, 1860–1914."

80. *Zikhroynes un maysim fun lines holim bialistok* (Bialystok, 1923), 4.

81. See Tomacz Wisniewski, "The Linat Hatsedek Charitable Fraternity in Bialystok," 122 and footnotes 4, 5.

82. Y.B. RG102, Box 15 Autobiography 178,14. YIVO Autobiography Collection. YIVO Institute for Jewish Research.

83. For a full discussion of rapid developments in the field of Jewish health care in this period see Epstein, "Caring for the Soul's House."

84. Herschberg, *Pinkes Bialistok* I, 331.

85. Sara Bender, *The Jews of Bialystok,* 5.

86. Herschberg, *Pinkes Bialistok* I, 331.

87. *Spradzowanii Kalender b belostok?* 65.

88. Concerning the rigid hierarchical organization of the kehilla, see Katz, *Tradition and Crisis,* 65–102.

89. Herschberg, *Pinkes Bialistok* II, 331–35.

90. Lindenmeyr, *Poverty Is Not a Vice,* 116; Louise McReynolds and Cathy Popkin, "The Objective Eye and the Common Good," 60.

91. *Bakasha me-Linat Hatzedek,* 1901 [Bialystok: July 10, 1901], Jewish National Library, L331; Dovid Sohn, ed., *Bialistoker bilder album,* 96.

92. "Hoda'at Lines Hatzedek, 1885" PL 331, Archives for the History of the Jewish People.

93. Dovid Klementinovski, *Dr. Yosef Khazanovitsh: der idealist, natsionalist un folksmentsh.*

94. Ibid, 9.

95. Ibid., 12–13.

96. For more on the haskalah movement that originated in Western Europe, see Michael Meyer's excellent overview in *Jewish Identity in the Modern World;* and David Sorkin, *The Transformation of German Jewry, 1780–1840.* In Eastern Europe, the haskalah followed different patterns. See Immanuel Etkes, ed., *ha-Dat veha-ḥayim: tenu'at ha-Haskalah ha-Yehudit be-Mizrach Eropah;* Shmuel Feiner, *Haskalah ve-Historyah: toldoteha shel hakarat-ʿavar Yehudit modernit;* Mordechai Zalkin, *Ba'alot ha-shahar: ha-Hasklah ha-Yehudit ba-Imperyah ha-Rusit ba-me'ah ha-tesha'esreh.*

97. Klementinovski, *Dr. Yosef Khazanovitsh,* 15–16.

98. Epstein, "Caring for the Soul's House."

99. Nancy Mandelker Frieden, *Russian Physicians in an Era of Reform and Revolution,* 333, based on V.I. Grebenshchikov, "Opyt razrabotki rezul'tatov registratsii vrachei v Rossii," I: 111–13. Even more remarkable, Jewish women represented 24 percent of Russia's female physicians. See Carole Balin, "The Call to Serve: Jewish Women Medical Students in Russia, 1872–1887."

100. G. Vol'tke, "Meditsinskiia professii po deistvuiushchemu russkomu zakonodatel'stvu," vol. 10, 780.

101. Herschberg, *Pinkes Bialistok* II, 432–42; "Hoda'at Lines Hatzedek, 1885," PL 331, Central Archives for the History of the Jewish People.

102. Klementinovski, *Dr. Yosef Khazanovitsh,* 31.

103. Wisniewski, "The Lines Hatsedek Charitable Fraternity, 1885–1939," 124.

104. Bialystok proverb quoted in ibid., 121.

105. Nahum Prylucki "Przemowienie na uroczystej akademii z okazji jubileuszu 50-lecia Lines Hatsedek," 6, quoted in Wisniewski, "The Lines Hatsedek Charitable Fraternity," 124.

106. *Nyu Yorker abend post,* June 28, 1900, 6.

107. Ibid.

108. Zvi Gitelman, ed. *The Emergence of Modern Jewish Politics: Bundism and Zionism in Eastern Europe,* 13; Nathans, *Beyond the Pale,* 201–307.

109. Gitelman, *The Emergence of Modern Jewish Politics,* 13. For discussions of similar developments in other cities in Imperial Russia, see Nathans, *Beyond the Pale,* 123–64; Meir "The Jewish Community of Kiev," 164–99.

110. Alexander Orbach, *New Voices of Russian Jewry: A Study of the Russian-Jewish Press of Odessa, 1860–1871;* Zipperstein, *The Jews of Odessa,* 96–113.

111. To be sure, the Bund, the Zionist movement, and to a lesser extent, the Esperanto movement have been discussed quite extensively by scholars of Jewish Eastern Europe; yet few scholars analyze these movements within the rubric of migration. See, for example, Frankel, *Prophecy and Politics;* Mendelsohn, *Class Struggle in the Pale;* Luz, *Parallels Meet;* Eli Lederhendler, *Jewish Responses to Modernity;* David Vital, *Zionism: The Formative Years.*

112. Mendelsohn, *Class Struggle in the Pale,* 31–46.

113. The Bund helped coordinate 78 percent of all strikes in Bialystok between 1901 and 1903; see Stanisław Kalabinski, "Białostockie Organizacje SDKPiL, PPS, Bundu, Socjalistów-Rewolucjonistów i Anarchistów w latach 1901–1903," 73.

114. Frank, "Der biterer kamf tsvishen de loynketniks un vebers," 371.

115. Y. B. RG102, Box 15, Autobiography 178, p.15. YIVO Autobiography Collection, 1939 Contest. YIVO Institute for Jewish Research Piotr Wróbel, "Na równi pochyłej. Żydzi Białegostoku w latach 1918–1939: demografia, ekonomika desintegracja, konflikty z Polakami," in *Studia Podlaskie,* 174–75.

116. "Kol Korai Me-Badatz" 1903 [Russian, Yiddish] Central Archives for the History of the Jewish People, PL 111.

117. The full text of this proclamation can be found in Stanisław Kalabiński, "Odezwy Białostockich Komitetów Partii Robotniczych do Proletariatu Żydowskiego z lat 1897–1900," 94–95. The quotation from the Jewish sage Hillel is derived from *Ethics of Our Fathers,* Chapter 1, Mishna 14.

118. "Di letzte nokh rikhten" *Der bialistoker arbeter* 1 (1899), 43, Bund Archives, YIVO Institute for Jewish Research.

119. "Di oyfgaben fun di veber," *Der bialistoker arbeter* 3 (1900) 5, Reel 190, Bund Archives. YIVO Institute for Jewish Research.

120. In fact, Sender Bloch's textile factory, the first Jewish-owned textile factory in Bialystok, was actually run by his widow, Malka-Rayzel. See Herschberg, *Pinkes Bialistok* II, 28–31, 34–35.

121. "Umziste sine," *Der bialistoker arbeter* 7 (1902), 7. Reel 190, Bund Archives. YIVO Institute for Jewish Research.

122. Bund leaders stated that "The disparagement of the shpuliarkes is merely a remnant from past times when workers were not class conscious and every individual sought to better his bitter state. . . . the stronger one hates the weaker one and considers him inhuman. . . . Those old times are, however, over." See *Der bialistoker arbeter* 7 (1902): 7. Reel 190, Bund Archives.

123. Bialystok was not the only city with such a newspaper. One can find similar regionalist rhetoric in *Der minsker arbeter* and *Der vilner arbeter*, Reel 190, Bund Archives. YIVO Institute for Jewish Research.

124. "Di osilennaya oyrana [*sic.*, read okhrana] in Bialistok," *Der bialistoker arbeter* 7 (1902), 1.

125. Ibid.

126. Compare proclamations 3, 4, 5, 7, and 8, published between 1898 and 1899; these can be found in "Odezwy Białostockich Komitetów Partii Robotniczych do Proletariatu Żydowskiego z lat 1897–1900," 91–98.

127. *Der bialistoker arbeter* 2 (1900), 1–4; *Der bialistoker arbeter* 6 (1901), 1. *Der bialistoker arbeter* 7 (1902), 1.

128. The Bund had scores of meetings in which thousands of workers participated between 1901 and 1904. See Kalabiński, "Białostockie Organizacje SDKPiL, PPS, Bundu, Socjalistów-Rewolucjonistów," 74–75.

129. In 1901, the head of the secret police, Zubatova, founded an Independent Jewish Workers Party to compete with the Bund, and many Jews joined this party. See Kalabiński, "Białostockie Organizacje SDKPiL, PPS, Bundu, Socjalistów-Rewolucjonistów," 75–78.

130. "Tsu ale Bialistoker arbeter," May 1905. Bund Archive: Mg 9. f 24. YIVO Institute for Jewish Research.

131. Kalabiński, "Białostockie Organizacje SDKPiL, PPS, Bundu, Socjalistów-Rewolucjonistów," 55–90.

132. Ibid., 79–81.

133. Luz, *Parallels Meet*, x.

134. Mohilever accepted this position reluctantly, for he feared it would interfere with his activism on behalf of Hibbat Zion, which he founded in 1882. He accepted on the condition that he could continue his traveling and fundraising for his cause. See Fishman, "Toldot Rebbe Shmuel," in *Sefer Shmuel Zikhron le-harav Shmuel Mohilever*, 28.

135. Luz, *Parallels Meet*, 63.

136. *Hibbat Zion* (Love of Zion) was the original term for the Zionist movement in Eastern Europe. Hibbat Zion was used both in reference to a particular ideology and to the loose organization of groups committed to this ideology which

came together at the Kattowitz conference of 1882. *Hovevei Zion* is the term used to refer to the adherents of Hibbat Zion; see M. Ben Zvi, *Rabbi Samuel Mohilever,* 7-8.

137. On the hundreds who joined the Bialystok Hibbat Zion chapter, see M. Dolitszky to E. Levin, August 24, 1881. Microfilm HM/1010, Central Archives for the History of the Jewish People, Jerusalem.

138. For more on the Polish nationalist rebellion and how it shaped discourse in the western Russian Empire, see Brian Porter, *When Nationalism Began to Hate: Imagining Modern Politics in Nineteenth-Century Poland;* and Weeks, *Nation and State in Late Imperial Russia,* 110-30.

139. Unless sanctioned by the tsar, all political organizations were illegal in tsarist Russia. M. Dolitszky to E. Levin, August 24, 1881. Microfilm HM/1010.

140. Hovevei Zion, Bialystok, to Kol Yisrael Hoveveim, Paris, May 15, 1883. Central Zionist Archives [CZA] Folder A9/63/2.

141. Yosef Katz, *The "Business" of Settlement: Private Entrepreneurship in the Jewish Settlement of Palestine,* 101-113, 141-42.

142. Dr. Leon Pinsker, one of these assimilated Jews, considered Mohilver an "impractical man who knew nothing about organizing a popular movement and was familiar only with the dicta of the *Shulḥan Arukh."* See Luz, *Parallels Meet,* 64.

143. On the impressive size of the Bialystok Hibbat Zion group, see M. Dolitszky to E. Levin, August 24, 1881. Microfilm HM/1010; Luz, *Parallels Meet,* 64.

144. Puah Rakovsky, *My Life as a Jewish Radical,* 72-78.

145. Sonia Mazny, Oral Interview, December 13, 2003.

146. Puah Rakovsky, *My Life as a Jewish Radical,* 94-102; "Sukenik-Feinsod, Hasya," in *Jewish Women: A Comprehensive Historical Encyclopedia.* I would like to thank Paula Hyman for pointing me to this source.

147. J. L. Fishman, ed., *Sefer Shemuel,* 138. Mohilever's tolerance of many different types of Jews (observant and nonobservant) differs drastically from other rabbinic leaders in his day. See Luz, *Parellels Meet,* 56-58.

148. See *Constitution fun Bialystoker Verein Somach Noflim* (1886), *Der bialistoker pioner,* 5.

149. Alejandro Portes and Rubén Rumbaut, *Immigrant America,* 181. Portes and Rumbaut summarize the general literature on this topic, 180-219.

150. For more on Zamenhof and the language of Esperanto, see Marjorie Boulton, *Zamenhof: Creator of Esperanto;* Edward Privat, *The Life of Zamenhof.*

151. Privat, *Life of Zamenhof,* 22.

152. Ludwig Zamenhof's address to the Esperanto Congress, August 18, 1906, Geneva, quoted in Boulton, *Zamenhof,* 108. Zamenhof noted several times the centrality of his childhood in Bialystok to his ideology concerning language and ethnic tension. See Privat, *Life of Zamenhof,* 22-23.

153. Ludwig Zamenhof's address, August 18, 1906, quoted in Boulton, *Zamenhof,* 108.

154. Quoted from Zamenhof's speech to the 1905 Esperanto Conference, Boulougne, France, in Ivo Lapenna's "Dr. Ludwig Zamenhof's Greatness," 5. Merhavia Archives.

155. Boulton, *Zamenhof,* 18-31.

156. Ludwig Zamenhof, *Linguo Internacia* (Warsaw, 1887), 7.

157. Zamenhof's 1906 speech to the International Esperanto Conference, Geneva, quoted in Boulton, *Zamenhof,* 108.

158. Ibid.

159. This is not peculiar to Bialystok, as Steven Zipperstein highlights in his discussion of Osip Rabinovich, editor of the Russian-language *Razsvet* in Odessa, "who viewed Russian Jewry through the prism of his beloved Odessa," and mistakenly assumed that all Russian Jewry knew the rudiments of the Russian language, when few actually did. See Zipperstein, *The Jews of Odessa,* 106.

160. Zamenhof's 1906 speech to the International Esperanto Conference, Geneva, 2; cited in Boulton, *Zamenhof: Creator of Esperanto,* 2.

161. Herschberg, *Pinkes Bialistok* I, 426.

162. For the numerous visitors and the plaque that marked Zamenhof's birthplace, see "Bialystok," Goskind Films (1939).

163. Zipperstein, *The Jews of Odessa,* 70–113, 129–50; Bemporad, "Red Star on the Jewish Street"; Keely Stauter-Halstead, *The Nation in the Village: The Genesis of Peasant National Identity in Austrian Poland, 1848–1914,* 2–17; Meir, "Jewish Community of Kiev."

164. S. Kalabinski, "Białostockie Organizacje SDKPiL, PPS, Bundu, Socjalistów-Rewolucjonistów i Anarchistów w Latach 1901–1903," *Rocznik Białostocki* X (1970), 55–90.

165. Bialystok was the PPS's center for the publication and distribution of its revolutionary Yiddish newspapers. See S. Kalabinski, "Białostockie Organizacje SDKPiL, PPS, Bundu"; and Joshua D. Zimmerman, "Poles, Jews and the Politics of Nationality: Relations between the Polish Socialist Party and the Jewish Labor Bund, 1892–1905."

166. S. Kalabinski, "Białostockie Organizacje SDKPiL, PPS, Bundu," 73.

167. In Lodz, for example, there was also a strong revolutionary fervor. See B. Mark, "Udział Proletariatu Żydowskiego w Czerwcowym Powstaniu Łódzkim I w Walkach Solidarnościowych," *Żydowskiego Instytutu Historycznego w Polsce* 23 (1957), 34–62.

168. The original report can be found in RGIA, f. 1284, d. 193, storage unit 136. This report is discussed in detail in Pawel Korzec's "Sviatopolk-Mirsky's Report to the Tsar on the Jewish Question in 1902–3," 92–94.

169. Bernard Mark, "Proletariat Żydowski w Okresie Strajków Ekonomicznych w Lutym-Marcu-Kwietniu 1905 r." [The Jewish Proletariat in the Period of Economic Strikes during February, March, and April 1905] *ZIH* 19–20 (1956), 4–9.

170. F. Kurtz, "Ha-pogrom bi-Bialistok bi-shnat 1906," 5 [unpublished manuscript], Merhavia Archives, Hebrew University.

171. Herschberg, *Pinkes Bialistok* II, 114–17.

172. Abraham Ascher, *The Revolution of 1905,* vol. I.

173. Boris Tsipin, "Zikroynes fun a bialistoker bundist," in Herman Frank, ed., *Natsyonale un politishe bavegungen bay yidn in byalistok: materyal tsu der geshikhte,* 45.

174. Herschberg, *Pinkes Bialistok* II, 114–17.

175. Ironically, the governor of the gubernia was present so that he could maintain order in Bialystok.

176. I. Michael Aronson, *Troubled Waters: The Origins of the 1881 Anti-Jewish Pogroms in Russia;* Hans Rogger, *Jewish Policies and Right-Wing Politics in Imperial Russia.* For more on this volatile period in Russian history, see Ascher, *The Revolution of 1905,* 142–61; Shlomo Lambroza, "The Pogroms of 1903–1906," in Jon Klier and Shlomo Lambroza, eds., *Pogroms: Anti-Jewish Violence in Modern Russian History,* 226–29, 238–42. Lambroza addresses this issue in much greater detail in his dissertation, "The Pogrom Movement in Tsarist Russia, 1903–1906" (Ph.D. Dissertation, Rutgers University, 1981).

177. Ascher, *The Revolution of 1905,* 148.

178. "Report of the Duma Commission on the Bialystok Massacre," *American Jewish Yearbook 1906–7,* 64–65; Ascher, *The Revolution of 1905,* 149.

179. "Report of the Duma Commission on the Bialystok Massacre," 73–74.

180. "Report of the Duma Commission on the Bialystok Massacre," 76.

181. In contrast to pogroms in the late nineteenth century, the Bialystok pogrom of 1906 clearly suggests the complicity of the tsarist government in anti-Jewish violence. See Aronson, *Troubled Waters;* Rogger, *Jewish Policies and Right-Wing Politics.*

182. For more on this volatile period in Russian history, see Ascher, *The Revolution of 1905,* 142–61. With specific relation to anti-Jewish violence, see Lambroza, "The Pogroms of 1903–1906," 226–29, 238–42; Kurtz, "Bialystok lifnei ha-Pogrom," 2.

183. Ascher, *The Revolution of 1905,* 146.

184. A full report of the pogrom and the months leading up to it appears in *Dielo o pogromie v Belostockie 1–3 Iunia 1906 goda,* 1–55. Also see "Report of the Duma Commission on the Bialystok Massacre," 71.

185. "Do obywateli miasta Białegostoku." Archives for the History of the Jewish People, PL113.

186. The press often discussed and hailed the more than six hundred pogroms that took place just between the signing of the October Manifesto in 1905 and September 1906. See Leo Motzkin's *Die Judenpogrome in Russland,* quoted in Lambroza, "The Pogroms of 1903–1906," 226–29.

187. "Report of the Duma Commission on the Bialystok Massacre," 72.

188. *Nasha zhizn,* June 6, 1906 quoted in Ascher, *The Revolution of 1905,* 149.

189. Ibid., 148–50.

190. Ibid., 148.

191. Aside from thanking the main perpetrators, the troops, for their "splendid service during the Belostok pogrom," the central government promoted the main organizer of the pogrom, police superintendent S. D. Sheremetev. See Lambroza, "The Pogroms of 1903–1906," 229, 237–38.

192. See the PPS's newspaper, *Robotnik,* June 29, 1906, no.129, quoted in Frankel, *Prophecy and Politics,* 153–55.

193. The PPS newspaper, *Robotnik,* June 19, 1906, no. 125, quoted in Frankel, 155.

194. Adam Dobroński, "The Pogrom against the Jews in Białystok and the Polish Press Attitude," 4 Merhavia Archives, Hebrew University.

195. The *Black Hundreds* is the generic term used for the many small right-wing groups that were founded during the spring and summer months of 1905.

They went under a wide variety of names, but all represented the basic conservative policies of Romanov nationalism, autocracy, and Orthodoxy. These groups played a central role in instigating attacks against Jews under the guise of patriotism and loyalty to the tsar.

196. Lambroza, "The Pogroms of 1903–1906," 238.

197. Kurtz, "Ha-pogrom bi-Bialistok bi-shnat 1906," 21–22.

198. *Der Fraynd* 120, 2 (15) July 1906.

199. Moses Eisenstein, *Der Pogrom von Bialystok*, 3, 19.

200. A. Litvak "Vegn di pogromen," *Folks-Tsaytung* (July 11, 1906) 86:1, quoted in Frankel, *Prophecy and Politics*, 155.

201. Eisenstein, *Der Pogrom von Bialystok*, 22.

202. Numerous articles discuss how the pogrom of 1906 prompted many Bialystoker Jews to emigrate and settle in new homes throughout the world. Moshe Kroll, "Der bialistoker pogrom: bleter fun mayn lebn," *Zukunft* (April 1939), 235–36; Dovid Klemintinovsky, "Der bialistoker pogrom in 1906," *Bialystoker Stimme* 260 (April 1956), 26–30; Zechariah Goldberg, "A kapital vegn bialistoker pogrom fun 1906," *Bialystoker Stimme* 254 (September 1951), 23; and Bensel Tsolevitsh, "In di blotige teg fun bialistoker pogrom," *Bialystoker Stimme* 260 (April 1956), 31–33.

203. A. Litvak's "Vegn di pogromen," *Folks-tsaytung* (July 11, 1906), no. 86, 1, quoted in Frankel, *Prophecy and Politics*, 155.

204. Lederhendler, ""Classless" 534.

205. Shaul Stampfer, "Internal Jewish Migration in the Russian Empire," 42.

206. Frank, "De goldene tekufa," 19–25. For statistical figures see Wisniewski, Appendix III.

207. The following schools were founded or expanded between 1906 and 1914, and each represents a wide range of political and cultural affiliations: Alexanderov's Gymnasia (1906), Gorevitch's Klasika Yidishe Gymnasia (1908), Beit Midrash Hevrah Tehilim (1910), Beit Midrash Torat Hesed (1912), Beit Midrash Torah Hayim (1912), Beit Midrash Mishna'ot (1914), Beit Midrash Tikhmoni (1914), Beit Midrash Bialystokci (1914), Yidishe-Rusisher Gymnasia (1914), and Gutman's Private Gymnasia for Girls (1914).

208. Bender, *The Jews of Bialystok*, 12–13.

209. Anna Gepner, Oral Interview, August 21, 1997, Melbourne, Australia.

210. Paula Hyman, *Gender and Assimilation in Modern Jewish History*, 50–63. The following schools founded in this period represent a wide range of political and cultural affiliations: Russian Girls' Gymnasia (Rusishe Frauen Gimnasia, 1897), Girls' Commerce School (Frauen Komers, 1905), Bund School for Girls (1905), Bogdanousky Polish School for Girls (1907), Feinsilber School for Girls (1908), and Gutman's Private Gymnasia for Girls (1914); Herschberg, *Pinkes Bialistok* II, 359.

211. Dori, Parnas, "80 lailah va-lailah: Ha Bimah; Yitzhah Norman, Be-reshit ha-Bimah: Nahum Tsemah meyased ha-Bimah.

212. For more on Simon Rawidowicz, see Noam Pianko, "Diaspora Jewish Nationalism and Identity in America, 1914–1967", 177–226.

213. Introduction: "The Life and Writings of Simon Rawidowicz," 16.

214. GARF f. 9529, op. 1, del. 2, 6, 22. For a larger statistical overview of the impact of the war, see Yakov Bachrach, *Demografie fun der yidisher befelkerung in bialistok,* 10.

215. Pesach Kaplan, "Unzer likhtige fargangenheyt," *Bialistoker Almanakh,* 37.

216. See Isaac Bashevis Singer, "Concerning Yiddish Literature in Poland (1943)," 21–22.

2. Rebuilding Homeland in Promised Lands

1. Yosef Lipnick, "Dovid Sohn's rol in der landsmanshaft," *Bialystoker Stimme* 25 (1932): 7.

2. Sohn, "A Half Century of Bialystoker Activity in America" (manuscript, 1928), Tel Aviv University Archives, A-18, 4.

3. Moshe Molotovski, "Dovid Sohn—mister bialistok," *Bialystoker Stimme* 287 (April 1961): 48.

4. A vast international literature exists on immigrant associations and the role they play in facilitating immigrants' economic adaptation to their new homes. For an excellent overview of recent historical literature, see Jose Moya, "Immigrants and Associations: A Global and Historical Perspective." For a survey of some earlier scholarship on immigrants and institutions, see George Pozzetta, ed., *Immigrant Institutions: The Organization of Immigrant Life.* Milton Gordon's *Assimilation in American Life: The Role of Race, Religion and National Origins* is one of the most influential explanations of how institutions aid immigrant acculturation the United States. Prior to the Second World War, several writers surveyed the landsmanshaftn movement, most notably the WPA's Yiddish Writers' Group led by Isaac Rontch. See I. Rontch, ed., *Di yidishe landsmanshaftn fun nyu york.*

5. Daniel Soyer, *Jewish Immigrant Associations and American Identity in New York, 1880–1939;* 1; P. Wald's "Di landslayt fereynen," *Der Avangard* (Buenos Aires), November 1916, 31–35; L. Zhitinsky, "Landsmanshaftn in Argentine," 155–57.

6. Aside from the WPA's study of landsmanshaftn organizations in New York (see note 4), there were few other major scholarly treatment of these institutions until the 1980s. In 1985, Michael Weisser's *Brotherhood of Memory: Jewish Landsmanshaftn in the New World* addressed these organizations, arguing that landsmanshaftn, because of their use of the Yiddish language, acted as bulwarks against East European Jewish immigrant acculturation. Recently, however, Daniel Soyer's *Jewish Immigrant Associations and American Identity in New York, 1880–1939* demonstrates the ways in which landsmanshaftn facilitated Jewish immigrant acculturation by introducing them to American civic culture through their modes of operation. He argues elsewhere that landsmanshaft organizations "constituted an American phenonmenon." Daniel Soyer, "Jewish Landsmanshaftn (Hometown Associations) in New York, 1880s to 1924" (Ph.D. dissertation, New York University, 1994), 492. Also see Susan Milamed, "Proskurover Landsmanshaftn," Hannah Kliger, "Communication and Ethnic Community: The Case of Landsmanshaftn" (Ph.D. dissertation, University of Pennsylvania, 1985); and Hannah Kliger, "Traditions of Grass-Roots Organization and Leadership."

There are even fewer studies of the landmanshaft movement in other countries. See P. Wald's "Di landslayt fereynen," *Der Avangard* (Buenos Aires), November 1916, 31–35; L. Zhitinsky, "Landsmanshaftn in Argentine," 155–57.

7. Since 1945, the numerous scholarly discussions of the migratory patterns of Jews from the lands of Eastern Europe (that in the early twentieth century fell under the political aegis of such diverse entities as the Russian Empire, the Austro-Hungarian Empire, or Romania) have almost universally deployed the universal category of "East European Jew," rarely taking into account the vast regional differences in this area. See, for example, Moses Rischin's pioneering monograph, *The Promised City;* and Gartner, *The Jewish Immigrant in England.* While scholars in the field of American Jewish history have recognized and discussed the formative role played by variables such as generation, gender, and class in understanding this mass population shift, few have yet seriously considered the importance of regionalism in molding this process. Indeed, within the wide swath of land known as Eastern Europe, regional identity provided a cornerstone for Jewish identity. See Lederhendler, "Did Russian Jewry Exist prior to 1917," 15–22. To be sure, regionalism played a similar role in identity definition in the larger European context; see Celia Applegate, "A Europe of Regions: Reflections on the Historiography of Sub-National places in Modern Times," 1157–82; Celia Applegate, *A Nation of Provincials: The German Idea of Heimat;* Alon Confino's *The Nation as a Local Metaphor: Württemberg, Imperial Germany, and National Memory, 1871–1918.*

8. Rukhl Rifkin, YIVO RG 102, Autobiography #79; Harry Sokol, YIVO RG 102: Autobiography #142. Both are part of the YIVO 1942 Autobiography Contest Collection, YIVO Institute for Jewish Research.

9. Rukhl Rifkin, Autobiography #79; 1952 Addendum, p. 3.

10. Max Pogorelsky, "Why I Left the Old Country and What I Achieved in the U.S." YIVO RG 102 Box 16:48. Autobiography #194, p. 16. By the 1880s, a commercial revolution had occurred in the women's clothing market. On the development of the American garment industry, see Egal Feldman, *Fit for Men: A Study of New York's Clothing Trade;* and Joel Seidman, *The Needle Trades; Reports of the Immigration Commission,* vol. 11, "Immigrants in Industry" (Clothing Manufacture), 61st Cong. (Senate) Second Session (Washington, D.C. 1911), 259–69.

11. Long periods of initial unemployment are discussed by many immigrant autobiographers. See YIVO RG 102 Autobiography Collection, YIVO Institute for Jewish Research. The dramatic growth in the women and children's garment sector is exemplified by the fact that in 1859 only 6,000 worked in this industry; by 1909 more than 150,000 workers were employed in just this sector of the garment industry; see Rischin, *Promised City,* 183–85; Glenn, *Daughters of the Shtetl,* 132–37.

12. B. Rosen YIVO RG 102, Autobiography #215. YIVO Autobiography Collection.

13. Arkadius Kahan, "Economic Opportunites," in *Essays in Jewish Social and Economic History,* 105–106.

14. Max Havelin, YIVO RG 102 Autobiography #21, pp. 17–21. Autobiography Collection, YIVO Institute for Jewish Research.

15. Max Pogorelsky, "Why I Left the Old Country and What I Achieved in the U.S." YIVO RG 102 Box 16:48. Autobiography #194. Autobiography Collection, YIVO Institute for Jewish Research.

16. Ibid.

17. A wide array of small garment factories were run by Jews from Bialystok, as can be seen through the advertisements in the souvenir journals of various Bialystoker organizations in New York and Chicago. For example, the anniversary journals of *Bialystoker Verein Somach Noflim* (1931) and the *Bialystoker Young Men's Association* (1936) contain advertisements by members for more than thirty different businesses associated with the garment industry. Alexander Brothers' Dress Manufacturers, 1369 Milwaukee Ave, Chicago; Wiesenfeld Men's Shirt Factory, 76 Delancey Street, New York; Jacob Wolf Dresses, Brooklyn, New York; Morse Avenue Tailors, Chicago, Illinois, are just a sampling of the numerous clothing enterprises opened by Bialystok's Jews in the United States.

18. Space does not allow for close analysis of all the Bialystoker organizations mentioned above or various others founded by Bialystoker émigrés to address their needs. For more on these different organization, see the overview provided in Kliger, "Traditions of Grass-Roots Organization and Leadership," 35–39.

19. *Bialistoker yizker bukh,* 166–67; Sohn, "A History of Bialystoker Jews in America," manuscript, 1934; Goren-Goldstein Center for the Study of Diaspora Jewry; Tel Aviv University Archives, A-18/38. Bialystok's Jews were far from exceptional. See Milamed, "Proskurover Landsmanshaftn," 41; Samuel Margoshes, "The Verband Movement in New York City," quoted in Daniel Soyer, "Between Two Worlds: The Jewish Landsmanshaftn and Immigrant Identity," 22.

20. Louis Cohen, "Zikhroynes fun a member," 3.

21. Many East European landsmanshaft groups framed their institution-building efforts as a strategy to avoid Christian charities. See Soyer, *Jewish Immigrant Associations and American Identity in New York,* 87–111.

22. Itsik Rybalovski, "Di yidishe bialistok in amerike," in *Bialistoker Yizker Bukh,* 335–38.

23. In the 1880s, a group of wealthy women in Bialystok founded Somech Noflim to provide basic financial support to workers' families in Bialystok during times of trouble. See Herschberg, *Pinkes Bialistok* I, 322.

24. Sohn, "Der bialistoker "pilgrims" in amerika," in *The Bialystoker Pioneer: 45th Anniversary Journal of the Bialystoker Verein Somach Noflim,* 5.

25. *Constitution fun Bialistoker Verein Somach Noflim,* Article III: Section V. Exceptions to the "Bialystok only" rule were made for sons of deceased members. They could be American-born and were allowed to join to ensure that their father's family would have resources in case they needed it. For other examples of landsmanshaftn's refusal to allow women to become members, see Soyer, *Jewish Immigrant Associations and American Identity,* 7.

26. *Constitution fun Bialistoker Verein Somach Noflim,* Article I: Section III, October 31, 1886 (New York, reprint, 1924), 5.

27. *Bialistoker Verein Somech Noflim Post Journal,* October 29, 1911. In this souvenir journal are published this organization's financial reports from 1886 to 1911.

28. *Bialistoker Verein Somach Noflim Post Journal* (1911), 8.

29. Ibid., 6.

30. Sohn, "Der bialistoker "pilgrims" in amerika," 3.

31. *Constitution fun Bialistoker Verein Somach Noflim,* Section III: 18.

32. Sohn, "Der bialistoker "pilgrims" in amerika," 5.

33. *Bikur Holim Anshei Bialystok: 18 Monatlicher Bericht, 1906–1908,* 18–19.

34. Ibid.

35. Louis Felder, "Di viktigtse pasirungen aroysgenumen fun protokoln fun unzer bialistoker bikur kholim fun broklin." This article is taken from *40th Anniversary: Bialystoker Bikur Cholim of Brooklyn* (New York, 1937).

36. Louis Felder, "Firtsik yor bialystoker bikur kholim in broklin,"in ibid., 6. Murray Brenner, "A Promise Kept," in ibid, 23. Morris Felder, "The Bialystoker Bikur Cholim—An Important Factor in the Community Life of Brooklyn," in ibid., 15.

37. The founders claimed they upheld the legacy of Lines HaTsedek, which served all people living in Bialystok regardless of religion, by serving all in Brooklyn. See Herman Rosenthal, "The Birth of the Bialystoker Bikur Cholim," in ibid., 9.

38. Bikur Cholim also ran classes that taught English or prepared individuals for citizenship and naturalization procedures. See Sidney Felder, "History of the Bialystoker Bikur Cholim of Brooklyn," 7.

39. Felder, "History of the Bialystoker Bikur Cholim," 5.

40. Rischin, *The Promised City,* 77.

41. Kliger, "Grass-Roots Organization and Leadership," 38.

42. *Bikur Holim Anshei Bialystok: 18 Monatlicher Bericht, 1906–1908,* 18–19.

43. Soyer, *Jewish Immigrant Association and American Identity,* 161–89.

44. Joseph Lipnick, "What David Sohn Has Done for Our Bialystok Landsmanschaft: An Appreciation of His Achievements and the Brief Review of the Development of Our Organization in the Past Thirteen Years," *Bialystoker Stimme* 25 (May 1932): 2.

45. Leon Elbe, "Di shlikhim fun folk," *Tog,* June 22, 1920. A social worker on the Lower East Side proclaimed there was a delegate "mania." See Soyer, *Jewish Immigrant Associations and American Identity in New York,* 175.

46. Between 1911 and 1919, Sohn wrote articles for the *Forverts, Morgen zhurnal, Tag,* and *Varheit.* See Yakov Cohen, "Dovid Sohn zvishen bede velt milkhamos," *Bialytoker Stimme* 1961: 7. For more on Sohn, see Lipnick, "What David Sohn Has Done for Our Bialystok Landsmanschaft," 2–4.

47. Moshe Molotivski, "David Sohn—mister bialistok," 61.

48. For more on the place of shdtadlanim in nineteenth-century Eastern Europe, see François Guesnet, *Polnische Juden im 19. Jahrhundert.*

49. Rontoch, *Di yidishe landsmanshaftn fun nyu york,* 397.

50. See *Byalistoker Froyen zhurnal* 1 (1930), and Ida Adack, "Greetings to David Sohn from the Ladies Auxiliary," *Bialystoker Stimme* 1961.

51. Lipnick, "What David Sohn has Done for Our Bialystok Landsman-schaft," 2.

52. Sohn, "A Half Century of Bialystoker Activity in America" (manuscript, 1928), Tel Aviv University Archives, A-18/67, 2.

53. Sohn, "Unzere oypgebn" *Bialystoker Stimme* 1 (November 1921): 1.

54. All monetary conversions were based on the value of the dollar linked to the Consumer Price Index. For the tools to produce such conversions, go to the economic history Web site http://www.eh.net or to http://www.measuringworth .com.

55. "The Bialystoker Center," 1 (manuscript, 1939), Tel Aviv University Archives, A-18/67. Heri Graf, "Tsu vos a bialistoker tsenter," *Bialystoker Stimme* 3 (March 1922): 1.

56. "Der bialistoker yom tov af ist brodvey," *Forverts,* February 15, 1923, 6.

57. Sohn, "Yakov Krepliak," *Bialystoker Stimme* (September 1955), 39. Also "Yakov Krepliak," in *Leksikon fun der nayer yidisher literature,* vol. 8, 788–90. For more information on this influential Yiddish literary journal, see Steven Cassedy, *Building the Future: Jewish Immigrant Intellectuals and the Making of Tsukunft;* Yakov Krepliak, "Khanukas ha-bayes," *Bialystoker Stimme* 6 (February 1923): 3.

58. Yakov Krepliak, "Khanukas ha-bayes," *Bialystoker Stimme* 6 (February 1923): 3.

59. Ibid.

60. "Bialistok, nyu york, patersun," *Bialistoker relif zhurnal,* 1.

61. Nathan Miler, "Di tetigkaytn fun bialistoker relif fun shikago," *Bialystoker Stimme* 1 (November 1921): 10.

62. Ibid.

63. Sohn, "A Half Century of Bialystoker Activity in America," 1.

64. Eiichiro Azuma, "Pioneers of Overseas Japanese Development," 1189.

65. "Unzer eygene velt," *Bialystoker Stimme* 5 (October 1922), 10. Also see Sohn, *Activities of the Bialystoker Community in America,* 17.

66. For a general overview of the importance of print in the creation of imagined communities in many locales, see Benedict Anderson, *Imagined Communities,* 37–46.

67. According to the personal files of David Sohn, during the 1920s and 1930s, 4,000 *Bialystoker Stimmes* were published in each run and by the 1940s the number of *Stimmes* published reached 5,000. See *Bialystoker Stimme* 239 (November 1945): 1 and Sohn, "The History and Achievements of the Bialystoker Center," undated manuscript, Tel Aviv University Archives A-18/63. In many communities, one or two Bialystoker émigré families would receive the *Bialystoker Stimme* and would share their copies with the other Bialystoker families in the community.

68. Interview with Anna Gepner, August 21, 1997, Melbourne, Australia.

69. Interview with Yehezkel Aran, April 15, 1999, Tel Aviv, Israel.

70. "Bialistok: a koloniol macht," *Bialystoker Stimme* 8 (February 1924): 1; "Der amerikaner royter kreys in bialistok," *Bialystoker Stimme* 2 (January 1922): 1; "Bialistok in argentine un argentine in bialistok," *Bialystoker Stimme* 13 (March 1926): 8; "Di bialistoker in berlin," *Bialystoker Stimme* 4 (June 1922): 12. The regular column on "Velt barimte bialistoker" debuted in the *Bialystoker Stimme* 4 (June 1922): 7–9, while the "Unzer eygene velt" column debuted in the *Bialystoker Stimme* 3 (March 1922): 12. Both soon became regular features. See, for example, *Bialystoker Stimme* 4 (June 1922): 14; *Bialystoker Stimme* 6 (February 1923): 22.

71. Soyer, "Between Two Worlds," 8.

72. Sohn, "A Half Century of Bialystoker Activity in America," 5.

73. Ibid., 10.

74. The Warschauer Haym Solomon Home for the Aged was founded in 1922. See *Warschauer Haym Salomon Home for the Aged Souvenir Journal, 1922–1938*. Also see *Souvenir Journal: Tenth Anniversary Dinner of the Mohilev-on-Dnieper and Vicinity Home for the Aged*. The proliferation of eldercare facilities in the 1920s reflected not only shifting demographics but the growing concern among many immigrant groups and the larger urban working class about how to care for aging family members who could no longer earn wages. See Michael Katz, *In the Shadow of the Poorhouse: A Social History of Welfare in America*.

75. See Katz, *In the Shadow of the Poorhouse*. Sohn's concern for the growing elderly population among the general immigrant Jewish community in New York is evident in his "Elter problemen bey yidn in nyu york," *Naye yom tov bleter* (June 1933), 28.

76. William Kavee, oral interview, July 29, 2007.

77. Ibid., 28. Sohn, reflecting on a recent report of the Welfare Council of New York, notes how there were only 2,500 beds in Jewish old age homes for this growing population.

78. Sohn, "Di tragedia fun eltern dur imigrantn," *Forverts*, July 1, 1934, 4. On the role the Bialystoker Center played in addressing this problem, see Sohn, "Di oyftungen [*sic.*, read *oyftuen*] fun der bialistoker landsmanshaft in di letste 15 yor," *Forverts*, May 26, 1934; Sohn, "Der nayer panim fun landsmanshaftn in amerika," *Naye yom tov bleter* (April 1933), 30.

79. Sohn, "A Half Century of Bialystoker Activity in America," 6.

80. Sohn, "Bialistok af ist brodvey" *Forverts*, June 21, 1931, 3.

81. The full transcript of this meeting can be found in the Goren-Goldstein Center for the Study of Diaspora Jewry; Tel Aviv University Archives, A-18/12. All statements in my following discussion are taken from this thirty-eight page transcript.

82. Ibid., 2.

83. Jacobson, *Special Sorrows*, 78–82; Susan Davis, *Parades and Power: Street Theatre in Nineteenth-Century Philadelphia*.

84. Arthur Goren, *The Politics and Public Culture of American Jews*, 30–31.

85. Sohn, "Bialistok af ist brodvey," *Forverts* June 21, 1931, 3.

86. Ibid.

87. Ibid.

88. Ibid.

89. Sohn, "A Half Century of Bialystoker Activity in America," 13.

90. The handwritten *Annual Report of the Bialystoker Center Old Age Home*, circa 1932 (Yiddish) reports that close to half of the home's twenty-three residents were born in Bialystok. See A-18/17, Tel Aviv University Archives.

91. Sohn, "A Half Century of Bialystoker Activity in America," 6.

92. William Herberg, *Protestant, Catholic, Jew: An Essay in American Religious Sociology*, 186. While there are many problems with Herberg's study and conclusions, he does correctly identify some general trends in early twentieth-

century immigrant America. Nonetheless, the case of Bialystok's Jews does reveal a major weakness in Herberg's reading of East European Jewish immigrant experience. Herberg saw East European Jewish émigrés as fundamentally different from other ethnic groups, such as Italians or Poles. As he wrote:

> But all that the third generation of the Italian or Polish group, for example, could, as Americans, remember, was the religion of the grandfather; the immigrant language and culture and way of life, were, of course, irretrievably gone. And so the emergence of the third generation meant the disappearance of the "Italianess" or "Polishness" of the group, or rather, its dissolution into the religious community. With the Jews, however, it was different. The first and second generation of Jews in America repeated the common immigrant pattern: immigrant foreignness followed by an anxious effort to overcome that foreignness and become American. But the third generation of American Jews, instead of somehow finally getting rid of their Jewishness, as Italians were getting rid of their "Italianness" and the Poles of their "Polishness," actually began to reassert their Jewish identification and to return to their Jewishness. (201)

The revolutionary process Herberg identified occurring among Polish and Italian immigrants was also transpiring among East European Jews. Herberg's inability to see the parallels was rooted in his conflation of East European Jews' ethnic and religious identities. However, for many Jews from Eastern Europe, as this study highlights, regional identity provided the main metaphors and central content of their religious identities. They would never identify as just Jews but rather as Bialystoker Jews.

93. Zvi Hirsch Masliansky, *Kitve Masliansky, neumin, zikhronot u-ma'asot,* 12.

94. Declaration of May 26, 1810 quoted in Avni, *Argentina and the Jews,* 2.

95. Ibid., 20.

96. Derek Penslar, *Shylock's Children,* 241.

97. Kurt Grunwald, *Türkenhirsch: A Study of Baron Maurice de Hirsch;* Theodore Norman, *An Outstretched Arm: A History of the Jewish Colonization Association.*

98. Delagacion de Asociaciones Israelitas Argentinas, *50 años de colonizacion judia en la Argentina.*

99. Osias Shijman, *Colonizacion judia en la Argentina;* Haim Avni, *Argentina and the Jews,* 36.

100. For more on the JCA and the critical role it played in shaping the Jewish immigrant experience in Argentina, see Avni, *Argentina and the Jews,* 32–92.

101. *Ha-melitz* 275 (December 15, 1889), 3.

102. See *Atlas des colonies et domaines de la Jewish Colonization Association en République Argentine et au Brésil [Supplément au rapport annuel pour 1913],* 3–5.

103. Yosef Yachnuk, "'Argentine' in bialistok un 'bialistok' in argentine," *Bialystoker Stimme* 13 (March 1926): 32.

104. M. Reisman, "Af di vegen fun 30 yor bialistoker mishpocha in argentina," *Bialystoker vegn* 5–6 (September 1950): 6.

105. Not only did the settlers arrive in Argentina before the JCA purchased sufficient lands, but the JCA had unrealistic expectations. For example, the JCA wanted the colonists to produce some items for the world market that were impossible to grow in Argentina's climate. See Avni, *Argentina and the Jews*, 34–38.

106. Yakov Beler, "Itsik Kaplan: 'pioner' fun yidisher kolonitzia in argentine," *Bialystoker Stimme* 326 (Sept 1956): 22.

107. Avni, *Argentina and the Jews*, 54–62, 81.

108. Yachnuk, "'Argentine' in bialistok un 'bialistok' in argentine," 32.

109. Ibid.

110. Avni, *Argentina and the Jews*, 81.

111. Victor Mirelman, *Jewish Buenos Aires, 1890–1930*, 187.

112. Argentine land owners contended that with large manufacturing empires, such as the United States, in easy shipping distance, there was no need to develop industry domestically. See W. Armstrong, "The Social Origins of Industrial Growth: Canada, Argentina and Australia, " in Desmond Platt et al., eds., *Argentina, Australia and Canada*, 88–90; and Eugene Sofer, *From Pale to Pampa*, 39–40.

113. Reisman, "Af di vegen fun 30 yor bialistoker mishpocha in argentine," 8; Shlomo Pat, "Zikhroynes zum 20-yorikn yuvile fun Bialystoker farband in Argentine," *Bialystoker vegn* 5–6 (September 1950), 10.

114. Itsik Gotlib, "Polishe yidn in der farmirung fun latin-amerikaner kehillos," in *Yorbukh*, S. Federbush, ed., 302.

115. Elkin, *The Jews of Latin America*, 215.

116. Avni, *Argentina and the Jews*, 15.

117. For more on this week of antisemitic violence and the poor response of the state see ibid., 16; Edgardo Bilsky, *La Semana Trágica*; Carlés Federico, *El Judaismo y La Semana Trágica: la verdadera histoira de los sucesos de enero de 1919;* Daniel Lvovich, *Nacionalismo y antisemitismo en la Argentina*.

118. Elkin, *The Jews of Latin America*, 201.

119. Ibid., 215.

120. Ibid.

121. While in 1886 the Argentine House of Representatives launched an aggressive immigration campaign to encourage European immigration to Argentina, including granting government loans to cover travel expenses for all "suitable" candidates, they offered little support once an émigré arrived in his or her new home. For more on these policies, see Avni, *Argentina and the Jews*, 9–12 and 26–32. Also see Elkin, *The Jews of Latin America*, 221.

122. Reisman, "Af di vegen fun 30 yor bialistoker mishpocha in argentine," 8; Pat, "Zikhroynes zum 20-yorikn yuvile fun bialistoker farband," 10.

123. Pat, "Zikhroynes zum 20-yorikn yuvile," 10.

124. Ibid.

125. Itsik Munacker, "Der bialistoker farband in boynes ayres," *Bialystoker Stimme* 250 (March 1948): 86.

126. Reisman, "Af di vegen fun 30 yor bialistoker mishpocha in argentine," 7.

127. Shelly Tenenbaum, "Immigrants and Capital: Jewish Loan Societies in the United States, 1880–1945," 67–77.

128. Oral interview with Luis Ovsejevich, Enrique Ovsejevich, Dina Ovsejevich, and Elsa Ovsejevich, July 7, 2008, Museo del Holocausto, Buenos Aires. All information discussed concerning the business enterprises of the Ovsejevich family was derived from this interview.

129. Reisman, "Af di vegen fun 30 yor bialistoker mishpocha in argentine," 10.

130. Roberto Pinkus, *Villa Lynch Era Una Fiesta*, 62–65.

131. Ibid., 79–80.

132. Reisman, "Af di vegen fun 30 yor bialistoker mishpocha in argentine," 7.

133. Hayim Shoshkes, "Vebstulen klapn, mashinen zingen in vila lintsh," *Bialystoker Stimme* 240 (January 1946): 16.

134. See the similar conclusion reached by Tenenbaum in "Immigrants and Capital," 77.

135. Shoshkes, "Vebstulen klapn, mashinen zingen in vila lintsh," *Bialystoker Stimme* 240 (January 1946): 16.

136. Reisman, "Af di vegen fun 30 yor bialistoker mishpocha in argentine," 7.

137. Ibid., 7.

138. Ibid., 9.

139. Ibid., 6.

140. Ibid., 7.

141. Mirelman, *Jewish Buenos Aires, 1890–1930*, 147–60.

142. Ibid., 61–75; 165–74; Federico Rivanera Carles, *El judaismo y la semana tragica: la verdadera historia de los sucesos de enero de 1919*.

143. Reisman, "Af di vegen fun 30 yor bialistoker mishpocha in argentine," 7.

144. Ibid., 8–9.

145. For more on Peretz, see Ruth Wisse, "Introduction," in *The I. L. Peretz Reader*.

146. "Hanukas ha-bayes fun der Y. L. Peretz-shul in v. lintsh" *Bialystoker vegn* 4 (September 1949), 68.

147. Itsik Munaker, "Der bialistoker farband in boyneys ayris," 86–87.

148. Emanuel Goldsmith, *Modern Yiddish Culture: The Story of the Yiddish Language Movement*.

149. Jeffrey Shandler, "Beyond the Mother Tongue," 102–112.

150. Cassedy, *Building the Future: Jewish Immigrant Intellectuals and the Making of Tsukunft*.

151. Itsik Munaker, "Farvos bialistoker vegn," *Bialystoker vegn* 1 (December 1947): 2.

152. Munaker, "Farvos bialistoker vegn," 2.

153. Ibid., 2.

154. Ibid., 1.

155. Founded in the 1870s, Petach Tikva would have been abandoned in 1880, had it not been for the influx of these committed settlers from Bialystok. See Katz, *"Business" of Settlement*, 16.

156. Luz, *Parallels Meet*, 141.

157. See Herzberg, *The Zionist Idea*, 368–88.

158. Since the land was located two kilometers away from a stop on the Jaffa–Jerusalem train line, the Bialystok Association for Land Purchases felt such a high price was fair. Katz, *The "Business" of Settlement*, 101–113, 141–42.

159. Club Bialystok, Tel Aviv to Bialystoker Center and Bikur Holim, New York, October 5, 1923, 1. Tel Aviv University Archives A-18/36.

160. Ibid.

161. Ibid.

162. Ibid.

163. Ibid. Emphasis in the original.

164. Hannah Kliger, "Ethnic Voluntary Associations in Israel," 117. See the writings of Max Nordau, Jacob Klatzkin, and A. D. Gordon for more on the desire to "build" a new type of Jew; translated in Hertzberg, *The Zionist Idea*, 232–42, 314–25, 368–87.

165. Yehuda Zar, "Bialistoker halutzim," *Bialystoker Stimme* 6 (February 1923): 45–46.

166. "Finanshal report fun der bialistoker relif komitet," *Bialystoker Stimme* 8 (February 1924): 30.

167. No records have survived that attest to any activities sponsored by Club Bialystok. This absence of records is probably the reason why the synthetic encyclopedia *Landsmanshaftn in yisroel* claims that the first Bialystoker organization in Israel was founded only in 1940. See L. Losh, ed., *Landsmanshaftn in yisroel*, 58–59.

168. Oral interview, Yehezkel Aran, Yisroel Prenski, Eliyahu Oran, Dov Chivak, Yisroel Adler, Yaakov Mikovsky, Yisroel Sokolowsky, Dr. Baruch Kaplan, Osher Gorfein, Pinchas Adler, and Zvi Yucht 6/22/97 and 6/29/97. After a "new" Bialystoker arrived, his friends from Bialystok would bring him or her food.

169. Oral interview, Yehezkel Aran 2/17/97, 5/13/97, and 6/29/97, Tel Aviv.

170. Bialystoker Landslayt in Palestine to Bialystoker Landslayt in Cuba, September 1941. Tel Aviv University Archives A-18/28. Interview, Yehezkel Aran, Yisroel Prenski, Eliyahu Oran, Dov Chivak, Yisroel Adler, Yaakov Mikovsky, Yisroel Sokolowsky, Dr. Baruch Kaplan, Osher Gorfein, Pinchas Adler, and Zvi Yucht 6/22/97 and 6/29/97.

171. *Landsmanshaftn in yisroel*, 58. This sentiment was also clearly echoed by one of the leaders of Irgun Yotzei Bialystok in 1981, who urged Bialystok émigrés not to think of the past but only to look forward and think about being full citizens of the State of Israel. See Kliger, "Ethnic Voluntary Associations in Israel," 112.

172. Ibid.

173. Bialystoker Landslayt in Palestine to Bialystoker Landslayt in Cuba, 1947 Tel Aviv University Archives, A-18/28

174. Oral interview with Yehezkel Aran, Yisroel Prenski, Eliyahu Oran, Dov Chivak, Yisroel Adler, Yaakov Mikovsky, Yisroel Sokolowsky, Dr. Baruch Kaplan, Osher Gorfein, Pinchas Adler, and Zvi Yucht 6/22/97 and 6/29/97, Tel Aviv.

175. Oral Interview, Mordechai Greenstein, May 19, 2009.

176. Ibid.

177. Oral interview, Mordechai Greenstein, June 18, 2009.

178. Ezra Mendelsohn, *The Jews of East Central Europe between the World Wars*, 68–83.

179. YIVO Autobiography quoted in Celia Heller, *On the Edge of Destruction: Jews of Poland between the Two World Wars*, 246.

180. Menakhem Linder, "Der khurbm funem yidishn handel in bialistoker rayon," 17–19.

181. Bialystoker Centre in Palestine to the Bialystoker Central Relief in New York, 1936. Tel Aviv University Archives A-18/36, 1. Emphasis in the original.

182. Ibid. Emphasis in the original.

183. "Zalman Yerushalmi," in *Bialistoker in yisroel*, 3.

184. Ibid., 3.

185. Ibid., 5.

186. *Yediot shel ha-va'ad le-'ezrat yehudei Bialistok*, No. 1 May 3, 1945. Tel Aviv University Archives A-18/72. Interview with Yehezkel Aran, Yisroel Prenski, Eliyahu Oran, Dov Chivak, Yisroel Adler, Yaakov Mikovsky, Yisroel Sokolowsky, Dr. Baruch Kaplan, Osher Gorfein, Pinchas Adler, and Zvi Yucht 6/22/97 and 6/29/97. Of the twenty Bialystoker émigrés I interviewed who arrived prior to 1945, none were aided by Irgun Yotzei Bialystok or knew of anyone who had been offered money by this organization.

187. Ibid.

188. "Zalman Yerushalmi," in *Bialistoker in yisroel*, 6.

189. *Landsmanshaftn in yisroel*, 63. *Kiryat Bialistok Buletin* 3 (1951), 1–2.

190. *Landmanshaftn in yisroel*, 63; Oral interview with Koppel Lev, 5/10/97.

191. "Kiryat bialistok," in *Bialistoker in yisroel*, 1.

192. S. Rutland, Edge of Diaspora, 76–77, 146–47.

193. W. Armstrong, "The Social Origins of Industrial Growth: Canada, Argentina and Australia," 88, 91.

194. Assimilation was the main problem facing Australian Jewry until 1920; see Rutland, *Edge of Diaspora*, 141–73.

195. Rutland, *Edge of Diaspora*, 188–201; aside from Germany, the growing strength of antisemitism in England clearly influenced the situation in colonial Australia.

196. C. Price, "Chain Migration and Immigrant Groups, with Special Reference to Australian Jewry," 161.

197. R. Benjamin, *A Serious Influx of Jews: A History of Jewish Welfare in Victoria*.

198. Oral interview, Anna Gepner, August 17, 1998.

199. For more on the Fink and Waks family businesses see, Australia's *Business Review Weekly*, August 15, 1986, 16–17. Also see Rutland, *Edge of Diaspora*, 222, 262–63.

200. Rutland, *Edge of Diaspora*.

201. Ibid., 169.

202. For more on the demographic growth of the Melbourne Jewish community and its impact on Jewish organizational life, see W. Lippmann, "The Demography of Australian Jewry."

203. Anna Gepner, Oral Interview, August 17, 1998.

204. See Yaakov Pat, "How Jews Live in Australia," quoted in H. Rubinstein, *The Jews in Victoria, 1835–1985*, 190–91; W. Lippmann, "The Demography of Australian Jewry"; Anna Gepner, Oral Interview, August 17, 1998. It is estimated there were approximately 3,000 Bialystokers living in Melbourne in this period.

While there are no exact statistics for the city of Melbourne, the population of the entire Victoria province Jewish community at this time was almost 10,000, suggesting that Bialystoker Jews comprised at least one-third of the Melbourne Jewish community. See Yaakov Pat, "How Jews Live in Australia"; W. Lippmann, "The Demography of Australian Jewry," 261.

205. Rubinstein had worked as an editor at *Unzer lebn* and therefore modeled many aspects of *Oystralisher idishe lebn* after this daily Yiddish newspaper in Bialystok. See Sohn, "A Bialistoker grindet a zeitung in Melborn, Oystralia," *Bialystoker Stimme* 16:38 (September 1933): 14.

206. P. Goldhar, "The Yiddish Press of Australia," in *Australian Jewish Almanac*, eds. Arthur Rose and Israel Sher, 268–74 [Yiddish].

207. The weekly reports on the Bialystoker landsmanshaft organization appeared regularly on the "society" page of *Oystralisher idishe lebn*. For an example of the prominence given the balance sheet of the Bialystoker society see *Oystralisher idishe lebn*, August 16, 1935, 1. On solicitations for charities in Bialystok, such as the Bialystok hospital, see the following issues of *Oystralisher idishe lebn*: July 12, 1935, 8; August 16, 1935, 8; August 30, 1935, 8; September 6, 1935, 8; September 27, 1935, 8. In general, on the difficult situation in Bialystok see *Oystralisher idishe lebn*, March 20 and April 10, 1936.

208. *Oystralisher idishe lebn*, December 12, 1935, 1.

209. Ibid.

210. Oral interview, Paula Hansky, August 18, 1998.

211. *Di Oystralisher idishe lebn*, January 3, 1935, 1.

212. Shelly Tenenbaum, "Immigrants and Capital: Jewish Loan Societies in the United States, 1880–1945," 67–77.

213. Isaac Kipen, *A Life to Live*, 149.

214. See in particular Pinhas Goldhar, "Ma Nishtana?" *Di Oystralishe idishe lebn*, April 9, 1934.

215. Oral interview, Paula Hansky, August 18, 1998.

216. Oral interview, Anna Gepner, August 17, 1998.

217. Ibid.

218. Ibid.

219. Oral interview, Ada Kagan, August 19, 1998.

220. Leon Kagan would later become the head of the Bialystoker Centre. Oral interview, Ada and Leon Kagan, August 19, 1998.

221. *Oystralisher idishe lebn*, July 9, 1937.

222. *Oystralisher idishe lebn*, June 16, 1937.

223. *Oystralisher idishe lebn*, September 27, 1935.

224. The popularity of this event among all members of the Melbourne Jewish community is evidenced by the fact that in 1935, the Bialystoker Lay Kassa was forced to publish a public apology to the whole community on the front page of *Oystralisher idishe lebn* after it accidentally distributed party favors manufactured in Germany. *Oystralisher idishe lebn*, December 27, 1935.

225. Bialystoker Centre Annual Report, 1947–1948.

226. Dr. Surowicz to the Bialystoker Centre, February 12, 1948, reprinted in the Bialystoker Centre Annual Report, 1948.

227. Oral interview, Paula Hansky, August 18, 1998.

228. Oral interview, Anna Gepner, August 17, 1998.

229. Benjamin, *A Serious Influx of Jews*, 154, 158–69.

230. Fink also believed the other major philanthropic organization in Melbourne, the Association of Jewish Immigrants, whose membership were mostly assimilated Australian-born Jews, lacked the drive to address this issue. See Suzanne Rutland, "I Never Knew a Man Who Had So Many Cousins," 395, quoting from an interview with Mrs. Mina Fink.

231. Australian immigration policy favored resettlement of refugees in order to strengthen Australia against any future Asian invasion, yet they did not want any Jews. For more on the antisemitic prejudices of Australian immigration policy in the postwar period, see Suzanne Rutland, "Waiting Room Shanghai: Australian Reactions to the Plight of the Jews in Shanghai after the Second World War," 407–411.

232. Rutland, "I Never Knew a Man Who Had So Many Cousins," 400.

233. Sohn, "Bialistoker yidn in amerike," 173. For a list of all the organizations founded by the transnational Bialystoker émigré community, see *Bialistoker yizker bukh*, 166–67.

234. Chaikan, "Bialystok Transplanted and Transformed," 41, 45. The actual number of Bialystoker émigrés, however, is probably closer to 80,000. David Sohn claimed that 50,000 Jews lived in America. See Sohn, "Bialystok," *Bialystoker Bilder Album*, 16. Michael Flicker, president of Irgun Yotzei Bialystok, claims that a survey conducted during the war (1944) found 15,000 Bialystoker Jews residing in Palestine. Although no surveys were conducted in Argentina, memoir materials and landsmanshaftn membership figures suggest that between 8,000 and 10,000 Jews from the Bialystok region settled in Argentina; see L. Zhitnitski, "Landsmanshaftn in Argentine," *Argentiner yivo shriftn* 3 (1945): 156–59. It is estimated there were approximately 3,000 Bialystokers living in Melbourne by 1939. See Yakov Pat, "Byalistoker yidn in oystralia," quoted in Howard Rubinstein, *The Jews in Victoria;* Anna Gepner, oral interview, August 17, 1998.

235. Jack Kugelmass, "Preface," *Going Home: YIVO Annual 21* (1993): viii–ix. A contention of scholars of East European Jewish migration is that Jews intended to separate themselves permanently from Eastern Europe when they settled in the United States, as opposed to other immigrants groups migrating in the same period. Most scholars tacitly assume that East European Jews wanted a permanent break with their past. This interpretation of East European Jews' motivations has become entwined with scholarly interpretations of East European Jewish immigrant economic and social mobility.

236. This plays a particularly important role in explaining phenomena among Jewish immigrants in the United States, such as their low rate of return migration and their rapid economic and social mobility See Rischin, *The Promised City;* Kessner, *The Golden Door.*

3. "Buying Bricks for Bialystok"

1. According to the personal files of David Sohn, director of the Bialystoker Center and editor of the *Bialystoker Stimme*, during the 1920s and 1930s, 4,000

*Bialystoker Stimme*s were published in each run and sent to Bialystoker Jews throughout the United States, Poland, Argentina, Australia, London, and Palestine. See *Bialystoker Stimme* 239 (November 1945): 1 and Sohn, "The History and Achievements of the Bialystoker Center," undated manuscript, Tel Aviv University Archives A-18/63. In many communities, one or two Bialystoker émigré families would receive the *Bialystoker Stimme* and would share their copy with other Bialystoker families in the community. Interview with Anna Gepner, August 21, 1997, Melbourne, Australia. Interview with Yehezkel Aran, April 15, 1999, Tel Aviv, Israel. Thus, the limited circulation numbers should not overshadow this periodical's wide influence, which as Matthew Frye Jacobson emphasizes in his study of the immigrant press, "circulation figures for immigrant journals are notoriously unreliable" because a single copy of an immigrant newspaper often reached "three, five or ten readers . . . [and] available figures understate the extent of a given journal's reach. See Jacobson, *Special Sorrows*, 57.

2. Archiwun Panstwowe w Bialymstoku, Zespol 1, sygnatura, 26. For more information on the Bialystok Clock tower, see Sohn, *Bialistoker bilder album*, 37.

3. The six-story Bialystoker Center (226–228 East Broadway) paled in comparison to the Forward Building (175 East Broadway), a twelve-story building that was home to the famous Yiddish newspaper. Atop the Forward Building was a bright *Forward* sign that was a landmark for Jews living on the Lower East Side.

4. Other landsmanshaft groups often compared giving money to their former home to observing a "great mitzvah." See Advertisement, *Tageblat*, April 6, 1917. For appeals using similar rhetoric, see *Tageblat*, February 15, 1917. Both are discussed in Soyer, *Jewish Immigrant Associations*, 166–67.

5. "The Bialystoker Center" (manuscript, 1939), 1. Tel Aviv University Archives, A-18/67. Heri Graf, "Tsu vos a bialistoker tsenter," *Bialystoker Stimme* 3 (March 1922): 1.

6. Steven Zipperstein, "The Politics of Relief: The Transformation of Russian Jewish Communal Life during the First World War"; Ezra Mendelsohn, *Zionism in Poland: The Formative Years*, 46–49.

7. There are many monographs on the history of interwar Jewish aid, mostly focusing on the American Joint Distribution Committee (JDC). See Yehuda Bauer, *My Brother's Keeper: A History of the American Jewish Joint Distribution Committee, 1929–1939* ; Naomi W. Cohen, *Not Free to Desist: The American Jewish Committee, 1906–1966;* Oscar Handlin, *A Continuing Task: The American Jewish Joint Distribution Committee, 1914–1964;* Zosa Szajkowski, "Private and Organized American Jewish Overseas Relief (1914–1938)"; Zosa Szajkowski, "Private and Organized American Jewish Relief and Immigration (1914–1938); Zosa Szajkowski, "Private American Jewish Overseas Relief (1919–1938): Problems and Attempted Solutions"; Selwyn Ilan Troen and Benjamin Pinkus, eds., *Organizing Rescue: National Jewish Solidarity in the Modern Period*. The vast sums raised and distributed during and following World War One were unprecedented. The JDC, for instance, disbursed $15 million during the war and more than $75 million between 1919 and 1939 (Bauer, 305–306).

8. A full accounting of Bialystoker émigré philanthropy can be found in the files and reports of the Bialystoker Relief Committee of America from 1919–1929 located in the Tel Aviv University Archives, A-18/3–9.

9. Safran, "Diasporas in Modern Societies," 83–84; Cohen, *Global Diasporas*, 26.

10. Rahel Rojanski, "The Influence of American Jewry on the Development of the Jewish Welfare System in Poland, 1920–1929", *Gal Ed* 11 (1989): 49–76; Yehuda Bauer, *American Jewry and the Holocaust: The American Jewish Joint Distribution Committee, 1939–1945*, 22. Such subversive behavior is common among many dispersed migrant groups. See Safran, "Diasporas in Modern Societies," 83–84; Cohen, *Global Diasporas*, 26. Jews had long been aware, Derek Penslar argues, that the application of Jewish power was economic in nature. See Penslar, *Shylock's Children*, 3.

11. Woocher, *Sacred Survival*, 1–63.

12. For more on how modern Jewish philanthropy differs from traditional forms of Jewish charity, see Woocher, *Sacred Survival*, 1–22. Michael Berkowitz argues in his study of the Zionist movement in Western Europe that philanthropic organizations and their fundraising materials played a central role in shaping how European Jews envisioned their identities. See Michael Berkowitz, *Zionist Culture and West European Jewry before the First World War*, 161–87.

13. John Higham, *Strangers in the Land*, 264–331: Patterns of American Nativism.

14. Andrew Heinze makes the argument that consumption enables East European Jews to fuse their American and Jewish identities. See his *Adapting to Abundance: Jewish Immigrants Mass Compsumption and the Search for American Identity*.

15. For two discussions of the Great War's devastating impact on Russian civilian life, resulting both from warfare and tsarist authorities' efforts to confront the challenges of war particularly in western borderlands of the Russian Empire where Jews primarily resided, see Peter Gattrell, *A Whole Empire Walking: Refugees in Russia during World War I*; and Eric Lohr, *Nationalizing the Russian Empire: The Campaign against Enemy Aliens during World War I*.

16. Gosudarstvennyi arkhiv Rossiiskoi Federatsii [GARF] (State Archives of the Russian Federation) GARF f. 9529, op. 1, del. 2, 6, 22. For a larger statistical overview of the impact of the war see Yakov Bachrach, *Demografie fun der yidisher befelkerung in bialistok*, 10; Piotr Wróbel, "Na równi pochyłej. Żydzi Biaegostoku w latach 1918–1939", 174–75.

17. Herschberg, *Pinkes bialistok* II: 175–224. For a personal account of the Jewish refugee crisis in Bialystok, see "Introduction: The Life and Writings of Simon Rawidowicz," in Benjamin Ravid, ed., *State of Israel, Diaspora and Jewish Continuity*, 15.

18. Herman Frank, "Daytshe yidn in bialistok beys der daytsher okupatsye, 1916–1917," 419–20.

19. More than 200,000 Jews flooded into Warsaw, overwhelming existing Jewish welfare agencies and creating a Jewish welfare crisis; see Gosudarstvennyi arkhiv Rossiiskoi Federatsii [GARF] (State Archives of the Russian Federation) f. 9529, op. 1, del. 5, 1.

20. The League to Aid Starving Jews in Enemy-Occupied Territories (*Liga pomoshi golodaivshchim evreiam v zaniatykh nepriatelem mestnostiakh*) dispensed

more than 200,000 rubles in aid between 1917 and 1919 with Bialystok receiving more than 50,000 rubles. See GARF f. 9529, op. 1, del. 5, 1 and in the same fond, op. 1, del. 2, 6, 22. For a larger statistical overview of the impact of the war, see Yakov Bachrach, *Demografie fun der yidisher befelkerung in bialistok*, 10.

21. Wróbel, "Na równi pochyłej. Żydzi Białegostoku w latach 1918–1939, 176–77.

22. Mendelsohn, *Jews of East Central Europe*.

23. The kehilla's authority was based on the stipulations of the Minorities Rights' Treaty that required Poland to set up institutions to protect the rights of all minority groups living within its borders. Concerned after the pogroms of 1918 and 1919, the League of Nations required Poland to set up separate governing bodies and schools for non-Polish nationals in order to maintain their independence. For more on the Minorities Treaty (including a translation of the treaty itself), see I. Lewin, *A History of Polish Jewry during the Revival of Poland, 1918–1919*, 167–205, 207–211.

24. Goldberg, "Bialistoker Textil Industria," *Unzer lebn*, October 8, 1937, 8.

25. Piotr Wróbel, "Na równi pochyłej. Żydzi Białegostoku w latach 1918–1939," 175.

26. For more on the Grabski reforms, see Antony Polonsky, *Politics in Independent Poland, 1921–1939*, 119–22; Pavel Korzec, *Juifs en Pologne*, 142–50.

27. The issue of Polish–Jewish relations has long been a topic of scholarly inquiry. Some pioneering studies on the subject include Magdalena Opalski, *Poles and Jews: A Failed Brotherhood*; Alina Cała, *Asymilacja Żydow w Krolestwie Polskim, 1864–1897*; Frank Golczewski, *Polnisch-Jüdische Beziehungen, 1881–1922: Eine Studie zur Geschichte des Anti-Semitismus in Osteuropa*; William W. Hagen, "Before the 'Final Solution': Toward a Comparative Analysis of Anti-Semitism in Interwar Germany and Poland," 351–81; Ezra Mendelsohn, "Interwar Poland: Good for the Jews or Bad for the Jews?" 130–39; Christopher Weber, "Towards Competitive Suffering: A Re-examination of the Historiography of Polish–Jewish Relations," 1–40. In recent years, Polish–Jewish relations during the Second World War have consumed the lion's share of scholarly interest. See Jan Gross, *Neighbors: The Destruction of the Jewish Community in Jedwabne, Poland*; Joshua D. Zimmerman, ed. *Contested Memories: Poles and Jews during the Holocaust and Its Aftermath*; Joanna Michlic and Anthony Polonsky, eds. *The Neighbors Respond: The Controversy over the Jedwabne Massacre in Poland*.

28. *Golos Belostoka* August 21, 1919, 2. Also see Piotr Wróbel, "Na równi pochyłej. Żydzi Białegostoku w latach 1918–1939," 193.

29. Marian Fuks, "Prasa żydowska w Białymstoku, 1918–1939," *Żydowskiego Instytutu Historycznego w Polsce* 145–46 (1988), 145–50.

30. *Dos naye lebn*, November 19, 1919, 2.

31. Stanislaw Mauersberg, *Szkolnictwo Powszechne Dla Mniejszoski Narodowych w Polsce w Latach 1918–1939*; Herschberg, *Pinkes bialistok* II: 269–89.

32. Wróbel, "Na równi pochyłej. Żydzi Białegostoku w latach 1918–1939," 192–94.

33. *Farvos hobn mir in der kehile dem proyekt vegn arbet far emigratsia un kolonitatsia?* (Bialystok 1919) Collection M-14/Folder 17, Bund Archives, YIVO Institute for Jewish Research, esp. 10.

34. Ibid., 3, 14–15.

35. Katarzyna Sztop-Rumkovska, "Konflikty polsko-żydowskie jako element kształtowania się ładu polityczno-społecznego w Białymstoku w latach 1919–1920 w świetle lokalnej prasy" *Studia Judaica* 5 (2002–03), 131–150.

36. *Dziennki Bialostocki* 1920, no. 257.

37. *Dziennki Białostocki* 1919, no. 43.

38. It is estimated that about 15 percent of the members of the sparse Polish Communist Party were of Jewish origin, but in Bialystok, as the local party leader complained, Jews comprised less than 5 percent of the ranks despite their overwhelming majority in the city; the strength of Zionism in the region, the local party leader reported, prompted those attracted to communism to join the Po'alei Zion party. See Zespol 266/ II-6, sygnature 98–105; Archiwun Akt Nowych, Warsaw. On this trend throughout Poland, see Alina Cała, Halina Węgrzynek, and Gabriela Zalewska, *Historia i kultura Żydów polskich: słownik*, 160. For a discussion of antisemitic portrayals of Jews in the interwar Polish press, see I. Kamińska-Szmaj, "Narodziny stereotypu bolszewika," 23–29.

39. Komisarz Rządu Rzeczpospolitej na Białystok, 14.07.1919. Archiwum Państwowe w Białmstoku [APB] Zespol 64, sygnature 305. This law mirrored Russian legislation of the last century that circumscribed use of Polish in the public sphere.

40. Piotr Wróbel, "Na równi pochyłej. Żydzi Białegostoku w latach 1918–1939," 195.

41. Ibid., 196.

42. Herschberg, *Pinkes bialistok*. Mendelsohn, *East Central Europe between the World Wars*, 43–63.

43. Sonia Mazny, oral interview, December 14, 2003. Also see the diary of writer Shimon Ravidowicz, who was active in establishing several new Jewish schools and organizations in Bialystok in 1918. See "Introduction: The Life and Writings of Simon Rawidowicz," in *State of Israel, Diaspora and Jewish Continuity*, Benjamin Ravid, ed., 15.

44. Bialystok had more Jews working in factories than any other town in Poland in 1918. Herschberg, *Pinkes Bialistok* II: 272–75, 291; Piotr Wróbel, "Na równi pochyłej. Żydzi Białegostoku w latach 1918–1939," 169.

45. A. Herschberg, *Pinkes Bialistok* II: 272–75, 291; Piotr Wróbel, "Na równi pochyłej. Żydzi Białegostoku w latach 1918–1939," 169.

46. *Dos naye lebn*, October 3, 5, 20, 31, 1919; December 11, 1919.

47. Szajkowski, "Private American Jewish Overseas Relief (1919–1938)," 301.

48. Samuel Kassow, "Communal and Social Change in the Polish Shtetl, 56–84.

49. Polonsky, *Politics in Independent Poland*, 108–109.

50. *Protokol-bukh fun Bialistoker Relif Komite*. Tel Aviv University Archives A-18/3.2. Babitsh, "A rizikalishe shlikhes in a kritisher tsayt," *Bialystoker yoyvelzamlbukh*, 19.

51. For a full accounting of how these funds were allocated, see "Protokol 100: July 30, 1920," *Protokol-bukh fun Bialistoker Relif Komite*. Tel Aviv University Archives A-18/3.2.

52. Wisniewski, "Lines HaTsedek," 129; Oral interview, M.A., Kiryat Bialystok, 3/26/99. Informant asked not to be identified.

53. Oral interview, M.A., Kiryat Bialystok 3/26/99.

54. Budżet Miasta Białegostoku na rok 1926/7, APB, Akta Miasta Białegostoku synatura 115.

55. See Budżet Miasta Białegostoku na rok 1927/8 and Budżet Miasta Białegostoku na rok 1929/30, APB, Akta Miasta Białegostoku, sygnatura 116 and 121.

56. Ibid.

57. Biuletyn Biblioteka im. "Szołem-Ałejchema" w Białymstoku (February 1937), 1–2. Folder M-14/17 Bund Archives, YIVO Institute for Jewish Research.

58. "Bericht fun Bialistoker senter," *Bialystoker Stimme* 1 (November 1921): 18.

59. "Unzer eygene velt," *Bialystoker Stimme* 5 (October 1922): 10. Also see Sohn, *The Activities of the Bialystoker Community in America*, 17.

60. Sohn, "A Half Century of Bialystoker Activity in America," 5.

61. Shaul Stampfer notes that the need to raise funds in America provoked many informally run institutions of Jewish education to formalize their curricula and to publish newsletters, balance sheets, and annual reports. See Shaul Stampfer, "Hasidic Yeshivot in Inter-war Poland," 3–25. Also see Rachel Rojanski, "American Jewry's Influence upon the Establishment of the Jewish Welfare Apparatus in Poland," 59–86.

62. Morris Sunshine Report to the Bialystoker Relief Committee, Tel Aviv University ArchivesA-18/3.

63. It is fascinating to compare the financial report of Białystok's Ezras yesoymim from the period before 1920 with that of the period following the intervention of the Bialystoker Relief Committee in Białystok. See *Ezras yesoymim, 1917–1920*, Białystok 1921, and *Raport fun Ezras yesoymin, 1923–1927*, Białystok 1928. Both of these booklets can be found in the Bund Archives, YIVO, M14/17. The impact that the requirements of American philanthropists had on institutions can also be seen by comparing the reports of Ezras yesomim with the report of the activities of the Peretz Children's Home and Work School from 1919 to 1920.

64. These transformations did not only take place in Bialystok but were prevalent throughout Poland. As Shaul Stampfer has noted in his study of interwar hasidic yeshivot, despite the fact that in earlier decades hasidic leaders had criticized the limitations of formal yeshiva study, many sects established formal yeshivot in the 1920s because they offered "an important advantage in fundraising." Because the informal hasidic *beis midrash* "certainly did not fit the Western patterns of formal education, organized study and certification of completion" as the yeshiva did, hasidic leaders chose to reorganize and recast their educational system in order to encourage American Jews to send funds. See Stampfer, "Hasidic Yeshivot in Interwar Poland," 3–25, esp. 20–21.

65. *Hoveret Likrat ha-Asefah Beys Midrash Beys Yosef;* Morris Sunshine, Report to the Bialystoker Relief Committee, DRC, A18/3.

66. See reports of the Jewish hospital in Bund Archives, YIVO, M14/17; also *Oystralisher idishe lebn*, July 12, August 16 and 30, September 6, and December 13, 1935.

67. See *Dos naye lebn*, October 6–8, 1919, 2.

68. *Dos naye lebn*, October 1919, 2.

69. Ibid.

70. There are dozens of letters to David Sohn from the editors of each of these newspapers in the Tel Aviv University Archives A-18/24.

71. See the following letters of Pesach Kaplan to David Sohn, August 8, 1923, October 8, 1924, July 1, 1925. The dozens of letters sent by Kaplan to Sohn can be found among Sohn's personal papers, Tel Aviv University Archives, A-18/38-18.

72. *Dos naye lebn*, November 19, 1919.

73. *Dos naye lebn*, November 19, 1919; April 20, 1925.

74. A column entitled "Gelt fun amerike," discussing the allocation of émigré funds, appeared daily between 1919 and 1922. Features entitled "Vos hert zikh in bialistok" and "Vos hert zikh in amerike?" appeared several times a week during this period. For several fine examples of the parallels, see *Dos naye lebn*, July 27 and August 24, 1919.

75. APB *Urząd Wojewódzki Białostocki: Sygnatura* 34, 69.

76. I. Kamińska-Szmaj, "Narodsiny stereotypu bolszewika," 23–29.

77. *Chata Polska* 20 (1919): 2. *Chata Polska* was a Polish weekly magazine published during the interwar period; it was read mostly by local villagers.

78. *Dziennik Białostoki* 123 (1919); *Dziennik Białostoki* 125 (1919).

79. Alina Cała, *The Image of the Jew in Polish Folk Culture*, 22–52.

80. Ibid.

81. *Dziennik Białostoki* 46 (1921).

82. See *Dziennik Białostoki* 25 (1919); *Dziennik Białostoki* 27 (1919); *Dziennik Białostoki*. 158 (1919); *Dziennik Białostoki* 183 (1919). The specific feature on Sohn and his compatriots appeared in *Dziennik Białostoki* on November 13, 1919; there, the editors constantly referred to these émigré philanthropists as "the Jewish activists from America."

83. See, for example, *Dziennik Białostoki* 25 (1919); *Dziennik Białostoki* 27 (1919); *Dziennik Białostoki* 158 (1919); and *Dziennik Białostoki* 183 (1919). On November 13, 1919, *Dziennik Białostoki* reported that "Dr. Margoszes, the activist of the Jews in America, arrived in Bialystok."

84. *Prożektor* 20, August 10–11, 1929.

85. See Berkowitz, *Zionist Culture and West European Jewry*; Beth Wenger and Jeff Shandler, *Encounters with the Holyland*. See also Kerri Steinberg, "Photography, Philanthropy and the Politics of American Jewish Identity."

86. Advertisement, *Bialystoker Stimme* 6 (March 1923): 44.

87. It is interesting to note that none of the Jewish men in Bialystok have beards, a trope common in these photos to highlight the clean-shaven modern attire of the visiting American Jews. For more on these photographs, see Jeffrey Shandler, *Going Home: How American Jews Invent the Old World*.

88. *Protokol-bukh fun Bialistoker Relif Komite*. Tel Aviv University Archives A-18/3.2. For a narrative description of the perils faced by representatives of the

Bialystoker Relief Committee, see Yosef Lipnick, "Dovid Sohn's rol in unzer lands-manshaft," 7–10.

89. For more on the links between philanthropy and class status in the United States, see Mary Ryan's *Cradle of the Middle Class;* Andrew Herman, *The Better Angels of Capitalism.*

90. Penslar, *Shylock's Jews,* 51–89.

91. John Higham, *Strangers in the Land;* Stanley Coben, "A Study of Nativism: The American Red Scare of 1919–1920"; Eli Lederhendler, "Hard Times: HIAS under Pressure," 125–27.

92. Muttel Dovesh, "Shmuses mit a faylerton," *Bialystoker Stimme* 9 (July 1924): 20.

93. Ibid., 20.

94. Editorial Staff, *Naye bialistoker Stimme,* Bialystok to David Sohn, New York, April 4, 1925. Tel Aviv University Archives A-18/24.

95. Dovesh, "Shmuses mit a faylerton," 21.

96. For just a glimpse into some of the hundreds of letters David Sohn received asking for financial aid during the interwar period, see A-18/21-5 Tel Aviv University Archives. On how these letters were read by the lay leadership of the Bialystoker Center, see Michael Arye, "A Meeting of the Board of Directors," *Bialystoker Stimme* 13, English supplement, March 1926, 12.

97. Yehuda Zar, "Bialistoker halutzim," *Bialystoker Stimme* 6 (Febraury 1923): 45.

98. Ibid., 45–46.

99. The Bialystoker Center sent more than $200 to Bialystokers in Berlin and Kovno. See "Bericht fun bialistoker relif," *Bialystoker Stimme* 8 (February 1924): 30.

100. Safran, "Diasporas in Modern Societies," 83–84; Cohen, *Global Diasporas,* 26.

101. "Bialistoker farband in berlin," *Bialystoker Stimme* 1 (November 1921): 8; "Bericht fun bialistoker relif," *Bialystoker Stimme* 1 (November 1921): 18.

102. Herman Frank, "Bialistoker farband in berlin," *Bialystoker Stimme* 3 (March 1922): 3; "Bialistoker in berlin," *Bialystoker Stimme* 4 (June 1922): 12; "Bialistoker in berlin," *Bialystoker Stimme* 5 (October 1922): 8; Herman Frank, "Di bialistoker in berlin," *Bialystoker Stimme* 7 (September 1923): 26.

103. "Bericht fun bialistoker tsenter," *Bialystoker Stimme* 1 (1921): 18; Tiltshe Tiktin, "Gedank vos geborn gevorn in bialistok un vilna," *Bialystoker Stimme* 179 (1938): 25–28.

104. Michael Arye, "A Meeting of the Board of Directors," *Bialystoker Stimme,* English supplement, March 1926, 12.

105. "Finanshal report fun bialistoker tsenter un bikur kholim," *Bialystoker Stimme* (March 1926): 54.

106. Ibid.

107. Itsik Iskolski, "Unzere bialistoker 'tokhter fun yisroel,'" *Bialystoker Stimme* 229 (March 1944): 16. For the larger context see Soyer, *Jewish Immigrant Associations and American Identity,* 192–93.

108. "The Bialystoker Ladies' Auxiliary," 6. Tel Aviv University Archives A-18/60.

109. Penslar, *Shylock's Children*, 191.

110. Ibid., 189–90.

111. "The Bialystoker Ladies' Auxiliary," in *The Bialystoker Ladies' Auxiliary Souvenir Journal* (1936), 3.

112. Sohn, "Dray yor laydis okzileri," *Bialystoker Stimme* 13 (March 1926): 2; Sohn, "The Bialystoker Center." Manuscript, 1934. Tel Aviv University Archives, A-18/63/4.1.

113. Sohn, "Dray yor laydis okzileri," *Bialystoker Stimme* 13 (March 1926): 2.

114. "The Bialystoker Ladies' Auxiliary," 4.

115. Ibid.

116. Ibid.

117. Sohn, "Dray yor laydis okzileri."

118. Sohn, "The Bialystoker Center." Manuscript, 1934. Tel Aviv University Archives, A-18/63/4.1

119. Ibid.

120. Ada Aidak, "Di laydis okzileri un unzer landmanshaftn," *Bialystoker Stimme* 18 (January 1928): 13.

121. *Bialystoker Frauen Journal* 2 (January 1931): 3.

122. Sohn, "Three Years' Work of the Ladies Auxiliary," *Bialystoker Stimme* 13 (March 1926), 7.

123. Wenger, *New York Jews and the Great Depression*, 71.

124. See Lori Ginzburg, *Women and the Work of Benevolence: Class, Politics and Morality in Nineteenth-Century America;* Kathleen McCarthy, *Noblesse Oblige: Charity and Cultural Philanthropy in Chicago, 1849–1929.* For more on Jewish women, philanthropy, and voluntarism, see Selma Berrol, "Class or Ethnicity: The Americanized Jewish Women and Her Middle-Class Sisters in 1895"; Deborah Grand Golumb, "The 1893 Congress of Jewish Women: Evolution or Revolution in American Jewish Women's History?"; William Toll, "A Quiet Revolution: Jewish Women's Clubs and the Widening Female Sphere, 1870–1920"; Beth Wenger, "Jewish Women and Voluntarism: Beyond the Myth of the Enablers."

125. Sohn, "Topics of the Day," *Bialystoker Stimme* 16, no. 38 (September 1933): 1.

126. Ibid.

127. Storch, "Women of Tomorrow," *Bialystoker lebn* 65 (June 1940), 3.

128. Shandler, "Producing the Future: The Impresario Culture of American Zionism before 1948," in *Divergent Jewish Cultures: Israel and America*, Deborah Dash Moore and Ilan Troen, eds., 57.

129. Shandler, "Producing the Future," 54–55.

130. See in particular, Shandler, "Producing the Future," M. Kaufman, "Envisaging Israel," and Deborah Dash Moore, "Bonding Images: Miami Jews and the Campaign for Israel Bonds," in *Envisioning Israel*, Allon Gal, ed., 219–70.

131. Lipnick, "Dovid Sohn's rol in unzer landsmanschaft," 12–14.

132. Ibid., 12.

133. "Der report fun Mr. ralf vin's bazukh in bialistok," *Bialystoker Stimme* 7 (September 1923): 14.

134. Ibid.

135. "Far vos bialistoker relif." Pamphlet, 1919. Merhavia collection, Hebrew University.

136. Ibid.

137. Sohn, "Roza raisa un dos pintele bialistok," *Bialystoker Stimme* 13 (March 1926): 24.

138. Weintraub, "Roza raisa," *Bialystoker Stimme* 3 (March 1922): 16.

139. Sohn, "Roza raisa un dos pintele bialistok," 24.

140. Event Program, May 20, 1920. Tel Aviv University Archives A-18/20.

141. "Prezident vilson's tokhter kumt heren roza raisa baym bialistoker avent," *Forverts*, May 23, 1920, 16.

142. Advertisement, *Bialystoker Stimme* 10 (October 1924): inside cover.

143. For example, in 1923, such concerts and theater benefits raised more than $11,000; "Finanshal report fun bialistoker tsenter un bikur kholim," *Bialystoker Stimme* 8 (February 1923): 22–23.

144. "Finanshal report fun 1926," *Bialystoker Stimme* 14 (1926): 21.

145. Sohn, "Roza raisa un dos pintele bialistok," 25.

146. Ibid., 24.

147. "Appeal to the Bialystoker Fellow Countrymen in America," *Bialystoker Stimme* 13 (March 1926): 10.

148. Ibid.

149. Sohn, "A Half Century of Bialystoker Activity in America," 6.

150. "Sigel, sigel far unzere hoyz," *Bialystoker Stimme* 15 (March 1927): 4.

151. Ibid.

152. *Bialystoker Haym* 1 (1930).

153. Elliot Willensky and Norval White, eds., *American Institute of Architects Guide to New York City*, 84.

154. Wenger, *New York Jews and the Great Depression*, 198–99.

155. "Durk a 10 dolar 'certifikeyt' vert a member fun bialistoker moshav zekanim far ire ganzen lebn," *Bialystoker Stimme* 28 (May 1931): 5.

156. Ibid.

157. Ibid.

158. Sohn, "At the Present Time," *Bialystoker Stimme* 28 (May 1931): 2.

159. The first example I found of the installation of such a tablet (and the fanfare surrounding it) was in *Bialystoker Stimme* 38 (Sept 1933), n.p. In almost every subsequent issue appears at least one article concerning the "dedication" or "installation" of another tablet.

150. Wenger, *New York Jews and the Great Depression*, 1–9.

161. "Der bialistoker relif," *Bialystoker Stimme* 34 (1932): 3.

162. These photographs can be found in the Tel Aviv University Archives A-18/44.

163. *Bialystoker Stimme* 202 (1947): 2. For more on the Bialystoker émigré community's interest in their mortgage, see *Bialystoker Stimme* 230, 231, 232, 233 (January, April, September and December 1944).

164. Tili Raskin, "Ve ich bin gevorn a mitglid fun der laydis okzileri," *Bialystoker Stimme* 13 (March 1926): 17.

165. *Dos naye lebn* was the only major newspaper until September 1939. For a list of all the newspapers, periodicals, and magazines published in Bialystok during the interwar period and their dates of publication, see Fuks, "Prasa żydowska w Białystoku, 1918–1939," 150–52.

166. Praca Centrali AJDC w Polsce: Wrkazy Demograficzne Mieszkańców Polski u uwzględnieniem Żydow, 1939–1941 (microfilm 1) ZIH Archives.

167. Menakhem Linder, "Der khurbn funem yidishn handel in bialistoker rayon," 17.

168. For more on Sektor films, see Eric Goldman, *Visions, Images and Dreams,* 83–87; J. Hoberman, *Bridge of Light,* 221–26.

169. "Bialystok," Yitzhak Goskind, Sektor Films, Poland, 1939.

170. See Zosa Szajkowski, "Private and Organized American Jewish Overseas Relief (1914–1938)"; Zosa Szajkowski, "Private and Organized American Jewish Relief and Immigration (1914–1938)"; Zosa Szajkowski, "Private American Jewish Overseas Relief (1919–1938): Problems and Attempted Solutions"; Troen and Pinkus, eds., *Organizing Rescue: National Jewish Solidarity in the Modern Period.*

171. Some scholarship addresses these interconnections, such as Bauer, *My Brother's Keeper;* Stampfer, "Hasidic Yeshivot in Inter-war Poland"; Rojanski, "American Jewry's Influence upon the Establishment of the Jewish Welfare Apparatus in Poland."

172. Several notable studies of the centrality of Zionism to East European Jewish immigrant life in America are Mark Raider, *The Emergence of American Zionism;* Sarah L. Schmidt, *Horace Kallen: Prophet of American Zionism;* Melvin Urofsky, *American Zionism from Herzl to Holocaust;* and Jacobson, *Special Sorrows.*

173. Shandler, "Producing the Future," 54–55.

174. Hoberman, *Bridge of Light,* 8.

4. Rewriting the Jewish Diaspora

1. Sohn, "Redaktsianele notitsen," *Bialystoker Stimme* 2 (January 1922): 14.

2. In many ways, the press functions in diasporic communities in similar ways as it did in the process of defining nation-states and national identity. See Benedict Anderson, *Imagined Communities.* Also useful are Jacobson, *Special Sorrows,* 94–137; Paul Gilroy, The *Black Atlantic: Modernity and Double Consciousness;* James Clifford, "Diasporas," in *Routes: Travel and Translation in the Late Twentieth Century,* 244–78; Khaching Tölölyan, "Rethinking Diaspora(s), 3–36.

3. Stein, *Making Jews Modern.*

4. Eva Morawska argues that immigrants' reconstructions of their homelands were directly related to their construction of ethnic identity. In addition to my extended discussion of this below, see: Morawska, "Changing Images of the Old Country," 273–345.

5. Daniel Wickberg, "What is the History of Sensibilities? On Cultural Histories, Old and New," argues cogently that historians need to get their readers "back to the cultural world" of their subjects, illuminating the "patterns of perception, feeling, thinking and believing" that came into play as historical actors

made important decisions (684). In trying to recapture the cultural world of the transnational Bialystok community, my study was greatly influenced by several exemplary models of this type of examination that address the American immigrant experience, most notably, Jacobson's *Special Sorrows,* Morawska's *For Bread with Butter,* and Orsi's *Madonna of 115th Street.*

6. David Weinberg, *Between Tradition and Modernity: Haim Zhitlowsky, Simon Dubnow, Ahad Ha-Am and the Shaping of Modern Jewish Identity;* and Sidra Ezrahi, *Booking Passage: Exile and Homecoming in the Modern Jewish Imagination.*

7. "Unzer oypgaben," *Bialystoker Stimme* 1 (November 1921): 1.

8. Oral interview with Anna Gepner, August 21, 1997, Melbourne, Australia. In many communities, one or two Bialystoker émigré families would receive the *Bialystoker Stimme* and would share their copy with other Bialystoker families. Oral interview with Sonya Mazny, Hartford, Connecticut, December 10, 2003. Oral interview with Yehezkel Aran, April 15, 1999, Tel Aviv, Israel.

9. "Bialistok: a koloniol macht," *Bialystoker Stimme* 8 (February 1924): 1; "Der amerikaner royter kreys in bialistok," *Bialystoker Stimme* 2 (January 1922): 1; "Bialistok in argentine un argentine in bialistok," *Bialystoker Stimme* 13 (March 1926), 32; "Di bialistoker in berlin," *Bialystoker Stimme* 4 (June 1922): 12. The regular column on "Velt barimte bialistoker" debuted in the *Bialystoker Stimme* 4 (June 1922): 7–9, while the "Unzer eygene velt" column debuted in the *Bialystoker Stimme* 3 (March 1922): 12. Both soon became regular features. See, for example, *Bialystoker Stimme* 4 (June 1922): 14; *Bialystoker Stimme* 6 (February 1923): 22.

10. Morawska, "Changing Images of the Old Country in the Development of Ethnic Identity among East European Immigrants, 1880s–1930s." Popular immigrant literature in English by East European Jewish immigrants, such as Abraham Cahan's novel *The Rise of David Levinsky,* buttressed this idea that the United States was fundamentally different from Eastern Europe. See Steven Zipperstein *Imagining Russian Jewry,* 21–23.

11. For a discussion of the role articles on national historical figures and national history played in the Slavic press and the construction of a Slavic ethnic consciousness see Morawska, "Changing Images of the Old Country," 276–77, 284–86.

12. Morawska, "Changing Images of the Old Country," 284–86.

13. The *Bialystoker Stimme* was not exceptional in this focus. *Der Vilner,* a publication supported by Jewish immigrants from the city of Vilna (or Vilnius) in Lithuania who resided in New York City also saluted its former home as it discussed current events, the town's history, and the biographies of important figures from Vilna's past and present. See, for example, *Der Vilner* (1922): 17–18; *Der Vilner* (1929): 13–19, 27, 33–34.

14. See *Biaylstoker Stimme* 1 (November 1921): 2; *Biaylstoker Stimme* 6 (February 1923): 46; *Biaylstoker Stimme* 8 (February 1924): 1. Such a vision of Eastern Europe as a Jewish motherland was not exclusive to Jews from Bialystok as can be seen in the Vilna landsmanshaft publication *Der Vilner.* See *Der Vilner* (1922): 22; *Der Vilner* (1929): 18, 27, 33, 58, 60.

15. For more on nostalgia and its functions see Suzanne Vromen, "Maurice Halbwachs and the Concept of Nostalgia"; and Suzanne Vromen, "The Ambiguity of Nostalgia."

16. Susan Matt, "You Can't Go Home Again: Homesickness and Nostalgia in U.S. History," 469.

17. As social theorist Maurice Halbwachs observes, group memory is a social construct built on individuals' common past experiences as well as their shared current needs. See Maurice Halbwachs, *The Collective Memory*. Daniel Soyer has explained landsmanshaftn groups' turn to writing about Eastern Europe in this period as representing a last-ditch effort to maintain group unity as interest in landsmanshaftn began to wane. See Soyer, *Jewish Immigrant Associations and American Identity*, 193–94.

18. Sohn, "Yakov Krepliak," *Bialystoker Stimme* (September 1955): 39; see also "Yakov Krepliak," in *Idishe leksikon*, vol. 8 (New York, 1956), 788–90. For an insightful analysis of the Yiddish literary journal and Krepliak's influence on it, see Cassedy, *Building the Future: Jewish Immigrant Intellectuals and the Making of Tsukunft*.

19. Yakov Krepliak, "Mayn heymish shtot," *Bialystoker Stimme* 14 (October 1926): 28. Emphasis in original.

20. Jacobson, *Special Sorrows*, 9.

21. Further discussion of female imagery and European nationalism can be found in George Mosse's *Nationalism and Sexuality;* and Maurice Agulhon's *Marianne into Battle: Republican Imagery and Symbolism in France, 1780–1880.*

22. Two insightful treatments of the complex relationship between landscape and national identity are Simon Schama, *Landscape and Memory* and Stephen Daniels, *Field of Vision: Landscape Imagery and National Identity in England and the United States.*

23. In fact, though, by using metaphors of landscape to articulate his feelings of loss and despair, Babitsh, despite his claims of alienation, illustrated how embedded he was in the American cultural landscape. Only in the cultural context of North America, where the American national character had long been linked with the landscape, did Bialystoker émigrés like Babitsh and Krepliak articulate their continued connection to Eastern Europe through narrative concerning landscape. See Daniels, *Fields of Vision*, 5–7, 180–97.

24. Mordechai Babitsh, "Der bialistoker vald," *Bialystoker Stimme* 1 (November 1921): 8.

25. Ibid.

26. The complex relationship between gender, sexuality, and nationalism was present in nationalist rhetoric in many different countries during the twentieth century. See Mosse, *Nationalism and Sexuality.*

27. Zalman Segelowitz, "Bialistok," 15.

28. This poem can be found in the following publications: *Bialystoker Stimme* 6 (February 1923): 15; *Bialystoker Stimme* 14 (October 1926): 24; *Bialystoker vegn* 1 (1947): 6; *Bialystoker vegn* 3 (1949): 1.

29. Natan Kaplan, "Oy bialistok," *Bialystoker Stimme* 2 (March 1922): 2.

30. Ibid.

31. Miron, "The Literary Image of the Shtetl," 1–43; David Roskies, *A Bridge of Longing: The Lost Art of Yiddish Storytelling;* Roskies, *The Jewish Search for a Usable Past,* 41–67.

32. Miron, "The Literary Image of the Shtetl," 1–3.

33. Anonymous, "Bialistok" *Bialystoker Stimme* 1 (November 1921): 22.

34. The different images of Bialystok presented in poetry, articles, and fictional vignettes of these newspapers illustrate clearly that the image of the city also served as a lightning rod for anxiety in the East European Jewish imagination, a topic few scholars have explored. In general, the "shtetlization" of the East European city is a subject deserving of much further research, but some suggestive insights about this phenomenon can be found in Roskies, *The Jewish Search for a Usable Past,* 49–54. Also see Zipperstein, *Imagining Russian Jewry,* especially his first essay, "Shtetls Here and There," 15–40.

35. B. Bialostocki, "Vilne," in *Di yidishe landsmanshaften fun nyu york,* 211.

36. Morris Aizenberg-Brodsky, "Pinsk," in *Di yidishe landsmanshaften fun nyu york,* 224.

37. Rabbi Jacob Eskolsky, "In Honor of the Fiftieth Anniversary of Bes Kneses Anshei Bialystok," *Bes Kneses Anshey Bialistok, 1878–1928* (New York, 1928), 2.

38. This phrase originally appears in Samuel II 20:19 to refer to the city of Abel, then a regional center, but by the nineteenth century it was used in reference to any town or city that was considered a great center of learning. See Even Shoshan, *"Ha-Milon ha-'Hadash,* vol. V, 1913. This image of Bialystok as a center of Jewish piety was elaborated upon by Louis Cohen in his, "Zikhroynes fun a member," 3; Rabbi Jacob Eskolsky, "In Honor of the Fiftieth Anniversary of Bes Kneses Anshei Bialystok," in Bes Kneses Anshei Bialystok, 1.

39. Zvi Hirsh Masliansky, *Maslianski's zikhroynes,* 66. Masliansky, a preacher who traveled throughout Eastern Europe before immigrating to the United States in 1895, where he became a regular speaker at the Educational Alliance, declared Bialystok "a daughter in Israel" in one of his talks on the Lower East Side.

40. Miron, "The Literary Image of the Shtetl."

41. Julius Gold, "Kapital fun yidisher tsrus in bialistok," *Bialistoker fraynd* (March 1925): 12–3; Nachum Konin, "Ikh hab gevolt zayn in bialistok," *Bialistoker fraynd* 11 (March 1925): 34; Yosef Yachnuk, "Di bund in der bialistoker pogrom," *Bialistoker fraynd* 11 (March 1925): 17–19.

42. Sohn, "In likhtigen fun yakov krepliak," *Bialystoker Stimme* (September 1955): 39; see also *Yidishe leksikon,* vol. 8 (New York, 1956), 788–90.

43. This Hebrew phrase literally means "the dedication of the house," but is used almost exclusively in reference to the consecration of holy sites. Yakov Krepliak, "Khanukas ha-bayes," *Bialystoker Stimme* 5 (February 1923): 3.

44. Herman Frank, "Bialistok: a kolonial macht," *Biaylstoker Stimme* 8 (February 1924): 1.

45. Anderson, *Imagined Communities,* 6.

46. Such a vision was not totally inconceivable, considering Bialystok had operated as an independent oblast in tsarist Russia, and relatively small, multinational regions like Lithuania were being recognized as their own independent political entities in this era. As Andrew Thompson highlights, "the terms empire

and imperialism were like empty boxes that were continuously being filled up and emptied of their meanings." See Thompson, "The Language of Imperialism and the Meanings of Empire," 147. The term *empire* was constantly being redefined during the interwar period. See R. Koebner and H. D. Schmidt, *Imperialism: The Story and Significance of a Political Word*, xiii–xiv. On Bialystok's operation as an independent oblast, see Edward Thadden, *Russia's Western Borderlands, 1710–1870*, 63–70.

47. Muttel Dovesh, "Shmuses mit a feyleton," *Bialystoker Stimme* 9 (July 1924): 20.

48. Ibid., 20.

49. Zelig Tigel, "Bialistok un varsha," *Bialystoker Stimme* 8 (1924): 8.

50. Ibid.

51. Similarly, an article in *Der Vilner*, portraying the dire situation in Lithuania, argued that even though "Vilna was never a rich city, like Odessa or Ekaterinoslav in the south, Minsk or Bialystok in the west or Lodz and Warsaw in Poland," the critical support and strong "bridge uniting Vilna in Europe with Vilna in America" has enabled this city to regain its former stature. See Dr. Ts. Shabad, "Vilne amol un itst," *Der Vilner* (1929), 16, 19.

52. A voluminous correspondence between David Sohn and the editors of Bialystok's three largest Yiddish newspapers, *Dos naye lebn, Unzer lebn*, and *Naye Byalistoker Stimme*, can be found among Sohn's personal papers. These letters contain both requests for more information and for copies of the *Bialystoker Stimme*. See Tel Aviv University Archives, A-18/38-18.

53. Anna Gepner, oral interview, August 17, 1997, Melbourne, Australia.

54. Sohn sent hundreds of contributions to almost every newspaper in Bialystok running the gamut from those that addressed larger topics such as American politics (see "Arbeitsozialistkeit in Amerike," *Byalistoker tageblat* [February 21, 1914]; "Amerikaner politisher partii," *Dos naye lebn* [May 7, 1920]) to those more focused on Bialystoker émigré life (see " A bialistoker frauen in amerike," *Byalistoker tageblat* April 2, 1914; "Der nayer moshav zekanim far di bialistoker landslayt," *Byalistoker tageblat*, July 2, 1930).

55. The transatlantic character of the Yiddish press is a quality rarely addressed by contemporary scholars but was abundantly clear to most interwar Jews. I. J. Singer, Yosef Tunkel, and Yankev (Jacob) Leschinsky were three writers who regularly contributed to papers both in New York and Warsaw. Even cartoonists, such as Zuni Maud, Saul Raskin, and Lola (Leon Israel) also regularly contributed to newspapers on both sides of the Atlantic. See Edward Portnoy's 2008 Jewish Theological Seminary dissertation entitled "The Creation of a Jewish Cartoon Space in the Yiddish Presses of New York and Warsaw." Studies of Yiddish performing arts highlight that as actors and troupes performed around the world, they engaged in a transatlantic dialogue that created an atmosphere of heightened creativity. See Edward Portnoy, "Modicut Puppet Theatre," 115–34; Nina Warnke, "Of Plays and Politics: Sholem Aleichem's First Visit to America"; Goldman, *Visions, Images and Dreams;* and Hoberman, *Bridge of Light.*

56. Anderson, *Imagined Communities*, 61–65. While Anderson's study deals with the emergence of print capitalism and nationalist consciousness in the eighteenth century, his theories about the ways in which newspapers construct worlds

along national lines can, I feel, be extended to Diaspora communities, who are even more dependent on print, because of their lack of territorial cohesiveness, in constructing their readers as members of one community.

57. *Dos naye lebn*, October 7, 1919, 2; November 8, 1919, 2.

58. *Dos naye lebn*, November 19, 1919; April 20, 1925.

59. A regular column entitled "Gelt fun amerike," which discussed the allocation of émigré funds, appeared daily between 1919 and 1922. Features entitled "Vos hert zikh in bialistok" and "Vos hert zikh in amerike?" appeared several times a week during this period. See *Dos naye lebn*, July 27 and August 24, 1919.

60. Pesach Kaplan, "Unzer likhtige fargangenheyt," 37.

61. Wenger, *New York Jews and the Great Depression*, 198.

62. Mendelsohn, *East Central Europe between the World Wars*, 74–76, 82.

63. *Forverts*, May 13, 1934, 5–6; and September 13, 1931.

64. Roza Nevodovska, "Heymvey," 20.

65. While widely read by members of the transnational Bialystok Jewish community, Nevodovska did not publish her poetry in the *Biaystoker Stimme* because the Depression had left the Bialystoker Center with few available funds, forcing it to radically pare down the length of the publication. Instead of the fifty-page issues of the 1920s that contained articles and poems solicited from around the world, the *Bialystoker Stimme* ran approximately five pages during the 1930s, focusing its articles almost exclusively on fundraising.

66. The dark pillar Nevodovska refers to is the memorial built for those Jews killed in the 1906 pogrom.

67. Rosa Nevodovska, "Tsu mayn heymstadt," 24–25.

68. Sohn, "Minutes from the First Years of the Bialystoker U.V. Somach Noflim," in *The Bialystoker Pioneer: 45th Anniversary Journal*, 5.

69. Ibid. A special photo-journalist series in the New York *Forverts* highlighted the penury of Bialystok's Jewish community; *Forverts*, September 13, 1931. Also see the issue of May 13, 1934, pp. 5–6, and Mendelsohn, *East Central Europe between the World Wars*, 74–76, 82.

70. Sohn, "Der bialistoker "pilgrims" in amerika," in *Der Byalistoker pionir*, 3, 6.

71. Sohn, "Bialistok a ist brodvey."

72. Anna Albert, "Unzer Yovilum," in *Bialystoker Ladies Aid Society of Harlem and Bronx 25th Anniversary Journal*, 1. Sohn, "Topics of the Day," *Bialystoker Stimme* 38 (September 1933): 1.

73. For more examples of this trend than discussed below, see "A monatliche stime,'" *Bialystoker Stimme* 22 (February 1932): 2, where the *Bialystoker Stimme* is described as the voice of the people (not the voice of Bialystok). The entire issue of *Bialystoker Stimme* 25 is devoted to Sohn, who is described several times as spreading Bialystok throughout the world through his activism and personality. See, in particular, *Bialystoker Stimme* 25 (1932): 4, 6, 8–10; Sohn, "Unzer bialistoker in dem oypboy fun rusland," *Bialystoker Stimme* 48 (1934): 8–9; Rivkin, "Der bialistoker tsenter—a muster landsmanshaft," *Bialystoker Stimme* 179 (1938): 6; Theodore Storch, "Women of Tomorrow," *Bialistoker lebn* 65 (June 1940): 3. Rosa Nevodovska went so far as to proclaim that "Bialystok is in all of us," in "Dem geyst fun unzer bialistok," *Bialystoker Stimme* 234 (January 1945): 3.

74. *Yidishe leksikon,* vol. 5, 22–23.

75. Solomon Kahan, "Strikhen fun bialistoker," *Bialystoker Stimme* 200 (September 1940): 4.

76. Miron, "Literary Image of the Shtetl," 19.

77. The Russian army, fearing that the Jews would ally with the Germans as they had in World War One, relocated thousands of Bialystok Jews to regions further east. Also, many Bialystok Jews fled to Vilna and their plight was described in "A brief fun de bialistoker pelitim in vilna," *Bialystoker Stimme* 197 (May 1940): 13.

78. Sohn, "Bialistoker in golus," *Bialystoker Stimme* 200 (September 1940): 3.

79. Roskies, *Against the Apocalypse,* 15–17.

80. Unlike the "relative disengagement" Hannah Kliger has identified among East European émigrés during these years, Sohn's evocative portrayal of the pain and anguish of "our brothers who are wandering around in exile" demonstrates how he appreciated the dire situation in Bialystok. See Kliger, "Communication and Ethnic Community," 23–28.

81. Abraham Shevach, "Bialistok mayn heym," *Bialystoker Stimme* 226 (December 1943): 9. This poem, slightly edited, was published on the cover page of the first issue of *Bialystoker vegn,* the magazine published by the Bialystoker émigré community in Argentina. See *Bialystoker vegn* 1 (December 1947): 1.

82. Shevach, "Bialistok mayn heym," *Bialystoker Stimme* 226 (December 1943): 9.

83. Chaikin, "Bialystok Transplanted and Transformed," 43.

84. Deborah Lipstadt, *Beyond Belief: The American Press and the Coming of the Holocaust.*

85. Sohn, "The Bialystoker Center," unpublished manuscript, 1944. Tel Aviv University Archives, 3.

86. Volf Garber, "Landsleyt shreyben" BS 246 March 1946, 39.

87. Their writings stand in contrast to what Jack Kugelmass and Jonathan Boyarin identified among other East European Jewish survivors, who turned to writing about their former homes to bury and memorialize their murdered brethren. See Kugelmass and Boyarin, *From a Ruined Garden,* 3–12, 15–17.

88. Terrence Des Pres, *The Survivor: An Anatomy of Life in the Death Camps.*

89. Sonia Rapalovsky, "Bialistok—mayn heym," *Bialystoker vegn* 3 (1949).

90. Elkin, *The Jews of Latin America,* 143.

91. Zalman Segelowitz, "Levana-nacht in tel-aviv," *Bialystoker Stimme* 221 (April 1943): 23–24.

92. Oral interview, Yisrael Prenski, Tel Aviv, 6/28/99.

93. Kiryat Bialystok Foundation Scroll, September 28, 1950. Kiryat Bialystok Archives, Yehud, Israel. I would like to thank Michael Flicker for bringing this source to my attention.

94. Miron, "The Literary Image of the Shtetl," 30.

95. Jonathan Sarna, "A Projection of America as It Ought to Be: Zion in the Mind's Eye of American Jews," 41–60.

96. Jacobson, *Special Sorrows,* 234–35.

97. Regional identity was the cornerstone of Jewish identity in Eastern Europe. See Lederhendler, "Did Russian Jewry Exist prior to 1917."

98. Kugelmass and Shandler, *Going Home: How American Jews Invent the Old World*, 4. Riv-Ellen Prell makes a similar point in her *Fighting to Become Americans*, 15.

99. Paul Novick, quoted in Soyer, *Jewish Immigrant Association and American Identity*, 196.

100. For more on the transformation of the shtetl into a Jewish polity, see Miron, "The Literary Image of the Shtetl," 35–37.

5. Shifting Centers, Conflicting Philanthropists

1. "Unzer erfalgreykhe konvenshon far 'kiryas bialistok,'" *Bialystoker Stimme* 255 (September 1949): 4.

2. With the exception of several studies of interwar Armenian refugees, who saw their ancestral homelands destroyed in the First World War, scholars have rarely considered this question with any group. On the Armenian case, see Rubina Peroomian, *Literary Reponses to Catastrophe: A Comparison of the Armenian and Jewish Experience;* on the specific ways Armenian refugees grappled with the great upheaval of genocide, see Anny Bakalian, *Armenian-Americans: From Being to Feeling Armenian;* and Susan Pattie, *Faith in History: Armenians Rebuilding Community.*

A virtual academic industry has grown around the topic of Holocaust memory, particularly in the United States, but most of the literature begins its discussions only in the 1960s. Some examples include Gerd Korman, "The Holocaust in American Historical Writing"; Leon Jick, "The Holocaust: Its Use and Abuse within the American Public"; Peter Novick, *The Holocaust in American Life;* Jeffrey Shandler, *While America Watches: Televising the Holocaust;* Edward T. Linenthal, *Preserving Memory: The Struggle to Create America's Holocaust Museum;* and Michael Staub, *Torn at the Roots: The Crisis of Jewish Liberalism in Postwar America.* For a comparative overview of Holocaust memory in Europe, see Tony Judt, *Postwar: A History of Europe Since 1945,* 803–831. While these studies are exemplary, few examine the immediate postwar period. Kirsten Fermaglich, for example, addresses "early Holocaust consciousness" in the era between 1957–1965, in her *American Dreams and Nazi Nightmares: Early Holocaust Consciousness in Liberal America.* One of the few synthetic treatments of visions of the Holocaust in American culture in the immediate aftermath of the war is in Hasia Diner's *We Remember: American Jewry and the Myth of Silence after the Holocaust.* I thank the author for sharing her manuscript with me.

3. David Engel, *Ben shiḥrur li-veriḥah: nitsole ha-Sho'ah be-Polin vehama'avak 'al hanhagatam, 1944–1946;* and Natalia Aleksiun, *Dokąd dalej?: ruch syjonistyczny w Polsce (1944–1950),* 2002.

4. Des Pres, quoted in Kugelmass and Boyarin, "Introduction," in *From a Ruined Garden,* 15.

5. "Unzer erfalgreykhe konvenshon far 'kiryas bialistok,'" *Bialystoker Stimme* 255 (September 1949): 4; Rezolutsoynes fun der velt bialistoker konferense, 1949. A-18/169 Tel Aviv University Archives.

6. Dash Moore, "Bonding Images, 255.

7. For more on the dominance and role of Polish Zionists in postwar Polish Jewish life, see Natalia Aleksiun's longer discussion in her dissertation ""Ruch syjonistyczny w Polsce w latach 1944–1950."

8. For more on this period, see Sara Bender, *Mul mavet orev;* Chaika Grossman, *The Underground Army: Fighters of the Bialystok Ghetto;* and Rafael Rayzner, *Der 'omkum fun bialistoker yidntum, 1939–1945.*

9. Oral interview, Koppel Lev, Kiryat Bialystok, May 1999.

10. Praca Centrali AJDC w Polsce: Wrkazy Demograficzne Mieszkańców Polski u uwzględnieniem Żydow, 1940 (microfilm 1) ZIH Archives, pp. 11–12.

11. B. Mark, *Der oyfshtand in Byalistoker geto;* Refa'el Rayzner: *Der umkum fun Byalistoker Yidntum, 1939–1945.*

12. Michael Flicker, oral interview, May 1999.

13. Because of the war, most of the funds were sent through the American Joint Distribution Committee's office in Warsaw, which was active in Poland until 1942 and which dispensed millions of dollars in aid and employed over forty people (including Emanuel Ringelblum) to work on their behalf. See Praca Centrali AJDC w Polsce: Wrkazy Demograficzne Mieszkańców Polski u uwzględnieniem Żydow, 1941 (microfilm 1) ZIH Archives, pp. 5–7, 21. For specific references to American funds sent to Bialystok via the Joint, see Praca Centrali AJDC w Polsce Dokumenty Finansowe: Wrkazy Demograficzne Mieszkańców Polski u uwzględnieniem Żydow, 1941, ZIH (microfilm 2) p. 33.

14. For the most expansive treatment of the experiences of Jews in the Soviet Union during the Second World War, see Yitzhak Arad, *Hashmadat Yehude Berit Ha-Moatsot Bi-Tekufat Ha-Sho'ah Ba-Shetahim She-Nikhbeshu Bi-Yede Ha-Natsim;* and his *Toldot ha-Sho'ah: Berit-ha-Mo'atsot yeha-shetahim ha-mesupahim.* Several excellent collections on this topic include Zvi Y. Gitelman, ed., *Bitter Legacy: Confronting the Holocaust in the USSR;* Vasilii Semenovich Grossman and Ilia Erenburg, *Chernaia Kniga: O Zlodeiskom Povsemestnom Ubilstve Evreev Nemetsko-Fashistskimi Zakhvatchikami Vo Vremenno Okkupirovannykh Raionakh Sovetskogo soiuza u v lageryakh Unichtozhenia Polshi Vo Vremia Voiny 1941–1945;* Zvika Dror, *Bi-Netive Hatsalah;* Israel Eichenwald, *Bi-Derakhim Uvi-Gevulot;* Rebecca Manley, "The Evacuation and Survival of Soviet Civilians, 1941–1946"; Ben-Cion Pinchuk, "Was There a Soviet Policy for Evacuating the Jews?" Tadeusz Piotrowski, ed., *The Polish Deportees of World War II: Recollections of Removal to the Soviet Union and Dispersal throughout the World.*

There are also many fascinating memoirs on these deportations and the experiences of Jews in the Soviet interior. See, for example, Fani Brener, *Di ershte helft lebn;* Toby Klodawski Flam, *Toby: Her Journey from Lodz to Samarkand (and Beyond);* Samuel Honig, *From Poland to Russia and Back, 1939–1946;* David Azrieli, *One Step Ahead: David J. Azrieli (Azrylewicz): Memoirs, 1939–1950.*

15. Chaika Grossman, *The Underground Army: Fighters of the Bialystok Ghetto.*

16. Tuvyah Tsitron, *Di geshikhte fun 'oyfshtand in bialistoker geto,* 47–72.

17. Dovid Bigelman, "Der itstiger poylisher ponim fun unzer idisher bialistok," *Bialystoker Stimme* 277 (September 1956): 16.

18. Ibid.

19. Yakov Makovski, *Zikhronotav shel partisn.*

20. Sohn, "Leafing through the Year," *Bialystoker Stimme* 202 (January 1941): 1.

21. Ibid.

22. "Unzere kinder in der armey," *Bialystoker Stimme* 221 (April 1943): 25; *Bialystoker Stimme* 224 (September 1943): 51; *Bialystoker Stimme* 226 (November 1943), n.p.; the advertisements to buy war bonds are present in every issue starting with the *Bialystoker Stimme* 220 (December 1942).

23. This was a larger trend in American Jewish life, explored in full by Deborah Dash Moore in her *GI Jews: How World War II Changed a Generation.*

24. Doniel Tsharne, "Bialistok, mir veln kumn," *Bialystoker Stimme* 232 (September 1944): 13–14.

25. Yakov Eyskolsky, "Peterson a tsveyte bialistok" *Bialystoker Stimme* 230 (April–May 1944): 43.

26. "Di bafrayte bialistok," *Bialystoker Stimme* 232 (September 1944): 4.

27. Joseph Chaikin, "Bialystok Transplanted and Transformed," *Bialystoker Stimme* 233 (November–December 1944): 39.

28. *Yediot shel ha-va'ad le-'ezrat yehudei Bialistok,* No. 1 May 3, 1945, Tel Aviv University Archives A-18/72.

29. Ibid.

30. Yehuda Bauer, *Out of the Ashes: The Impact of American Jews on Post-Holocaust European Jewry,* xxi.

31. "Helft di bialistoker milkhome karbanus," *Bialystoker Stimme* 233 (November–December 1944): 1.

32. J. Lightman [The American Joint Distribution Committee in Argentina] to Joint Distribution Committee New York, August 7, 1945; J. Lightman to American Joint Distribution Committee, August 30, 1945. YIVO Archives RG335.7 Folder 531.

33. "Helft unz in der shvere zumer monaten oyftsuhalten di lebens fun unzere zekanim un zekanos," *Bialystoker Stimme* 223 (July 1943): 1.

34. Sohn, "Di tragedia fun alt veren in amerike," *Bialystoker Stimme* 228 (February 1944), n.p.

35. "Azkare-ovent far di ked fun bialistok," *Bialystoker Stimme* 229 (March 1944): 25.

36. For more on American Jewish organizations' postwar efforts to rebuild Poland, see Handlin, *A Continuing Task;* Tom Schachtman, *I Seek my Brethren: Ralph Goldman and "The Joint";* Joseph Tenenbaum, *Let My People In;* and Cohen, *Not Free to Desist,* 265–93. Many representatives wrote and published travelogues recounting their journeys. See, for example, the account of the president of the American Federation of Polish Jews, Joseph Tenenbaum, *The Road to Nowhere;* and Louis Segal, representative of the World Jewish Congress, *Bey unzere sheyres hapleyte in poylen un ma'arav europye.*

37. Sohn, "Vos Dr. Shoskes derseylt (fun zeyn shlikhuts in bialistok)," *Bialystoker Stimme* 241 (March 1946): 28–33.

38. Sohn, "Vos Dr. Shoskes derseylt (fun zeyn shlikhuts in bialistok)," 29.

39. Lucjan Dobroszycki, "Re-emergence and Decline of a Community," 23, 27–28. It is estimated that between 1944 and 1947, approximately 275,000 Jews lived in Poland. This large number should not obscure the demographic irregularities of this group: this population contained relatively few older people and

children and many fewer women since women were less likely to have fled to the Russian interior in 1941.

40. Dobroszycki, "Re-emergence and Decline of a Community), 7–9; Aleksiun, "Ruch syjonistyczny w Polsce w latach 1944–1950."

41. Oral interview, Zev Olshak, March 27, 1999. Kiryat Bialystok, Israel; Dobroszycki, "Re-emergence and Decline of a Community," 4–12.

42. For a discussion of Zionism and its implications in postwar Poland, see Aleksiun, "Ruch syjonistyczny w Polsce w latach 1944–1950"; David Engel, *Ben shiḥrur li-veriḥah: nitsole ha-Sho'ah be-Polin yeha-ma'avak 'al hanhagatam, 1944–1946;* and Avinoam Patt, *Finding Home and Homeland: Jewish Youth and Zionism in the Aftermath of the Holocaust).*

43. Dr. Shimon Datner to Editor of the New York *Tog,* December 17, 1945. In A-18/169 Goren-Goldstein Center for the Study of Diaspora Jewry, Tel Aviv University.

44. Jan Gross, *Fear: Anti-Semitism in Poland after Auschwitz,* 248–49.

45. Oral interview, Ewa Kracowski, May 19, 2009.

46. Dovid Bigelman, "Der itstiger poylisher ponim fun unzer idisher bialistok," *Bialystoker Stimme* 277 (September 1956): 16.

47. Records of the OZE-TOZ (Obshchestvo Zdravookhraneniia Evreev/Society for the Protection of Jewish Health); YIVO Institute of Jewish Research RG 53; folders 3, 4, 6, 7, 9.

48. For the complete reports of TOZ in Bialystok, see Zespół: Towarzystwo Ochrony Zdrowia Ludności Żydowskiej: Sygnatura 324/514–515 ZIH Archives Warsaw.

49. Voivodisher Yidisher Komitet in Bialystok: Report fun der Kinder shul, July 1, 1946. Wydziału Oświaty: File 951. ZIH Archives, Warsaw.

50. Oral interview, Malka Ostrobuski Lawrence, Melbourne, 1998.

51. Gross, *Fear,* 164.

52. *Yediot shel ha-va'ad le-'ezrat yehudei Bialistok,* No. 2, September 12, 1946 Tel Aviv University Archives A-18/72. For more on this wave of anti-Jewish violence, see Stanisław Meducki, "The Pogrom in Kielce on 4 July 1946"; and Joanna Milhlic-Coren, "Anti-Jewish Violence in Poland, 1918–1939 and 1945–1947."

53. Stanisław Meducki, "The Kielce Pogrom, 4 July 1946," 165.

54. Albert Stankowski, "Emigracja Żydów z Pomorza Zachodniego w latach, 1945–1960," in August Grabski, Maciej Pisarski, and Albert Stankowski, eds., *Studia z dziejów i kultury Żydow w Polsce po 1945 roku,* 83–141. For the larger context see Natalia Aleksiun, *Dokąd dalej?: Ricj syjonistyczny w Polsce.* 55. Shimon Datner, "Vegn a bialistoker velt farband," *Bialystoker Stimme* 243 (September 1946): 36; "A protest fun bialistok," *Bialystoker Stimme* 245 (January 1947): 33.

56. "A protest fun bialistok," 33.

57. Datner, "Vegn a bialistoker velt farband," 36; "A protest fun bialistok," 33.

58. Australian immigration policy favored resettlement of refugees in order to strengthen Australia against any future Asian invasion, yet they did not want any Jews. For more on the antisemitic prejudices of Australian immigration policy in the postwar period, see Suzanne Rutland, "Waiting Room Shanghai," 407–411.

59. Fink acquired these visas; Minister Caldwell commented how "he never knew a man who had so many cousins," but Fink stood by all the refugees he

sponsored, for he believed "all Jews were family." See Rutland, "I Never Knew a Man Who Had So Many Cousins," 400.

60. See the correspondence between Fink and the American Joint Distribution Committee in the Joint Distribution Committee Archives, Collection AR33/44: Folder 438b.

61. Aside from the work of Suzanne Rutland, few have discussed this topic. See Rutland, "I Am My Brother's Keeper"; see also Rutland, "Are You Jewish? Post-war Jewish Immigration to Australia, 1945–1954"; and Rutland, "Subtle Exclusions: Postwar Jewish Emigration to Australia and the Impact of the IRO Scheme." These efforts are briefly mentioned in Bauer, *Out of the Ashes*, 77, 199, and 256; Mark Wischnitzer, *Visas to Freedom: The History of HIAS*, 226–28; and Ronald Sanders, *Shores of Refuge: A Hundred Years of Jewish Emigration*, which has a number of brief references to the Australian story, but nothing on the post-war period.

62. Oral interview, Paula Pitt Hansky, August 18, 1998; *Bialystoker Centre Annual Report* (Melbourne 1946), 1; Benjamin, *A Serious Influx of Jews*, 154, 158–69.

63. Rutland, "I Never Knew a Man Who Had So Many Cousins," 401.

64. To fully understand the extent of this economic stress, one needs to look at the fifty letters Abraham Zbar sent to David Sohn between January 1946 and December 1947. I would like to thank Paula Pitt Hansky for providing me with copies of these letters.

65. Abraham Zbar to David Sohn, November 4, 1947.

66. Abraham Zbar to the Bialystoker Refugee Organization, Los Angeles, October 1947.

67. Oral interview, William Kavee, July 16, 2007.

68. Ibid., and "Sylvia Sohn," *Bialystoker Stimme* 240 (January–February, 1946): 54.

69. *Bialystoker Stimme* 246 (1947): 63.

70. Ibid., 62.

71. "Vegn Bialistoker emigratsia kayn oystralia," *Bialystoker Stimme* 247 (June 1947): 2.

72. "Finanshal bericht fun bialistoker relif komitet," *Bialystoker Stimme* 248 (1947): 64.

73. Sohn and Zbar's evolving relationship is eloquently narrated in the fifty letters Abraham Zbar sent to David Sohn between January 8, 1946 and December 22, 1948. Oral interview, Willaim Kavee, July 29, 2007.

74. Bialystoker Centre Annual Report, 1947–8 (Melbourne, 1948), n.p.

75. David Sohn to Abraham Zbar, December 17, 1950 A-18/38.11, Tel Aviv University Archives.

76. *Bialystoker Stimme* 247 (March 1947): 55.

77. Ibid., 55–57.

78. See Michael Berkowitz, "Art in Zionist Popular Culture and Jewish National Self-Consciousness, 1897–1914," in Ezra Mendelsohn, ed., *Art and Its Uses*, 9–42.

79. Alfred M. Lilienthal was the first Jew to publicly oppose Zionism out of the specter of dual loyalty. In the September 1949 issue of *Reader's Digest*,

Lilienthal maintained that "the future happiness of the Jews in America depends on their complete integration as citizens of this—our true—country." See Alfred Lilienthal, "Israel's Flag Is Not Mine," 49.

80. Oral interview, William Kavee, July 19, 2007.

81. Kliger, "Traditions of Grass-Roots Organization and Leadership, 32.

82. Samuel Rabinowitch (London) to David Sohn (New York), September 1, 1946. Tel Aviv University Archives A-18/38-18.

83. *Bialystoker Stimme* 253 (January 1949): 32.

84. "Unzer erfalgreykhe konvenshon far 'kiryas bialistok,'" *Bialystoker Stimme* 255 (September 1949): 4.

85. National Labor Committee, Israel to David Sohn, August 20, 1949. Tel Aviv University Archives, A-18/41.

86. Rezalushons fun der alveltlicher bialistoker konvenshon, August 21, 1949. Tel Aviv University Archives A-18/41, 1–2.

87. Oral interview, Lev Koppel, March 26, 1999.

88. Ibid., 2–5.

89. *Bialystoker Stimme* 18 (September 1928): 33.

90. *Kiryas bialistok buletin*, 1 (December 1949): 1; Rezalushons fun der alveltlicher bialistoker konvenshon, 4.

91. Ibid.

92. *Kiryas bialistok buletin* 1 (December 1949): 3. Tel Aviv University Archives A-18/72.

93. Ibid.

94. *Kiryas bialistok buletin* 2 (July 1950): 1. Tel Aviv University Archives A-18/72.

95. Ibid.

96. Volf Onin, "Der emes vegn "kiryas bialistok," *Bialystoker Stimme* 264 (January 1952): 9–21.

97. Ibid., 9–10.

98. Oral interview, Michael Flicker, March 26, 1999. Lev Koppel, oral interview, March 26, 1999.

99. Oral interview, Michael Flicker, March 26, 1999.

100. Ibid.

101. Ha-Va'ad shel Kiryat Bialistok to David Sohn.

102. "Grus fun yisroel" *Bialystoker Stimme* 268 (December 1952): 10.

103. "We read in the *Bialystoker Stimme* and other newspapers," wrote one anonymous member of the board to David Sohn, "that over $5000 was raised for Kiryat Bialystok at a Hanukah Bazaar in New York to build a community center . . . but it has been six months since Hanukah and we have seen no money yet." Also see "Grus fun yisroel."

104. *Kiryas bialistok buletin* 5 (1952): 4–5.

105. William Kavee, oral interview, July 19, 2007.

106. *Kiryas bialistok buletin* 5 (1952): 5.

107. "Tsum shand slup," *Bialystoker Stimme* 266 (June 1952): 2.

108. Oral interview, Michael Flicker, March 26, 1999; Lev Koppel, oral interview, March 26, 1999; Oral interview, Zev Olshak, March 26, 1999.

109. "Yisroel band dreyv," *Bialystoker Stimme* 265 (April 1952): 2.

110. This was the original goal of erecting Kiryat Bialystok. *Kiryas bialistok buletin* 1 (December 1949): 1.

111. Kugelmass and Boyarin, *From a Ruined Garden*, 5.

112. Des Pres, quoted in Kugelmass and Boyarin, *From a Ruined Garden*, 15.

113. The Jewish tradition of writing memorial works for destroyed communities stretches back to the medieval period. See Robert Chazan, *Crusade Chronicles;* indeed, even the Bialystok diaspora produced three memorial books: the *Byalistoker bilder album* (New York, 1952); *Seyfer Byalistok* (New York, 1963–64); *Byalistoker Yizker Bukh* (New York, 1982).

114. Shimon Datner's column, "Hurban byalistok un umgegent" debuted in *Bialystoker Stimme* 246 (1947):18–21; also see *Bialystoker Stimme* 247 (1947): 18–20; *Bialystoker Stimme* 249 (Jan 1948), 15–19; *Bialystoker Stimme* 250 (April 1948), 78–82; *Bialystoker Stimme* 254 (April 1949): 51–54; *Bialystoker Stimme* 255 (September 1949): 41–48.

115. Yehoshua Rapaport, "A vort fun di aroysgeber," in Rayzner, *Der umkum fun Byalistoker Yidntum*, 3.

116. Ibid., 10–14.

117. Samuel Rabinowitch, Middlesex England, to David Sohn, May 23, 1946. A-18/ Tel Aviv University Archives.

118. Samuel Rabinowitch, Middlesex England to David Sohn, New York, October 2, 1946. A-18/ Tel Aviv University Archives.

119. Oral interview, William Kavee, July 29, 2007. He joined a chorus of intellectuals with his concern; see Uriah Zevi Engleman, "The Fate of Yiddish in America"; Alter Brody, "Yiddish: A Childless Language"; and I. Brill, "Can Yiddish Survive?" *Yidishe gazetn*, May 25, 1923, 16.

120. *Bialystoker Stimme* 246 (March–April 1947): 33.

121. *Bialystoker Stimme* 256 (Jan 1950) : 67–68.

122. Barbie Zelizer, *Remembering to Forget: Holocaust Memory through the Camera's Eye*, 6. For more on the increased importance of visual images in the narration and conceptualization of the Holocaust in the 1950s and 1960s, see Shandler, *While America Watches;* Andrea Liss, *Trespassing through Shadows: Memory, Photography, and the Holocaust;* and Richard Raskin, *A Child at Gunpoint: A Case Study in the Life of a Photo.*

123. *Bialystoker Stimme* 256 (Jan 1950): 67–68.

124. Maurice Samuel, *The World of Sholem Aleichem.*

125. Heschel's emotional YIVO lecture, which even provoked his avowedly secularist audience to break out into a spontaneous *kaddish* (mourner's prayer) at its conclusion, was originally published as an essay in *Yivo bleter* 25 no. 2 (1945) and in English translation in the *YIVO Annual of Jewish Social Science* 1 (1946). An expanded version, *The Earth Is the Lord's: The Inner World of the East European Jew*, came out several years later.

126. Barbara Kirshenblatt-Gimblett, "Introduction," to Mark Zborowski and Elizabeth Herzon's *Life is with People: The Culture of the Shtetl*, xii.

127. *Di farshvundene velt* [The Vanished World].

128. Roman Vishniac, *Polish Jews: A Pictorial Record*. The photographs in this volume were taken in Poland in 1938 and were later exhibited at New York's YIVO Institute for Jewish Research in 1944 and 1945.

129. Roman Vishniac, *Polish Jews*, back cover.

130. Barbara Kirshenblatt-Gimblett, "Imagining Europe: The Popular Arts of American Jewish Ethnography," in *Divergent Jewish Cultures*, Dash Moore and Troen, eds., 175.

131. Diner, *We Remember*, 126.

132. J. M. Kersht, "An eygenartiger denkmol nokh der shtot Bialystok," *Forverts*, May 11, 1951.

133. Yakov Letchinsky, "Byalistoker bilder album," *Forverts*, June 3, 1951.

134. Osip Dimov, "Byalistoker Album," *Di presse*, May 4, 1951. Also see these other reviews: "A moment far Byalistok," *Tog*, April 17, 1951; "Byalistoker Album," *Novy Ruskaya Slovo*, June 10, 1951; *Idishen zhurnal* (Toronto), May 8, 1951.

135. Aviv and Shneer, *New Jews*, xv.

136. Steven M. Cohen, "Ties and Tensions: The 1986 Survey of American Jewish Attitudes Towards Israel and Israelis;" Charles Liebman and Steven Cohen, *Two Worlds of Judaism: The Israeli and American Experiences*.

Epilogue

1. Oral Interview, Michael Flicker, Minna Flicker, Malka A., Lev Koppel, Yisroel Sokolowsky. May 18, 1999, Kiryat Bialystok.

2. Eva Hoffman, *Lost in Translation*, 274. Magdalena Zaborowska highlights this point in her reading of Hoffman's memoir. See Magdalena Zaborowska, *How We Found America: Reading Gender through East European Immigrant Narratives*, 249–250.

3. Hoffman, *Lost in Translation*, 275.

4. Nathans, *Beyond the Pale*, 397.

5. Shaul Stampfer, "Patterns of Internal Jewish Migration in the Russian Empire," 43–44.

6. Several doctoral studies illuminate how the upheaval and transformations set in motion in Bialystok were far from unusual. See Elissa Bemporad, "Red Star on the Jewish Street"; Natan Meir, "The Jews in Kiev"; Robert Shapiro, "Jewish self-government in Poland: Lodz, 1914–1939"; Scott Ury, "Red Banner, Blue Star."

7. I discuss the confluence of forces animating mass Jewish migration more fully in Kobrin, "The 1905 Revolution Abroad: Mass Migration, Russian Jewish Liberalism and American Jewry, 1903–1914," in *The 1905 Revolution: A Turning Point in Jewish History?* Ezra Mendelsohn and Stefani Hoffman, eds., 227–246.

8. Madeline Hsu, *Dreaming of Gold, Dreaming of Home*, 9.

9. Hasia Diner, "The Local and the Global: Lombard Street and the Modern Jewish Diaspora," in *Voices of Lombard Street: A Century of Change in East Baltimore*, D. Weiner, A. Kassof, and A. Decter, eds., 11.

10. Sara Stein, *Making Jews Modern*, 214. Other fine examples of the rich insights offered by a comparative approach to the study of Jewish migration are Anna Lipphardt's "Vilne, yidishlekh fartrakht . . . Kulturelle Erinnerung,

Trauma, Migration. Die Vilne-Diaspora in New York, Israel und Vilnius nach dem Holocaust" (University of Potsdam, 2006). Devin Naar's forthcoming Stanford University dissertation, "Inventing the 'Jerusalem of the Balkans': Competing Visions of Salonika, 1876–1945" explores in a cross-cultural context the conflicting images of Salonika deployed by its Jewish émigrés to achieve a variety of political goals. Lara Rabinovich's forthcoming New York University dissertation, "Feeding Identity: Romanian Jewish Immigrants in New York City and Montreal, 1900–1939," uses a comparative framework to assess Jewish immigrant food culture.

11. Salo Baron, *Steeled by Adversity*, 144.

12. Bender, *A Nation among Nations*, 298.

13. Shalom Asch, *Kiddush ha-shem*, quoted on the front page of the periodical *Polin* (1986), xi.

14. Jonathan Boyarin, *Polish Jews in Paris*, 17–18.

15. Most scholars agree that the above criteria make a dispersed group into a diasporic group. For a good review of the literature see Robin Cohen, *Global Diasporas;* and William Safran, "Comparing Diasporas," 255–291.

16. Hasia R. Diner, *Lower East Side Memories;* Hasia R. Diner, Jeffrey Shandler, and Beth S. Wenger, eds. *Remembering the Lower East Side.*

17. Boyarin and Boyarin, "Diaspora: Generation and the Ground of Jewish Identity," 713.

18. Stratton, "Displacing the Jews: Historicizing the Idea of Diaspora," 312.

19. It is no coincidence that the renowned Russian Jewish historian Simon Dubnov turned to describing the Pale of Settlement as "the greatest [Jewish] center, following Babylon and Spain, in the historical diaspora." See the text of Dubnov's inauguration speech for the Jewish Historical-Ethnographic Society in *Evreiskaia Starina*, 1, no. 1 (1909): 154.

20. Adam Mendelsohn, "Tongue Ties: The Emergence of the Anglophone Jewish Diaspora in the Mid-Nineteenth century," *American Jewish History* 93, no. 2 (2007): 177–209. Marcie Ferris, "Dining in the Dixie Diaspora: A Meeting of Region and Religion," *Jewish Roots in Southern Soil* (2006) 226–254; and Ira Sheskin, "The Dixie Diaspora: The "Loss" of the Small Southern Jewish Community," *Dixie Diaspora* (2006), 165–188. Diaspora as a concept has also been increasingly deployed by scholars seeking to study trade networks and commodity chains. See Chiara Betta, "The Baghdadi Jewish Diaspora in Shanghai: Community, Commerce and Identities," *Sino-Judaica* 4 (2003): 81–104; Sara Stein, *Plumes: Ostrich Feathers, Jews, and a Lost World of Global Commerce.*

21. Sandhya Shukla, *India Abroad*, 252.

22. Eva Hoffman, *Lost in Translation*, 3–4.

23. Ibid., 274–75.

24. Deborah Dash Moore, *To the Golden Cities: Pursuing the American Dream in Miami and Los Angeles.*

25. On the importance of organizations, philanthropy and literary reinvention in contemporary Jewish life, see Allon Gal, ed., *Beyond Survival and Philanthropy: American Jewry and Israel*; Allon Gal, ed., *Envisioning Israel: The Changing Ideals and Images of North American Jews*; Arnold Dashefsky, *Ethnic*

Identification among American Jews: Socialization and Social Structure; Roberta Farber and Chaim Waxman, eds., *Jews in America: A Contemporary Reader;* David Brauner, *Post-war Jewish Fiction: Ambivalence, Self-Explanation and Transatlantic Connections;* Daniel Breslauer, *Creating a Judaism without Religion: A Post-Modern Jewish Possibility*; Sidra Dekoven Ezrahi, *Booking Passage: Exile and Homecoming in the Modern Jewish Imagination;* Linda Nochlin et al., eds., *The Jew in the Text: Modernity and the Construction of Identity.*

26. For discussions of fundamental shifts in migration in our current age of "globalization," see Emory Elliott, Jasmine Payne, and Patricia Ploesch, eds., *Global Migration, Social Change, and Cultural Transformation*; Rey Koslowski, ed., *International Migration and the Globalization of Domestic Politics;* Stephen Castles, *Ethnicity and Globalization: From Migrant Worker to Transnational Citizen.* For some historical perspective on this discussion, see Adam McKeown, *Melancholy Order: Asian Migration and the Globalization of Borders.* For more information on contemporary migrant groups remittances see www.worldbank.org/prospects/migrationandremittances.

Bibliography

Primary Sources

Archival Material

ARGENTINA
Fundación IWO, Buenos Aires

Box 30: Bund, Colección

Box 35: Colonias Agrícolas de Jewish Colonization Association [in particular 35.8 which focuses on Moisesville and the Bialystok settlement]

Box 180: Sociedades de ex residentes. Colección. Ladslait fareinen. [28, 29, 34] Bialystok, Federación de sociedades de Residentes, Poilisher Farband. Archivo institucional. Editó *Landsmanshaftn* en español desde 30 Jul. 1950

ISRAEL
Archive for the Study of Diaspora Jewry, Tel Aviv University

Collection A-18: Bialystoker Center and Old Age Home

Folders 1–3: Bialystoker Unterstitzung Verein Somach Noflim, papers, 1877–1924

Folders 3–9: Bialystoker Relief Committee of America, papers, 1919–1926

Folders 10–15: Papers of the Bialystoker Center and Old Age Home, 1933–1951

Folders 16–15:Bialystoker Center, correspondences, 1919–1959

Folder 26: Verband der Bialystoker in Berlin, 1921–1923

Folder 29: Union Residentes de Bialystok y alrededores en la Argentina, 1931–1966

Folder 30: Bialystoker Centre in Australia, papers, 1947–1961

Folder 31: Bialystoker Farband in Mexico, 1954

Folder 34: Comitato di Assistenza per profughi Ebrei di Bialystok, 1947–1948

Folder 35: Bialystoker Farband, Cyprus, 1947–1948

Folder 36–38: Bialystoker Organizations in Israel, papers, 1923–1958

Folder 41: Bialistoker velt konvenshon, protokols, 1949

Folder 42: 35th Yovileum bericht fun Bialistoker Tsenter, 1954

Folder 43–4: Photographs, Bialystoker Center and Bialystok, 1921–1966

Folder 47: Relif fun bialistoker in yisroel, 1950–1952

Folders 57–60: Bialystoker Ladies Auxiliary, papers, 1930–1966

Folder 61: Yakov Krepliak, personal papers, 1928–1946

Folder 62: Herman Frank, personal papers, 1921–1952

Folder 63: David Sohn, personal papers, 1921–1966

Folder 66: Photographs, Bialystoker Center and Old Age Home, 1934

Folder 70–79: Kiryat Bialystok, correspondences, minute books, 1949–1968

Folder 87–88: Bialystoker Young Men's Association, papers, 1906–1946

Folder 90: Bialystoker Culture Society, 1922

Folder 91: Bialystoker Verein Somach Noflim, reports and papers, 1911–1936

Folder 93: Bialystoker Relief Society, Paterson, N.J., journals, 1935–1956

Folder 94: Bialystoker Aid Society, Detroit, papers, 1940–1955

Folder 96: Bialystoker Relief Committee, Rescue Chain Division, 1946–1948

Folder 104–105: Bialystoker Branch 88, Arbeter Ring, papers, 1910–1955

Folder 110: Bialystoker Centre in Australia, annual reports, 1947–1953

Folder 111–113: Farband fun bialistoker in Argentina [Union Israelite Residentes de Bialystok] (Buenos Aires), papers, correspondences, and publications, 1947–1964

CENTRAL ARCHIVES OF THE HISTORY OF THE JEWISH PEOPLE, JERUSALEM

File PL 5: *Księga ślubów Rabinatu: Protóklarne Oświadczenie 1923–1933*

File PL111-4: Bialystok, 1905–1906

Microfilm HM/1010: Hibbat Zion, 1881–1903

CENTRAL ZIONIST ARCHIVES, JERUSALEM

Folder A9/63: Rabbi Shmuel Mohilever

Folder AK278/1: Kaplan Family Papers

THE DEPARTMENT OF MANUSCRIPTS AND ARCHIVES, JEWISH NATIONAL LIBRARY (JNULA), JERUSALEM

Chen Merhavia collection

POLAND
ŻYDOWSKI INSTYTUTU HISTORYCZNY, WARSAW

I: Centralnego Komitetu Żydow w Polse, 1945–1950

Wydział Repatriacji: Wojewódzki Komitet Żydowski—Białystok, 1946

303/V/10 303/XVIII/15 Korespondencja WKŻ do CKS Warsawa, 1946–1947

303/XVIII/27 Plany sytuacyjne Białegostoku, 1946

303/XVIII/ 28 Plany sytuacyjne obiektów—Białystok, 1946

BIBLIOGRAPHY

303/XVIII/48 WKŻ w Białymstoku, 1946–1947

303/XIX/31 Wydziału Ziomkstw: Sprawozdania okresowe z dzialalności ziom-kostw—Białystok, 1946–1948

Wydziału Oświaty: [Education committee, correspondences with WKZ of Bialystok]

Files 951–954, WKŻ w Białymstoku

Files 956–960 Hebrajska Szkoła Powszechna

Wydziału Opieki Społecznej [Social Welfare Committee]

File 249: Białystok WKŻ. Program uroczystośću żałobnej, 16.08.1949

File 250–258: Białystok Opieki Społecznej, 1946–1948

File 259: Białystok. Dom Starców

Towarzystwa Ochrony Zdrowia Ludności Żydowskiej w Polse przy CKZP [Special Commission for the protection of the Jewish population in Poland]

File 26: Sprawozdania statystyczne z działalności TOZ, 1948

File 39: Informacja na temat działalności TOZ

File 238: Pomoc dla dzieci. Korespondencja z Oddziałem Wojewódzkim w Białymstoku, 1946–1948

File 417: Akta personalne pracowników. Korespondencja z Oddziałem Wojewódzkim w Białymstoku, 1946–1948

Files 513–517: Wojewódzki Komitet Żydowski (Oddział TOZ)

ARCHIWUM PAŃSTWOWE W BIAŁYMSTOKU, BIALYSTOK

47 Urząd Wojewódzki Białostocki, 1918–1939

48 Okręgowy Urząd Ziemski w Białymstoku, 1919–1933

57 Tygodniowe sprawozdania sytuacyjne, 1927–1930

58 Komenda Wojewódzka Policji Państwowej w Białymstoku, 1920–1939

62 Okręgowa Komisja Wyborcza do Sejmu i Senatu w Białymstoku, 1922

63 Okręgowa Komisja Wyborcza do Sejmu i Senatu w Białymstoku, 1927–8

op. 31, d.1–2

64 Akta miasta Białegostoku, 1838–1944

117–121 Budzet Miasta Bialystok 1928/9–1934/5

D441 Szpital Okręgowy w Białymstoku, 1913

733.2 Rząd Guberniały Grodzieński, 1819–1853

Domeradzki, E. ed. Sprawozdanie Zarządu Głównego T-wa Białostockiego Opieki and Sierotami Żydowskiemi za lata 1923–1928. Bialystok: Miszondznika, 1929.

Sprawozdanie roczne Statystyki Ministerstwa Finansów *Annual of Statistics of the Ministry of Finance, 1924*. Warsaw: Ministerstwo Skarbu, 1926.

315

Statut Toawazystwa Białostockiego Opieki nad Sierotami Zydowskiemi. Bialystok: Miszondznika, 1923.

Ustav Belostokou talmud torah, 1901.

ARCHIWUM AKT NOWYCH, WARSAW

Zespol 266/II-3 Urząd Wojewódzki Białostocki, 1929–1931

RUSSIA
GOSUDARSTVENNYI ARKHIV ROSSIISKOI FEDERATSII [GARF]
(STATE ARCHIVES OF THE RUSSIAN FEDERATION)

Fond. 9529, *Liga pomoshi golodaivshchim evreiam v zaniatykh nepriatelem mestnostiakh*, 1914–1917

UNITED STATES
CENTER FOR JEWISH HISTORY, NEW YORK

Bund Archives: Box M-14

Folder 17: Records of Ezras Yesomim, Bialystok (1917–1920); Peretz Children's Home and Work School, Bialystok [1920]

Folder 19: Bialystoker Workers Bank (*Byalistoker arbeter bank*), Annual report and account books, 1920

Folder 20: Report of the Bialystok Society for Orphans, 1923–1928

Demography of the Jewish Population in Bialystok, 1919–1935

Folder 21: Statutes of Bialystok Factories, 1910–1937. Reports on the textile industry in Bialystok, undated. Jewish workers in Bialystok, 1921

Bund Photograph Collection, unsorted materials interwar Poland

YIVO INSTITUTE FOR JEWISH RESEARCH, NEW YORK

Autobiography Collection, 1934. Vilna Archive

Autobiography Collection, 1939. New York

Joint Distribution Committee Collection

Ustav obshestva po otkretiyo u v gorod Belostok obshestvenux bibliotek

RG335.7 Folder 600–601: Joint Distribution Committee, Bialystok, 1919–1947

RG335.7 Folder 531: Joint Distribution Committee, Argentina, 1938–1947

RG 123 Landsmanshaft Archive, Box 2

RG 53; folders 3, 4, 6, 7, 9 OZE-TOZ (Obshchestvo Zdravookhraneniia Evreev/ Society for the Protection of Jewish Health);

Newspapers, Periodicals, Bulletins
(available at the National Library, Jerusalem, The New York Public Library, and the YIVO Institute for Jewish Research)

Australisher yidishe lebn, Melbourne, 1933–1950

Bialistoker arbeter, Bialystok, 1899–1903

Bialistoker fraynd, New York, 1925–1945

Bialistoker handles zeitung, Bialystok, 1928

Bialystoker heym, New York 1930–1931

Bialystoker lebn, Brooklyn, 1932–1945

Bialistoker mort, Bialystok, 1913–1915

Bialystoker Stimme, New York, 1921–1969

Bialistoker tageblat, Bialystok, 1913–1915

Bialistoker vegn, Buenos Aires, 1947–1951

Bialistoker veker, Bialystok, 1925

Der tog, New York, 1914–1953

Der vilner, New York, 1929–1941

Dos naye bialistoker stimme, Bialystok, 1921–1925

Dos naye lebn, Bialystok, 1921–1939

Dziennik Białostocki, Bialystok, 1919–1939

Forverts, New York, 1901–1951

Golos Belostoka, Bialystok, 1919–1921

Ha-melits, Odessa; St. Petersburg, 1861–1901

Kiryat bialistok buletin, New York, 1949–1951

Naye yom tov bleter, New York, 1931–1934

Nyu Yorker abend post, New York, 1899–1930

Prożektor, Bialystok, 1925–1929

Unzer lebn, Bialystok, 1924–1934

Oral Interviews

Malka A., Kiryat Bialystok, 1999. Informant asked to not be identified by surname.

Pinchas Adler, Tel Aviv, 1999

Yisroel Adler, Tel Aviv, 1999

Yehezkel Aran, Tel Aviv, 1999

Miriam Birnbaum, New York, 1997

Moises Borowicz, Buenos Aires, Argentina, 2008

Dov Chivak, Tel Aviv, 1999

Stilla Feigin, Buenos Aires, Argentina, 2008

Manya Firsheim, New York, 2000

Michael Flicker, Kiryat Bialystok, Israel, 1999

Anna Gepner, Melbourne, Australia, 1998

Mario Ginzburg, Buenos Aires, Argentina, 2008

Nora Ginzburg, Buenos Aires, Argentina, 2008

Osher Gorfein, Tel Aviv, 1999

Paula Pitt Hansky, Melbourne, Australia, 1998

Avi Jaworowski, Melbourne, Australia, 1998

Ada Kagan, Melbourne, Australia, 1998

Sol Kagan, Melbourne, Australia, 1998

Dr. Baruch Kaplan, Tel Aviv, 1999

Steven Kavee, Westbury, Long Island, 2007

William Kavee, Westbury, Long Island, 2007

Mira Kniaziew, Buenos Aires, Argentina, 2008

Ewa Kracowski, Bialystok, Poland, 2008

Koppel Lev, Kiryat Bialystok, Israel, 1999

Menachem Lewin, New York, 2007

Sonya Mazny, New York, 2002

Yaakov Mikovsky, Tel Aviv, 1999

Rona Moyer, Westbury, Long Island, 2007

Zev Olshak, Kiryat Bialystok, 1999

Eliyahu Oran, Tel Aviv, 1999

Malka Ostrobuski Lawrence, Melbourne, Australia, 1998

Dina Ovsejevich, Buenos Aires, Argentina, 2008

Elsa Ovsejevich, Buenos Aires, Argentina, 2008

Dr. Enrique Ovsejevich, Buenos Aires, Argentina, 2008

Dr. Luis Ovsejevich, Buenos Aires, Argentina, 2008

Julio Pitluk, Buenos Aires, Argentina, 2008

Yisroel Prenski, Tel Aviv, 1999

Yisroel Sokolowsky, Tel Aviv, 1999

Sam Solarz, New York, 1997

Malka [Mary] Taubman, Melbourne, Australia, 1998

Zvi Yucht, Tel Aviv, 1999

Printed Primary Sources

GENERAL

Aguda li-yesod moshava ve-'ir ganim li-mofet bi-erets yisrael (Bialystok, Farlag "Meg"l, 1919).

American Jewish Yearbook 1906–1907. Philadelphia: Jewish Publication Society, 1907.

Berikht fun der yidisher kehile in byalistok far di yorn 1933–1937, Bialystok: Nakład Zarzadu Gminy Żydowskiej w Białymstoku, 1937.

Berikht fun voyevodishn hilf-komitet far di gelitene yidisher yishuvim in byalistoker rayon, 1937.

Bialistoker Komitet fun der fareynigter yidishe sosialistisher arbeter parti, *Di imigratsia un di kehila*. Bialystok: B. Mirsky, 1919.

Delagacion de Asociaciones Israelitas Argentinas. *50 años de colonizacion judia en la Argentina*. Buenos Aires: Sarmiento, 1939.

Eisenstein, Moses. *Der Pogrom von Bialystok*. Sniatyn: Pohorilles, 1907.

Frank, Herman. *Dray yor fun byalistoker konsum-kooperasia, 1915–1918*. Bialystok, 1918.

Heller, Eliezer, *Żydowskie Przedsiębiorstwa Przemysłowe w Polsce z 1921 Roku* Di Welt Publishing:Warsaw 1922.

Hilzer, N. *Hurban Bialistok*. Bialystok, 1906.

Kaplan, Pesach, ed. *Byalistok zamelheft*. Bialystok: Buchdruckerei Sch. & A. Sbar, 1917.

———. *Almanakh*. Bialystok: Farlag Dos Naye Lebn, 1931.

———. *Byalistoker yor bukh*. Bialystok: Farlag Dos Naye Lebn, 1932.

———. *Byalistoker leksikon: biografis fun bialistoker yidishe perzenlakhkaytn*. Bialystok: Unzer Prese, 1935.

Kremer, Yosef. *Masa Byalistok, Kneset Yisroel*. Warsaw, 1886.

Masliansky, Zvi Hirsh. *Maslianski's zikhroynes: firtsik yohr lebn un kemfn*. New York: Farlag Zerubavel, 1924.

Nevodovska, Rosa. *Azoy ve ikh bin: lider fun roza nevodovska*. Los Angeles: Rosa Nevodovska Book Committee, 1936.

———. *Lider mayne*. Tel Aviv: I.L. Peretz Publishing, 1971.

Shmulevitsh, Y., Ribalovski, I., Ḳronik, S. eds. *Der Byalistoker yizker bukh*. New York: Aroysgegebn fun dem Byalistoker Tsenter, 1982.

Sohn, David. *Di tetinkayt fun der bialistoker landsmanshaft in amerike*. New York: Bialystoker Center, 1934.

———. *Sefer Byalistok*. New York: Bialystoker Book Committee, 1951.

————, ed. *Der Byalistoker fundament: aroysgegeben lekoved dem draytsig yorigen yubileum banket fun di Byalistoker Brikleyers Progresiv Benevolent Assn.,* Montag, dem 10ten Martsh, 1935. New York: n.p., 1935.

————, ed. *Byalistoker Bilder Album: bilder album fun a barimter shtot on ire iden iber der velt.* New York: Bialystoker Center, 1952.

Yerushalimski, Ya'akov, *Zikkroynes un shriftn fun a byalistoker.* Y. L. Peretz Publishing House: Tel Aviv, 1984.

NEWSPAPERS AND BIALYSTOKER LANDSMANSHAFT SOUVENIR JOURNALS
(Available at YIVO Institute for Jewish Research or New York Public Library Jewish Division)

Bes Kneses Anshei Bialistok, 1878–1928 (New York, 1928).

Byalistoker yung mens asosieyshon zhurnal: 30 yoriker yovileum fun di bialistoker yung mens asosieyshon (New York, 1936).

Byalistoker yung mens asosieyshon zhurnal: finf-un-svansik yoriker yovileum (New York, 1931).

Byalistoker zhurnal (Paterson, N.J., 1935).

Bialystoker Centre Annual Report (Melbourne, 1947–1950).

Byalystoker froyen zhurnal (New York: 1930).

Byalystoker Relif Journal

Bialystoker unterstitzungs verein somach noflim post zhurnal (New York, 1911).

Bikur Holim Anshei Bialystok: 18 montlicher bericht, 1906–1908 (New York, 1908).

Khroniker Voskhoda, St. Petersburg

Kiryas bialistok bulletin (New York, 1949–1953)

The Bialystoker Synagogue, 1878–1978 (Dallas, 1978).

Sohn, David, ed. *Der byalistoker pionir: 45 yoriker yovileum zhurnal fun unterstitzungs verein somach noflim* (New York, 1931).

Souvenir Journal: Tenth Anniversary Dinner of the Mohilev-on-Dnieper and Vicinity Home for the Aged (New York, 1937).

————. *50 yor bialistoker somach noflim* (New York, 1936).

Bialystoker Ladies Aid Society of Harlem and Bronx 25th Anniversary Journal, New York, 1933.

SECONDARY SOURCES

Abramowitcz, Hirsz. *Farshvundene geshtaltn: siluetn un zchrunut.* Buenos Aires: [Union Central Israelita Polaca en la Argentina], 1958.

Abramsky, Chimen, Maciej Jachimczyk, and Antony Polonsky. *The Jews in Poland.* Oxford: B. Blackwell, 1986.

BIBLIOGRAPHY

Agulhon, Maurice. *Marianne Into Battle: Republican Imagery and Symbolism in France, 1780–1880*. Cambridge, Cambridge University Press, 1981.

Aleksiun, Natalia. *Dokąd dalej? Ricj syjonistyczny w Polsce (1944–1950)*. Warsaw: Wydawnictwi TRIO, 2002.

Alroey, Gur. *ha-Mahpeka ha-Shektah: Hagirah ha-Yehudit 'meha-Imperyah ha-Rusit, 1875–1924*. Tel Aviv: Am 'Oned, 2007.

Anderson, Benedict. *Imagined Communities: Reflections on the Origin and Spread of Nationalism*. London: Verso, 1983.

Applegate, Celia. *A Nation of Provincials: The German Idea of Heimat*. Berkeley: University of California Press, 1990.

———. "A Europe of Regions: Reflections on the Historiography of Sub-National Places in Modern Times." *American Historical Review* 104, no. 4 (1999): 1157–82.

Arad, Yitzhak. *Hashmadat Yehude Berit Ha-Moatsot Bi-Tekufat Ha-Sho'ah Ba-Shetahim She-Nikhbeshu Bi-Yede Ha-Natsim*. Jerusalem: Misrad ha-hinukh veha-tarbut, 1991.

———. *Toldot ha-Sho'ah: Berit-ha-Mo'atsot vÚeha-sheṭaḥim ha-mesupaḥim*. Jerusalem: Yad va-Shem, 2004.

Armstrong, W. "The Social Origins of Industrial Growth: Canada, Argentina and Australia." In *Argentina, Australia and Canada: Studies in Comparative Development, 1870–1965*, ed. D.C.M. Platt and Guido di Tella. London: Macmillan, 1985, 161–76.

Aronson, I. Michael. *Troubled Waters: The Origins of the 1881 Anti-Jewish Pogroms in Russia*. Pittsburgh: University of Pittsburgh Press, 1990.

Asch, Shalom. *Kiddush ha-shem* Philadelphia: Jewish Publication Society, 1926.

Ascher, Abraham. *The Revolution of 1905*. 2 vols. Stanford, Calif.: Stanford University Press, 1988–1992.

Avineri, Shlomo. *The Making of Modern Zionism: Intellectual Origins of the Jewish State*. New York: Basic Books, 1981.

Aviv, Caryn and David Shneer, *New Jews: The End of the Jewish Diaspora*. New York: New York University Press, 2005.

Avni, Haim. *Argentina and the Jews: A History of Jewish Immigration*. Tuscaloosa: University of Alabama Press, 1991.

Azrieli, David. *One Step Ahead: David J. Azrieli (Azrylewicz): Memoirs, 1939–1950*. Ed. Leah Aharonov and Danna J. Azrieli. Jerusalem: Yad Vashem, 2001.

Azuma, Eiichiro. "'Pioneers of Overseas Japanese Development': Japanese American History and the Making of Expansionist Orthodoxy in Imperial Japan." *Journal of Asian Studies* 67, no. 4 (November) 2008: 1187–1226.

Bachrach, Jacob. *Demografie fun der yidisher befelkerung in bialistok*. Bialystok: Viktoria Press, 1937.

Baer, Yitzhak. *Galut*. Schocken Library. New York: Schocken Books, 1947.

————. *A History of the Jews in Christian Spain*. Philadelphia: Jewish Publication Society of America, 1961.

Band, Arnold. "The New Diasporism and the Old Diaspora." *Israel Studies* 1 (1996): 323–31.

Baily, Samuel L. *Immigrants in the Lands of Promise: Italians in Buenos Aires and New York City, 1870–1914*. Ithaca, N.Y.: Cornell University Press, 1999.

Bakalian, Anny. *Armenian-Americans: From Being to Feeling Armenian*. New Brunswick, N.J.: Rutgers University Press, 1993.

Balin, Carole. "The Call to Serve: Jewish Women Medical Students in Russia, 1872–1887." *Polin* 18 (2005): 133–152.

Baron, Salo Wittmayer. *Steeled by Adversity; Essays and Addresses on American Jewish Life*. Philadelphia: Jewish Publication Society of America, 1971.

Bauer, Yehuda. *My Brother's Keeper: A History of the American Joint Distribution Committee, 1929–1939*. Philadelphia: Jewish Publication Society of America, 1974.

————. *American Jewry and the Holocaust: The American Jewish Joint Distribution Committee, 1939–1945*. Jerusalem: The Institute of Contemporary Jewry, Hebrew University, 1981.

————. *Out of the Ashes: The Impact of American Jews on Post-Holocaust European Jewry*. New York: Pergamon Press, 1989.

Beker, Israel. *Y. Beker, di bine fun mayn lebn*. Tel-Aviv: Y. Beker, 1979.

Benbassa, Esther, and Aron Rodrigue. *The Jews of the Balkans: The Judeo-Spanish Community, 15th to 20th Centuries*. Oxford: Blackwell, 1995.

Bender, Sara. "From Underground to Armed Struggle: The Resistance Movement in the Bialystok Ghetto." *Yad Vashem Studies* 23 (1993): 145–71.

————. *Mul Mavet Orev: Yehude Bialistok bi-Milkhamet 'Olam ha-Sheniyah*. Tel Aviv: Am Oved Publishers, 1997.

————. *The Jews of Białystok during World War II and the Holocaust*. Waltham, Mass: Brandeis University Press, 2008.

Bender, Thomas. *A Nation among Nations: America's Place in World History*. New York: Hill and Wang, 2006.

————, ed. *Rethinking American History in a Global Age*. Berkeley: University of California Press, 2002.

————, and Carl Schorske, eds. *Budapest and New York: Studies in Metropolitan Transformation, 1870–1930*. New York: Russell Sage Foundation, 1994.

Benjamin, Rodney. *A Serious Influx of Jews: A History of Jewish Welfare in Victoria*. Welfare Studies. St Leonards, NSW, Australia: Allen & Unwin, 1998.

Ben-Zvi, Mordecai. *Rabbi Samuel Mohilever*. [London]: Bachad Fellowship & Bnei Akivah, 1945.

Berger, David, ed. *The Legacy of Jewish Migration: 1881 and Its Impact*. New York: Columbia University Press, 1983.

Berkowitz, Michael. "Art in Zionist Popular Culture and Jewish National Self-Consciousness, 1897–1914." In *Art and Its Uses: The Visual Image and Modern Jewish Society*, ed. Ezra Mendelsohn. New York: Oxford University Press, 1990, 9–42.

———. *Zionist Culture and West European Jewry before the First World War*. Cambridge: Cambridge University Press, 1993.

Berrol, Selma. "Class or Ethnicity: The Americanized Jewish Women and Her Middle-Class Sisters in 1895." *Jewish Social Studies* 47 (Winter 1985): 21–32.

Biale, David, Michael Galchinsky, and Susannah Heschel, eds. *Insider/Outsider American Jews and Multiculturalism*. Berkeley: University of California Press, 1998.

Bilsky, Edgardo J. *La Semana Trágica*. Biblioteca Política Argentina, 50. Buenos Aires: Centro Editor de América Latina, 1984.

Bodian, Miriam. *Hebrews of the Portuguese Nation: Conversos and Community in Early Modern Amsterdam*. Bloomington: Indiana University Press, 1997.

Boggs, Colleen Glenney. *Transnationalism and American Literature*. New York: Routledge, 2008.

Bohning, W. R. "Elements of a Theory of International Economic Migration to Industrial Nation States." In *Global Trends in Migration*, ed. Mary Kritz et al. New York: Center for Migration Studies, 1981, 28–43.

Boulton, Marjorie. *Zamenhof: Creator of Esperanto*. London: Routlege and Kegan Paul, 1960.

Boyarin, Daniel, and Jonathan Boyarin. "Diaspora: Generation and the Ground of Jewish Identity." *Critical Inquiry* 19, no. 4 (Summer 1993): 693–726.

Boyarin, Jonathan. *Polish Jews in Paris: The Ethnography of Memory*. Bloomington: Indiana University Press, 1991.

Boyarin, Jonathan, and Daniel Boyarin. *Powers of Diaspora: Two Essays on the Relevance of Jewish Culture*. Minneapolis: University of Minnesota Press, 2002.

Brauner, David. *Post-War Jewish Fiction: Ambivalence, Self-Explanation and Transatlantic Connections*. Houndmills, Basingstoke, Hampshire: Palgrave, 2001.

Braziel, Jane Evans, and Anita Mannur. *Theorizing Diaspora*. New York: Blackwell, 2003.

Brener, Fani. *Di ershte helft lebn: Araynfir-Vort—Dr. Y. H. Biletski*. Jerusalem: Farlag Y. L. Perets, 1989.

Briggs, John. *An Italian Passage: Immigrants to Three American Cities, 1890–1930*. New Haven: Yale University Press, 1978.

Brill, I. "Can Yiddish Survive?" *Yidishe gazetn*, May 25, 1923, 16.

Brody, Alter. "Yiddish: A Childless Language." *The Nation*, June 9, 1926, 631–33.

Cała, Alina. *Asymilacja Żydów w Królestwie Polskim, 1864–1897: postawy, konflikty, stereotypy.* Warsaw: Państwowy Instytut Wydawniczy, 1989.

———. *The Image of the Jew in Polish Folk Culture.* Jerusalem: Magnes Press, 1995.

———, Hanna Wegrzynek, and Gabriela Zalewska. *Historia i kultura Żydów polskich: słownik.* Warsaw: Wydawnictwa Szkolne i Pedagogiczne, Spółka Akcyjna, 2000.

Campell, Malcolm. "The Other Immigrants: Comparing the Irish in Australia and the United States." *Journal of American Ethnic History* 14, no. 3 (Spring 1995): 3–22.

Cassedy, Steve. *To the Other Shore: The Russian Jewish Intellectuals Who Came to America.* Princeton, N.J.: Princeton University Press, 1997.

———. *Building the Future: Jewish Immigrant Intellectuals and the Making of Tsukunft.* New York: Holmes and Meier, 1999.

Chaikin, Joseph. "Bialystok Transplanted and Transformed." *Bialystoker Stimme* 233 (1944): 41, 45.

———. *Yidishe bleter in Amerike: a tsushteyer tsu der 75 yoriker geshikhte fun der Yidisher prese in di Fareynikte Shtatn un Kanada.* New York : M. Sh. Shklarski, 1946.

Chlebowczyk, Jozef. *On Small and Young Nations of Europe: Nation-Forming Processes in the Ethnic Borderlands in East-Central Europe.* Wrocław: Zaklad Narodowy im. Ossonlinskich Wydawnictwo Polskie Akademii Nauk, 1980.

Clifford, James. "Diasporas." In *Routes: Travel and Translation in the Late Twentieth Century,* ed. James Clifford. Cambridge, Mass.: Harvard University Press, 1997, 244–77.

Coben, Stanley. "A Study of Nativism: The American Red Scare of 1919–1920." *Political Science Quarterly* 79, no. 1 (1964): 52–75.

Cohen, Israel. *Vilna.* Philadelphia: Jewish Publication Society of America, 1943.

Cohen, Naomi. *Not Free to Desist: The American Jewish Committee, 1906–1966.* Philadelphia: Jewish Publication Society, 1972.

Cohen, Naomi. *Encounter with Emancipation: The German Jews in the United States, 1830–1914.* Philadelphia: Jewish Publication Society, 1984.

Cohen, Robin. *Global Diasporas: An Introduction.* Seattle: University of Washington Press, 1997.

Cohen, Steven M. *Ties and Tensions: The 1986 Survey of American Jewish Attitudes towards Israel and Israelis.* New York: American Jewish Committee, 1987.

Confino, Alon. *The Nation as a Local Metaphor: Württemberg, Imperial Germany, and National Memory, 1871–1918.* Chapel Hill: University of North Carolina Press, 1997.

Corrsin, Stephen. *Warsaw before the First World War: Poles and Jews in the Third City of the Russian Empire, 1880–1914.* Boulder, Colo.: East European Monographs, 1989.

Cygielman, Shmuel. *Jewish Autonomy in Poland and Lithuania until 1648.* Jerusalem: Zalman Shazar Center, 1997.

Danek, Wincenty. *Józef Ignacy Kraszewski: Zarys biograficzny.* Warsaw: Ludowa Spółdzielnia Wydawnicza, 1976.

Daniels, Stephen. *Field of Vision: Landscape Imagery and National Identity in England and the United States.* Princeton, N.J.: Princeton University Press, 1993.

Dashefsky, Arnold, and Howard M. Shapiro. *Ethnic Identification among American Jews: Socialization and Social Structure.* Lanham, Md.: University Press of America, 1993.

Datner, Szymon. *Pamiece 200,000 Żydow Wojewodztwa Bialostockiego wymordowanych przez Niemcow.* Warsaw: Centralna Żydowska Komisja Historyczna, 1945.

————. "Szkice do studiow nad dziejami żydowskiego ruchu partyzanckiego w okregu Bialystokiego." *Biuletyn ZIH* 100 (1976): 4.

Davies, Norman. *God's Playground: A History of Poland.* Oxford: Clarendon Press, 1979.

————. *Heart of Europe: A Short History of Poland.* Oxford: Clarendon Press, 1984.

Davis, Susan. *Parades and Power: Street Theatre in Nineteenth-Century Philadelphia.* Philadelphia: Temple University Press, 1986.

Dawson, Ashley, and Malini Johar Schueller. *Exceptional State: Contemporary U.S. Culture and the New Imperialism.* Durham, N.C.: Duke University Press, 2007.

de Grazia, Victoria. *Irresistible Empire: America's Advance through Twentieth-Century Europe.* Cambridge, Mass.: Harvard University Press, 2005.

Des Pres, Terrence. *The Survivor: An Anatomy of Life in the Death Camps.* New York: Oxford University Press, 1977.

Dielo o pogromie v Belostokie 1–3 iiunia 1906 goda. St. Petersburg, n.p., 1907.

Diner, Hasia. *A Time for Gathering: The Second Migration, 1820–1880.* Baltimore: Johns Hopkins University Press, 1992.

————. *Lower East Side Memories: A Jewish Place in America.* Princeton, N.J.: Princeton University Press, 2000.

————. *The Jews of the United States, 1654 to 2000.* Berkeley: University of California Press, 2004.

————. *We Remember with Reverence and Love: American Jews and the Myth of Silence after the Holocaust, 1945–1962.* New York: New York University Press, 2009.

Diner, Hasia, Jeffrey Shandler, and Beth Wenger, eds. *Remembering the Lower East Side: American Jewish Reflections.* Bloomington: Indiana University Press, 2000.

Dobronski, Adam. *Białystok: Historia Miasta*. Białystok: Zarzad Miasta Białegostoku, 1998.

———, and Jolanta Szczygieł-Rogowska. *Białystok: Lata 20-te, lata 30-te*. Bialystok: Instytut Wydawniczy Kreator, 2007.

Dobroński, Adam. "The Pogrom against the Jews in Białystok and the Polish Press Attitude." Merhavia Archives, Hebrew University.

Dobroszycki, Lucjan. "Re-emergence and Decline of a Community: The Numerical Size of the Jewish Population in Poland, 1944–1947." *YIVO Annual* 21 (1993): 3–32.

Dolistowska, Małgorzata. *Architektura rezydencjalna i mieszkaniowa Białegostoku na przełomie XIX i XX wieku (1890–1914)*. Bialystok: Studia i materiały do dziejów miasta Białegostoku, 2001.

Dotterer, Ronald L., Deborah Dash Moore, and Steven Cohen. *Jewish Settlement and Community in the Modern Western World*. Selinsgrove, Pa.: Susquehanna University Press, 1991.

Doyle, Michael W. *Empires*. Ithaca, N.Y.: Cornell University Press, 1986.

Dror, Zvika. *Bi-Netive Hatsalah*. Tel Aviv: ha-Kibuts ha-meuhad, 1988.

Dubnov, Simon. [Inauguration speech for the Jewish Historical-Ethnographic Society]. *Evreiskaia Starina* 1, no. 1 (1909), 154.

Dubnov, Simon. *History of the Jews in Russia and Poland, from the Earliest Times until the Present Day*. 2 vols. Philadelphia: Jewish Publication Society, 1916.

———. *Nationalism and History: Essays on Old and New Judaism*. Philadelphia: Jewish Publication Society, 1958.

Dubnov-Erlich, Sophie. *The Life and Work of S. M. Dubnov: Diaspora Nationalism and Jewish History*. Bloomington: Indiana University Press, 1991.

Eichenwald, Israel. *Bi-Derakhim Uvi-Gevulot*. Ed. Levi Deror. Tel-Aviv: Sifriyat poalim, 1989.

Eisen, Arnold. *Galut: Modern Jewish Reflections on Homelessness and Homecoming*. Bloomington: Indiana University Press, 1986.

Eisenberg, Ellen. "Argentine and American Jewry: A Case for Contrasting Immigrant Origins." *American Jewish Archives* 47, no. 1 (Spring 1995): 1–16.

Eisenstein, Moses. *Der Pogrom von Bialystok*. Sniatyn: Pohorilles, 1907.

Elkin, Judith. *Jews of the Latin American Republics*. Chapel Hill: University of North Carolina Press, 1980.

———. *The Jews of Latin America*. New York: Holmes and Meier, 1998.

Endelman, Todd, ed. *Comparing Jewish Societies*. Ann Arbor: University of Michigan Press, 1997.

Encyclopedia Judaica. Jerusalem: Keter, 1971.

Engel, David. *Ben shiḥrur li-veriḥah: nitsole ha-Sho'ah be-Polin veha-ma'avaḳ 'al hanhagatam, 1944–1946*. Tel Aviv: Am 'oved, 1996.

Engleman, Uriah Zevi. "The Fate of Yiddish in America." *Menorah Journal* 15 (July 1928): 22–32.

Etkes, Immanuel ed. *ha-Dat veha-hayim: tenu'at ha-Haskalah ha-Yehudit be-Mizrach Eropah.* Jerusalem: Merkaz Zalman Shazar, 1993.

Even Shoshan. *ha-Milon ha-'Hadash.* Vol. V. Jerusalem: Kiryat Sefer, 1969.

Evreiskoe Statisticheskoe Obshchestvo. *Evreiskoe naselenie Rossii po dannym perepisi 1897 g. i po noveishim istochnikam.* Petrograd, 1917.

Ezrahi, Sidra. *Booking Passage: Exile and Homecoming in the Modern Jewish Imagination.* Berkeley: University of California Press, 2000.

———, "Our Homeland, the Text . . . Our Text, the Homeland: Exile and Homecoming in the Modern Jewish Imagination." *Michigan Quarterly Review* 31 (1992): 463–97.

Farber, Roberta, and Chaim Waxman, eds. *Jews in America: A Contemporary Reader.* Hanover, N.H.: Brandeis University Press, 1999.

Di farshvundene velt [The Vanished World]. New York: Forward Association, 1947.

Feiner, Shmuel. *Haskalah ve-Historyah: toldoteha shel hakarat-'avar Yehudit modernit.* Jerusalem: Merkaz Zalman Shazar, 1995.

———, and David Sorkin, eds. *New Perspectives on the Haskalah.* London: Littman Library of Jewish Civilization, 2000.

Feldman, Egal. *Fit for Men: A Study of New York's Clothing Trade.* Washington, D.C.: Public Affairs Press, 1960.

Fermaglich, Kirsten. *American Dreams and Nazi Nightmares: Early Holocaust Consciousness and Liberal America, 1957–1965.* Hanover, N.H.: Brandeis University Press, 2006.

Fishman, Yehuda. *Sefer Shmu'el: Zikharon leha-Rav Shmu'el Mohiliver.* Jerusalem: Histadrut Mizrachi, 1923.

Flam, Toby Klodawski. *Toby: Her Journey from Lodz to Samarkand (and Beyond).* Toronto: Childe Thursday, 1988.

Frank, Herman. *Statistik fun der yidisher befelkerung in Bialystok far 10 yor: 1909–1918.* Bialystok: Viktoria Press, 1920.

———. *Di yidishe befelkerung in bialistok 1914–1924.* Bialystok: Kehila Farvaltung in Bialistok, 1928.

———. *Natsionale un politishe bavegungen bey yidn in bialistok.* New York: Bialystok Jewish Historical Association, 1951.

———. *Geklibene shriftn.* New York: Bialystok Historical Society, 1954.

———, ed. *Geshikhte fun di yidn in bialistok.* New York: Bialystok Historical Society, 1951.

———. "De goldene tekufa fun de in der geshikte fun der yidisher byalistok," n.d., 19–25.

Frankel, Jonathan. *Prophecy and Politics: Socialism, Nationalism and the Russian Jews, 1862–1917.* Cambridge: Cambridge University Press, 1981.

Frenkiel, A. *Sytuacja zydów w polsce w chwili obecnej.* Warsaw: Druk. Stołeczna R. Belke i S-ka,1923.

Frieden, Nancy Mandelker. *Russian Physicians in an Era of Reform and Revolution, 1856–1905.* Princeton: Princeton University Press, 1981.

Fuks, Marian. "Prasa żydowska w Białystoku, 1918–1939." *Żydowskiego Instytutu Historycznego w Polsce* 145–146 (1988): 145–53.

Gabaccia, Donna, R. "Is Everywhere Nowhere? Nomads, Nations and the Immigrant Paradigm of United States History." *Journal of American History* 86, no. 3 (December 1999): 1115–34.

———. *Italy's Many Diasporas.* Seattle: University of Washington Press, 2000.

——— and Fraser M. Ottanelli, eds. *Italian Workers of the World: Labor Migration and the Formation of Multiethnic States.* Urbana: University of Illinois Press, 2001.

Gafni, Isaiah M. *Land Center and Diaspora: Jewish Constructs in Late Antiquity.* Sheffield: Sheffield Academic Press, 1997.

Gal, Allon, ed. *Envisioning Israel: The Changing Ideals and Images of North American Jews.* Detroit.: Wayne University Press, 1996.

———. *Beyond Survival and Philanthropy: American Jewry and Israel.* Cincinnati: Hebrew Union College, 2000.

Gampel, Benjamin R. *Crisis and Creativity in the Sephardic World, 1391–1648.* New York: Columbia University Press, 1997.

Garrett, Leah. "Shipping the Self to America: The Perils of Assimilation in Glatshteyn's and Shapiro's Immigration Novels." *MELUS* 26, n. 3 (2001): 203–230.

Gartner, Lloyd. *The Jewish Immigrant in England, 1870–1914.* London: Allen & Unwin, 1960.

Gattrell, Peter. *A Whole Empire Walking: Refugees in Russia during the First World War.* Bloomington: Indiana University Press, 1999.

Gilman, Sander. "The Frontier as a Model for Jewish History." In *Jewries at the Frontier: Accommodation, Identity, Conflict,* ed. Sander Gilman and Milton Shain. Urbana: University of Illinois Press, 1999, 1–27.

Gilroy, Paul. *The Black Atlantic: Modernity and Double Consciousness.* Cambridge, Mass.: Harvard University Press, 1993.

Ginzberg, Lori D. *Women and the Work of Benevolence: Morality, Politics, and Class in the Nineteenth-Century United States.* New Haven, Conn.: Yale University Press, 1990.

Gitelman, Zvi. *Bitter Legacy: Confronting the Holocaust in the USSR.* Bloomington: Indiana University Press, 1997.

———. *The Emergence of Modern Jewish Politics: Bundism and Zionism in Eastern Europe.* Pittsburgh: University of Pittsburgh Press, 2003.

Glazier, Ira A. *Migration from the Russian Empire: Lists of Passengers Arriving at the Port of New York.* Baltimore: Genealogical Pub. Co., 1995.

Glenn, Susan. *Daughters of the Shtetl: Life and Labor in the Immigrant Generation.* Ithaca, N.Y.: Cornell University Press, 1990.

Golczewski, Frank. *Polnisch-jüdische Beziehungen 1881–1922: eine Studie zur Geschichte des Antisemitismus in Osteuropa.* Quellen und Studien zur Geschichte des östlichen Europa, Bd. 14. Wiesbaden: Steiner, 1981.

Goldman, Eric. *Visions, Images and Dreams: Yiddish Film Past and Present.* Ann Arbor: UMI Research Press, 1983.

Goldscheider, Calvin, and Alan Zuckerman. *The Transformation of the Jews.* Chicago: University of Chicago Press, 1984.

Goldsmith, Emanuel. *Modern Yiddish Culture: The Story of the Yiddish Language Movement.* New York: Shapolsky Publishers and Workmen's Circle Education Dept., 1987.

Golumb, Deborah Grand. "The 1893 Congress of Jewish Women: Evolution or Revolution in American Jewish Women's History." *American Jewish History* 70 (September 1980): 52–67.

Gordon, Milton. *Assimilation in American Life: The Role of Race, Religion and National Origins.* New York: Oxford University Press, 1964.

Goren, Arthur. "The Jewish Press." In *The Ethnic Press in the United States: A Historical Analysis and Handbook,* ed. Sally M. Miller. New York: Greenwood Press, 1987, 203–228.

———. *The Politics and Public Culture of American Jews.* Bloomington: Indiana University Press, 1999.

Gotlib, Itsik. "Polishe yidn in der farmirung fun latin-amerikaner kehillos," in *Yorbukh,* S. Federbush, ed. New York, 1964.

Graf, Heri. "Tsu vos a bialistoker tsenter." *Bialystoker Stimme* 3 (March 1922).

Grebenshchikov, V. I. "Opyt razrabotki rezul'tatov registratsii vrachei v Rossii." *Spravochnaia kniga dlia vrachei.* 2 vols. St. Petersburg, 1890.

Green, Nancy. *The Pletzl of Paris: Jewish Immigrant Workers in the Belle Epoque.* New York: Holmes & Meier, 1986.

———. "L'histoire comparative et le champ des études migratoires." *Annales: ESC* 45, no. 6 (November 1990): 1335–50.

———. "The Comparative Method and Post-structural Structuralism—New Perspectives for Migration Studies." *Journal of American Ethnic History* 13, no. 4 (Summer 1994): 13–23.

———. "The Modern Jewish Diaspora: East European Jews in London, Paris and New York." In *Comparing Jewish Societies,* ed. T. Endelman. Ann Arbor: University of Michigan Press, 1997.

———, ed. *Jewish Workers in the Modern Diaspora.* Berkeley: University of California Press, 1998.

———, ed., with François Weil. *Citizenship and Those Who Leave: The Politics of Emigration and Expatriation.* Chicago: University of Illinois Press, 2007.

Greene, Victor. *For God and Country: The Rise of Polish and Lithuanian Ethnic Consciousness in America, 1860–1910.* Madison: State Historical Society of Wisconsin, 1975.

Grewal, Inderpal. *Transnational America: Feminisms, Diasporas, Neoliberalism.* Durham, N.C.: Duke University Press, 2005.

Grinberg, Daniel. "Migracje i emigracja Żydów wschodnioeuropejskich w latach 1795–1939." *Biuletyn Żydowskiego Instytutu Historycznego w Polsce* 165/166 (1993): 95–104.

Gross, Jan. *Neighbors: The Destruction of the Jewish Community in Jedwabne, Poland.* Princeton, N.J.: Princeton University Press, 2001.

————. *Fear: Anti-Semitism in Poland after Auschwitz.* New York: Random House, 2006.

Grossman, Chaika. *The Underground Army: Fighters of the Bialystok Ghetto.* Trans. S. Beeri; ed., S. Lewis. New York: Holocaust Library, 1987.

Grossman, Vasilii Semenovich, Il'iaËrenburg, and Margarita Aliger. *Chernaia kniga: o zlodeĭskom povsemestnom ubiistve evreev nemetsko-fashistskimi zakhvachikami vo vremenno-okkupirovannykh raionakh Sovetskogo Soiuza i v lageriakh unichtozheniia Pol'shi vo vremia voiny 1941–1945 gg.* Jerusalem: Izd-vo "Tarbut," 1980.

Gruen, Erich S. *Diaspora: Jews amidst Greeks and Romans.* Cambridge, Mass.: Harvard University Press, 2002.

Grunwald, Kurt. *Türkenhirsch; A Study of Baron Maurice De Hirsch, Entrepreneur and Philanthropist.* [Jerusalem]: Israel Program for Scientific Translations, 1966.

Guesnet, François. *Polnische Juden im 19. Jahrhundert: Lebensbedingungen, Rechtsnormen und Organisation im Wandel.* Cologne: Bohlau, 1998.

Gurock, Jeffrey. *When Harlem Was Jewish, 1870–1930.* New York: Columbia University Press, 1979.

————. *The American Rabbinate: A Century of Continuity and Change, 1883–1983.* Hoboken, N.J.: Ktav, 1985.

Gutiérrez, David. *Walls and Mirrors: Mexican Americans, Mexican Immigrants, and the Politics of Ethnicity.* Berkeley: University of California Press, 1995.

Hagen, William W. "Before the 'Final Solution:' Toward a Comparative Analysis of Anti-Semitism in Interwar Germany and Poland." *Journal of Modern History* 68 (1996): 351–81.

Halbwachs, Maurice. *The Collective Memory.* New York: Harper & Row, 1980.

Hamm, Michael, ed. *The City in Late Imperial Russia.* Bloomington: Indiana University Press, 1986.

Handlin, Oscar. "New Paths in American Jewish History." *Commentary* 7, no. 4 (April 1949): 388–94.

————. "America Recognizes Diverse Loyalties." *Commentary* 9, no. 3 (March 1950): 220–26.

———. "American Views of the Jew at the Opening of the Twentieth Century." *American Jewish Historical Society* 40, no. 3 (1951): 323–44.

———. "We Need More Immigrants." *The Atlantic* 191, no. 5 (May 1953): 27–31.

———. *Adventures in Freedom: Three Hundred Years of Jewish Life in America.* New York: McGraw-Hill, 1954.

———."The American Jewish Pattern, after 300 Years." *Commentary* 18, no. 4 (1954): 296–307.

———. *American Jews: Their Story.* New York: Anti-Defamation League of B'nai B'rith, 1958.

———. *The Dimensions of Liberty.* Cambridge: Harvard University Press, 1961.

———. *A Continuing Task: The American Jewish Joint Distribution Committee, 1914–1964.* New York: Random House, 1964.

———. *The Uprooted.* 2d ed. Boston: Little Brown, 1973.

———. "A Twenty Year Retrospect of American Jewish Historiography." *American Jewish Historical Quarterly* 65, no. 4 (June 1976): 295–309.

Hayashi, Brian. *For the Sake of Our Japanese Brethren: Assimilation, Nationalism and Protestantism among the Japanese of Los Angeles.* Stanford, Calif.: Stanford University Press, 1995.

Heinze, Andrew. *Adapting to Abundance: Jewish Immigrants, Mass Consumption and the Search for American Identity.* New York: Columbia University Press, 1990.

Heller, Celia. *On the Edge of Destruction: Jews of Poland between the Two World Wars.* New York: Columbia University Press.

Herberg, William. *Protestant, Catholic, Jew: An Essay in American Religious Sociology.* New York: Doubleday, 1955.

Herman, Andrew. *The Better Angels of Capitalism: Rhetoric, Narrative and Moral Identity among Men of the American Upper Class.* Boulder, Colo.: Westview Press, 1999.

Hersch, Liebmann. "Jewish Migrations during the Last Hundred Years." In Jewish Encyclopedic Handbooks, Inc., New York. *The Jewish People, Past and Present.* New York: Jewish Encyclopedic Handbooks, 1946.

Herschberg, Abraham. *Pinkes bialistok: grunt-materyaln tsu der geshikhte fun di idn in Bialistok biz nokh der ershter velt-milhomeh.* New York: Bialystoker Jewish Historical Association, 1949.

Hertzberg, Arthur. *The Zionist Idea: A Historical Analysis and Reader.* New York: Atheneum, 1984.

Heschel, Abraham Joshua. *The Earth Is the Lord's: The Inner World of the Jew in East Europe.* New York: H. Schuman, 1950.

Higham, John. *Strangers in the Land: Patterns of American Nativism, 1860–1925.* New York: Atheneum, 1981.

Hoberman, J. *Bridge of Light: Yiddish Film between Two Worlds.* New York: Museum of Modern Art, 1991.

Hobson, J. A. *Imperialism: A Study*. New York: Cosimo, 2005.

Hoffman, Eva. *Lost in Translation: A Life in A New Language*. New York: Penguin Books, 1989.

Honig, Samuel. *From Poland to Russia and Back, 1939–1946: Surviving the Holocaust in the Soviet Union*. Windsor, Ont.: Black Moss Press, 1996.

Horowitz, Khaym. "Mir bialistoker (gedanken un gefilen)." *Bialystoker Stimme* 1 (November 1921): 2.

Howe, Irving. *World of Our Fathers*. New York: Harcourt Brace Jovanovich, 1976.

Hsu, Madeline Yuan-yin. *Dreaming of Gold, Dreaming of Home: Transnationalism and Migration between the United States and South China, 1882–1943*. Stanford: Stanford University Press, 2000.

Hyman, Paula. *Gender and Assimilation in Modern Jewish History: The Roles and Representation of Women*. Seattle: University of Washington Press, 1995.

Ianovskii, S. Ia. *Evreiskaia blagotvoritel'nost'.* St. Petersburg: Gosudarstvennaia tipografiia, 1903.

Jacobson, Matthew. *Special Sorrows: The Diasporic Imagination of Irish, Poland Polish, and Jewish Immigrants in the United States*. Cambridge, Mass.: Harvard University Press, 1995.

Jacobson, Matthew Frye. "The Quintessence of the Jew: Polemics of Nationalism and Peoplehood in Turn-of-the-Century Yiddish Fiction." In *Multilingual America: Transnationalism, Ethnicity and the Languages of American Literature*, ed. Werner Sollors. New York: New York University Press, 1998.

Jewish Colonization Association. *Atlas des colonies et domaines de la Jewish Colonization Association en République Argentine et au Brésil*. Paris: Jewish Colonization Association, 1914.

Jick, Leon. "The Holocaust: Its Use and Abuse within the American Public." *Yad Vashem Studies* 14 (1981): 303–318.

Johanson, Christine. *Women's Struggle for Higher Education in Russia, 1855–1900*. Kingston, Ont.: McGill-Queen's University Press 1987.

Johnpoll, Bernard. *The Politics of Futility: The General Workers Bund of Poland, 1917–1943*. Ithaca, N.Y.: Cornell University Press, 1967.

Joka, Jerzy. "Z dziejów walk klasowych proletariatu Białegostoku w latach 1918–1939." In *Studia i materialy do dziejów miasta Białegostoku*. Bialystok, 1968, 285–352.

Joselit, Jenna Weisman. *New York's Jewish Jews: The Orthodox Community in the Interwar Years*. Bloomington: Indiana University Press, 1990.

———, *The Wonders of America: Reinventing Jewish Culture, 1880–1950*. New York: Hill and Wang, 1994.

Judt, Tony. *Postwar: A History of Europe since 1945*. New York: Penguin 2005.

Kahan, Arcadius. *Essays in Jewish Social and Economic History*. Chicago: University of Chicago Press, 1986.

————, and Roger Weiss, *Essays in Jewish Social and Economic History*. Chicago: University of Chicago Press, 1986.

Kalabiński, Stanisław. "Początki ruchu robotinczego w białostockim okregu przemysłowym w latach 1870–1887." *Rocznik Białostocki 2* (1961): 143–94.

————. "Odezwy białostockisch komitetów partii robotniczych do proletariatu Żydownskiego z lat 1897–1900." *Biuletyn Żydowskiego Institutu Historycznego* 56 (1965): 83–113.

————. "Odewy Białostockich Komitetów Partii Robotniczych do Robotników Żydowskich (II)." *Biuletyn Żydowskiego Institutu Historycznego* 57 (1966): 63–103.

————. "Białostockie Organizacje SDKPil, PPS, Bundu, Socjalistów-Rewolucjonistów i Anarchistów w Latach 1901–1903." *Rocznik Białostocki* X (1970): 55–90.

————. *Pierwszy okres przemyslu i klasy robotniczej Białostocczyzny 1807–1870*. Warsaw: Panstwowe Wydawn. Nauk, 1986.

————. "Stan Zatrudnienia w Prsemyśle Białostocczyzny w latach 1870–1914." *Studia Histoyczne II*, n.d., 42–87.

Kamińska-Szmaj, I. "Narodsiny stereotypu bolszewika." *Poradnik Językowy* 3 (1993): 23–29.

Kaplan, Amy. *The Anarchy of Empire in the Making of U.S. Culture*. Cambridge, Mass.: Harvard University Press, 2002.

————, and Donald Pease, eds. *Cultures of United States Imperialism*. Durham, N.C.: Duke University Press, 1993.

Kaplan, Pesach. "Unzer likhtige fargangenheyt." In *Byalistoker almanakh*. Bialystok: Farlag, 1931.

Kaplan, Yosef. *Jews and Conversos: Studies in Society and the Inquisition: Proceedings of the Eighth World Congress of Jewish Studies Held at the Hebrew University of Jerusalem, August 16–21, 1981*. Jerusalem: World Union of Jewish Studies, 1985.

Karp, Abraham, J., ed. *Golden Door to America: The Jewish Immigrant Experience*. New York, Viking Press, 1976.

Kassow, Samuel. "Communal and Social Change in the Polish Shtetl, 1900–1939." In *Jewish Settlement and Community in the Modern Western World*, ed. Ronald Dotterer, Deborah Dash Moore, and Steven Cohen. London: Susquehanna University Press, 1991, 56–84.

Katz, Jacob. *Tradition and Crisis: Jewish Society at the End of the Middle Ages*. New York, Schocken Books 1971

Katz, Michael. *In the Shadow of the Poorhouse: A Social History of Welfare in America*. New York: Basic Books, 1986.

Katz, Yosef. *The "Business" of Settlement: Private Entrepreneurship in the Jewish Settlement of Palestine*. Jerusalem: Magnes Press, 1994.

Kaufman, David. *Shul with a Pool: The Synagogue Center in American Jewish History.* Hanover, N.H.: University Press of New England, 1999.

———. "The Construction of Memory: The Synagogues of the Lower East Side." In *Remembering the Lower East Side: American Jewish Reflections*, ed. Hasia R. Diner, Jeffrey Shandler, and Beth S. Wenger. Bloomington: Indiana University Press, 2000.

Kaufmann, Yehezkel. *Golah ve-Nekhar.* 2 vols. Tel Aviv: D'vir, 1962.

Kazal, Russell. "Revisiting Assimilation: The Rise, Fall and Reappraisal of a Concept in American Ethnic History." *American Historical Review* 100 (April 1995): 437–71.

Kazdan, H. S. "Der Bund: Biz dem finftn tsuzamenfor," in *Di Geshikhte fun Bund*, ed. G. Aronson. New York: Unzer Tsaty, 1960.

Kessner, Thomas. *The Golden Door: Italian and Jewish Immigrants in New York City, 1880–1915.* New York: Oxford University Press, 1977.

———, and Betty Caroli. "New Immigrant Women at Work: Italians and Jews in New York City, 1880–1915." *Journal of Ethnic Studies* 4 (Winter 1978): 19–31.

Kipen, Isaac. *A Life to Live.* Sydney. n.p., 1989.

Kirshenblatt-Gimblett, Barbara. "Imagining Europe: The Popular Arts of American Jewish Ethnography." In *Divergent Jewish Cultures: Israel and America*, ed. Deborah Dash Moore and S. Ilan Troen. New Haven, Conn.: Yale University Press, 2001.

———. "Introduction," to Mark Zborowski and Elizabeth Herzon, *Life is With People: The Culture of the Shtetl.* New York: Schocken, 1995.

Klementinovski, David. *Dr. Yosef Khazanovitsh: der idealist, natsionalist un folksmentsh.* New York: Bialystoker Historical Association, 1956.

Klier, John. *Imperial Russia's Jewish Question, 1855–1881.* Cambridge: Cambridge University Press, 1995.

Kliger, Hannah. "Traditions of Grass-Roots Organization and Leadership." *American Jewish History* 76 (1986): 25–39.

———. "Ethnic Voluntary Associations in Israel." *Jewish Journal of Sociology* 31, no. 2 (December 1989): 109–119.

Kobrin, Rebecca. "Contested Contributions: Émigré Philanthropy, Jewish Communal Life, and Polish-Jewish Relations in Interwar Bialystok, 1919–1929," *Gal-Ed* (2006) 43–62.

———. "Rewriting the Diaspora: Images of Eastern Europe in the Bialystok Press," *Jewish Social Studies* 12:3 (2006) 1–38.

———. "The 1905 Revolution Abroad: Mass Migration, Russian Jewish Liberalism and American Jewry, 1903–1914." In *The 1905 Revolution: A Turning Point in Jewish History."* Philadelphia: University of Pennsylvania Press, 2008.

Koebner, Richard, and Helmut Dan Schmidt. *Imperialism: The Story and Significance of a Word, 1840–1960.* Cambridge: Cambridge University Press, 1964.

Korman, Gerd. "The Holocaust in American Historical Writing." *Societas* 2 (Summer 1973): 259–65.

Korzec, Paweł. "Rzemiosło żydowskie w Białymstoku." *Biuletyn Żydowskiego Institutu Historycznego* 50 (1964): 23–35.

———. "Svatopolk-Mirsky's Report to the Tsar on the Jewish Question in 1902–3." *Soviet Jewish Affairs* 2:2 (1972): 86–95.

Korzec, Paweł. *Juifs en Pologne: la question juive pendant l'entre-deux-guerres.* Paris: Presses de la Fondation nationale des sciences politiques, 1980.

Kotik, Yehezkel. *Mayne zikhroynes.* Vol. 1. Warsaw: A Gitlin, 1913.

Krasowski, K. *Zwiazki Wyznaniowe w Rzeczypospolitej Studium Historycznopprawne.* Warsaw: Panstwowe Wydawn, 1988.

Krause, Corianne. "Urbanization without Breakdown: Italian, Jewish and Slavic Immigrant Women in Pittsburgh, 1900–1945." *Journal of Urban History* 4, no. 3 (May 1978): 291–306.

Kritz, Mary. *Global Trends in Migration: Theory and Research on International Population Movements.* New York: Center for Migration Studies, 1981.

———, Hania Zlotnick, and Lin Lean Lim. *International Migration Systems: A Global Approach.* New York: Oxford University Press, 1992.

Krutikov, Mikhail. *Yiddish Fiction and the Crisis of Modernity, 1905–1914.* Stanford. Calif.: Stanford University Press, 2001.

Kugelmass, Jack. *Going Home. YIVO annual,* vol. 21. Evanston, Ill: Northwestern University Press and the YIVO Institute for Jewish Research, 1993.

———, and Jonathan Boyarin, eds. *From a Ruined Garden: The Memorial Books of Polish Jewry.* Bloomington: Indiana University Press, 1988.

Kurtz, F. "Ha-pogrom bi-Bialistok bi-shnat 1906. Unpublished manuscript, 5. Merhavia Archives, Hebrew University.

Kuznets, Simon. "Immigration of Russian Jews to the United States: Background and Structure." *Perspectives in American History* 9 (1975): 35–124.

Lambroza, Shlomo. "The Pogroms of 1903–1906." In J. Klier and S. Lambroza, eds., *Pogroms: Anti-Jewish Violence in Modern Russian History.* Cambridge: Cambridge University Press, 1992, 195–247.

Lavie, Smadar, and Ted Swedenberg. *Displacement, Diaspora and the Geographies of Identity.* Durham, N.C.: Duke University Press, 1996.

Lederhendler, Eli. *The Road to Modern Jewish Politics: Political Tradition and Political Reconstruction in the Jewish Community of Tsarist Russia.* New York: Oxford University Press, 1989.

———. *Jewish Responses to Modernity: New Voices in America and Eastern Europe.* New York: NYU Press, 1994.

————. "Hard Times: HIAS under Pressure." *YIVO Annual* 22 (1995): 105–130.

————. "Classless: On the Social Status of Jews in Russian and Eastern Europe in the Late Nineteenth Century." *Contemporary Studies in Society and History* 50, no. 2 (2008): 507–535.

Leskov, N. S. *Polnoe sobranie sochinenii v tridtsati tomakh.* Moscow: Terra, 1996.

Lestchinsky, Jacob. "Die Zahl der Juden auf der Erde." *Zeitschrift für Demographie und Statistik der Juden* (Berlin, 1925): 1–8.

Lestchinsky, Jacob. "Yidn in di gresere shtet fun poyln." *Yivo Bleter,* 1943.

————. *Jewish Migration for the Past Hundred Years.* New York: YIVO, 1944.

————. "Jewish Migrations, 1840–1956." In *The Jews: Their History, Culture and Religion,* ed. Louis Finkelstein. New York: Harper 1960, 1536–96.

————, *Prezesledlenie i przewarstowienie Żydów ostatniem stuleciu.* Warsaw: ORT, 1933.

Lewin, Isaac. *A History of Polish Jewry during the Revival of Poland, 1918–1919.* New York: Shengold Publishers, 1990.

————, and N. M. Gelber. *A History of Polish Jewry during the Revival of Poland.* New York: Shengold Publishers, 1990.

Lieberson, Stanley. *A Piece of the Pie: Blacks and White Immigrants since 1880.* Berkeley: University of California Press, 1980.

Liebman, Charles, and Steven Cohen. *Two Worlds of Judaism: The Israeli and American Experiences.* New Haven, Conn.: Yale University Press, 1990.

Liedtke, Rainer. *Jewish Welfare in Hamburg and Manchester, c. 1850–1914.* Oxford: Clarendon Press, 1998.

Lilienthal, Alfred. "Israel's Flag Is Not Mine." *Reader's Digest* (September 1949): 49.

Lindenmeyr, Adele. *Poverty Is Not a Vice: Charity, Society, and the State in Imperial Russia.* Princeton, N.J.: Princeton University Press, 1996.

Linder, Menakhem. "Der khurbm funem yidishn handel in bialistoker rayon." *Yidishe ekonomik* 1 (1937): 17–19.

Linenthal, Edward T. *Preserving Memory: The Struggle to Create America's Holocaust Museum.* New York: Viking, 1995.

Lippmann, W. "The Demography of Australian Jewry." *Australian Jewish Historical Society* 6, no. 5 (1968).

Lipstadt, Deborah. *Beyond Belief: The American Press and the Coming of the Holocaust, 1933–1945.* New York: Free Press, 1993.

Liss, Andrea. *Trespassing through Shadows: Memory, Photography, and the Holocaust.* Minneapolis: University of Minnesota Press, 1998.

Litvak, Olga. *Conscription and the Search for Modern Russian Jewry.* Bloomington: Indiana University Press, 2006.

Lohr, Eric. *Nationalizing the Russian Empire: The Campaign against Enemy Aliens during World War I.* Russian Research Center Studies, 94. Cambridge, Mass: Harvard University Press, 2003.

Losh, L., ed. *Landsmanshaftn in Yisroel*. Tel Aviv: World Congress of Polish Jews, 1961.

Łukasiewicz, Juliusz. "Białystok w XIX Wieku." *Studia i Materiały do Dziejów Miasta Białegostoku*. Bialystok: Białostockie Towarzystw Naukowe, 1972, 59–71.

Lundestad, Geir. *Empire by Integration: The United States and European Integration 1945–1997*. Oxford: Oxford University Press, 1998.

———. *The United States and Western Europe since 1945: From Empire by Invitation to Transatlantic Drift*. Oxford: Oxford University Press, 2003.

Luz, Ehud. *Parallels Meet: Religion and Nationalism in the Early Zionist Movement, 1882–1904*. Philadelphia: Jewish Publication Society, 1988.

Lvovich, Daniel. *Nacionalismo y antisemitismo en la Argentina*. Biografía e historia. Buenos Aires: Javier Vergara, Grupo Zeta, 2003.

Mahler, Raphael. *Toldot ha-Yehudim be-Polin*. Merhavyah, Palestine: Hashomer Hatzair Sifriyat Poalim, 1946.

Maier, Charles S. *Among Empires: American Ascendancy and Its Predecessors*. Cambridge, Mass.: Harvard University Press, 2006.

Makovski, Yakov. *Zikhronotav shel partisn*. Tel-Aviv: private publication, 1997.

Małek, Ariusz. "Żydzi w Nowych Prusach Wschodnich." *Białostocczyzna* 1 (1997): 133–35.

Mark, B. "Proletariat Żydowski w Okresie Strajków Ekonomicz nych w Lutym-Marcu-Kwietniu 1905 r." *ZIH* 19–20 (1956): 4–9.

———. "Udział Proletariatu Żydowskiego w Czerwcowym Powstaniu Łódzkim I w Walkach Solidarnościowych." *Żydowskiego Instytutu Historycznego w Polsce* 23 (1957): 34–62.

Masliansky, Zvi Hirsch. *Kitve Masli'anski: ne'umim, zikhronot u-masa'ot*. New York: Hibru Pob. Ko, 1929.

Matt, Susan. "You Can't Go Home Again: Homesickness and Nostalgia in U.S. History." *Journal of American History* 94, no. 2 (September 2007): 469–97.

Mauersberg, Stanislaw. *Szkolnictwo Powszechne Dla Mniejszoski Narodowych w Polsce w Latach 1918–1939*. Wroław: Zaklad Nardowy im. Ossolinskich, 1968.

McCaffray, Susan. *The Politics of Industrialization in Tsarist Russia: The Association of Southern Coal and Steel Producers, 1874–1914*. DeKalb: Northern Illinois University Press, 1996.

McCarthy, Kathleen. *Noblesse Oblige: Charity and Cultural Philanthropy in Chicago, 1849–1929*. Chicago, University of Chicago Press, 1982.

McGreevy, John. *Parish Boundaries: The Catholic Encounter with Race in the Twentieth-Century Urban North*. Chicago: University of Chicago Press, 1996.

McKeown, Adam. "Global Migration, 1846–1940." *Journal of World History* 15, no. 2 (June 2004): 151–90.

Medoff, Rafael. *Militant Zionism in America: The Rise and Impact of the Jabotinsky Movement in the United States, 1926–1948*. Tuscaloosa: University of Alabama Press, 2002.

Meducki, Stanisław. "The Pogrom in Kielce on 4 July 1946." *Polin* 9 (1996): 158–63.

Mendelsohn, Ezra. *Class Struggle in the Pale: The Formative Years of the Jewish Workers' Movement in Tsarist Russia*. Cambridge: Cambridge University Press, 1970.

———. "A Note on Jewish Assimilation in the Polish Lands." In *Jewish Assimilation in Modern Times*, ed. Bela Vago. Boulder, Colo.: Westview Press, 1981, 141–49.

———. *Zionism in Poland: The Formative Years, 1915–1926*. New Haven, Conn.: Yale University Press, 1981.

———. *The Jews of East Central Europe between the World Wars*. Bloomington: Indiana University Press, 1983.

Meyer, Michael. *Jewish Identity in the Modern World*. Seattle: University of Washington Press, 1990.

Michlic, Joanna, and Anthony Polonsky, eds. *The Neighbors Respond: The Controversy over the Jedwabne Massacre in Poland*. Princeton, N.J., Princeton University Press, 2004.

Milamed, Susan. "Proskurover Landsmanshaftn: A Case Study in Jewish Communal Development." *American Jewish History* 76 (September 1986): 40–55.

Milhlic-Coren, Joanna. "Anti-Jewish Violence in Poland, 1918–1939 and 1945–1947." *Polin* 13 (2000): 34–62.

Miller, Kerby, A. *Emigrants and Exile: Ireland and the Irish Exodus to North America*. New York: Oxford University Press, 1985.

Mirelman, Victor. *Jewish Buenos Aires, 1890–1930: In Search of an Identity*. Detroit: Wayne State University Press, 1990.

Miron, Dan. *A Traveler Disguised: The Rise of Modern Yiddish Fiction in the Nineteenth Century*. New York: Schocken Books, 1973.

———. "Literary Image of the Shtetl." *Jewish Social Studies* 1, no. 3 (1995): 1–43.

Mishkinsky, Moshe. "Regional Factors in the Formation of the Jewish Labor Movement in Czarist Russia." *YIVO Annual* 14 (1969): 51–72.

———. *Reshit Tenuat ha-poalim ha-yehudit bi-rusiya: megamot yesod*. Tel Aviv: University of Tel Aviv Press, 1981.

———. "'Al tafkidah shel Bialystok be-tekufat ha-ʿisuv shel tenuʾat ha-poʾalim ha-yehudit be-kesarut ha-rusit." *Shvut* 13 (1988): 65–70.

———. "Rola Białegostoku w okresie formowania sie Żydowskiego ruchu Robotniczego w Imperium Rosyjskim." *Studia Podlaskie* 2 (1989): 98–99.

Monroy, Douglas. *Rebirth: Mexican Los Angeles from the Great Migration to the Great Depression.* Berkeley: University of California Press, 1999.

Moore, Deborah Dash. *At Home in America: Second-Generation New York Jews.* New York: Columbia University Press, 1981.

———. *B'nai Brith and the Challenge of Ethnic Leadership.* Albany: State University of New York Press, 1981.

———. *To the Golden Cities: Pursuing the American Dream in Miami and L.A.* New York: Free Press, 1994.

———. *GI Jews: How World War II Changed a Generation.* Cambridge, Mass.: Harvard University Press, 2004.

———, and S. Ilan Troen. *Divergent Jewish Cultures: Israel and America.* Studies in Jewish Culture and Society. New Haven, Conn.: Yale University Press, 2001.

Morawska, Ewa. *For Bread with Butter: The Life-worlds of East Central European Immigrants in Johnstown, Pennsylvania, 1890–1940.* Cambridge: Cambridge University Press, 1985.

———. "Changing Images of the Old Country in the Development of Ethnic Identity among East European Immigrants, 1880s–1930s: A Comparison of Jewish and Slavic Representations." *YIVO Annual* 21 (1993): 273–345.

———. *Insecure Prosperity: Small-Town Jews in Industrial America.* Princeton, N.J.: Princeton University Press, 1996.

———. "Immigrants, Transnationalism, and Ethnicization: A Comparison of This Great Wave and the Last." In *E pluribus unum?: Contemporary and Historical Perspectives on Immigrant Political Incorporation,* ed. Gary Gerstle and John Mollenkopf. New York: Russell Sage Foundation, 2001.

Mościcki, Henryk. *Białystok Zarys Historyczny.* Białystok: Wydawn. Magistratue Bialegostoku, 1933.

Mosse, George. *Nationalism and Sexuality: Respectability and Abnormal Sexuality in Modern Europe.* New York: H. Fertig, 1985.

Moya, José. "Immigrants and Associations: A Global and Historical Perspective." *Journal of Ethnic and Migration Studies* 31, no. 5 (2005): 833–64.

Nathans, Benjamin. *Beyond the Pale: The Russian-Jewish Encounter in Late Imperial Russia.* Berkeley: University of California Press, 2002.

Nevodovska, Rose Z. *Azoi wi ich bin, lider . . . 1933–1936.* Los Angeles: Rose Nevodovska buch-komitet, 1936.

Ngai, Mae. *Impossible Subjects: Illegal Aliens and the Making of Modern America.* Princeton, N.J.: Princeton University Press, 2004.

Niger, Samuel, and Jacob Shatzky. *Leksikon fun der nayer yidisher literatur.* New York: Alveltlekhn Yidishn Kultur-Kongres, 1956.

Ninkovich, Frank. *The United States and Imperialism.* Malden, Mass.: Blackwell, 2001.

Nochlin, Linda, and Tamar Garb. *The Jew in the Text: Modernity and the Construction of Identity: with 72 Illustrations.* New York, N.Y.: Thames and Hudson, 1996.

Nolt, Samuel. "Formal Mutual Aid Structures among American Mennonites and Brethren: Assimilation and Reconstructed Ethnicity." *Journal of American Ethnic History* 17, no. 3 (1998): 71–86.

Norman, Theodore. *An Outstretched Arm: A History of the Jewish Colonization Association.* London: Routledge & Kegan Paul, 1985.

Novick, Peter. *The Holocaust in American Life.* Boston: Houghton Mifflin, 1999.

Opalski, Magdalena, and Yisrael Bartal. *Poles and Jews: A Failed Brotherhood.* The Tauber Institute for the Study of European Jewry Series, 13. Hanover, N.H.: University Press of New England, 1992.

Orbach, Alexander. *New Voices of Russian Jewry: A Study of the Russian-Jewish Press of Odessa in the Era of Great Reforms, 1860–1871.* Leiden: Brill, 1980.

Orsi, Robert. *The Madonna of 115th Street: Faith and Community in Italian Harlem, 1880–1950.* New Haven, Conn.: Yale University Press, 1985.

Palter, Luis. *Byalissṭoker leben.* [Brooklyn]: Byalistoker bikher ḥoylim fun Bruklin, 1937.

Pat, Shlomo. "Zikhroynes zum 20-yorikn yuvile fun Bialystoker farband in Argentina," *Bialystoker vegn* 5–6 (September 1950), 10.

Pat, Yakov. "Bialistoker yidn in oystralia." In Hilary L. Rubinstein, *The Jews in Victoria, 1835–1985.* Sydney: Allen & Unwin, 1986, 190–91.

Patt, Avinoam J. *Finding Home and Homeland: Jewish Youth and Zionism in the Aftermath of the Holocaust.* Detroit: Wayne State University Press, 2009.

Pattie, Susan. *Faith in History: Armenians Rebuilding Community.* Washington, D.C.: Smithsonian Press, 1997.

Penkalla, Adam. "Poles and Jews in the Kielce Region and Radom, April 1945–February 1946." *Polin* 13 (2000): 236–52.

Penslar, Derek. *Shylock's Children: Economics and Jewish Identity in Modern Europe.* Berkeley: University of California Press, 2001.

Peroomian, Rubina. *Literary Reponses to Catastrophe: A Comparison of the Armenian and Jewish Experience.* Atlanta: Scholars Press, 1993.

Pervaia vseobshchaia perepis' naseleniia Rossiiskoi imperii, 1987 g. Vol. 11. St. Petersburg, 1904.

Pinchuk, Ben-Cion ."Was there a Soviet Policy for Evacuating the Jews? The Case of the Annexed Territories." *Slavic Review* 39, no. 1 (1980): 44–55.

Pinkus, Roberto. *Villa Lynch Era Una Fiesta.* Buenos Aires: De Los Cuatro Vientos, 2007.

Piotrowski, Tadeusz. *The Polish Deportees of World War II: Recollections of Removal to the Soviet Union and Dispersal throughout the World.* Jefferson, N.C.: McFarland & Co, 2008.

Polonsky, Antony. *Politics in Independent Poland, 1921–1939: The Crisis of Constitutional Government*. Oxford: Clarendon Press, 1972.

Pomeranz, Kenneth. "Empire and Civilizing Missions Past and Present." *Daedalus* 134, no. 2 (Spring 2005): 34–45.

Porter, Brian. *When Nationalism Began to Hate: Imagining Modern Politics in Nineteenth-Century Poland*. New York: Oxford University Press, 2000.

Portes, Alejandro, and Rubén G. Rumbaut. *Immigrant America: A Portrait*. Berkeley: University of California Press, 1990.

Portnoy, Edward. "Modicut Puppet Theatre: Modernism, Satire, and Yiddish Culture." *The Drama Review* 43, no. 3 (Fall 1999): 115–34.

Pozzetta, George, ed. *Immigrant Institutions: The Organization of Immigrant Life*. New York: Garland, 1991.

Prell, Riv-Ellen. *Fighting to Become Americans: Jews, Gender and the Anxiety of Assimilation*. Boston: Beacon Press, 1999.

Price, C. "Chain Migration and Immigrant Groups, with Special Reference to Australian Jewry." *Jewish Journal of Sociology* 6, no. 2 (1964): 157–71.

Privat, Edmond. *The Life of Zamenhof*. London: George Allen, 1931.

Rabinowitz, Benjamin. "The Young Men's Hebrew Association (1854–1913)." *PAJHS* 37 (1947): 222–47.

Raider, Mark A. *The Emergence of American Zionism*. New York: New York University Press, 1998.

Rapalovsky, Sonia. "Bialistok—mayn heym," *Bialystoker vegn* 3 (1949).

Rapaport, Yehoshua. "A vort fun di aroysgeber." In *Der umkum fun Byalistoker Yidntum, 1939–1945*. Melbourne: Bialystoker Centre, 1948, 3.

Raskin, Richard. *A Child at Gunpoint: A Case Study in the Life of a Photo*. Aarhus: Aarhus University Press, 2004.

Rawidowicz, Simon, and Benjamin C. I. Ravid. *State of Israel, Diaspora, and Jewish Continuity: Essays on the "Ever-Dying People."* The Tauber Institute for the Study of European Jewry series, 26. Hanover, NH: Published by University Press of New England [for] Brandeis University Press, 1998.

Rayzner, Rafael. *Der umkum fun Byalistoker yidntum, 1939–1945* [The Annihilation of Bialystok Jewry, 1939–1945]. Melbourne: Byalistoker Tsenter in Oystralye, 1948.

Reisman, M. "Af di vegen fun 30 yor bialistoker mishpocha in argentina." *Bialystoker vegn* 5–6 (September 1950).

Rischin, Moses. *The Promised City: New York's Jews, 1870–1914*. Cambridge, Mass.: Harvard University Press, 1962.

Rivanera Carleïs, Federico. *El judaísmo y la semana trágica: la verdadera historia de los sucesos de enero de 1919*. [Buenos Aires, Argentina]: Instituto de Investigaciones sobre la Cuestión Judía, 1986.

Rodriguez, Marc S., ed. *Repositioning North American Migration History: New Directions in Modern Continental Migration, Citizenship, and Community.* Rochester, N.Y.: University of Rochester Press, 2004.

Rogger, Hans. *Jewish Policies and Right-Wing Politics in Imperial Russia.* Basingstoke, Hampshire: Macmillan, 1986.

Ro'i, Yaacov. *Jews and Jewish Life in Russia and the Soviet Union.* The Cummings Center series. Ilford, Essex, England: F. Cass, 1995.

Rojanski, Rachel. "American Jewry's Influence upon the Establishment of the Jewish Welfare Apparatus in Poland, 1920–1929." *Gal-Ed* 11 (1989): 59–86.

Rollet, Henry. "The Polish Borderlands and Nationality Problems." *Polin* 3 (1988): 343–47.

Rontch, Itsak. "Der itstiger matsev fun di landsmanshaftn." In *Di yidishe landsmanshaftn fun nyu york* [Jewish Hometown Associations in New York] New York: I. L. Peretz Publishing, 1938.

———. "The Present State of the Landsmanschaften." *The Jewish Social Service Quarterly* 15, no. 4 (June 1939): 620–34.

Rose, Arthur, Israel Sher, and Melech Ravitch. *Oystralish-Yidisher Almanakh.* Melbourne: A. Rose and I. Sher, 1937.

Rosenfeld, Alvin. "Promised Land(s): Zion, America, and American Jewish Writers." *Jewish Social Studies* 3, no. 3 (1997): 111–31.

Roskies, David. *Against the Apocalypse: Responses to Catastrophe in Modern Jewish Culture.* Cambridge, Mass.: Harvard University Press, 1984.

———. *A Bridge of Longing: The Lost Art of Yiddish Storytelling.* Cambridge, Mass.: Harvard University Press, 1995.

———. *The Jewish Search for a Usable Past.* Bloomington: Indiana University Press, 1999.

Rossino, Alexander. "Polish 'Neighbours' and German Invaders: Anti-Jewish Violence in the Bialystok District during the Opening Weeks of Operation Barbarossa." *Polin* 16 (2003): 431–52.

Rothschild, Joseph. *East Central Europe between the Two World Wars.* A History of East Central Europe, vol. 9. Seattle: University of Washington Press, 1974.

Rouse, Roger. "Mexican Migration and the Social Space of Post-Modernism." *Diaspora* 1 (1991).

———. "Thinking through Transnationalism: Notes on the Cultural Politics of Class Relations in the Contemporary United States." *Public Culture* 7, no. 2 (1995): 353–402.

Rubinstein, Hilary L. *The Jews in Victoria, 1835–1985.* Sydney: Allen & Unwin, 1986.

Ruppin, Arthur. *Soziologie der Juden.* Berlin: Jüdischer Verlag, 1930.

Rutland, Suzanne D. "Waiting Room Shanghai: Australian Reactions to the Plight of the Jews in Shanghai after the Second World War." *Leo Baeck Annual* 23 (1987): 407–411.

———— *Edge of the Diaspora: Two Centuries of Jewish Settlements in Australia.* Sydney: Collins, 1988.

————. "Are You Jewish? Post-war Jewish Immigration to Australia, 1945–1954." *Australian Journal of Jewish Studies* (1991): 35–58.

————. "I Am My Brother's Keeper: The Central Role Played by Overseas Jewry in the Reception and Integration of Post-war Jewish Immigration to Australia." *Australian Jewish Historical Society Journal* XI, part 4 (1992): 687–702.

————. "I Never Knew a Man Who Had So Many Cousins": Differing Attitudes to Postwar Survivor Migration—Melbourne and Sydney." *Australian Jewish Historical Society* Journal 12, no. 2 (1994) 394–406

————. "Subtle Exclusions: Postwar Jewish Emigration to Australia and the Impact of the IRO Scheme." *The Journal of Holocaust Education* 10, no. 1 (Summer 2001): 50–66.

Ryan, Mary. *Cradle of the Middle Class: The Family in Oneida County, New York, 1790–1865.* New York: Cambridge University Press, 1981.

Rydell, Robert W. and Rob Kroes, *Buffalo Bill in Bologna: The Americanization of the World, 1869–1922.* Chicago: University of Chicago, 2005.

Safran, Gabriella. *Rewriting the Jew: Assimilation Narratives in the Russian Empire.* Stanford, Calif.: Stanford University Press, 2000.

Safran, William. "Diasporas in Modern Societies: Myths of Homeland and Return." *Diaspora* 1 (Spring 1991): 83–99.

————. "Comparing Diasporas: A Review Essay." *Diaspora* 8, no. 3 (1999): 255–91.

Sahlins, Peter. *Boundaries: The Making of France and Spain in the Pyrenees.* Berkeley: University of California Press, 1989.

Samuel, Maurice. *The World of Sholem Aleichem.* New York: Knopf, 1943.

Sanchez, George. *Becoming Mexican American: Ethnicity, Culture, and Identity in Chicano Los Angeles, 1900–1945.* New York: Oxford University Press, 1993.

Sanders, Ronald. *Shores of Refuge: A Hundred Years of Jewish Emigration.* New York, Holt, 1988.

Sarna, Jonathan. "The Myth of No Return: Jewish Return Migrants to Eastern Europe, 1891–1914." *American Jewish History* 71 (1981): 256–69.

————. *People Walk on Their Heads: Moses Weinberger's Jews and Judaism in New York.* New York: Holmes & Meier, 1981.

————. "A Projection of America as It Ought to Be: Zion in the Mind's Eye of American Jews." In *Envisioning Israel: The Changing Ideals and Images of North American Jews,* ed. A. Gal. Detroit: Wayne State University Press, 1996, 41–60.

————. *American Judaism: A History.* New Haven, Conn.: Yale University Press, 2004.

Schachtman, Tom. *I Seek My Brethren: Ralph Goldman and "The Joint."* New York: Newmarket Press, 2001.

Schama, Simon. *Landscape and Memory.* New York: Knopf, 1996.

Schiller, Nina Glick. *Towards a Transnational Perspective on Migration: Race, Class, Ethnicity and Nationalism Reconsidered.* New York: New York Academy of Sciences, 1992.

———. *Nations Unbound: Transnational Projects, Postcolonial Predicaments, and Deterritorialized Nation States.* New York: Gordon and Breach, 1994.

———, Linda Basch, and Cristina Szanton Blanc. "From Immigrant to Transmigrant: Theorizing Transnational Migration." *Anthropological Quarterly* 68, no. 1 (1995): 48–63.

Schmidt, Sarah L. *Horace M. Kallen: Prophet of American Zionism.* Brooklyn, N.Y.: Carlson Publishing, 1995.

Schuler-Springorum, Stephanie. "Assimilation and Community Reconsidered: The Jewish Community in Konigsberg, 1871–1914." *Jewish Social Studies* 5, no. 3 (Summer 1999): 104–132.

Segal, Louis. *Bey unzere sheyres hapleyte in poylen un ma'arav euroype.* New York, Farband, 1947.

Seidman, Joel. *The Needle Trades.* New York: Farrar & Rinehart, 1942.

Shabad, Ts. "Vilne amol un itst." *Der Vilner* (1929): 16, 19.

Shandler, Jeffrey. *While American Watches: Televising the Holocaust.* New York: Oxford University Press, 1999.

———. "Beyond the Mother Tongue: Learning and the Meaning of Yiddish in America." *Jewish Social Studies* 6, no. 3 (Spring 2000): 102–112.

———. "Producing the Future: The Impresario Culture of American Zionism before 1948." In *Divergent Jewish Cultures: Israel and America,* ed. Deborah Dash Moore and Ilan Troen. New Haven, Conn.: Yale University Press, 2001.

———. *Adventures in Yiddishland: Postvernacular Language and Culture.* Berkeley: University of California Press, 2006.

Sheraton, Mimi. *The Bialy Eaters: The Story of a Bread and a Lost World.* New York: Broadway Books, 2000.

Shijman, Osías. *Colonización judía en la Argentina.* [Buenos Aires: n.p.], 1980.

Shukla, Sandhya. *India Abroad: Diasporic Cultures of Postwar America and England.* Princeton, N.J.: Princeton University Press, 2003.

Singer, Isaac Bashevis. "Concerning Yiddish Literature in Poland (1943)." Trans. Robert Wolf. *Prooftexts* 15 (1995): 113–28.

Slezkine, Yuri. *The Jewish Century.* Princeton, N.J.: Princeton University Press, 2004.

Smith, Judith. *Family Connections: A History of Italian and Jewish Immigrant Lives in Providence, Rhode Island, 1900–1940.* Albany: State University of New York Press, 1985.

Sofer, Eugene. *From Pale to Pampa: A Social History of the Jews of Buenos Aires.* New York: Holmes & Meier, 1982.

Sohn, David. "Redaktsianele notitsen." *Bialystoker Stimme* 2 (1922): 15.

———. "Bialistok af ist brodvey." *Forverts*, June 21, 1931, 3.

———. "Der bialistoker "pilgrims" in amerika." in *The Bialystoker Pioneer: 45th Anniversary Journal of the Bialystoker Verein Somach Noflim.* New York, 1931.

———. "Minutes from the First Years of the Bialystoker U.V. Somach Noflim." In *The Bialystoker Pioneer: 45th Anniversary Journal of the Bialystoker Verein Somach Noflim.* New York, 1931, 5.

———. "Der nayer panim fun landsmanshaften in amerika." *Naye yom tov bleter* (April 1933).

———. "Di tragedia fun eltern dur imigrantn." *Forverts*, July 1, 1934.

———. "Unzer bialistoker in dem oyfboy fun rusland," *Bialystoker Stimme* 48 (1934), 8–9

Soloveitchik, Haim. "Migration, Acculturation, and the New Role of Texts in the Haredi World." In *Accounting for Fundamentalisms: The Dynamic Character of Movements*, ed. M. Marty and R. Appleby. Chicago: University of Chicago Press, 1994, 197–235.

Sorin, Gerald. *American Jewish Immigrant Radicals, 1880–1920.* Bloomington: Indiana University Press, 1985.

Sorkin, David. *The Transformation of German Jewry, 1780–1840.* Oxford: Oxford University Press, 1987.

Soyer, Daniel. "Between Two Worlds: The Jewish Landsmanshaftn and Immigrant Identity." *American Jewish History* 76, no. 1 (1986): 5–25.

———. *Jewish Immigrant Associations and American Identity in New York, 1880–1939.* Cambridge, Mass.: Harvard University Press, 1997.

Stampfer, Shaul. "The Geographic Background of East European Jewish Migration to the United States before World War I." In *Migration across Time and Nations*, ed. I. Glazier and L. De Rosa. New York: Holmes & Meier Press, 1986, 220–30.

———. "Patterns of Internal Jewish Migration in the Russian Empire." In *Jews and Jewish Life in Russia and the Soviet Union*, ed. Yaakov R'oi. Portland: Frank Cass, 1995, 28–47.

———. "Hasidic Yeshivot in Inter-war Poland." *Polin* 11 3–25.

Stanislawski, Michael. *Tsar Nicholas I and the Jews: The Transformation of Jewish Society in Russia, 1825–1855.* Philadelphia: Jewish Publication Society, 1983.

Stankowski, Albert. "Emigracja Żydów z Pomorza Zachodniego w latach, 1945–1960." In *Studia z dziejów i kultury Żydow w Polsce po 1945 roku*, ed. August Grabski, Maciej Pisarski, and Albert Stankowski. Warsaw: Wydawnictwo Trio, 1997, 83–141.

Staub, Michael. *Torn at the Roots: The Crisis of Jewish Liberalism in Postwar America.* New York: Columbia University Press, 2002.

Stauter-Halstead, Keely. *The Nation in the Village: The Genesis of Peasant National Identity in Austrian Poland, 1848–1914.* Ithaca, N.Y.: Cornell University Press.

Stein, Sarah Abrevaya. *Making Jews Modern: The Yiddish and Ladino Press in the Russian and Ottoman Empires.* Bloomington: Indiana University Press, 2004.

———. *Plumes: Ostrich Feathers, Jews, and a Lost World of Global Commerce.* New Haven: Yale University Press, 2008.

Storch, Theodore."Women of Tomorrow." *Bialystoker lebn* 65 (June 1940): 3.

Stratton, Jon. "(Dis)placing the Jews: Historicizing the Idea of Diaspora." *Diaspora* 6 (1997): 301–329.

Szajkowski, Zosa. "Dos yidishe gezelshaftlekhe lebn in Pariz tsum yor 1939." In *Yidn in Frankraykh,* ed. E. Tcherikower. New York: YIVO, 1942.

———. "Private and Organized American Jewish Overseas Relief (1914–1938)." *American Jewish Historical Quarterly* 57, no. 1 (September 1967): 52–106.

———. "Private American Jewish Overseas Relief (1919–1938): Problems and Attempted Solutions." *American Jewish Historical Quarterly* 57, no. 3 (March, 1968): 285–352.

Telushkin, Joseph. *The Golden Land: The Story of Jewish Immigration to America: Experience the Achievements of American Jews through Removable Documents and Artifacts.* New York: Harmony Books, 2002.

Tenenbaum, Joseph. *The Road to Nowhere.* New York: American Federation of Polish Jews, 1947.

———. *Let My People In.* New York: American Federation of Polish Jews, 1947.

Tenenbaum, Shelly. "Immigrants and Capital: Jewish Loan Societies in the United States, 1880–1945." *American Jewish History* 76, no. 1 (1986): 67–77.

Terent'ev, P. N. *Prokhorovy: materialy k istorii Trekhgornoi manufaktury i torgovo-promyshlennoi deiatelnosti sem'i Prokhorovykh, 1799–1915 gg.* Predprinimateli Rossii. Moscow: Terra, 1996.

Thadden, Edward. *Russia's Western Borderlands, 1710–1870.* Princeton, N.J.: Princeton University Press, 1984.

Thompson, Andrew, S. "The Language of Imperialism and the Meanings of Empire: Imperial Discourse in British Politics." *Journal of British Studies* 36 (April 1997): 147–77.

Toll, William. "A Quiet Revolution: Jewish Women's Clubs and the Widening Female Sphere, 1870–1920." *American Jewish Archives* (Summer 1989): 7–26.

Tölölyan, Khaching. "Rethinking Diaspora(s): Stateless Power in the Transnational Moment." *Diaspora* 5 (1996): 3–36.

Troen, Selwyn Ilan, and Benjamin Pinkus, eds. *Organizing Rescue: National Jewish Solidarity in the Modern Period.* London: Frank Cass & Co., 1992.

Tsipin, Boris. "Zikroynes fun a bialistoker bundist." In *Natsyonale un politishe bavegungen bay yidn in byalistok: materyal tsu der geshikhte*, ed. Herman Frank. New York: Gezelshaft far geshikhte fun Byalistok, 1951.

Tsitron, Tuvyah. *Di geshikhte fun 'oyfshtand in bialistoker geto*. Tel Aviv: Bialystoker Center, 1995.

United States, and William P. Dillingham. *Reports of the Immigration Commission 1907–1910: Senate Documents*. Washington, D.C.: U.S. G.P.O., 1911.

Vishniac, Roman, and Abraham Joshua Heschel. *Polish Jews: A Pictorial Record*. New York: Schocken Books, 1965.

Vital, David. *Zionism: The Formative Years*. New York: Oxford University Press, 1982.

Vol'tke, G. "Meditsinskiia professii po deistvuiushchemu russkomu zakonodatel'stvu." In *Evreiskaia Entsiklopediia: Svod znanii o evreistve i ego kul'ture v proshlom i nastoiashchem*. St. Petersburg: Izdanie Obshchestva dlia nauchnykh evreiskikh izdanii i Izdatel'stva Brokhaus-Efron, 1906–1913.

Vromen, Suzanne. "Maurice Halbwachs and the Concept of Nostalgia." *Knowledge and Society: Studies in the Sociology of Culture Past and Present* 6 (1986): 55–66.

———. "The Ambiguity of Nostalgia" *YIVO Annual* 21 (1993): 69–86.

Walicki, Andrzej. *The Enlightenment and the Birth of Modern Nationhood: Polish Political Thought from Noble Republicanism to Tadeusz Kosciuszko*. Notre Dame, Ind.: University of Notre Dame Press, 1989.

Wandycz, Piotr. *The Lands of Partitioned Poland, 1795–1918*. Seattle: University of Washington Press, 1974.

Warnke, Nina. "Of Plays and Politics: Sholem Aleichem's First Visit to America." *YIVO Annual* 20 (1991): 240–51.

Weeks, Theodore. *Nation and State in Late Imperial Russia: Nationalism and Russification on the Western Frontier, 1863–1914*. DeKalb: Northern Illinois University Press, 1996.

Weinberg, David. *Between Tradition and Modernity: Haim Zhitlowsky, Simon Dubnow, Ahad Ha-Am and the Shaping of Modern Jewish Identity*. New York: Holmes and Meier, 1996.

Weinberg, Sydney. *World of Our Mothers: The Lives of Jewish Immigrant Women*. Chapel Hill: University of North Carolina Press, 1988.

Weiner, Deborah R., Anita Kassof, and Avi Y. Decter. *Voices of Lombard Street: A Century of Change in East Baltimore*. Baltimore: Jewish Museum of Maryland, 2007.

Weinreich, Max. *Geshikhte fun der Yidisher shprakh: bagrifn, faktn, metodn*. Bibliotek fun YIVO. New York: Yidisher Visnshaftlekher Institut, 1973.

Weisser, Michael. *Brotherhood of Memory: Jewish Landsmanshaftn in the New World*. New York: Basic Books, 1985.

Wenger, Beth. "Jewish Women and Voluntarism: Beyond the Myth of the Enablers." *American Jewish History* 79:1 (1989), 16–36.

———. *New York Jews and the Great Depression: Uncertain Promise.* New Haven, Conn.: Yale University Press, 1996.

———, and Jeffrey Shandler. *Encounters with the Holyland: Place, Past and Future in American Jewish Culture.* Philadelphia: National Museum of American Jewish History, 1997.

Wettstein, Howard, ed. *Exiles and Diasporas: Varieties of Jewish Identity.* Berkeley, University of California Press, 2002.

Wickberg, Daniel. "What is the History of Sensibilities? On Cultural Histories, Old and New." *American Historical Review* 112, no. 3 (June 2007): 661–84.

Willcox, Walter F. *International Migrations.* Vol. 2: *Interpretations.* [New York: National Bureau of Economic Research], 1931.

Willensky, Elliot, and Norval White, eds. *American Institute of Architects Guide to New York City.* San Diego: Harcourt Brace Jovanovich, 1988.

Wischnitzer, Mark. *Visas to Freedom: The History of HIAS.* Cleveland: World. Pub. Co., 1956.

Wisniewski, Tomasz. "The Lines Hatsedek Charitable Fraternity in Bialystok, 1885–1939." *Polin* 7 (1992).

———.Wisniewski, Tomasz. *Jewish Bialystok and Surroundings in Eastern Poland: A Guide for Yesterday and Today.* Ipswich, Mass.: Ipswitch Press, 1998.

Wisse, Ruth. "Introduction." *The I. L. Peretz Reader.* New York: Schocken Books, 1990.

Woocher, Jonathan. *Sacred Survival: The Civil Religion of American Jews.* Bloomington: Indiana University Press, 1986.

Wróbel, Piotr ."Na równi pochyłej. Żydzi Białegostoku w latach 1918–1939: demografia, ekonomika desintegracja, konflikty z Polakami." *Studia Podlaskie* (Bialystok, 1989), 125–97.

Zabłotniak, Ryszard. "Niektóre Wiadomości O Żydowskiej Służbie Zdrowia w Białymstoku." *Żydowskiego Instytutu Historycznego w Polsce* 60 (1966): 111–15.

Zaborowska, Magdalena. *How We Found America: Reading Gender through East European Immigrant Narratives.* Chapel Hill: University of North Carolina Press, 1995.

Zak, Abraham. *Knekht mir zaynen geven.* Buenos Aires, 1956.

Zalkin, Mordechai. *Ba'a lot ha-shahar: ha-Hasklah ha-Yehudit ba-Imperyah ha-Rusit ba-me'ah ha-tesha'esreh.* Jerusalem: Magnes Press, 2000.

Zbikowski, Andrzej. *Zydzi.* Wroclaw: Wydawnictwo Dolnoslaskie, 1999.

Zelizer, Barbie. *Remembering to Forget: Holocaust Memory through the Camera's Eye.* Chicago: University of Chicago Press, 1998.

Zilberblat, Eli. "Yidisher tekstil-pioneyren in bialistok un umgegent." *Bialystoker Almanakh*. Bialystok: "Naye lebn," 1931.

Zimmerman, Joshua. *Poles, Jews, and the Politics of Nationality: The Bund and the Polish Socialist Party in Late Tsarist Russia, 1892–1914*. Madison: University of Wisconsin Press, 2004.

———, ed. *Contested Memories: Poles and Jews during the Holocaust and Its Aftermath*. New Brunswick, N.J.: Rutgers University Press, 2003.

Zipperstein, Steven. *The Jews of Odessa: A Cultural History 1794–1881*. Stanford, Calif.: Stanford University Press, 1985.

———. "The Politics of Relief: The Transformation of Russian Jewish Communal Life during the First World War." *Studies in Contemporary Jewry* 4 (1988): 22–40.

———. *Elusive Prophet: Ahad Ha'am and the Origins of Zionism*. Berkeley: University of California Press, 1993.

———. *Imagining Russian Jewry: Memory, History, Identity*. Seattle: University of Washington Press, 1999.

Zolberg, Aristide. *A Nation by Design: Immigration Policy in the Fashioning of America*. Cambridge, Mass.: Harvard University Press, 2006.

Zunz, Olivier. *The Changing Face of Inequality: Urbanization, Industrial Development, and Immigrants in Detroit, 1880–1920*. Chicago: University of Chicago Press, 1982.

Unpublished Dissertations

Bemporad, Elissa. "Red Star on the Jewish street: The Reshaping of Jewish Life in Soviet Minsk, 1917–1939." Stanford University, 2006.

Epstein, Lisa. "Caring for the Soul's House: The Jews of Russia and Health Care, 1860–1914. Yale University, 1995.

Gately, M. "The Development of the Russian Cotton Textile Industry, 1861–1913." University of Kansas, 1968.

Kliger, Hannah. "Communication and Ethnic Community: The Case of Landsmanshaftn." University of Pennsylvania, 1985.

Lipphardt, Anna. "Vilne, yidishlekh fartrakht . . .kulturelle Erinnerung, Trauma, Migration: Die Vilne–Diaspora in New York, Israel, und Vilnius nach dem Holocaust." University of Potsdam, 2006.

Manley, Rebecca. "The Evacuation and Survival of Soviet Civilians, 1941–1946." University of California, Berkeley, 2004.

Meir, Natan. "The Jews in Kiev, 1859–1914: Community and Charity in an Imperial Russian City." Columbia University, 2004.

Pianko, Noam. "Diaspora Jewish Nationalism and Identity in America, 1914–1967." Yale University, 2004.

Portnoy, Edward. "The Creation of a Jewish Cartoon Space in the Yiddish Presses of New York and Warsaw." Jewish Theological Seminary, 2008.

Shapiro, Robert. "Jewish Self Government in Poland: Lodz, 1914–1930." Columbia University, 1987.

Soyer, Daniel. "Jewish Landsmanshaftn (Hometown Associations) in New York, 1880s to 1924." New York University, 1994.

Steinberg, Kerri. "Photography, Philanthropy and the Politics of American Jewish Identity." University of California, Los Angeles, 1998.

Ury, Scott. "Red Banner, Blue Star: Radical Politics, Democratic Institutions and Collective Identity amongst Jews in Warsaw, 1904–1907." Hebrew University, 2006.

Weber, Christopher. "Towards Competitive Suffering: A Re-examination of the Historiography of Polish–Jewish Relations." M.A. thesis, University of Guelph, 1996.

Weiser, Keith. "Noyekh Prulitski and the Folkspartey in Poland, 1900–1926." Columbia University, 2001.

Wisniewski, Tomasz, "Misja Barbizanska w Białymstoku, 1924–1939." University of Bialystok, 1989.

Zimmerman, Joshua D. "Poles, Jews and the Politics of Nationality: Relations between the Polish Socialist Party and the Jewish Labor Bund, 1892–1905." Brandeis University, 1998.

Index

REBECCA KOBRIN is Assistant Professor of Jewish History at Columbia University. She is author (with Adam Shear) of an exhibition catalog, *From Written to Printed Text: The Transmission of Jewish Tradition*. She lives in New York with her husband and two daughters.

Printed and bound by CPI Group (UK) Ltd, Croydon, CR0 4YY

13/04/2025

14656545-0003